# WINNING INVESTORS OVER

# WINNING INVESTORS OVER

SURPRISING TRUTHS ABOUT HONESTY, EARNINGS GUIDANCE, AND OTHER WAYS TO BOOST YOUR STOCK PRICE

## Baruch Lev

HARVARD BUSINESS REVIEW PRESS

Boston, Massachusetts

Copyright 2012 Harvard Business School Publishing Corporation

Printed in the United States of America

10 9 8 7 6     5 4 3 2 1

Library of Congress Cataloging-in-Publication Data

Lev, Baruch.
  Winning investors over : surprising truths about honesty, earnings guidance, and other ways to boost your stock price / Baruch Lev.
      p. cm.
  ISBN 978-1-4221-1502-2 (alk. paper)
  1. Corporations—Valuation. 2. Stocks—Prices. 3. Corporate governance. 4. Intangible assets. I. Title.
  HG4028.V3L4854 2012
  658.15'224—dc23

                                                                              2011022454

The paper used in this publication meets the requirements of the American National Standard for Permanence of Paper for Publications and Documents in Libraries and Archives Z39.48-1992.

To Ilana, Eli, and Racheli

# Table of Contents

# Acknowledgments

"Capital markets are for us, CEOs of public companies, the most important thing," the CEO of an innovative pharmaceutical company stated to me over lunch in San Francisco. Crossing the Bay Bridge back to Berkeley, I decided to write a book on this very topic: how to make the interactions between managers and investors mutually beneficial.

I thankfully received considerable assistance and support writing this book. The extensive research underlying practically every chapter was facilitated by highly capable colleagues: Richard Carrizosa, Peter Demerjian, Feng Gu, Kalin Kolev, Alina Lerman, Theodore Sougiannis, Jennifer Tucker, and Emanuel Zur. Many colleagues provided vital information, including Massimiliano Bonacchi, Mary Billings, Dan Cohen, Melissa Lewis, and Suresh Radhakrishnan.

Various experts read parts of the manuscript and enlightened me with insightful comments: Rachel Corn, Kenneth Jensen, April Klein, Sarah McVay, Richard Passov, Christine Petrovits, and Stephen Ryan. Special thanks to Gene Epstein for extensive comments on the book, extending even to its title, and for his wisdom. I was particularly fortunate to obtain the administrative support of my highly professional and dedicated assistant Autherine Allison, as well as that of the equally dedicated and professional Shevon Estwick. Nancy Kleinrock edited the manuscript very skillfully and wisely, and Jing Chen assisted with the numerous references. Joanne Hvala, Stern School's associate dean, provided valuable marketing advice.

My rough manuscript was transformed into a much improved book by Harvard Business Review Press editor Justin Fox, who was ably assisted by Jennifer Waring, Erin Brown, Stephani Finks, and Kevin Evers at HBRP. Kirsten Sandberg, a former HBRP editor, helped me in the planning of the book.

My wife Ilana and children Eli and Rachel, to whom I collectively dedicate the book, were a constant source of encouragement and wisdom, as were our grandchildren—Netanel, Daniel, Gregory, Maor, Jason, and Michael—and daughter- and son-in-law, Ayala Lev and Tom Corn. Of these, our lovely granddaughter Daniel (age 12) provided the real impetus to conclude the book. While staying with us, she greeted me every morning with a smile and the ever-present and guilt-inducing query, "Did you finish the book already?"

# Why Restoring Investors' Trust in Managers Is Now Critical

Capital markets during the first decade of the twenty-first century were hostile territory for investors. From the debacles of Enron and World-Com early in the decade to the collapse of Bear Stearns, Lehman Brothers, and Countrywide Financial at its end, and from the vanished investments in dot-coms and high-techs in 2000 to the massive losses of funds sunk into stocks, subprime mortgages, and commercial real estate, equity investors suffered mightily. Many corporate managers meanwhile enjoyed ever-increasing, sometimes detached-from-performance compensation, some even abusing stock option grants and helping themselves to outrageous perks and golden parachutes, all enabled by complacent, often incompetent directors. Investors' disillusionment, ire, and loss of trust in corporate leaders were the inevitable outcome. And a seriously costly outcome it is. Consider:

- Investors' discontent brought new costly regulations: first, after the stock market collapse of 2001 and 2002, the wide-reaching Sarbanes-Oxley Act and, later, after the 2007–2008 financial crisis, the Dodd-Frank Wall Street Reform and Consumer Protection Act, which reached far beyond the financial sector with its "say on pay" provision, enhancing regulators' and shareholders' reach at the expense of managers'.

1

- Shareholders' and boards' increasing impatience is shrinking the tenure of top managers. Mean CEO tenure in the United States was cut by a quarter—from eight to six years—in just the last decade. And not only in the United States. In February 2010, SAP, the world's third-largest software producer, broke the world record for speed-firing CEOs of major companies by ousting Léo Apotheker after just nine months at the helm as sole chief (not to worry, he landed at Hewlett-Packard).

- The relentless drive for director independence—the cure du jour for governance ills—and the rising number of thumbs-down votes by shareholders at directors' elections transformed many corporate boards from managers' counselors and advisers into supervisors and monitors, and sometimes even into adversaries. Frank information sharing and competent advice in board meetings are the victims.

- Sensing investors' discontent and managers' loss of power, hedge funds and other activists preyed on companies to gain board seats, deplete cash reserves, and change corporate strategies. Recently, even some long-dormant mutual funds joined the activists' ranks.

- The increasing number and success of shareholder proposals and proxy contests aimed at changing corporate bylaws, separating the CEO and board chair positions, curbing compensation, as well as enacting a slew of social and environmental provisions, obviously encroach on managers' prerogatives and restrict their decision space.

All this—primarily the outcome of investors' and the public's loss of trust—impinge on the ability of managers to do their jobs. The power and stature of executives have declined during the past decade, as Marcel Kahan and Edward Rock, leading law professors, document in their recent and widely read paper, "Embattled CEOs."[1] While a certain shift of power from executives to corporate constituencies may be desirable, there is always the danger of the pendulum of change swinging too far. Perhaps it already has.

Regaining investors' and the public's confidence is the most critical issue facing corporate executives in the early twenty-first century. How else will they be able to secure investors' and lenders' backing for investments in growth (R&D, IT, brands), corporate restructurings, or strategic shifts? How else will they fend off disruptive activist investors and trial lawyers? For managers, it's about protecting the core of their businesses—not to mention their jobs.

Alas, there is no magic bullet here, no quick PR fix. Rebuilding confidence requires a concerted effort to repair relations with investors and the public: improve the quality and integrity of financial disclosure, restructure managerial compensation systems and governance design, and rethink corporate social responsibility. And above all, root out earnings manipulation, compensation abuses, false promises and hype, and self-serving managerial activities. These issues are what this book is about.

This book is a survival kit, outlining systematically the way managers can regain and sustain investors' confidence. Drawing on voluminous state-of-the-art research in finance, economics, accounting, and management, and plugging numerous knowledge gaps with my own research conducted for this book, I analyze a broad spectrum of issues and strategies related to managers' interaction with capital markets, along with the consequences of such interaction, leading to practical actions. This comprehensive evidence-based approach focuses on *proactive* policies—how to avoid disappointing investors—as well as *reactive* actions—what to do when bad things happen. This, then, provides the basis for the specific actions—"operating instructions"—I prescribe at the end of each chapter, building up to the comprehensive capital markets strategy presented in the final chapter. While this book is primarily aimed at corporate managers, the wide scope of evidence and experience of what works and doesn't work in capital markets, laid out next, will also be of great interest to investors, financial analysts, and business students, as well as to the business-minded public.

## The Critical Role of Capital Markets

I have recently analyzed, with a group of doctoral students, the detailed transcripts of hundreds of quarterly earnings conference calls of managers with investors and analysts. As this book unfolds, I will share with you what I learned from this fascinating, albeit laborious (that's where the students come in handy), endeavor. One startling observation: with but one exception, all the conference calls, lasting about two hours each, were conducted by the CEO along with the CFO—sometimes with other executives present—and watched over, of course, by legal counsel. These are not special events, mind you. Conference calls, made soon after the release of quarterly results, have been, in recent years, routine events, yet the top corporate guns conducted them all.

Can you think of another corporate activity that is never delegated? Subordinates usually make crucial production, investment, marketing, or R&D decisions, and important relations with legislators and governmental institutions are often assigned to lobbyists. Talking to investors, in contrast, obviously cannot be entrusted to underlings. And, come to think of it, for good reason.

The capital markets arena is where the success or failure of public companies is largely determined: the company's cost of capital—the all-important price and, often, the availability of external funds to finance investment and growth—is determined in the capital markets, based on the information available to investors.[2] Share prices—the outcome of investors' expectations and trades—directly affect managers' compensation and increasingly their tenure: research consistently shows that poor share performance significantly increases the likelihood of top managers' termination.[3] Moreover, investor discontent, sparked by disappointing news and chronically depressed equity values, is the prime trigger for activist shareholders: Carl Icahn at Motorola, Nelson Peltz at Cadbury Schweppes, Eric Knight targeting HSBC Bank, Steel Partners at Japanese beer maker Sapporo, Ralph Whitworth at Sprint Nextel, and CalPERS, the giant California pension fund targeting multiple companies each year, are but a few examples of shareholder activists intruding in recent years on managerial turf, primarily because of share underperformance.[4] And when investor discontent persists, a takeover and managerial overhaul ensues. Not the least of the adverse consequences of dropping stock prices are the consequent class-action lawsuits filed against managers and board members. All serious consequences indeed.

Less appreciated, yet equally important is the fact that share price patterns—growth or decline—are a beacon for highly qualified employees to join, stay, or leave the organization. The "war for talent" is fought partially with stock. Google's spectacular stock price rise from 2005 to 2007 facilitated its raids on top software engineers and programmers employed by stock-price-lagging technology companies, including mighty Microsoft and Intel, while Google's subsequent price decline from 2008 to 2009 contributed to its own brain drain. And Morgan Stanley's mediocre performance from 2004 to 2005 was a major reason for the defection of top banking talent to competitors.

While capital markets affect the fortunes of all public enterprises, they are most crucial to the survival and growth of "equity-dependent companies," those young, small and midsize, earnings- and cash-flow-starved businesses that nevertheless have attractive investment opportunities. These are high-tech, biotech, Internet–based, and health-care companies, as well as entrepreneurial transportation, telecommunications, and energy companies. They all rely on capital markets to fund their investment and growth.[5] Downcast investors' perceptions and lethargic stock performance are particularly damaging to these companies, which are vital to the nation's economic growth.

No company is immune to the vagaries of the capital market. Even if it doesn't rely on the stock market for continuous fund-raising—having no plans for stock or bond issues in the foreseeable future—the performance of the company's shares, lagging or leading comparable firms, is an influential operating and solvency signal to lenders, suppliers, and customers, affecting their relations with the company. Suppliers are known, for example, to restrict sales and credit to retailers with depressed share prices. No wonder, then, that interaction with investors, such as in conference calls, is invariably conducted by the Cs: CEO and CFO.

## Ephemeral Growth and Investors' Discontent

It's all well and good as long as managers report profits and growth—increasing sales, earnings, and margins, beating analysts' consensus forecasts—and predict a bright future. But practically every growth company sooner or later sees its core businesses mature and ultimately decline, and rejuvenating the growth so craved by investors is difficult. For doubters, the investment research firm Morningstar demonstrates how ephemeral growth is.[6] Out of 2,179 public companies that had a one-year rise in earnings-per-share (EPS), only 41 percent saw their EPS increase over three consecutive years, and for five-year running growth, the number dwindles to 16 percent. Only 67 companies of the original 2,179—a mere 3 percent—reported EPS increases for ten years running. These sobering findings concerning the transitory nature of corporate growth are corroborated by comprehensive empirical research.[7]

The picture is even bleaker for corporate performance tracked by free cash flows (operating cash flows minus capital expenditures). Of the 1,787 companies in Morningstar's study with a one-year free cash flow growth, only 3 percent managed to report five-year running increases of this widely used performance indicator, and for ten years the number of consistent enhancers of free cash flow is virtually nil. If you wonder why cash-flow growth decays much faster than EPS growth, you will meet a major culprit starring prominently in later chapters—information manipulation. The closely watched EPS figure is manipulated more intensely than are the less scrutinized cash flows, thereby giving the appearance of a longer-lasting EPS growth. By now, the picture should be clear: your likelihood of sooner rather than later disappointing investors with an EPS or cash flow decline or, heaven forbid, a miss of the consensus analyst forecast of earnings is overwhelming.

It happens to the mightiest, too. Consider figure I-1, portraying the number of annual EPS and return on equity (ROE) decreases for *Fortune's* ten most-admired companies in 2008, during the fifteen-year period from 1994 to 2008. One would think that "the most admired" don't disappoint. Far from it. Berkshire Hathaway, Warren Buffett's famously successful enterprise, had no less than six EPS reversals and seven ROE declines in fifteen years. No wonder Buffett adamantly refuses to provide earnings guidance to investors. Southwest Airlines, the most successful U.S. carrier of all time, experienced no less than five years of disappointing EPS growth and nine reversals of ROE, followed by Procter & Gamble (three and five disappointments) and Toyota (three and six). Apple and Federal Express, celebrated growth stories, also saw their fortunes reverse frequently. Even Google, which enjoyed a meteoric stock price rise from its IPO in 2004 through 2007, has experienced one EPS and five ROE disappointments in its short history.[8] Have one last look at the figure and note that, for each company, the number of ROE reversals is substantially larger than EPS decreases. The reason: the closely watched EPS is easier to "manage" than is ROE (by a stock repurchase, for example), and even without manipulation, it often overstates the company's profitability (since it ignores the capital increase from periodic retained earnings).

Given the overwhelming likelihood of disappointing investors, what's a manager to do? I devote a considerable part of the book to answer this critical question. From outlining how best to conduct conference calls after disappointing earnings, through immunizing your company against trial lawyers and activist hedge funds preying on companies in distress, to guiding investors on the company's prospects and providing them with valuation-relevant information not required by accounting rules, I prescribe the ways to avoid capital market setbacks and ride them out when they do occur.

FIGURE I-1

**Number of year-to-year decreases of EPS and ROE for the 2008 *Fortune* most admired companies, 1994–2008**

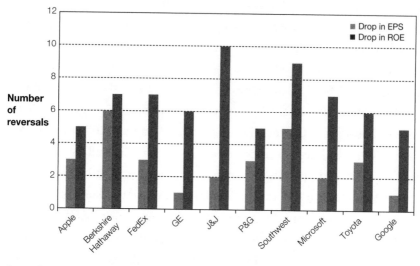

*Source:* Compustat database.

## What, Me Worry?

Some managers profess to be largely unconcerned with investors, claiming that shareholders are just one class of stakeholders managers should answer to, and perhaps not even the most important class. Furthermore, say managers, most investors are short-term oriented, and catering to their whims interferes with advancing the long-term growth of companies. Others claim they don't plan to issue stock in the foreseeable future, so why bother about stock prices? And then there are the ideologues arguing that Wall Street should be kept separate from Main Street: managers should do their thing—run the business—and investors will follow. Such "isolationist" views reflect a fundamental misconception of capital markets and are hazardous to companies and their managers' careers.

This is why: the premises underlying the isolationists' arguments are factually flawed. Take investors' myopia. As I demonstrate later, while some investors are indeed short-term oriented, the market as a whole is clearly *dominated* by long-term investors, as evidenced by my finding that about half of the typical stock price reflects the long-term growth prospects of companies. Or, consider the attitude of "we don't plan to issue stock in the foreseeable future, hence . . ."—an unwise posture, to put it mildly. One never knows when an attractive investment opportunity—a business acquisition or a major R&D project—will present itself, but if the company's shares at the moment are seriously undervalued, managers will be deprived of a ready source of financing. And when credit markets dry up, as was the case from 2008 to 2009, where will investment funding come from? Here, as elsewhere in the book, empirical evidence speaks loudly. As prominent finance scholars Gene Fama and Ken French document in a 2004 study, the likelihood of any firm tapping into the stock market is high: from 1993 through 2002, 86 percent of their sample (3,000 to 4,500 U.S. companies) issued some equity—seasoned equity offerings, equity issues in mergers, private placements, or employee stock options—*each year.*[9] Fama and French end their study in 2002, but even in the financial crisis years, from 2007 to 2008, the total volume of stock issues in the United States (IPOs and seasoned equity) exceeded $100 billion a year, only slightly below the average of the early 2000s. Very few managers can credibly claim that they will not access capital markets in the foreseeable future.

Essentially, an isolationist attitude toward capital markets reveals a fundamental misunderstanding of their role in advanced economies. In addition to the obvious function—raising funds for corporate investment and growth—capital markets generate crucial information about business enterprises and their prospects, and serve important monitoring and governance roles affecting managers' compensation and careers, whether they access these markets frequently or not.

How do capital markets do all this? Consider: where do investors get reliable information on prospective risks and returns of securities?

Certain raw data originates from companies through IPO prospectuses and periodic financial reports. But such accounting-based information suffers from serious deficiencies; recall the inflated valuations of subprime mortgages in financial institutions' reports from 2007 to 2008, necessitating ever-increasing asset write-offs and restatements.[10] No wonder the usefulness of financial report data decreases continuously, as I show in chapter 7. Capital market intermediaries (buy- and sell-side analysts, and various shareholder advisory services, among others) analyze and adjust the raw data reported by companies and blend it with other information and analyses—macro-economic statistics, industrial trends and prospects, and competitive position evaluations—to provide actionable data for investors.[11] This extensive information processing and generation of new data in capital markets enhance considerably the quality and usefulness of information on prospective risks and returns available to investors, as evidenced, for example, by the significant stock price reaction to analysts revising their earnings forecasts and recommendations.[12]

Such information generation about your company and its performance—affecting its stock prices, your compensation and sometimes tenure, the terms of bank loans, shareholder activists' interventions, class-action lawsuits, and even SEC actions—will take place *with or without* your participation. In the latter case, however, you deny yourself the crucial opportunity to shape and correct investors' information. Research has shown, for example, that financial analysts are often overly optimistic about companies' sales or earnings, leading to investor disappointments when the reported numbers fall short of expectations. Guiding analysts in such cases will prevent the disappointment. Research also shows that the shares of intangibles-intensive (R&D, brands) companies are often undervalued by investors, leading, if uncorrected, to excessive cost of capital and lower corporate investment and growth. Disclosure of supplementary information and certain timely actions like a stock buyback or a dividend change will correct the undervaluation of shares. And, when short sellers spread negative rumors about your company, hedge fund activists publicly call for an unjustified change of strategy, or analysts fail to fully appreciate your company's prospects, it is, in my opinion, a dereliction of your duties as a manager not to intervene in the information processing taking place in capital markets, even if you believe your investors are myopic or if you don't plan a stock issue. The bottom line is that you can't retreat from an institution—capital markets—that affects your company's performance and your career. Remember, in capital markets, silence is *not* golden. No news is bad news. Disengagement from investors is not an option.

## A U.S.-Centric or a Global Book?

Is a book like this dealing with capital market strategies restricted to U.S. and U.K. and perhaps Japanese audiences? Absolutely not. Practically every major topic in this book—be it earnings management, mispriced shares, voluntary information disclosure, investors' alleged short-termism, hedge fund activism, effective corporate governance, managers' compensation, corporate social responsibility, or capital markets and cyberspace—is as relevant to French, German, Chinese, Korean, Brazilian, and other developed countries' managers as it is to U.S. and U.K. executives and investors.[13] In fact, capital markets are crucial to the investment and growth of public companies in all countries where the majority of corporate ownership is *diffused*, that is, held by other than founders, governments, or large blockholders. Rene Stulz, in a 2005 study, provides country-by-country data on the mean percentage of shares held by corporate insiders, relative to the remainder owned by diffused shareholders.[14] Selected examples: in the U.S., U.K., and Ireland, diffused ownership of public companies exceeds 80 percent, on average; in the Netherlands, Australia, Switzerland, Canada, and Korea, it exceeds 70 percent; and in Taiwan, Sweden, Finland, and France, diffused ownership is higher than 60 percent. In Japan, Italy, Israel, Belgium, Brazil, and Spain, diffused ownership surpasses 50 percent, and it is a shade below 50 percent in India, Singapore, and Thailand.[15]

In all these countries, spanning the globe, investors wield considerable influence on the cost and availability of investment funds, on managers' compensation and tenure, and on corporate governance and strategies via activist shareholders. A 2008 study of thirty-eight countries by Woojin Kim and Michael Weisbach documents that equity offerings for capital expenditures and R&D (both IPOs and seasoned stock offerings) are prevalent throughout the world, and with equity issuance comes the monitoring of companies by investors and often intervention in companies' activities.[16] Accordingly, the topics I discuss and analyze in this book, and particularly the actionable prescriptions I provide, are essentially universal, relevant to executives of public companies and their shareholders throughout the world.

Much of the research I use in this book, is, however, based on U.S. data. The reason: U.S. financial databases—for corporate financial reports, stock prices, executive compensation, analyst forecasts, and R&D—are more comprehensive and cover longer time periods than in most other countries. Also, many trends, such as earnings forecasts and guidance, litigation, and stock options, start, for better or worse, in America. In addition, more researchers in the United States engage in empirical financial markets and accounting research than in other countries, accounting for the abundance of capital markets research using U.S. data. I strongly believe, however, that with few exceptions this research is relevant across the globe. Nevertheless, wherever available I use research from non-U.S. countries.

## The Shape of Things to Come

There are three major themes in this book. The first deals with handling emergencies—putting out fires. The company's performance unexpectedly stalls—earnings decline, consensus analysts' forecast is missed, an IPO bombs, or a drug is rejected by the FDA. I prescribe what to do in such cases, particularly when you fail to meet the consensus analysts' forecast or otherwise disappoint investors, and how best to communicate with investors. I outline the detrimental consequences of earnings management and information manipulation, and advance strategies to fend off class-action lawyers.

The second theme takes the long view: how to regain and maintain investors' trust. I outline strategies to prevent share prices from deviating systematically from intrinsic values and the consequent shocks when inflated prices revert to fundamentals. I delineate circumstances in which to guide investors concerning the future, what information beyond that legally required is beneficial to disclose to capital markets, the actions to take to bolster managers' message to investors, and the specific corporate social responsibility policies that are good for both businesses and society.

The third theme deals with the prickly issues of conflicts between owners and managers. First, I debunk the perennial and distracting allegation that investors are myopically obsessed with quarterly earnings, forcing short-termism on managers. I then proceed to address the important questions of how to deal with activist investors—hedge funds, in particular—and those pesky short sellers, and how to achieve an optimal shareholder mix. Next I focus on corporate governance and conduct—the presumed solution to shareholder-manager conflicts. I then turn to a major point of shareholder-manager contention—executives' compensation—and outline the contours of an equitable compensation system. Finally, I summarize and distill the specific action plans concluding each chapter into a coherent, operational, corporate capital markets strategy.

Throughout the book, I emphasize "critical thinking," that is, a systematic reliance on state-of-the-art empirical evidence, carefully separating fact from fiction and causality from mere association. For example, do corporate charitable contributions *enhance* sales and profits (causation), or are corporate contributions just *correlated* with sales and profits, since profitable companies tend to give more to charities? Separating causation from association is important. The former informs managers about the benefits of actions, such as charitable contribution or share purchases by managers, whereas the latter—association—doesn't tell managers much. Debunking widespread myths—that shareholder litigation proliferates, that share overpricing is good, that charitable contributions are a waste of corporate resources, that earnings guidance is dysfunctional, that investors are short-term oriented, to name a few—is a major objective of this book. It's fun, too. As to details, here is a brief chapter-by-chapter outline.

I begin chapter 1, "It's Not the End of the World," with the worst-case scenario: your company hits the skids—earnings stall, margins shrink, revenues stagnate—and you are facing a miss of the consensus analysts' forecast of earnings. What's a manager to do? Contrary to popular belief, investor reactions to earnings disappointments are in most cases both mild and temporary, and hasty measures to "make the numbers," legit or not, are often counterproductive. The best course of action is to warn investors, outline clearly and credibly the remedial action plan, and focus on improving the business.

Chapter 2, "Do We Have a Story for You," deals with mending fences with investors, focusing on conference calls and other investor communication venues. I outline what works and doesn't work in investor communications, and how to handle tough questions by analysts. I also discuss managerial communication in cyberspace—financial blogs, chat rooms, and investment communities.

When performance stalls and shareholders are disillusioned, it is often difficult to resist the temptation to manage (manipulate) sales and earnings, particularly when managers believe—and who doesn't?—that the slump is temporary. In chapter 3, "To Manage or Not to Manage Earnings?" I tackle the ethically charged and practically complex issue of information manipulation. Analyzing an array of SEC-sanctioned manipulation cases, I show that unless the business slowdown is short-lived—most, unfortunately, are not—earnings manipulation exacerbates the predicament, thereby hastening a painful blowout. Earnings "management" is, in fact, gross mismanagement.

Earnings disappointments, restatements, and information manipulation are sure to draw the attention of class-action lawyers. In chapter 4, "Kill All the Lawyers?" I present both good and bad news: the myth that shareholder lawsuits automatically follow sharp stock price drops is just that, a myth. However, in certain industries (high-tech and biotech, for example) and circumstances (large, previous share price increases), the probability of being sued following bad news is rather high. Accordingly, I develop a research-based profile of litigation risk factors—akin to cardiac arrest signs—enabling you to assess litigation risk. For high-exposure companies, I design an immunization strategy to thwart lawsuits.

From putting out fires, I shift gears to the second theme—the proactive, longer view: how to regain investors' confidence and avoid the predicament of further disappointing them? In chapter 5, "Nothing in Excess," I take up the sure recipe for investor letdown—an inflated stock price, rare in recessions, yet frequent in normal times. An overvalued stock, by definition, leads to investor disillusionment, steep price declines, and sometimes to shareholder litigation and managerial turnover. Accordingly, I outline techniques to determine the extent of overvaluation—as well as undervaluation—and propose the means to *safely* revert the price of both under- and overvalued companies to fundamentals.

Providing consistent and credible guidance—performance forecasts—to investors is an effective, yet hotly debated way to prevent prices from straying from fundamentals (intrinsic values) and regain managers' credibility. In chapter 6, "Guiding the Misguided," I analyze earnings guidance and show that, despite the vehement objection by various business associations and sage investors like Warren Buffett, guidance under the right circumstances is a very effective tool for narrowing the information gap between managers and investors and keeping the stock price close to fundamentals.

Guidance refers to near-term earnings or sales prognostications. In chapter 7, "Life Beyond GAAP," I considerably expand the scope of disclosure to deal with the voluntary release of information that complements and sometimes substitutes for the statutorily required, yet often deficient disclosures. I show that beyond-GAAP disclosures—such as on the scope and depth of the product pipeline of biotech and pharmaceutical companies, royalty income from patent licensing, or customer growth rates and churn of subscription-based companies—are richly rewarded by investors in reduced cost of capital, lower stock price volatility, and higher analyst following.

Actions, goes the saying, speak louder than words. Indeed. In chapter 8, "Put Your Money Where Your Mouth Is," I switch from communications to real managerial actions, such as dividend changes, stock splits, and stock repurchases; the use of reputable (and expensive) underwriters; and increases in managers' and directors' stock ownership in their company. I bring to bear extensive research documenting which actions work and which fail to change investor perceptions.

In chapter 9, "Is Doing Good, Good for Business?" I examine whether it makes sense for corporations to engage in environmental, community, poverty-reduction, and health-care activities, even if they don't enhance the bottom line. I conclude that these days it's irresponsible not to be socially responsible and offer answers on how much, where, and when.

Chapter 10, "In the Long Run, We're All Dead" (John Maynard Keynes's immortal—or, rather, mortal—quip), opens the third theme: owners versus managers. I start by removing a major obstacle to effective interaction with shareholders: the popular belief in investor myopia (short-termism). The evidence I present conclusively shows that long-term investors dominate the market, and most shareholders care a lot about your company's long-term prospects. Accordingly, don't waste time and energy lamenting investor myopia and appeasing short-term-oriented investors. But, while most investors aren't myopic, short sellers definitely are, and I suggest how to deal with them.

While not necessarily myopic, "activist" investors can make life hell for managers and directors. In chapter 11, "Breathing Down Your

Neck," I deal with the worldwide rise in shareholder activism, particularly the recent strain led by hedge funds. I show that, contrary to widespread belief, hedge fund and institutional investor activism is often a good thing, driving up shareholder value and improving corporate governance. Based on a profile of targets of activism that I develop, you will be able to ascertain how vulnerable your company might be to activist attack, and what you should do if it were to happen.

In the wake of the corporate scandals of the early 2000s and the ensuing legislation, some boards are coming to resemble shareholder activists. Directors are increasingly assertive in overseeing corporate performance and managerial conduct, evidenced by growing managerial turnover. In chapter 12, "Looking Out for You, Dear Shareholder," I take the unconventional view that the relentless move toward a full *monitoring* board has gone too far. In many cases, independent directors lack expertise in the company's business and technology, depriving managers of much-needed advice. I call for a rebalancing of the board and other governance mechanisms to enhance *both* the monitoring and advising of managers. A friendlier, more effective board, so to speak.

Managers' compensation is a major irritant to shareholders and the public at large. I analyze the thorny issues of compensation in chapter 13, "Excess or Excellence?" and conclude, based on evidence, that the major problem with managers' pay is the prevalent weak link between compensation and company performance. I point at the urgent need to substantially restructure managerial compensation systems to strengthen their link with long-term value enhancement and to curb manipulation and abuse.

Chapter 14, "What Then Must We Do?" distills the specific prescriptions and action plans—operating instructions—that conclude each chapter into a coherent corporate capital markets strategy. Essentially, I provide a comprehensive prescription for what to do and not do to satisfy investors.

## Chapter 1

# It's Not the End of the World

## What to Do—and Not Do—When Faced with Missing the Consensus Earnings Estimate

➡ Why a one-penny miss of the consensus is so deleterious.

➡ What factors determine investors' reaction to companies' results.

➡ Why high-growth companies that disappoint investors are hit hard.

➡ What actions managers can take to avoid a consensus miss, and its consequences.

➡ What course mitigates investors' response to disappointments.

On June 26, 2007, the Kroger Company reported a 10 percent rise in first-quarter profits. The supermarket chain's shares, however, fell 4.7 percent (the S&P 500 rose 0.6 percent).[1] What gives? Kroger's EPS, coming at $.47, missed the analysts' consensus earnings estimate by a penny—the dreaded consensus miss.[2] What happens to other companies that miss the consensus? Will their price drop further and linger on in a funk, or pick up with the improvement in business fundamentals? What types of companies are penalized harshly for missing the consensus and which remain largely unscathed? On the bright side, what happens when you "make the numbers"—meet or beat analysts' estimates, or surpass last year's EPS? And does it all matter beyond the few days surrounding the earnings release? The extensive evidence on these and related questions dealing with what is often dubbed "the earnings game"—managers' continuous struggle to meet investors' expectations—is highly revealing and will be analyzed next. At the chapter's end, I advance a consequence-mitigation action plan for executives facing the specter of disappointing investors. In a nutshell, as indicated by this chapter's title, missing the consensus, if dealt with appropriately, is not the end of the world. Far from it. In contrast, desperate attempts frequently taken to avoid disappointing investors by a last-minute sales blitz or cost cuts, an earnings boost from a change of accounting procedure, or—worst of all—manipulating the numbers are at best ineffective and often seriously counterproductive.

## The Not-So-Bell-Shaped Earnings Surprises

Many wonder why investors take so seriously an earnings consensus miss, even by a penny. Simply, because relatively few companies get entrapped in this predicament. Look at figure 1-1 from Mei Feng's 2008 study of quarterly EPS surprises, which displays the difference between reported EPS and the last consensus estimate available prior to earnings release. Feng's sample is very large and representative: 180,000 quarterly observations from 1988 through 2005, an average of 2,500 companies per quarter. The highest bar, situated in the center of the graph, indicates that roughly 24,000 observations (about 13 percent of the sample) were perfect hits, where reported EPS matched the consensus to the penny. Many companies fared even better: the three successively decreasing bars to the right of zero surprise indicate that about 47,000 cases—over a quarter of the sample—beat the consensus by $.01 to $.03.

FIGURE 1-1

## Earning surprises: Reported EPS minus analyst consensus estimate, 1988–2005

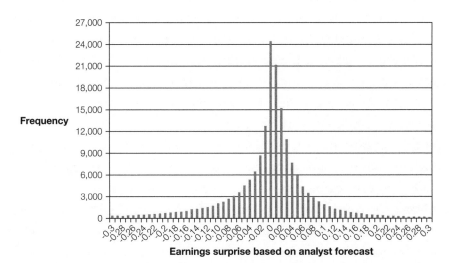

**Earnings surprise based on analyst forecast**

*Source:* Mei Feng, "Why do managers meet or slightly beat earnings forecasts in equilibrium? An endogenous mean-variance explanation," working paper, Katz Graduate School of Business, University of Pittsburgh, 2008.

Thus, a whopping 71,000 cases, almost 40 percent of the sample, meet or beat by $.01 to $.03 the analysts' forecasts. This, mind you, is the optimal play of the earnings game. You want to beat the consensus, but not handily, lest analysts raise the bar substantially for next quarter or year.

In sharp and painful contrast, the three bars to the left of the perfect hit indicate that only about 27,000 cases (15 percent of the sample) miss the consensus by $.01 to $.03. Herein lies the main answer to the opening question: missing the EPS consensus estimate even by a few pennies takes a heavy toll on the stock because it places you in the minority of underperformers. Not good company to keep. Moreover, given that the majority of companies manage to avoid missing the consensus, those who get entrapped are presumed not only to come short of expectations, but also to have tried every means available, legit or not, to get over the consensus hump and failed. This obviously suggests to investors the existence of serious business issues lurking in the background, causing the strong negative reaction to even a one-penny miss.[3]

There is another remarkable feature in figure 1-1. In such a large sample of EPS surprises, encompassing eighteen years of boom and bust and including thousands of companies operating in most economic sectors, it is reasonable to expect the earnings surprises to be bell-shaped—symmetrically distributed around zero: a certain number of consensus matches at the center, flanked on both sides by a roughly equal and decreasing number of negative and positive surprises. But look closely at the figure and you will see a surprising—no pun intended—pattern of earnings surprises. Centered on top of zero surprise is, as expected, the highest bar, but to its right are the two next-highest columns, indicating that beating analyst forecasts by $.01 to $.02—a dream come true—is the second most-frequent occurrence. Missing the consensus by a penny is only the fourth-highest bar in the graph. In fact, the ratio of $.02 consensus hits to misses is 1.7:1—hardly a bell-shaped phenomenon.

Clearly, something other than chance is going on here. If the outcomes of repeated rolls of a dice would resemble the figure, the inescapable conclusion would be that the dice are loaded. So what's going on with the earnings game between managers and analysts? Are analysts chronically pessimistic, systematically underestimating earnings, thereby creating an overwhelming number of consensus beats? Highly unlikely, since analysts and their employers profit primarily from people *buying* stocks, and downcast earnings forecasts are hardly a recipe for investment. Moreover, pessimistic forecasts—driving away investors—will bring down on analysts the wrath of managers, likely severing the all-important managers–analyst information channel.[4] In fact, my evidence indicates that analysts are, if anything, optimistic. More likely, the unexpectedly large number of consensus beaters is caused by suave "earnings gamers" who either succeed in guiding—"walking down"—analysts to lower the forecast bar sufficiently for them to surpass it, and/or those who "manage" (simply put, manipulate) reported earnings to meet or slightly beat the forecast. The former manage the consensus, whereas the latter manage earnings. And then there are those who manage both. The 1.7:1 asymmetry between consensus beaters and missers strongly suggests that earnings gamers are far from an endangered species.[5]

The widespread earnings game poses a serious ethical and practical dilemma for honest managers. What to do when competitor managers are manipulating earnings and, in the process, are securing investors' favor and low-cost funds? Persist with a depressed stock—an invitation to activist shareholders and takeover specialists—or join the manipulators? A vivid example of this dilemma involved a superstar of the early 2000s scandals, WorldCom, and its fierce competitors AT&T and Sprint. In the late 1990s and early 2000s, WorldCom engaged in one of the most brazen accounting scams in history, inflating reported earnings by more than $10 billion through the capitalization (recorded as assets) of regular operating expenses. The fraudulently "superior" performance of WorldCom—fast-growing earnings and enviable margins—totally spooked financial analysts and placed heavy pressure on AT&T and Sprint managers to shape up and match the "performance" of their star competitor, which, to their credit, they refrained from doing. The twenty-five-year prison term given in 2005 to Bernie Ebbers, World-Com's CEO at the time of the fraud, was probably a small consolation to AT&T's and Sprint's beleaguered executives, and to their shareholders living dangerously for several years with depressed share prices. Research on "scandal companies" depressingly indicates that executives of competing firms saw their compensation drop as the manipulators "outperformed" them.[6] I will return to the intriguing issue of earnings manipulation in this chapter and in chapter 4, but first let's examine briefly the partners to the earnings game: financial analysts.

## How Good Are Analysts Anyway?

Is the focus that investors and managers have on analysts' consensus estimates warranted? To answer this question, I computed for every year, 1995 through 2006, the percentage of analysts' forecast error—the difference between *reported* annual EPS and the *consensus* EPS, relative to reported EPS—for four thousand to five thousand companies a year. I examined two forecast horizons: a twelve-month horizon using the first consensus estimate after the previous year's earnings release, and a three-month (fourth quarter) horizon, using the first consensus estimate after the third-quarter earnings release. To provide a benchmark, I repeated the forecast error computation with an "extrapolation (naive) forecast," where the prior year's reported EPS (or the mean of the prior four quarters' EPS, for the three-month prediction) competed with the analysts' consensus. I thus compared analysts to a "dummy," predicting that history repeats itself perfectly (someone quipped that history doesn't repeat itself, only historians do).

My results showed that analysts' (the consensus) median forecast error was 14.5 percent of reported earnings for the twelve-month horizon and 3.9 percent for the three-month horizon. The corresponding median forecast errors for the extrapolation forecast—which is free of charge, of course—are 23.7 percent for the yearly horizon and 13.8 percent for the three-month horizon. Analysts' forecasts are obviously better than a simple extrapolation, and they show an improvement from 2002 to 2006. Also, in every year the mean errors are negative, indicating that analysts' forecasts are optimistic, on average. Other research indicates that analysts' forecasts improve with experience, breadth of industry coverage, and size of employer; and that following analysts' stock recommendations (buy, hold, sell) will get you about 4 percent abnormal (above-market) gain annually, although much of it will be eaten up by transaction costs.[7] (Findings for European analysts are quite similar.[8]) The lesson is, don't rush to dismiss analysts as quacks.

## Anatomy of Hits and Misses

Investor reaction to the release of financial results is often hard to predict; it's surely not a Pavlovian reaction to whether reported earnings miss, meet, or beat the consensus. Sometimes the reaction to a miss is harsh, other times mild, or even positive. It may be temporary or long-lasting.

The following cases, focusing on the consequences of hits and misses, are instructive for the proactive managerial action I outline later.

- **EBAY'S ONE-PENNY MISS.** On January 19, 2005, eBay—the world's leading online auction company—posted fourth-quarter EPS (excluding one-time items) of $.33, compared with $.24 a year earlier, an enviable 37.5 percent growth. Analysts' consensus estimate, however, was $.34, leading to the nasty one-penny miss. eBay's stock tumbled on the disappointment by 21.7 percent (S&P 500 decreased 1.7 percent), despite the fact that other eBay indicators were positive: quarterly sales, for example, were up 44 percent from the year earlier, slightly beating analysts' sales forecast, and, in an attempt to mollify investors and perhaps distract them from the one-penny miss, the company announced a 2:1 stock split, generally considered a harbinger of good things to come (not really; see chapter 8). But all to no avail—eBay's stock was hammered.

    What explains the fury that greeted eBay's earnings? A postmortem by market mavens suggested that the earnings disappointment was aggravated by eBay's lukewarm outlook for the rest of 2005: an annual EPS range of $1.48 to $1.52 against analysts' estimate of $1.50 to $1.72. But this could hardly justify a 22 percent price drop lasting three months until the subsequent earnings announcement. The real culprit, corroborated by the research I present in the next section, was the 80 percent price rise of eBay's stock over the ten months preceding the January 2005 earnings announcement (the S&P 500 index over the corresponding period increased by a mere 5 percent). What gets a stock clobbered upon a consensus miss is not so much the severity of the earnings shortfall, but rather the shattering of investors' erstwhile growth dreams—the more enticing the dream, reflected by the price rise, the larger the disappointment upon wake-up. This, we will see, has important implications for proactive management.

- **WALMART ALSO MISSES BY A PENNY.** On May 12, 2005, Walmart Stores—the world's largest retailer—released first-quarter 2005 EPS (excluding one-time items) of $.55 against a consensus forecast of $.56. Once more—a one-penny miss. However, in contrast to eBay, Walmart also slightly missed the sales target, $71.7 billion versus an estimate of $72.0 billion, and, like eBay, issued a gloomy guidance for the following quarter: an EPS range estimate of $.03 to $.07 below the analysts' estimate. Surely, an all-around disappointing quarter, yet, the hit to Walmart's stock was rather mild: a 3 percent drop (S&P 500 dropped 1.5 percent). Why the different reaction by investors to a penny miss between eBay and Walmart? Once more, the clue lies in investors' expectations *prior* to the earnings announcement. Over the year preceding Walmart's earnings release, its stock *decreased* by 12.6 percent.[9] Disappointment in the wake of disillusionment apparently is easier to bear.

- **A SHOCKER—CATERPILLAR'S $.12 DISAPPOINTMENT.** On October 21, 2005, Caterpillar—a large earthmoving and farm machinery producer—reported third-quarter 2005 EPS of $.94 against a consensus estimate of $1.06. No longer a penny, rather a serious $.12 shortfall. Investors clearly vented their disapproval. Caterpillar's stock price dropped 6.9 percent (S&P 500 increased 1.8 percent) on the earnings announcement. However, and this is important, within a couple of days, Caterpillar's price started rising, gaining all the lost ground in ten days, and continued its ascent thereafter. The reasons for this were solid business conditions and sustained efficiency improvements. The increased demand for Caterpillar's products post-Hurricane Katrina didn't hurt either. The lesson is that even a serious consensus miss is a nonevent (except to panicky investors) when the business fundamentals are solid.

- **GOOGLE'S FIRST DISAPPOINTMENT.** Since its 2004 IPO at $80 a share, Google released an uninterrupted stream of good news and received investors' adulation, catapulting its stock price to $470 in early 2006. Then, on February 1, 2006, came the first reality check. Google released a fourth-quarter 2005 EPS of $1.54 against the consensus estimate of $1.76. Google's price dropped 8.5 percent (S&P 500 decreased by less than 1 percent) and stayed flat throughout February and March 2006. The intriguing feature here is that Google may have avoided the sharp price drop with an earnings guidance, which the company declines to give, on principle. In a repeat performance, Google announced a January 31, 2008, fourth-quarter EPS of $4.43, a penny short of the consensus estimate, and its price dropped 8.6 percent (S&P 500 rose 1.2 percent).

- **GOOD NEWS FOR A CHANGE—WILLIAMS-SONOMA'S ONE-PENNY BEAT.** Enough with the gloom and on to the rewards of making the numbers, such as this home furnishing retailer that released, on August 23, 2005, a second-quarter EPS of $.26, beating the consensus estimate by a penny. These earnings, moreover, increased by 11.6 percent from a year earlier. Surely good news, although not for shareholders, who reacted with a yawn—a price drop of 1.2 percent (S&P 500 decreased 1.0 percent). The presumed reason was that revenues, which increased 13 percent to $776 million from a year earlier, fell short of analysts' forecasts of $783 million. The lesson is that it's obviously not just "the earnings consensus, stupid"; revenue hits or misses matter too.[10]

- **GENERAL MOTORS ROARS TO ... A PRICE DROP.** On October 25, 2006, GM announced, for a change, a profit of $.93 a share (excluding one-time items) against a $.49 consensus estimate. Revenues also topped the forecast. Delirious investors drove the price *down* 5.1 percent (S&P 500 was up almost 1.0 percent). While never at a loss for "Monday morning" explanations, analysts interviewed by CNN appeared puzzled. The best they could offer was that the CFO's answer to a question about GM's profit outlook was: "I can't promise anything."[11] Investors' reaction to earnings surprises sometimes surprises even expert analysts.

- **H&R BLOCK'S $.04 BEAT—THINGS AS USUAL.**  On June 29, 2009, the tax adviser announced a fourth-quarter EPS of $2.09, beating the consensus by $.04. Revenue, at $2.47 billion, however, fell a little short of analysts' expectation ($2.52 billion). Investors nevertheless reacted to the bright side. H&R Block's stock price advanced 11.7 percent on the announcement (the S&P 500 was virtually unchanged). The takeaway is that anything is relative; in the depressed market from 2008 to 2009, any positive news looms large.

These seven cases of consensus hits and misses with their consequences clearly indicate that there is much more to investors' reactions than a mechanical response to the earnings surprise. Context is crucial, in particular, the stock price pattern prior to the earnings release, to which I turn next.

## Riding a Tiger

Why are some earnings disappointments punished severely, while others escape unscathed? The long answer is that there are many reasons. A sales, cash flow, or gross margin disappointment jointly disclosed with the earnings miss obviously paints a particularly bleak picture of things to come. So is an earnings miss coupled with a downcast management outlook of the future. But there is an equally important, although less appreciated, determinant of the reaction to an earnings miss and, importantly, one that managers can proactively alleviate: investors' pre-miss growth expectations.

In a comprehensive study of the consequences of missing, meeting, or beating consensus quarterly estimates, published in 2002, accounting researchers Doug Skinner and Richard Sloan documented that the stocks of companies that missed the consensus dropped by 5 percent, on average, whereas those that beat the consensus increased 5.5 percent (prices of companies that exactly met the forecast rose by 1.6 percent), over the three months ending with the earnings release (thereby reflecting investors' aggregate reaction to managers' guidance and analysts' forecast revisions made prior to the final earnings announcement).[12] The important insight of Skinner and Sloan came from ranking the disappointing companies by investors' growth expectations prior to the earnings release, as measured by the market-to-book ratio (the ratio of the forward-looking stock price to the historical-based book or equity value per share). Whereas the disappointers with low prior growth expectations saw their stock prices decrease by 3.6 percent, the earnings disappointers with high prior growth expectations experienced a double price whammy: a 7.3 percent drop.[13]

Even more surprising, the price hit to an earnings miss is only slightly affected by the *magnitude* of the disappointment, and even small shortfalls of a penny or two by erstwhile highfliers result in sharp price declines, as in eBay and Google. Moreover, whereas for all stocks, investor reaction to positive and negative surprises is roughly symmetrical, for high-growth stocks, the negative reaction to an earnings disappointment is substantially more severe than the reward for a similar positive surprise. Paraphrasing Willing Congreve in *The Mourning Bride*, hell hath no fury like a shareholder scorned. The price hit to disappointing highfliers is accentuated by "momentum investors," that breed of market players riding the growth tiger, who are quick to bail out on the first sign of the end of growth—often an earnings disappointment. This helps explain why the magnitude of the consensus miss matters little. Any miss signals the end of the dream.

There are two important lessons for managers here. The first is reflected in the familiar adage, there is no free lunch. Investors' growth expectations and the consequent elevated stock price have their obvious benefits—lower cost of capital, high managerial stock-based compensation, employment attraction—while the favorable situation lasts, but the retribution for even minor faltering of the growth is commensurately high. Second, the research I discuss in the next section indicates that investors and financial analysts tend to be *overly optimistic* about the growth prospects of companies with good track records, believing that the fast-growing sales and earnings will persist far into the future. The steep stock price decline upon a consensus miss is, therefore, not just a reaction to the disappointing earnings, but primarily a *correction* of the overly optimistic growth expectations. The message to managers is that if you suspect that your company's stock is overheated, outstripping the business fundamentals, resist the temptation to ride the tiger—go along with the market—and instead gradually cool off investors' enthusiasm to avoid their wrath when the inevitable end-of-growth materializes. In chapter 5 I provide diagnostics on how to identify overheated stocks and prescribe safe means of dismounting the tiger.

## A Brief but Important Detour on Value Versus Glamour Stocks

The sharp investor reaction to an earnings miss of the erstwhile growth company I discussed earlier is related to a major puzzle in capital markets: the consistent, yet counterintuitive superior performance of "value stocks" relative to their "glamour" (growth) counterparts. Drawing attention to the different performance of value and glamour stocks is often attributed to Benjamin Graham, a successful money manager and Columbia University finance professor from 1928 to 1957, whose reputation has resurfaced in recent years by the claim that the legendary investor Warren Buffett developed his finance acumen in Graham's class. Graham defined value and glamour by relating stock prices to various financial indicators, such as earnings, book value, or cash flows. Glamour stocks have relatively *high* valuations—high market-to-book (M/B) or price-to-earnings (P/E) ratios—while value stocks are characterized by *low* valuations.[14]

It isn't surprising, of course, that investors favor certain stocks, while others are in the doghouse. If investors expect company A to grow faster than B, they will bid up the shares of the former, resulting in a higher valuation ratio (P/E or M/B) for A than B. However, and this is the basic tenet of efficient (rational) capital markets—one of the fundamental concepts of modern finance theory—if investors properly price securities, taking into account all available information about growth and risk, then the *future* risk-adjusted returns on the stocks of companies A and B (and, in general, the returns on high- and low-growth stocks) should be virtually identical, despite their current different valuations.[15] The different growth expectations are fully reflected in current prices. Stated differently, in efficient markets, one cannot profit from widely known information—in this case, the higher M/B or P/E ratios of company A relative to B—*after the fact*.[16] But here comes the value–glamour puzzle: during most of the post-World War II period, investment in value stocks—out-of-favor equities with *low* market valuation relative to fundamentals—yielded *higher* returns than glamour stocks, which investors favored.[17] During the period from 1990 to 2008, value stocks yielded, on average, 11.5 percent annually, while glamour stocks returned 9.5 percent only.[18] Josef Lakonishok and colleagues documented in 1994 that from 1968 to 1989, stocks with low M/B (value stocks) outperformed high M/B (glamour stocks) on average by 6.3 percent in the year following the valuation and founded a successful fund operation on this principle.[19]

How can the lowly value stocks consistently outperform their glamour counterparts? The traditional explanation is: compensation for risk. When the market is in positive territory, risky investments yield higher returns than do lower-risk securities, and the higher return on value stocks just reflected their higher risk than growth stocks. The problem with this explanation is that the documented value–glamour return differential is already risk-adjusted, accounting for known risk factors, such as beta (market risk), size, and the market-to-book ratio. Alternatively, the behavioral explanation to the value-growth conundrum rests on investors' excessive optimism regarding growth stocks. They systematically overvalue the stocks of glamour companies, believing that their past sizzling record of sales and earnings growth will persist into the distant future and undervalue the prospects of the lagging value stocks.[20] Thus, for example, the impressive sales and earnings growth rates of the likes of Microsoft, Dell, Vodafone, and Walmart in the 1990s led many investors to believe that these glamour companies would continue to grow briskly well into the twenty-first century, according them high valuation multiples (M/B and P/E ratios). However, as I noted in the introduction, corporate growth is ephemeral, and sooner or later the highfliers stall, inevitably leading to investor disappointment and stock price declines. The *reversal* of investors' excessive optimism about glamour stocks and the undue pessimism regarding many value shares explain nicely the value–glamour return differential.

What does all this have to do with missing the earnings consensus? A lot, in fact. Skinner and Sloan document that much of the superior performance of value versus glamour stocks is due to consensus misses of the glamour highfliers when their earnings disappoint investors.[21] Thus, the serious retribution to an earnings disappointment of a growth company is largely a correction of investors' excessive, erstwhile optimism.

## Who Is Afraid of Missing the Consensus?

CFOs are afraid of missing the consensus, according to an extensive CFO survey published in 2005 by John Graham and colleagues.[22] A majority of the CFOs surveyed considered a consensus miss a serious setback to the company, and some indicated that they would even sacrifice certain future growth (by, say, cutting R&D) to meet the consensus. The specter of missing the consensus, say CFOs, is also a major driver of information manipulation. But, as this chapter's title indicates and the following evidence corroborates, missing the consensus is far from the end of the world, and its consequences can be mitigated. Thus, even CFOs have something to learn.

## So, What's a CEO to Do?

A nightmare scenario: the quarter-end is approaching; you huddle with the CFO over the forthcoming earnings report and realize that earnings will fall short of the consensus estimate. Overcoming the initial panic, you recognize that something must quickly be done. But what? Here are the frequently followed courses of action managers take when facing the specter of the consensus miss, along with their consequences (see figure 1-2).

**SALES BLITZ–COST CUTS (SHIFTS).** The knee-jerk reaction to an earnings shortfall is to boost revenues and income by an end-of-quarter sales offensive, offering unusually large discounts, particularly common among medium-size and small technology companies, which finalize most of their sales in the last days of the quarter by offering exceptionally favorable terms. The obvious downside is that customers, aware of the vendor's predicament from missing the numbers, wait until the end of the quarter to squeeze the last penny of the seller's profit. In general, large price incentives surrender substantial economic value to customers and condition them to expect similar discounts in the future, and, while the sales blitz may boost EPS by a few pennies, the lower prices

FIGURE 1-2

**Actions and their consequences**

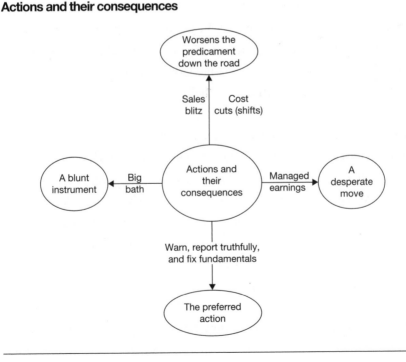

often shrink the margins—a closely watched indicator—leading to a price drop despite the EPS "hit."[23] Most ominously, the artificially enhanced end-of-quarter sales cannibalize the next quarter's revenues, thereby exacerbating the forthcoming EPS shortfall.

Managers encounter similar issues with another favorite action: last-minute cost cuts—distinct from carefully-thought-through efficiency measures—aimed at meeting the consensus estimate. Such cost cuts or shift of expenses—advertising, maintenance, travel—to the following quarters also exacerbate the problems down the road. Thus, both the sales blitz and last-minute cost cuts (shifts) make sense only if the EPS shortfall is small and temporary. Most shortfalls unfortunately are not.[24]

THE BIG BATH. This course of action is tempting when you face a *substantial* earnings deficiency. Here is how it works. Couple the earnings shortfall with a massive asset write-off—decrease of the book value of inventory, goodwill, or long-term assets—or with sizable restructuring charges (employee layoff costs, plant-closing expenses), thereby reporting an eye-popping loss that detracts investor attention from the consensus miss. An added advantage is that the large write-offs and restructuring charges boost future earnings by lowering asset values and depreciation. Arthur Levitt, Securities and Exchange Commission (SEC) chairman in the 1990s, describes an additional "benefit" of the big bath:

> These charges help companies "clean up" their balance sheet—giving them a so-called "big bath." Why are companies tempted to overstate these charges? When earnings take a major hit, the theory goes, Wall Street will look beyond a one-time loss and focus only on future earnings. And if these charges are conservatively estimated [namely, future expenses are overstated] with a little extra cushioning, that so-called conservative estimate is miraculously reborn as income when estimates change or future earnings fall short (emphasis mine).[25]

Thus, overstated write-offs, when reversed, boost future reported earnings. However, the "gains" from reversing previous exaggerated restructuring charges have to be fleshed out in the financial report and are thus obvious to the careful investor.[26] Essentially, asset write-offs and restructuring charges are strategically important events called for by Generally Accepted Accounting Principles (GAAP) when fundamental economic circumstances, like competitive position, worsen. The infrequent nature of write-offs makes them too blunt an instrument to smooth out temporary earnings shortfalls (although some companies, like Eastman Kodak—dubbed a serial restructurer—"bathe" their financials frequently).

MANAGED EARNINGS. Although often tempting, this is the worst course of action when facing a consensus miss. A distinction is frequently made between earnings *management*—changes in reported earnings made within the boundaries of GAAP, such as switching accounting procedures or tweaking income statement estimates—and earnings *manipulation* or *fraud*, which involve GAAP-violating schemes, such as front-loading revenues or capitalizing expenses (a WorldCom favorite). In practice, however, the boundaries between earnings management and manipulation are often blurred. Consider, for example, the ploy Sarah McVay documented in 2006, in which companies shift regular expenses from their natural abode—cost of sales, or general and administrative expenses—to the income statement category of "special items," generally reserved for nonrecurring, unusual items (such as the consequences of a strike).[27] Such a shift doesn't affect the bottom line, yet inflates the closely watched "core (recurring) earnings." Is this earnings management or manipulation? Judging by the shared intent to deceive investors, who cares?

Chapter 3 is devoted to the follies of management or manipulation of financial information, showing that such practices are both ethically wrong and highly likely to be surfaced sooner or later by whistleblowers, auditors, or the SEC. Once disclosed, information manipulation is very detrimental to the company's operations and reputation and often devastating to the perpetrating managers.[28]

**RECOMMENDED COURSE: WARN, REPORT TRUTHFULLY, AND FIX THE FUNDAMEN-TALS.** As soon as you realize you are going to disappoint investors—miss the consensus, or report an earnings or sales drop—preferably well before quarter-end, issue a public warning to this effect along with a detailed and credible plan of how you intend to fix the business funda-mentals. Then, report the grim results truthfully and keep investors engaged, sharing with them the progress of the corrective moves, whether successful or not. A warning will not mollify investors, though; your stock will be hit on the announcement. Vodafone, the leading wireless communications company, lost almost 6 percent (S&P 500 dropped less than 1 percent) when it warned in February 27, 2006, of slowing revenues and a gross margin drop for the year ending March 31, 2007.[29] Sometimes the price hit on the warning is temporary, as in Voda-fone's case. On March 3, 2006, a mere week after the warning, Voda-fone's stock price returned to its pre-warning level. Of course, if investors aren't convinced of the efficacy of the corrective measures, the price drop will last longer. The main advantages of the warning are that it enhances managers' credibility as straight shooters and as execu-tives who are on top of things (they weren't surprised by the shortfall), and that the warning often lessens the company's exposure to share-holder litigation and the estimated damages to investors, as I show in chapter 6.

Most importantly, in financial reporting, honesty prevails. How do I know? In 2009, Sanjeev Bhojraj and colleagues examined empirically what happens to companies that miss the consensus estimate by a penny *without managing earnings*, compared with companies that beat the con-sensus by a penny *with the help of earnings management*.[30] A few research particulars of this smart exercise: The study examined 1,390 companies that missed the consensus and 2,125 firms that beat it. The researchers assessed whether a company managed its earnings or not by tracking unusual changes in the major expense items that are susceptible to manipulation—accounting accruals (subjective reserves, provisions, estimates), R&D, and advertising expenses. Thus, for example, an unusual (relative to comparable firms) decrease in R&D, advertising expense, or in the bad-debt reserve (an accrual) at a company that beat the consensus by a penny leads to the presumption of earnings management.

The outcome of this analysis is both surprising and reassuring. First, the manipulators that beat the consensus received as a group a temporary 3 percent to 4 percent bump in stock price but lost it by year-end.[31] This corroborates my earlier argument that beating the consensus by manipulation is a temporary fix, and sooner rather than later the true adverse fundamentals can no longer be masked. In sharp contrast, the one-penny missers that resisted the temptation to manage earnings didn't suffer price decline, and from roughly a year after the consensus miss their share prices increased significantly. Thus, refusal to manipulate earnings prevails and will even be rewarded.

## Operating Instructions

- **RISING STOCK PRICES CAN ALSO BITE.** The mother of all stock hits on a consensus miss happens to growth companies whose share prices are stoked by inflated investor expectations (recall eBay's 22 percent price drop upon a penny miss). Accordingly, resist the temptation of riding an inflated stock price tiger, and deflate investors' overly optimistic expectations well before the inevitable disappointment.

- **AVOID QUICK FIXES.** Unless the earnings shortfall is small and temporary, you should resist quick fixes—last-minute sales blitz, cost cuts, or shifts to future periods—for the sake of making the numbers. When such moves are not part of a carefully planned restructuring, they will only exacerbate future sales and earnings shortfalls.

- **THE ONE THING YOU SHOULDN'T MANAGE.** You should avoid earnings manipulation or the better-sounding yet equally deleterious earnings management at all costs, on both ethical and practical grounds. Since most manipulation schemes "borrow from the future," they soon spiral out of control and, when ultimately revealed, the consequences to the company and its managers are harsh.[32]

- **JUST DO THIS.** The recommended course when facing a consensus miss is to warn investors of the impending shortfall as soon as practicable, share with them the corrective actions planned, report the financials honestly, and follow with detailed and credible progress reports.

## Chapter 2

# Do We Have a Story for You

## How Soft Information Can Change Stock Prices

➡ How to overcome investors' "limited attention."

➡ What makes a conference call effective?

➡ How the tone of managerial communications matters, not just the numbers.

➡ How investor relations make a difference.

The Children's Place, a retailer of—what else?—children's apparel and accessories, opened the year 2003 with a quarter to forget: its EPS, at $.21, missed analysts' consensus estimate by $.04 and fell far short of the year-earlier EPS of $.56. If this was not enough, same-store sales, a key retailers' performance measure, fell 13 percent, and gross profit decreased to 38.6 percent of sales from 45.7 percent a year earlier. The May 15, 2003, conference call following this grim news opened with the CFO tersely pointing out several reasons for the financial results—a decrease in average transaction size, sales price decreases, increases in employee training and payroll costs, and severe winter weather.

(Wouldn't you expect an *increasing* demand for children's clothes as the weather worsens?) The CFO went on to expand on the future: "Looking ahead, we remain confident that our business is moving in the right direction, as evidenced by our improved sales and transaction trends ..." The CEO then joined the call and, abstracting from inconvenient details, had this to say on the quarter: "We are pleased with the progress we made in the first quarter ... We made progress in our strategic initiatives and they remain on track yielding positive results in the following key performance indicators, as compared to last year."

What followed was a litany of presumably positive indicators, such as increases in customer conversion rates and units per transaction. As for the large increase in inventory levels during the quarter—a frequent indicator of deteriorating business—the CEO said: "Inventory levels are now well positioned to support our business." And, he concluded, "we are further streamlining our operations to leverage our infrastructure while at the same time supporting our growth. As we reflect on the challenges that we have been facing, we look forward to the many opportunities that lie ahead of us. Our early signs of progress encourage us and we remain confident about achieving our long-term objective of making the Children's Place the number-one brand in children's clothing. We believe we have the right formula and the right strategies to achieve this ambitious goal."

All this optimism and progress notwithstanding, during the conference call, Children's Place executives adamantly refused to provide any quantitative earnings or expense guidelines for the next quarter. To an analyst's question about the main components of the deteriorating gross profit, an inquiry about past operations, not a request for prediction, the CFO replied: "John, on the gross profit breakdown, we don't specify the amounts, but we do list them in order." All this, in reaction to an all-around disappointing quarter.[1] No wonder that the cheerful, forward-looking message of Children's Place executives didn't do much to lift the spirits of investors: Children's stock price fell by over 5 percent during the call day and the following couple of days.[2]

While reading the transcripts of scores of conference calls I was occasionally reminded of the classic *On Bullshit*, by the renowned

Princeton philosopher Harry Frankfurt who equates his book's theme to the more palatable term *hot air*, and explains: "When we characterize talk as hot air, we mean that what comes out of the speaker's mouth is only that. It is mere vapor. His speech is empty, without substance or content. His use of language, accordingly, does not contribute to the purpose it purports to serve. No more information is communicated than if the speaker had merely exhaled."[3] Frankfurt goes on to distinguish bullshit from a lie: "When an honest man speaks, he says only what he believes to be true; and for the liar, it is correspondingly indispensible that he considers his statements to be false. For the bullshitter, however, all these bets are off: he is neither on the side of the true nor on the side of the false. His eye is not on the facts at all, as the eyes of the honest man and of the liar are, except in so far as they may be pertinent to his interest in getting away with what he says."[4]

Chapter 3 is devoted to truths and lies in financial reporting and their consequences. Here, I deal with a subtler dimension of communication with investors—soft information—and show, among other things, that bullshit often defeats the communicator's purpose, whereas relevant, credible information—details later—will improve investors' perceptions of the company, even in the wake of a disappointing quarter or year. Soft information, not just data, matters, as well as its tone and delivery. Above all, investors' seriously limited cognitive capacity, which economists often ignore, has to be carefully accommodated by the communicator or executive.

## Surprise, Investors Are Human After All

Mainstream economists and finance scholars implicitly assume that investors, at least those that rely on information in making decisions, possess a perfect capacity to collect and process that information. They expeditiously read and digest the voluminous quarterly and annual financial reports of companies (including the generally indecipherable notes); attend conference calls and press meetings; read the various SEC filings of companies; learn about new technologies, innovations, and changes in the competitive environment of firms from governmental, research, and consultants' reports; speak with customers and suppliers; and do all this and more on a regular basis for fifteen to twenty companies typically followed by financial analysts and active investors. If investors were indeed able to achieve this physical and intellectual phenomenal feat, how could one explain the following research findings:

- On Sunday, May 3, 1998, a *New York Times* front-page article about a promising drug developed by EntreMed, a biotech company, catapulted its stock price from $12 to $52, despite the fact that "the new-news content of the *Times* story was nil."[5] The attributes and prospects of this drug were thoroughly analyzed months earlier in scientific journals, and covered by the popular media, including the *New York Times*, though not on its front page. If investors process information fully and in a timely manner, the *New York Times* article, which didn't contain any new scientific or commercial information, should have been stale news, exerting no effect on EntreMed's stock price. And yet, the stock price more than quadrupled.

- Research shows that pro forma (non-GAAP) earnings prominently displayed in the title or the first paragraph of a company's news release have a substantially stronger impact on stock prices than pro forma earnings reported less prominently in earnings releases.[6] However, efficient information processors react only to the content of a message and are indifferent to the order of information release, or where it is placed in the message. And yet …

- During the 1990s, managers of high-tech companies fought tooth and nail against the FASB's proposal to expense the value of employee stock options—namely, subtract it from earnings—yet were indifferent to reporting the same information in a footnote to the financial report. Evidently, managers believe that an item affecting net income will draw investors' attention, whereas they will largely ignore the same item disclosed in a footnote a few pages later in the report. But, surely, astute investors read financial report footnotes carefully and can easily subtract the value of stock options reported in a footnote from earnings.[7] Managers clearly beg to differ.

- A textual analysis of managers' narrative in earnings press releases indicates that the narrative's tone—level of optimism or pessimism—has a significant effect on investors' (price) reaction to the earnings release, beyond the quantitative, hard component of the message.[8] Shouldn't hardened, rational investors be indifferent to the tone of a message, focusing only on its substance?

- Last, companies tend to release poor earnings news on Fridays because the stock price reaction to Friday's news is significantly more muted than on Monday through Thursday. Indeed, studies have shown that there is a catch-up (delayed) stock price reaction to earnings announcements on Friday, occurring over several weeks.[9] It's hard to believe that sophisticated, alert investors are distracted on Fridays by the approaching weekend; isn't fund management 24/7? And yet …[10]

Surprise, surprise: investors are evidently not the bloodless, efficient automatons populating economic and finance textbooks. They obviously suffer from what behavioral researchers call "limited attention," namely, a seriously restricted ability to process and analyze the vast amount of information relevant to companies' values. In the Nobel Laureate economist Herbert Simon's words, "the scarce resource is not information, it is processing capacity to attend to information."[11] That's why investors focus on *salient cues*, information items that stand out in the crowded data mess, such as a front-page *New York Times* article about a promising drug, devoid of new information, or react strongly to pro forma earnings and restatements flashed in the heading of a news release, while reacting with reserve to similar information buried in the text of the release. Limited attention also implies that investors will use an information item *as displayed* to them, rather than engage in an extensive modification of the information,[12] corroborating managers' belief that when the stock options expense is in the P&L report (displayed information), it will have a substantially stronger impact on investors than a footnote disclosure requiring investors to modify reported earnings.[13] These are all important lessons for executives striving to communicate effectively to investors.

A more subtle yet equally serious manifestation of investors' limited attention and constrained information-processing capacity is their frequent failure to draw inferences from the *absence* of information, such as when a company that used to provide quarterly earnings guidance to investors stops doing so, often because of deteriorating performance.[14] Similarly, investors rarely realize in time that some widely touted drugs while under development never made it to the market because the developers kept mum about the failure of these drugs in clinical tests.[15] It's the same with companies that announce with fanfare plans for large stock repurchases (usually triggering stock price increases), yet never fulfill the promise. However, since the absent information was apparent (earnings guidance that was subsequently stopped), efficient information processors are expected to notice the change. They don't.

I dwell on the severe information-processing constraints and limited attention of investors because a comprehensive understanding of these limitations is central for designing effective capital-market communications policies. The tone (sentiment) of a message, where it is placed in a news release, when to keep mum, or what works in a conference call are essential components of an effective disclosure strategy to investors with limited attention, as I show next.[16]

## Speak Softly and Carry a Big (Hard) Stick

Investors' limited attention and constrained cognitive capacity naturally sway them toward *hard information*, which is easily reduced to numbers and thereby made salient, and away from *soft information*, which is hard to summarize by a quantitative score.[17] Moreover, institutional investors—investment managers, banks, insurance companies—prefer hard information, like earnings or sales, because it is easy to transmit across their hierarchies to researchers and investment managers and will be interpreted uniformly by the various employees and executives on the decision-making team. Soft information, such as a description of the competitive position of the company or the strength of its intellectual property, may be lost in translation across hierarchical channels. Soft information is also easier to hype and misinterpret relative to hard data. And yet, soft information or narrative is extensive in managerial communications, such as earnings press releases and conference calls, and is potentially very useful. So, what is the impact of soft information on investors and how can you enhance this impact?

As Mitchell Petersen points out, there is more to the distinction between hard and soft information than numeric versus narrative (text).[18] After all, any soft information, like a discussion of the company's competitive position, can be transformed to a numeric score, say, on a one-to-ten scale, based on the receiver's assessment. The main difference between hard and soft information lies elsewhere. Truly hard information is *uniform*—has the same meaning to different persons—like a company's annual sales number, whereas soft information, like the subjective scores of customer or employee satisfaction, is rarely uniform and will be interpreted differently by different people. The reason is that "with soft information the context under which it is collected and the collector of the information are part of the information."[19] This "information baggage" (context and collector) limits significantly the usefulness of soft information and the ability to delegate decisions based on soft information (one collects, another decides, a third oversees execution). To fully appreciate a customer satisfaction or a social responsibility score, you need to know how and by whom the underlying surveys were conducted. Hard information, on the other hand, like a company's earnings or liabilities, can be interpreted without context or knowledge of the collector.

Another important advantage of hard information, particularly a forward-looking one, is its *verifiability*. A management forecast of

25 percent gross margin next year can be easily compared later on with the actual gross margin, whereas a soft statement such as, "We remain confident that AOL is on the right track,"[20] is largely unverifiable. The verifiability of a message effectively disciplines and keeps the communicator honest, mitigating manipulation and hype, thereby enhancing the credibility of the message. Effective communication strategy should therefore strive to harden soft information as far as possible, such as the use of an industry-standardized methodology for measuring the all-important book-to-bill ratio (order backlog in the semiconductor industry) and the use of a common data collector (a major accounting firm) for this indicator, disposing of the need to specify the context (methodology) and the collector of the information in each book-to-bill communication. Or, accompanying a reassurance such as, "the company is on the right track," with measurable and verifiable milestones, such as an expected 12 percent return on equity next year. Hardening soft information is critical to effective communication.

Hard information is not a panacea, however. In the process of transforming soft to hard information, certain valuable knowledge is lost, adversely affecting decisions based on the information.[21] And when decisions are entirely based on hard data, it's easy to distort them by manipulating the information. Thus, for example, when the creditworthiness of a loan or credit card applicant is solely determined by a hard, numeric score based on several attributes (e.g., income, age, place of residence), considerable relevant information, such as the applicant's wealth, family resources, or social network, is lost. And when some of the attributes of the score are known to applicants, they can easily misrepresent them (e.g., claim a higher income, say, as was frequently done during the mortgage boom preceding the 2007 to 2008 subprime debacle). The choice, therefore, is not between hard or soft information, but rather finding the right combination of hard and *hardened* soft information.[22]

The important role that soft information plays in investors' decisions is evidenced by the startling finding that the key, hard corporate data—earnings and book values (net assets)—account statistically for no more than 10 percent of stock price changes around the financial report release.[23] Clearly, the soft information conveyed in the financial report (in the management, discussion, and analysis section, for example), as well as in managers' press releases and conference calls, drives many investors' decisions. The key issue for managers then is how to effectively communicate soft information to investors suffering from limited attention and constrained information-processing capacity. Let's start with the ubiquitous earnings conference call.

## Analyze This ... Earnings Conference Calls

Managers' conference calls with analysts and investors that are held soon after the release of quarterly earnings are now routine. Almost all large companies and many medium-size and small firms conduct quarterly conference calls. But are these interactive and impromptu communications with investors an idle ritual, like most annual shareholder meetings, or a vital channel of communication? And even more important, how can managers turn the conference call into an effective tool for changing investors' perceptions, particularly in the wake of a dismal quarter? Research has lots to say about these questions.

### The Secrets of Effective Conference Calls

The evidence is unanimous that, by and large, conference calls impart useful information to investors. Studies have documented, for example, an abnormally high volume of stock trade and price volatility during and immediately after the calls, indicating that new information was released in the calls.[24] Such findings aren't really surprising. Why else would analysts and investors continue to attend conference calls? The important question for managers is how to enhance the effectiveness of calls. For this, you have to actually listen and analyze the *content* of the calls, not just record their impact.

Although Marshall McLuhan famously claimed that "the medium *is* the message," the conference calls' narrative and tone are crucial to their impact on investors. The Children's Place conference call I described earlier disappointed investors because of largely irrelevant content—particularly managers' refusal to provide meaningful details and prospective guidelines. Two studies, using advanced linguistic-analyzing software, delved into the content of conference calls, providing important insights.

Dawn Matsumoto, Maarten Pronk, and Erick Roelofsen analyzed over ten thousand transcripts of earnings conference calls held between 2003 and 2005, considering the two segments of the calls—the management presentation and the subsequent Q&A.[25] The researchers focused on the length (word count) of the call and on two content dimensions: financial (earnings, sales) versus nonfinancial (e.g., competitive position, economic outlook) information, as well as retrospective (e.g., past earnings) versus prospective (sales guidance) information.[26] The findings indicate that the worse the company's performance disclosed before the call, the longer the discussion will be in both segments of the calls. Either managers attempt to distract disappointed investors with hot air, and/or poor performance requires more explaining than good performance. Similarly, when performance is poor, managers' presentations are less financially oriented (more bullshit?) and more focused on the future. Not unexpectedly, in the Q&A segment of the call, which is initiated by analysts, the worse the company's performance, the more the discussion is financially oriented and focused on the past. Clearly, analysts and investors are less interested in managers' "castles in the air" and more concerned with hard, financially oriented information about the things that went wrong.

But what exactly makes a conference call click? To answer this question, I performed (with a group of doctoral students—Karthik Balakrishnan, Richard Carrizosa, and Alina Lerman—all young professors now) an intensive content analysis of a large sample of effective versus ineffective calls. What's our definition of an effective call? One that creates a buzz and triggers an abnormally high volume of stock trade.[27] Better yet, a call coming in the wake of a disappointing quarter, yet results in a stock price increase during and immediately after the call.

Using conference call transcripts from the Thomson StreetEvents database, we identified thousands of quarter-end calls conducted from 2001 to 2007, all following disappointing results—a miss of analysts' consensus earnings estimates. Since corporate earnings are released before the conference call, our measure of the reaction to the call—the stock price change from the start to the end of the call, or to the end of the call day—reflects the call's message rather than the disappointing earnings.[28] We focused on both the stock price change and the trading volume generated by the call, the latter, reflecting its buzz.[29]

We examined the following attributes of conference calls: (1) *participation*—the number of analysts participating, number of questions asked, and number of managers' answers (some questions got multiple answers; others, mainly related to managers' compensation, were sometimes left unanswered); (2) *quantity*—the total number of figures (quantities) relative to the number of words (narrative) in the presentation and the Q&A sections; and (3) *content and tone*—examined by automated linguistic algorithms based on various established and self-constructed "dictionaries." To differentiate between effective and ineffective calls, we compared the one-third of the calls with the largest stock price increase during and after the call—obviously effective calls—to the one-third of the calls with the largest price decrease—ineffective (or adverse) calls. Similarly, we compared high-buzz calls—generating a large volume of trade—with low-buzz calls. (Recall that all our conference calls came in the wake of a disappointing quarter.) Our main findings and managerial lessons are:

- Effective (buzz-creating and price-increasing) calls have substantially more analysts participating, more questions asked, and more responses given (several executives chiming in), as well as managers' lengthier discussion and responses, than ineffective calls.

  *Lesson:* To enhance call effectiveness, encourage wide participation by analysts and investors in the call by extensively publicizing it and by being responsive to questions. Foster a lively

Q&A session by providing new information and original insights on the business. Notwithstanding frequent advice from legal council, don't be overly cryptic or bland in your presentation and answers. Focus on providing useful information, rather than on avoiding lawsuits. A defensive stance may sometimes work in boxing, but not in conference calls.

- Effective calls are characterized by more quantitative responses (a higher ratio of numbers to total words) and by fewer big-picture words (like *growth*, *strategy*, or *reputation*) that many CEOs favor. Also, in effective calls, managers spend less time on discussion of competitive position and pricing issues than in ineffective calls.

  *Lesson:* Stick to the facts and don't blather. In conference calls, forget the concepts and models you learned in MBA strategy and leadership classes. Most analysts skipped these classes anyway.

- Interestingly, buzz-creating calls (high volume of trade) contain more negative words (like *abandon* or *abolish*)—recall, all these calls follow a disappointing quarter—and less reassuring, buoyant expressions than less-effective calls.[30]

  *Lesson:* Honesty and specificity in face of adversity are more informative and credible than vagueness using big-picture words and sugarcoating with a positive tone. This makes sense, yet is often overlooked by executives under duress.

- Finally, effective buzz-creating calls contain more forward-looking quantitative guidance, not flights of fancy, than low-buzz calls.

  *Lesson:* Hard, forward-looking information (unlike "we look forward to the many opportunities that lie ahead") is central to an effective conference call. With the legal protection (safe harbor) given to such information, why decline to provide it?[31]

In summary, two major themes emerge from our analysis of effective conference calls: both the setting of the call and its tone matter. Wide participation by analysts (number of analysts as well as number of questions) and hard information—data, guidance, and less discussion of big issues or the economy at large—are the main determinants of call effectiveness. Honesty and negative expressions when called for trump obfuscation, here, as elsewhere.

## Other Communication Channels

When investors attend shareholder meetings, read quarterly or annual reports, or participate in initial public offering (IPO) road shows, do they pay attention to the soft information imparted and to its tone, or just focus on the numbers? Is the narrative accompanying quantitative information cheap talk or does it convey a meaningful message?[32] The latter, say Elizabeth Demers and Clara Vega, based on a study of twenty thousand quarterly earnings announcements made from 1998 to 2006, using linguistic algorithms.[33] The researchers focus on two tone dimensions of the narrative: *optimism* (words of praise, satisfaction, inspiration) versus *pessimism* (blame, hardship, denial), and *certainty* expressions (tenacity, insistence) versus *wavering* (ambivalence, self-reference, variety). The results are instructive.

- An optimistic managerial tone in earnings announcements positively affects investors' reaction (the stock price change around the announcement date) beyond the impact of the hard numbers.[34] And this contagious effect of optimism is greater for high-tech firms, whose complex operations are not fully captured by a single number of earnings or sales, and companies with a lower quality of earnings (having large one-time and transitory items).[35] Furthermore, the stock price impact of optimism is higher, the larger the number of analysts following the company and the more extensive the media coverage of the earnings announcement.

  *Lesson:* Don't hesitate to sound optimistic *when warranted*, particularly when the hard data like earnings or sales don't fully capture your company's performance and potential, as when earnings are depressed by large, yet promising R&D or brand-enhancing expenditures. This is important because lawyers frequently caution managers that optimism enhances exposure to litigation. Yet optimism has its rewards, as documented by Demers and Vega (optimistic persons also live longer, say researchers). But beware of baseless hype, which definitely attracts litigation. Optimism is based on facts and positive documented developments, such as a new major contract, a recent sales pickup, or a successful drug test, whereas hype is an empty ballyhoo. Recall that financial analysts and reporters will verify your optimism later on against subsequent developments, enabling them to distinguish optimism from hype.

- Demers and Vega also report that a wavering, ambivalent tone (frequent use of *maybe, approximately, uncertainty*) is contagious too; it increases the volatility of the stock price, a reflection of investors' uncertainty.

    *Lesson:* Shielding yourself with vagueness and equivocation, which so often characterizes managerial communications, exacts a price in increased investor uncertainty and likely lower stock prices.[36]

## Meet the Relatives: Investor Relations

On a flight to London a few years back, as I pretended to be engrossed in a book, my neighbor asked about the purpose of my trip. Giving a talk at an investor relations (IR) conference, I said, to which my neighbor, who turned out to be a CEO, responded, "We have superb IR people. They organize our press conferences and road shows well, book great hotels, and are effective gatekeepers against pestering investors and analysts." My next-day audience was, understandably, less than thrilled to hear the CEO's "praise" of their functions. Like Rodney Dangerfield, they believe they deserve more respect. Since most medium-size and large companies have in-house IR departments, and many small firms engage IR consultants, managers would surely like to know if there is more to the IR function than the facilitation of executives' communication with investors.[37] Is IR more than a glorified PR? Should we invest more in IR, upgrade its personnel, or keep it a bare-bones function? There is only scant systematic research on these important questions, but here is what we know.

IR activities are mostly aimed at enhancing the company's visibility and management's credibility in capital markets and the economic community at large: familiarizing investors with the company, its operations, performance and growth potential; targeting the desired investor base (e.g., institutional investors, sovereign funds); and attracting financial analysts to cover the company.[38] Due to investors' limited attention (discussed earlier), company visibility and familiarity count a lot in capital markets. How else to explain the pervasive phenomenon known as "home bias"—the widely documented tendency of investors worldwide to invest mostly in the familiar domestic equities or in companies headquartered locally, despite the demonstrated benefits of international diversification.[39] Enhancing companies' visibility, particularly of medium-size and small companies, often translates to increased demand for their securities. Wide visibility, large institutional holding, and a significant following of analysts—all objectives of investor relations—come in handy when managers issue stocks or bonds, acquire companies, or ward off activist investors and hostile acquirers. So, does IR effectively enhance a company's visibility and analysts' following, and what are the consequences of wide visibility? Brian Bushee and Gregory Miller in a comprehensive study of IR effectiveness provide interesting insights.[40]

Based on interviews with IR professionals, the researchers found that companies seek IR help primarily when managers believe the firm's shares are undervalued or when they want to change the composition of shareholders (e.g., increase institutional investors' share). The SEC's Regulation Fair Disclosure (2001), which prohibited restricted communication with investors, increased the demand for IR professionals to navigate public communication to capital markets. Raising the awareness of buy-side analysts and investors, said the interviewees, is the most important part of the IR function, generally aimed at creating a stable and sophisticated investor base and boosting trading activity (stock liquidity). Catering to sell-side analysts and the media follows the buy-side as IR objectives. Enhancing the credibility of managers as straight shooters is also a major target of IR, coming in handy when scandals, like earnings restatements, erupt or a proxy contest with activist investors looms. Clearly, IR professionals aspire to do more than just book good hotels for managers. But are these elevated objectives achieved with IR help?

The empirical part of the Bushee-Miller study takes up this issue. It examined a sample of 210 midsize and small companies—those with the largest potential benefit from IR in terms of visibility—that hired IR consultancies. The researchers compared the companies that hired IR consultants with a control group of companies of the same exchange listing, industry, and institutional ownership, which didn't hire IR professionals. The researchers first examined the *determinants* of the decision to initiate an IR activity and found once more that perceived share undervaluation and low company visibility were the major reasons for hiring IR consultants. As for the *consequences* of this decision, the findings will surely please IR professionals:

> *We find that media coverage increases almost immediately [after the IR initiation]. The increase is maintained over the next year, but does not grow over time. Analyst coverage also increases; however, it takes several quarters to develop and is not always sustained ... Firms initiating IR activities experience a significant and persistent increase in both the number of institutions and the percentages of institutional ownership that is greater than for the control firms ... Moreover, we document that firms initiating IR programs experience significant improvements in their market valuation ... Overall, these results suggest that IR activities play a significant role in helping small and mid-cap companies to overcome their low visibility.*[41]

But wait, before you rush to hire an IR consultant, consider first that IR is not a one-shot affair. For the positive outcomes noted by Bushee and Miller to persist, you have to maintain a sustained and costly IR effort. Since Bushee and Miller didn't match the cost of IR against the benefits, the issue of IR's cost-effectiveness is still an open one. Second, as always, statistical results are "on average"; there is no assurance that in your particular case all the documented IR benefits will materialize. Nevertheless, this preliminary research does suggest a considerable potential for IR activities to create value, particularly for small, "neglected" firms starting from a low visibility level.

And what about larger companies with ongoing IR activities? Agarawal et al. examined companies with high IR quality ratings from 2000 to 2008 in the "Best Overall IR" survey of *Investor Relations Magazine*, a trade journal.[42] Their main finding is that companies in the "Best IR" list have a higher market value (capitalization) than similar companies not rated by the magazine, and the "best" companies also enjoyed a positive abnormal stock return (adjusted for risk, size, etc.) during the year following their appearance on the "Best IR" list. As frosting on the cake, nominated companies also saw an increase in the number of analysts following them. This is a strong endorsement of the effectiveness of IR activities, although (sorry for the downer) the documented relation between good IR and high market value could also reflect a certain reverse causal effect—from successful companies to better IR. It stands to reason that profitable companies with higher market values can better afford advanced IR activities. While it is notoriously difficult to determine *causation* (as opposed to correlation) with statistical tools, the relation between good IR and the *subsequent* increase in the number of analysts and share performance does suggest a causation, from IR to positive outcomes.

## A Final Note on Visibility, Disclosure, and Stock Prices

Empirical findings, I learned long ago, have to make sense in addition to being statistically significant. How can the hiring of an IR consultancy increase share prices, as Bushee and Miller document? What's the process that leads from enhanced visibility and improved transparency, both important IR objectives, to higher market capitalization? Financial hocus-pocus? Not really. Here, briefly, is the important chain of events, where each link is supported by empirical research.[43]

- An effective IR program reduces analysts' and institutional investors' *costs* of obtaining and processing information about companies and their growth prospects. This is done by improving the quality of information, such as systematically disclosing beyond-GAAP data, like drug companies' product pipeline or data on the effectiveness of restructuring efforts (see chapter 7). Also, improving information quality involves securing wide analyst participation and the quality of presentation in quarterly and annual conference calls, arranging media coverage for important company events, and making executives available for background discussions with analysts and major investors. The objective here is to reduce information costs for analysts and investors who are seeking information yet have limited attention.

- Next, evidence indicates that improving information quality and investors' accessibility to information sources increases the number of analysts following the company and enhances institutional demand for its shares. This, in turn, increases the *liquidity* of the company's shares—the ability to buy or sell stock without a considerable price impact—a highly coveted share attribute by institutional investors, reflected by a high volume of share trade.[44] The key here is that more analysts, buy- and sell-side, and improved analysts' product—earnings forecasts and stock valuations—enhance the stock's liquidity.

- And, finally, since investors, institutions in particular, highly value liquidity, they are willing to pay a premium for it, requiring a lower rate of return on the stock. This ends the virtuous cycle, from effective investor relations to a higher shareholder value.

In sum, the various communication channels (conference calls, earnings releases) and information facilitators (investor relations, business media) I have analyzed in this chapter work their magic, when effective, through the following chain:

Reduction of information costs → increasing the number of analysts following and institutional investors' visibility → enhancing share liquidity → stock price and volume improvements

A company can achieve all this without a formal IR function, but trained and capable IR professionals undoubtedly facilitate the process from information to higher value, and conserve precious CEO and CFO time.

## Operating Instructions

I opened this chapter with a dysfunctional conference call, long on rosy assertions, short on details, and mum on forward-looking guidance. In contrast, TCF Financial, a bank, held a conference call on January 15, 2004, that also followed a disappointing quarter and year—decreasing earnings and missing the consensus estimate—yet its stock price increased during the call by about 2 percent. What gives?

TCF's call opened with the CEO's brief, matter-of-fact presentation providing a clear outline of the causes of the earnings shortfall (primarily low interest rates, causing enhanced loan prepayments) and proceeding with specific curative plans for next year (such as opening twenty-four branches). No fluff, no empty reassurances. Giving truth to sharing the pain, TCF's CEO announced during the call that since the 2003 earnings goal was missed, "TCF management will not be receiving incentive compensation this year." How refreshing. Furthermore, the CEO set a tough earnings goal for incentive compensation for 2004: $3.70 EPS versus the disappointing $3.05 EPS in 2003. The answers to analysts' questions during the call were equally informative, quantitative, and, more important, forward looking. To a question about debit card revenue next year, the answer was, "net debit card revenues will increase next year by approximately 10 percent"—a verifiable target, enhancing managers' credibility. Regarding the outlook of the bank's leasing equipment business, the important forward-looking indicator of a leasing backlog of $187 million at the end of 2003 was given. A question about the 2004 tax rate triggered a terse "34.25ish" answer.[45] No wonder that investors were pleased with TCF's conference call, and analysts are likely to participate in subsequent calls.

My specific operating instructions for managers' communications are:

- **HARDEN SOFT INFORMATION.** When possible, replace or augment narrative with numbers that are comparable across companies and computed the same way by your competitors, like earnings or order backlog. The numbers should be verifiable and audited, or aligned with subsequent facts. For example, TCF's CEO succinctly quantified the major reason for the disappointing year thus: "Big impact for the year for us was the 44 million dollars that we spent in debt cancellation, mostly in the third quarter, which impacted on an after-tax basis about 41 cents per share for the year."[46] Not exactly Shakespearean, yet straight to the point.

- **PAY ATTENTION TO TONE AND STYLE.** Most managers focus on the subject matter of the communication, or *what* the message is, and leave to an afterthought its tone and style, *how* it is communicated. The evidence is unanimous: tone and style—pessimism or optimism, certain or wavering, crisp or foggy—count in changing investors' perceptions and their actions. In particular, frankness enhances credibility.[47] Here is Warren Buffett in a 2007 shareholder letter discussing a table showing that Berkshire's pretax EPS rose from 1965 to 2007 from $4 to an astounding $4,093: "Berkshire's past record can't be duplicated or even approached. Our base of assets and earnings is now far too large for us to make outsized gains in the future." (p. 4) Typical no-hype Warren.

- **FOSTER INTERACTIVE COMMUNICATION.** I documented earlier that the effectiveness of conference calls increases with the number of participants and the number of questions asked. It's important, therefore, to engage analysts and investors as much as possible in interactive discussion. *Ex cathedra* preaching is better left to the clergy.

- **ENHANCE COMPANY RECOGNITION (VISIBILITY).** Investors' limited attention adversely affects their demand for small and mid-cap companies' shares and lowers their prices. Effective investor relations and positive media exposure mitigate investors' limited attention, positively affecting IPOs' outcomes and companies' capitalization.[48] Feed the business press interesting stories about exciting products and business ventures; don't be coy about important social responsibility initiatives; and turn the usually dull shareholder meetings into media events.

- **AND, YES, LIGHTEN UP.** The somber, sometimes grim atmosphere of investor communications is contagious and counterproductive; lighten up the discussion. Here are several vignettes from Warren Buffett's 2007 letter to shareholders:

  *John Stumpf, CEO of Wells Fargo, aptly dissected the recent behavior of many lenders: "It is interesting that the industry has invented new ways to lose money when the old ways seemed to work just fine." (p. 3)*

  *A footnote: We paid the IRS tax of $1.2 billion on our PetroChina gain. This sum paid all costs of the U.S. government—defense, social security, you name it—for about four hours. (p. 16)*

  *(I've reluctantly discarded the notion of my continuing to manage the portfolio after my death—abandoning my hope to give new meaning to the term "thinking outside the box.") (p. 18)*

  But note, no humor is better than lame humor (this writer exempted).

- **AND, DON'T PLAY GAMES.** Angela Davis and Isho Tama-Sweet examined fourteen thousand quarterly earnings releases and report that managers' pessimistic tone in the widely watched preliminary earnings release, concerning declining earnings or missing analysts' estimates, was substantially tamer than their pessimistic tone in the subsequent, less followed management discussion and analysis (MD&A) section in the financial report.[49] Obviously, managers tried to soften the blow in the earnings release and protect themselves against litigation in the subsequent MD&A. Shareholders generally wise up to such games, and when they do, your integrity is seriously hurt.

## Chapter 3

# To Manage or Not to Manage Earnings?

## Why You Shouldn't Even Think of Manipulating Financial Information

➡ Surprise, there is no "truth" in accounting information.

➡ GAAP to the rescue of truth, sort of.

➡ Why do managers manipulate financial information and how do they do it?

➡ The harsh consequences of manipulation for investors and managers.

➡ Just don't manipulate; there are better alternatives.

On September 12, 2007, the SEC charged former top executives of Nortel Networks, a Canadian telecommunications equipment maker, with accounting and reporting fraud aimed at beautifying reported earnings.[1] Specifically, the SEC alleged that in 2002 Nortel executives created accounting reserves, in violation of GAAP, by artificially lowering the company's earnings, which happened to be higher than internal and analysts' estimates. These reserves were quickly put to good use: nearly $350 million of them were reversed and credited to income to inflate reported earnings—magically turning losses in the first two quarters of 2003 into profits—to impress investors and generate executive bonuses.

You will see in this chapter that Nortel is far from an aberration. In fact, financial reporting manipulation, ranging all the way from small tweaks of accounting estimates to beat analysts' consensus forecasts by a penny to egregious multibillion-dollar frauds, is quite common. Manipulation is perhaps even increasing, as indicated by the frequency of corporate restatements of previously reported information, mostly, corrections of previous misreporting: from 614 restatements in 2001 to a whopping 1,795 in 2006, decreasing gradually thereafter to 1,217, to 923, and to 674 in 2007, 2008, and 2009, respectively.[2] The total number of restatements from 2006 to 2008, a staggering 3,935, indicates that over half of public companies corrected previously reported earnings during those years. That's seriously disturbing. The number of annual SEC Accounting and Auditing Enforcement Releases is rising too—from 134 in 1997 to 180 in 2009. You will see later that the incentives to manipulate reported information are strong and varied, making "earnings management"—an elegant euphemism for manipulation—an issue that most managers face. Yet, the costs of manipulation to investors, employees, society at large and, not the least, to managers are onerous. I focus in this chapter on the most critical circumstance leading to manipulation—a business slowdown causing managers to miss the consensus estimate or report decreasing earnings—discuss the means and consequences of manipulation, and conclude with operating instructions.

## Truth in Accounting?

Lying in financial reporting as elsewhere is universally condemned. An absolutist rejection of lying, on moralistic grounds, has a long-standing tradition. The ninth of the ten commandments delivered by Moses from Mount Sinai states emphatically: "You shall not bear false witness against your fellow." St. Augustine adds: "Now it is evident that speech was given to man, not that men might therewith deceive one another, but that one man might make his thoughts known to another. To use speech, then, for the purpose of deception, and not for its appointed end, is a sin." Fast-forward fourteen centuries to hear Immanuel Kant declare that a lie is "a crime of man against his own person and a baseness which must make a man contemptible in his own eyes." When asked if a lie is permitted to save a life, Kant answered: "To be truthful (honest) in all declarations, therefore, is a sacred and absolutely commanding decree of reason, limited by no expediency."[3]

Realists, keen observers of life and human nature, have taken a more pragmatic and nuanced approach to deception. Plato "had allowed that in his ideal Republic, rulers, the very topmost executives of the state, might find it 'necessary' to lie for the good of the community, and Machiavelli most wholeheartedly agreed with him."[4] Iris Murdoch sarcastically noted: "We have to mix a little falsehood into truth to make it plausible."[5] In a competitive environment, marked by the struggle to survive, lies and deceptions are often a part of life. Jeremy Campbell notes the following:

> In the world of life, even fairly primitive life, Darwin recognized that falsehood and chicanery are part of the game of survival. Writing in the Descent of Man, he commanded as "admirable" a paper by the entomologist Henry Walter Bates on mimicry in nature.... Mimicry in effect was a pretense, a form of lying, a means of gaining an edge on survival by deceiving predators as to the "real" character of their potential victims[6] ... Adaptation to the conditions of life ... can and does involve deception. That is a major theme of evolutionary studies today. Certain species flourishing now might be extinct if they had depended on truthfulness to increase and multiply.[7]

It may seem a short step from deception by species for survival to the fiercely competitive business world, where the struggle to prevail and prosper is as fierce as in nature. This, however, is a step fraught with danger. Truthfulness is the bedrock of all social and economic arrangements. No economic institution, be it a corporation or a stock market, can survive if falsehood in loan or labor contracts, manipulation in financial statements, or fraud in auditors' reports are tolerated. Who will work, lend money, or invest in securities when lies are permitted in contractual agreements? Obviously, for economic and social institutions to survive, truth must govern all arrangements, a theme I emphasize throughout this book. But, and this is the crux of the issue, what *is* truth and its converse—a lie?

Simple. Truth is universally believed to be *correspondence with facts*. Lying, with misstating facts. Thus, for example, in the early 2000s when Parmalat, a large Italian dairy company, presented on its balance sheets multibillion-dollar deposits in the Bank of America, where there were none, it lied. Things become murkier with accounting estimates, prevalent in financial reports. Consider a 12 percent annual depreciation expense on a firm's machinery. True, or deceptive expense intended to inflate earnings? That's hard to say, since depreciation is an estimate derived from a prediction of the future useful life and productivity of the machinery. There are no facts to substantiate the 12 percent rate and, therefore, no unequivocal answer to the true-or-false question.[8] The situation is similar to a bank's loan loss reserve, a major expense item, which is based on estimated future losses from delinquent borrowers. There are no corresponding facts here either at the time the estimate is made—just managers' *judgment* of the creditworthiness of borrowers. Even if it were to turn out later on that managers had seriously underestimated the loan loss reserve, it would be next to impossible to prove that *at the time* they made the estimate it was fraudulent. And what about the impairment or loss of value charges of long-term assets or goodwill, which are based on estimated future cash flows from these assets? There are no facts here either. And how about the ultimate noncorrespondence with facts—the marked-to-market toxic assets of banks during the financial crisis from 2007 to 2008, when no market for these assets in fact existed? Mark-to-myth would be a better description, quipped Warren Buffett. The list of estimates, forecasts, and subjective judgments underlying financial information covers most balance sheet and income statement items. Thus, unbeknownst to nonaccountants, in corporate financial reports, there are very few facts to establish truth or duplicity.[9] What then substitutes for correspondence with facts as a truth criterion in financial information?

## GAAP to the Rescue, Sort Of

Consider i2 Technologies, a developer and marketer of supply chain management solutions, which, according to the SEC, "overstated approximately $1.0B of software license revenues" by frontloading sales from 1998 to 2002.[10] This enabled i2 to report an increasing revenue stream, portraying itself as a fast-growing company and being rewarded as such by investors. What is front-loading of revenues, you ask? Complex software programs, such as i2's, usually require significant updating and servicing over an extended time after sale. Recording the total value of the software package, including payments for *future services*, as revenue at the time of sale is front-loading. But is front-loading a lie? No, if the relevant fact is a finalized software sale, and i2's front-loading indeed related to finalized sales. However, GAAP—the accounting "law" in the United States—requires the allocation of revenue and income from multiperiod projects over the respective delivery and subsequent service periods (quarters, years) to properly match periodic revenues and expenses. Recording the total revenue of the software in the delivery period and the cost of servicing and updating it in subsequent periods distorts such matching and the consequent income number. Thus, according to GAAP, i2 Technologies' front-loading of revenues violated truthful reporting and was accordingly sanctioned by the SEC.[11] That's how GAAP substitutes for the missing or hazy facts, in the establishment of truth or falsehood in financial reporting. A GAAP violation *is* manipulation.

This may seem clear-cut, but nothing in accounting is. There are no clear criteria in GAAP for making reliable estimates, except for the general dictum—use the best information available—which is as helpful as "buy low and sell high." This is serious, because most financial information items are based on managerial estimates. Not surprisingly, studies have shown that many manipulations of financial information, particularly the "fine tuning" of EPS to beat the consensus analysts' estimate by a penny or two, are done through "massaging" accounting estimates and projections.[12] The upshot is that GAAP is often an insufficient benchmark for investors and regulators to establish truth or trickery in financial reporting, particularly for emerging industries, such as software in the 1980s, biotech in the 1990s, and the Internet services in the 2000s, and for new technologies, such as risk hedging or securitization of intellectual property, where GAAP is lagging considerably behind business developments. For example, in 2002, the FASB started its "revenue recognition" project to update the measurement rules for this key income statement item. As of early 2011 (yes, nine years later), work on this project continues.

GAAP's inadequacy exposes managers and directors to considerable risk: what may seem truthful reporting to them, the SEC or class-action lawyers might claim later on to be fraudulent.[13] AOL is an early case in point. Starting in 1995, the company capitalized, justifiably in my opinion, certain advertising and promotion expenses, claiming that they create an asset—customer franchise—generating future benefits. Trial lawyers and the SEC challenged this practice, which reduced substantially AOL's reported losses, as manipulative, finally forcing the company in 1998 to reverse the capitalization and write off (charge to expenses) close to $400 million of customer acquisition costs. This early experience with the hazards of intangibles' capitalization had detrimental effects even when GAAP was clear. The software industry provides an example. GAAP in FASB Statement 87, 1986, calls for the capitalization of software development costs—recognizing them as an asset, rather than an expense—when a project successfully passes the technological feasibility stage. Many software companies, however, particularly the large ones like Microsoft, expense all their software development costs, lest analysts accuse them of earnings manipulation. And yet the evidence shows that software capitalization, when justified, yields earnings that better predict future performance than software expensing.[14]

Thus, except for clear-cut frauds, such as Parmalat's claim of having billions of dollars in an empty bank account, or obvious GAAP violations, such as WorldCom's multibillion-dollar capitalization of regular expenses in the late 1990s, many cases of managed or manipulated information are in a gray area, difficult to ascertain and prosecute. This vagueness poses a serious challenge to managers wishing to make sure that the information they disclose and certify, a Sarbanes-Oxley requirement, is truthful, and to financial information users who rely on the presumed integrity of the information. A thorough analysis of the motives to manipulate financial information and the means of manipulation—both vividly demonstrated by the following cases—goes a long way in drawing a bright line between truth and falsity in financial reporting.

## Why and How They Do It

The closest one gets to a proven manipulation (defendants rarely admit wrongdoings) are the SEC's Accounting and Auditing Enforcement Releases (AAERs), which report on cease-and-desist orders concerning accounting and financial reporting issues imposed on companies, their managers, and auditors for violations of the 1933 and 1934 Securities Acts. These actions are generally the culmination of elaborate and extended investigations by the SEC. Here is a varied selection of such actions from the early 2000s, a period ripe with manipulations, each followed by my message for managers.

### GE Brings Good Things to Life, Yet Not to Accounting

In 2009, the SEC filed a suit against General Electric, alleging that it had misreported revenues and earnings during 2002 and 2003 in order to beat analysts' consensus earnings estimates, partially explaining a "world record." From 1995 through 2004, GE met or exceeded the consensus estimate in practically every quarter: forty consecutive hits! The SEC alleged several manipulations, some of which, while involving millions of dollars, require an advanced accounting degree to fully comprehend. One was a plain-vanilla accelerated revenue recognition scheme. In the fourth quarters of 2002 and 2003, GE purportedly sold locomotives to financial institutions (heavy users of locomotives) to the tune of $223 million and $158 million, respectively. These transactions, the SEC alleged, were not real sales and shouldn't have been recorded as revenue, because they were structured in a way that didn't transfer the risk of ownership to the institutions, a GAAP requirement for revenue recognition. The financial institutions were, of course, expected to subsequently deliver the locomotives to real customers, but GE needed immediate delivery to boost fourth-quarter sales and earnings to beat the consensus estimates. GE settled the SEC's lawsuit by paying a $50 million penalty without, as is customary in such cases, admitting to wrongdoing.[15]

The major lesson learned is that many manipulative schemes cannibalize future revenues and earnings, necessitating an ever-increasing intensity of trickery, soon to spiral out of control. This was evident in 2007 when GE restated its 2002 and 2003 reports for the locomotives "sales," stating that the 2002 fourth-quarter segment revenues and profits were overstated by 8.8 percent and 14.6 percent, respectively, while the corresponding 2003 overstatements were substantially higher: 22.6 percent and 16.7 percent, respectively. This cannibalization renders most reporting manipulations unsustainable.

### How Gateway "Immunized Itself from the Vagaries of the Market"

In 1999, Gateway Inc., a direct marketer of personal computers and related products, embarked on a diversification strategy—dubbed venturing beyond the box—offering software, Internet access services, and training and support programs to customers. By the end of 1999, Gateway's beyond-the-box income reached 20 percent of total earnings, seemingly demonstrating the success of the diversification program.

Soon, however, things turned ugly. The tech bubble burst in 2000, the economy fell into a recession, and demand for computers and related products plummeted. Gateway, however, continued to present a happy face. While competitors reported a significant softening of demand and the consequent reduction in revenues and earnings, Gateway managers consistently claimed they were bucking the trend and reported increasing revenues and earnings to boot. How did Gateway manage, in the words of an analyst, to immunize itself from the vagaries of the market?

The SEC provides the answer.[16] In late 1999, Gateway initiated a program to sell computers on credit to persons who were previously rejected because of poor-credit status. At first, management characterized the program "a test" and limited it to $10 million. Soon, however, as Gateway's revenues declined and the specter of missing analyst estimates loomed large, it aggressively accelerated the program. In the second quarter of 2000, this high-risk sales drive—for which Gateway's internal delinquencies estimates reached 40 percent—generated sales of $112 million (5 percent of second-quarter revenues). The SEC contends that Gateway violated securities regulations—the requirement to disclose known trends and uncertainties that could have an unfavorable impact on earnings—by failing to inform investors that a significant part of revenues came from a new, high-risk customer group. Nor did Gateway adequately provide for the expected loan losses for this program. But this wasn't all.

The third quarter of 2000 saw further business deterioration, yet Gateway assured investors that its sales "remain robust" and the consensus revenue growth estimate of 16 percent would be achievable, despite a Gateway internal document, dubbed "Gap to Consensus," to the contrary. How did Gateway close the gap? You guessed it. By accelerating sales to poor-credit customers, thereby adding $84 million to quarterly revenues.[17] While the quality of Gateway's receivables continued to deteriorate—poor-credit receivables reached 37 percent of total receivables at the end of the third quarter—management reduced the loan loss reserve by $34.5 million, inflating reported income by the same amount. This enabled the company to report $0.46 EPS, precisely meeting the consensus estimate. For good measure, Gateway improperly booked a gain of $4.3 million from receivables sales in the second quarter and shipped $21 million worth of PCs to warehouses at the end of the third quarter in 2000, improperly recording this channel stuffing as revenues.

Analysts celebrated Gateway's third-quarter "performance"—meeting the consensus against all odds—leading one analyst to state that the company's business model "gives them an advantage over everyone." On October 13, 2000, the day following the third-quarter earnings release, Gateway's stock followed suit, increasing 22 percent. So much for analysts' prescience. Less than a couple of months later, however, Gateway's manipulations ran out of steam, and its stock plummeted by two-thirds: from $53.11 in October 13, 2000, to $17.99 on December 31, 2000.

Note that Gateway engaged in a combination of *accounting* manipulations (cutting the bad-debt reserve) and *real* manipulative activities (increasing sales to poor-credit customers). The latter schemes, such as cutting R&D or maintenance to "make the numbers," are particularly damaging because they exacerbate an already deteriorating business.[18]

### Things Go Better with Coke (When Pushed a Bit)

From 1997 to 1999, Coca-Cola engaged in an elaborate program of "gallon pushing" in Japan, which made the difference, according to the SEC, "between Coca-Cola meeting or missing analysts' consensus or modified consensus earnings estimates for 8 out of 12 quarters."[19] What was this innovative gallon-pushing strategy that was kept secret—as is the venerated Coke formula—from the public? In 1997 and onward, the Coca-Cola (Japan) Company substantially improved credit terms to Coke bottlers to induce them to purchase increased quantities of concentrates, beyond those required by customer demand. According to the SEC, these gallon-pushing efforts increased bottlers' inventory of concentrates by 60 percent between 1997 and 1999, while sales rose by 11 percent only. The enhanced "pushed gallons" augmented Coca-Cola's revenues and earnings from 1997 to 1999, a period of intensifying competition. The gallon-pushing program enabled Coca-Cola, according to the SEC, to "publicly maintain between 1996 and 1999 that it expected its earnings per share to continue to grow between 15 percent and 20 percent annually [despite the challenging competitive environment]."[20]

Typical to most revenue-enhancing schemes, borrowing from the future leads to deficits in subsequent quarters, requiring an acceleration of the manipulation. Unless business improves dramatically, this is bound to crash sooner rather than later. Indeed, by the end of 1999, as concentrate inventories at Coke bottlers reached exorbitant levels, it was no longer feasible to continue the gallon-pushing program, and, on January 26, 2000, Coca-Cola filed a Form 8-K with the SEC, announcing a worldwide concentrate-inventory-reduction plan, stating that "the management of Coca-Cola and its bottlers, specifically including bottlers in Japan, had jointly determined that opportunities exist to reduce concentrate inventory carried by bottlers." This, artfully worded statement, says the SEC, was false and misleading, "describing the inventory reduction as a joint proactive efficiency measure between Coca-Cola and its bottlers," while omitting any reference to the multiyear gallon-pushing program that created the urgent need to drastically reduce inventory levels.

The important lesson from this case is that when you cease manipulating, come out with a clear and complete mea culpa, rather than painting the pig with lipstick (i.e., "an inventory reduction plan").

### Charter Communications: No Customer Left Behind

Charter Communications is a provider of basic and digital cable, high-speed Internet, and telephone services. The SEC contends that in 2001, Charter inflated the number of its subscribers—a key performance and growth indicator for communications and Internet companies—to meet analyst growth expectations and portray itself as a reasonably successful enterprise.[21] From 1999 to 2001, Charter reported annual customer growth rates of 3.1 percent, 2.5 percent, and 1.1 percent, respectively. The meager 2001 growth, however, was enabled by a process dubbed internally as "holding disconnects." This original "growth strategy" was surprisingly simple. Facing an increasing number of customers switching to satellite television and otherwise delinquent or terminating customers, Charter responded by—doing nothing, that is, retaining the deserting customers. This, says the SEC, enabled Charter to pretend that, in 2001, "it was meeting and, at times, exceeding analysts' expectations for subscriber growth when, in fact, Charter actually experienced flat to negative growth."[22] Whereas the "holding the disconnects" policy took care of the pretense of subscriber growth, Charter also needed to show revenue growth—"show me the money." This was facilitated by fictitious barter transactions. Charter entered into agreements with set-top box providers adding $20 to the price of a box, and in return the box providers purchased $20 in advertising from Charter, which was duly recorded as revenues to the tune of $17 million in the fourth quarter of 2000. In fact, says the SEC, "no real revenue was generated by these transactions."[23]

This scheme highlights yet another aspect of manipulations that makes them unsustainable: manipulating one performance indicator—in this case, subscriber growth—generally requires doctoring other indicators, such as revenue growth.

### CMS Energy: Brag-a-Watts

CMS Energy, an integrated energy company, overstated its revenues in 2000 and 2001 by $1.0 billion (10 percent of revenues) and $4.2 billion (36 percent of revenues), respectively.[24] This manipulation, however, didn't affect earnings because it entailed round-trip trades with counterparties, simultaneously purchasing and selling electric power or natural gas in identical volumes and prices, with no deliveries in sight. The purpose of these sham transactions, which were quite popular in the late 1990s and early 2000s in the energy sector, was, according to the SEC, "to elevate MS&T [CMS's trading division] into the top-20 tier ("top 20") of the industry publication volume ranking," expecting that the top-tier status would enhance CMS's business. As in the Coca-Cola case, the end-of-day contrition was halfhearted. When CMS's revenues were restated downward on March 29, 2002, to eliminate the effect of the round-trip trades, the explanation CMS gave investors was materially misleading, according to the SEC, because it did not state that the transactions causing the restatement—dubbed in the industry as "brag-a-watts"—lacked economic substance. Nor was the full magnitude of the round-trip transactions—$5.2 billion—properly disclosed.

Both the Charter and CMS cases demonstrate the wide range of manipulated items in addition to earnings and sales, like subscriber growth or oil reserves,[25] and the varied target audiences, like customers and suppliers, in addition to investors.

### Daisytek International: Driving Miss Daisy to Bankruptcy

Daisytek, a distributor of office products and computer supplies, engaged in an elaborate manipulation of earnings from 2001 to 2003, according to the SEC.[26] The company regularly released earnings forecasts it could not meet and made the numbers by a practice euphemistically called "booking to budget." This, stripped to its essence, meant recording fictitious "budgeted" revenues and expenses instead of the actual numbers. At the end of each quarter, the increasing gaps between real and booked (budgeted) amounts were bridged by income from vendors' allowances and rebates granted on large inventory purchases Daisy had made.[27] The vendor allowances recorded as income were substantial, often exceeding reported earnings, such as in 2002, when Daisytek reported net income of $10.85 million, while vendor allowances were $22 million. Reported earnings were thus significantly inflated by rebates from the acquisition of unnecessary, often obsolete inventory.

Not surprisingly, inventory levels at Daisytek spiraled: $83.6 million, $115.4 million, and $190.7 million at the end of 2001, 2002, and the first nine months of 2003, respectively. Total revenues for the corresponding periods rose only slightly: $1.01 billion, $1.19 billion, and $1.33 billion. Throughout, Daisytek assured investors that "Our purchases of inventory generally are closely tied to sales." As an aside, since both inventories and sales figures were publicly reported and prominently displayed, one wonders about the gullibility of investors and analysts who failed to realize the increasing misalignment between Daisytek's inventories and sales. Ultimately, the large inventory purchases, often of hard-to-sell items, had a devastating effect on the company's liquidity and operations, leading suppliers to place it on a credit hold, until it mercifully filed for Chapter 11 in May 2003.

Daisytek's schemes, aimed at meeting its own performance forecasts, demonstrate the recklessness and shortsightedness of some managers, willing to mortally hurt the company—purchasing large quantities of unneeded, obsolete inventory—to temporarily mask a deteriorating business, and even paying taxes on fictitious income. Daisytek's managers apparently believed that they were immune to detection because they manipulated earnings by real actions—excess inventory purchases—rather than by twisting accounting rules. Managing earnings by actions like R&D cuts or deeply discounted sales, some managers believe, is safer than by misapplying accounting techniques, because business decisions are rarely second guessed.[28] Earnings manipulation by actions, however, is often more costly than by accounting means, as clearly demonstrated by Daisytek's bankruptcy.

## Made in America?

Finally, lest you think from the previous cases that information manipulation is made in the United States, thirty countries, mostly developed, suffer from more acute cases of manipulitis (see figure 3-1). The researchers producing the graph in the figure, Christian Leuz, Dhananjay Nanda, and Peter Wysocki, developed an earnings manipulation score that reflects various characteristics of managed earnings, such as high volatility relative to cash flows (managed earnings deviate from cash flows more than truthful earnings) and loss avoidance (managed earnings frequently transform small losses to profits).[29] By this score, earnings management is, surprisingly, less prevalent in the

FIGURE 3-1

# Earnings management around the world

## AGGREGATE EARNINGS MANAGEMENT SCORE

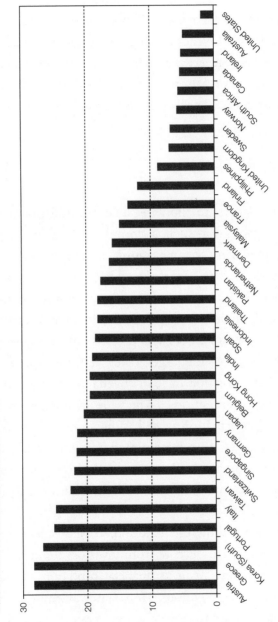

*Source:* Christian Leuz, Dhananjay Nanda, and Peter Wysocki, "Earnings management and investor protection: An international comparison," working paper, Wharton School of the University of Pennsylvania, 2002.

United States than in other countries, including Switzerland, Denmark, Germany, Japan, and the United Kingdom. Nor are manipulations by large companies restricted to the United States. Royal Dutch Shell (U.K. and the Netherlands); Parmalat (Italy); Nortel (Canada); Nikko Cordial, Sanyo Electric, and Livedoor (Japan); Bawag Bank (Austria); and Ahold (the Netherlands)—a very partial list of sizeable offenders—attest to the globalization of information manipulation. And yet, not being the worst offender is, of course, hardly a consolation for Americans.

## Why They Do It?

Why do managers manipulate financial information? There are numerous reasons for such a complex, widespread phenomenon. Enhancing managers' compensation, which is frequently based on reported performance (earnings, sales) as well as on stock price changes—which in turn are affected by corporate performance—is a frequent manipulation motive.[30] Others include thwarting proxy contests or activist shareholders by a pretense of improved performance; inflating share prices for larger takes at IPOs and secondary stock issues; avoiding violation of loan covenants; or deflecting regulatory (e.g., antitrust) interventions.[31] The wide array of incentives to manipulate financial information as well as the items manipulated arise from the varied uses of this information in contractual arrangements between the company and its employees (to determine bonuses), lenders (loan covenant violations), patent licensees (royalty amounts), and other stakeholders.

But, as the cases show, the major objective of information manipulation is undoubtedly to obscure from investors the deterioration in the company's operations or in its financial condition, thereby preserving managers' jobs and reputations. Thus, Gateway embellished its reported revenues and earnings to conceal from investors the decline in demand for its computers after the tech bubble burst, and Coca-Cola aggressively pushed its concentrates on Japanese bottlers to mask the adverse effects of the intensified competition in the mid-1990s. Often, particularly companies in growth sectors (high-tech, biotech, environmental), manipulate reported information to preserve the image of the growth so coveted by investors. Thus, i2 Technologies, while growing reasonably well, front-loaded revenues to meet the increasingly aggressive growth expectations of analysts, and Charter Communications attempted to maintain the growth facade by refusing to disconnect delinquent and switching customers. My research on companies that restate their earnings corroborates the growth-at-all-costs objective. Restatements offer a unique opportunity to compare previously reported (misstated) earnings with true ones.[32] A sample of 189 restating companies shows that the *originally reported* mean earnings growth rates in the two restated years were 3.8 percent and 6.7 percent, whereas the mean growth rates of the restated (true) earnings were rather anemic: 0.3 percent and 3.2 percent. Masking the end of growth is clearly the major objective of the manipulators.

This leaves us with a nagging question: don't managers—on the whole, a smart lot—know that report manipulation is fraught with dangers (see next section) and is unsustainable, as the preceding cases show? How can rational persons engage in such a self-destructive activity? The answer probably lies in a prevalent cognitive trait of managers: *overconfidence*. Studies have shown that overconfidence—possessing unrealistically positive beliefs about the future performance of the company—is pervasive among executives, leading to both positive (increased investment in basic R&D) and negative (reckless acquisitions) outcomes.[33] Here is the common scenario of report manipulation perpetrated by an overconfident manager:

The company's operations hit a snag: sales growth flattens or operating costs unexpectedly increase. To avoid missing the consensus or their own guidance, managers front-load or bring forward a modest amount of revenue from next quarter to make the numbers. They, of course, know that next quarter's revenue will start with a deficit, but here is where overconfidence comes in. Managers are convinced that revenues in the next quarter or year will be sufficiently high to cover the front-loading and then some. It rarely is, however, and small frauds quickly mushroom and burst. This was vividly confirmed by the CEO of Satyam, a large Indian information services company, who in his 2009 letter to the board disclosing the massive manipulation that he perpetrated over several years wrote: "What started as a marginal gap between actual operating profit and the one reflected in the books of accounts [and publicly reported] continued to grow over the years. It has attained unmanageable proportions."[34]

## Innocent Victims

Who bears the cost of financial information manipulations? Primarily the innocent bystanders—shareholders. James Lockhart, Fannie Mae's regulator, told the U.S. Senate in June 2006 that Fannie's $11 billion mis-statement cost shareholders up to $30 billion.[35] These huge shareholder losses are, of course, dwarfed by the cost of Fannie's and Freddie's implosion in the 2007–2008 financial crisis to investors and taxpayers. Jonathan Karpoff, Scott Lee, and Gerald Martin carefully estimated the loss to shareholders of 585 companies that were targets of SEC enforcement actions from 1978 to 2002 for financial-reporting violations.[36] They estimated the shareholder loss by summing the stock price drops on the various public announcements related to the manipulations, such as the initial disclosure of investigation by the board or the SEC, subsequent announcements of SEC or Department of Justice actions, "Wells Notices" (SEC intent to file charges), and civil or criminal actions against perpetrators. The total estimated loss to shareholders from managers cooking the books is an astounding 38 percent share price decline, on average.[37] Translated to dollars, the mean market-value loss per company is almost $400 million, and the aggregate loss over all enforcement targets exceeds $150 billion.[38] Not all shareholders, of course, suffered a 38 percent loss on their investment. Some bought shares at low prices before the manipulation kicked in, others sold before the price drop upon discovery, and some were partially compensated from lawsuit settlements. Nevertheless, it's safe to say that a price correction of such magnitude has very serious consequences for most shareholders.

These shareholder losses, estimated from stock price declines, reflect real costs, of course. According to Karpoff et al.'s computations, 9 percent of the overall shareholder value loss reflects legal penalties[39]; a quarter of the value loss represents a reality check—the correction of the erstwhile manipulation that inflated the stock price. The remaining two-thirds of the shareholder value loss represents, in the researchers' phrase, reputational loss: investors' expectation of the cost of customers bailing out or adversely changing business terms with a company caught cheating and whose survival prospects have diminished; the cost from suppliers reassessing their relationship with the company; the increased cost of capital charged by lenders concerned with the integrity of the firm and its managers; and the obvious impediments to future stock or bond issues. Key talent leaving a business tarnished by scandal coupled with the considerable and protracted distraction of management dealing with investigations and lawsuits add to the heavy reputational loss.

In case these "averages" seem abstract, consider Computer Associates, renamed CA, after its massive information manipulation. A *Fortune* article recounted how, two years after the revelation of the multiyear manipulation of reported sales and earnings and the installment of a new management, the company—a large supplier of software for businesses—is still struggling with restatements, consensus misses, bonds downgraded to junk, cash flow shortfalls, and, perhaps most seriously, "an exodus of executive talent."[40] The company was in probation, operating under a court-appointed monitor, as a condition of deferring prosecution, and the new CEO expects the cleanup to last five years! As for CA's reputation, the article quoted a Gartner analyst saying, "I think this whole image perception is going to take years to get by."

In the meantime, at Nortel—another prominent manipulator of the early 2000s—a *Wall Street Journal* lead article described earnings restatements stretching back several years and predicted that internal controls and financial reporting problems "will continue to take significant time and effort"; quoting the new CEO, "It's going to take three to five years to recreate a great company."[41] Hope springs eternal; in January 14, 2009, Nortel filed for bankruptcy. A mercy killing.

The root cause of the downfalls of Computer Associates, Nortel, Fannie Mae, and the multitude of less illustrious cookers of books was, of course, a business deterioration that the manipulators intended to mask. Manipulations, however, not only fail to mask serious business deterioration for long, but also exacerbate the deterioration and wreak havoc on efforts to reverse the downward trend. Skeptical, often hostile shareholders, suppliers, and customers, harmed by the manipulation, along with disillusioned employees, vengeful prosecutors, and class-action lawyers, are often reluctant to participate in restructuring plans and sever credit and supply lines, distract managers' attention, and cost a fortune to mollify. No wonder that this "reputational loss" shaves a quarter of shareholders' value by Karpoff et al.'s estimates (two-thirds of 38 percent price decline).

But it's not only shareholders who pay the price of financial misrepresentation; employees and the economy at large are seriously damaged, too. Simi Kedia and Thomas Philippon highlight an intriguing facet of the social cost and waste wrought by reporting manipulation.[42] They argue that earnings manipulation is not convincing unless it is accompanied by real increases in corporate investment and employment. Thus, in order to persuade investors that the reported (manipulated) sales and earnings growth is real, the manipulators must mimic the investment and employment patterns of their genuinely high-performing counterparts. High reported earnings with employee layoffs don't seem credible. Using a sample of four hundred companies that restated earnings for misreporting reasons from 1997 to 2002, Kedia and Philippon demonstrate that these companies increased their head count during the manipulation period by 3.7 percent *more* than similar (same size, age, industry) nonrestating companies and boosted their property, plant, and equipment by 5 percent *more* than honest comparables. Alas, after restatement, both employment and investment plummeted relative to the nonrestating companies.[43] Keeping the business-as-usual facade led the manipulators to shed between 250,000 and 600,000 jobs from 2000 to 2002. Heavy are the costs of manipulation.

## Crime and Punishment

And what about the perpetrators of reporting manipulations? Jonathan Karpoff, Scott Lee, and Gerald Martin examined all the SEC and Department of Justice (DOJ) enforcement actions for financial misrepresentations from 1977 to 2006, in all 788 actions, documenting the fate of persons targeted by these actions: 2,206 employees of the companies involved, 723 of whom were CEOs, presidents, or board chairs.[44] The turnover rate of these corporate chiefs should give a long pause to any manager contemplating cooking the books. Almost 80 percent of the targeted executives left or were terminated *before* the public announcement of the SEC or DOJ action, and an additional 11 percent were dismissed by the end of the regulatory proceedings.[45] The turnover rate was even higher (96 percent) for the nonexecutives targeted by the SEC or DOJ (it's easier to dump those without golden parachutes). Thus, the likelihood of survival for an executive or employee targeted by an enforcement action is even slimmer than Evel Knievel's chance of motorcycle jumping over fourteen Greyhound buses (he actually made it on October 25, 1975, in Kings Island, Ohio).

But losing one's job is by no means the end of travails. The SEC initiated civil litigation against 87 percent of the 723 CEOs, presidents, and board chairs, resulting in a third of them barred from serving as officers or directors of public companies and a quarter being criminally indicted, 102 of whom were sentenced to an average of 5.7 years in prison. On top of all this, most of the targeted executives paid substantial fines. Even more bad news for perpetrators: the prosecutorial zeal and severity of punishment increased substantially in the wake of the early-2000s accounting scandals and the Sarbanes-Oxley Act. Justice Department data indicates that, between July 2002 and March 2006, there have been more than 1,000 convictions (including plea bargains) in corporate-fraud cases, including 82 CEOs, 85 presidents, 36 CFOs, and 102 vice presidents.[46] Pretty scary stuff.

Trying to see the bright side, you may ask, what about all the unde-tected and unpunished manipulations? Don't shareholders of these firms enjoy higher stock prices and managers richer compensation? In some cases, they do, when the business slowdown triggering the manipulation is temporary, and a quick recovery allows managers to "mend their ways" with nobody the wiser. But, one rarely knows *ahead of time* the duration of a slowdown, so that embarking on a manipulation gets you on a very risky path. And even if the manipulation somehow escapes exposure, the potpourri of SEC enforcement actions discussed earlier indicates that most manipulations adversely affect business operations. Thus, Gateway achieved its revenue targets by selling computers to previously rejected, poor-credit customers, essentially at a loss. Coca-Cola's gallon-pushing program was enabled by a significant extension of credit to bottlers, "typically … from eight to twenty-eight or thirty days," increasing Coke's cost of funds. Charter Communications, striving to portray solid cus-tomer growth, continued to provide costly services to delinquent cus-tomers as well as to those who asked to be disconnected, obviously with no revenues to match. Daisytek's large acquisitions of slow-moving, obsolete inventories ultimately drove it to bankruptcy. And i2 Technolo-gies' front-loading of revenues was costly too, as the SEC notes: "To close certain sales, i2 sales representatives exaggerated or oversold what certain software products could actually do. After these deals closed, i2 techni-cians were, in many instances, able to write code to create the promised functionality, but *these efforts took much time, effort and expense* … and i2's relationship with some customers had been strained, due in part to the substantial post-license work i2 had to perform to make its software deliver what had been agreed upon" (emphasis mine).[47] And don't forget the taxes—actual cash outflows—paid on the inflated earnings.

These substantial costs of the SEC-sanctioned cases are clearly also present in manipulations that don't see the light of day. Add to this the costs of needless investment and recruiting to portray an image of success, documented by Kedia and Philippon,[48] and the loss from postponement or cancelation of R&D, advertising, or maintenance to make the numbers, and the weighty burden of information manipulation, *detected or not*, becomes clear. Obviously, there is no free lunch in information manipulation.

## Manipulation in Good Cause

Like the Allies' deceptions that helped win World War II, or a butterfly's trickery to avoid a predator, there surely are "good earnings managements"—information manipulations in good causes. Here they are:

*This part intentionally left blank.*

## Operating Instructions

- **DON'T EVEN THINK ABOUT IT.** When operations stall and the specter of falling stock prices, intervention by activist investors, defection by disgruntled employees holding useless options, and adverse actions by concerned customers and suppliers loom large, the temptation to manipulate financial information naturally arises. Being convinced, like most executives, that the slump is temporary, you may even think that you do shareholders a favor by "smoothing out" the downturn in the financials so they don't worry their pretty heads about it.

  Consider that many business slowdowns are prolonged affairs exacerbating the fraud, and that the likelihood of being caught cheating is constantly increasing in the post–Sarbanes-Oxley environment, further enhanced by the 2010 Dodd-Frank legislation encouraging whistle-blowers to go directly to the SEC and obtain rich rewards.[49] And, when caught, you are almost sure to lose your job. Remember, even if not detected, the act of manipulation, as I've shown abundantly, is costly and exacerbates the downturn. So, like the warning at the top of the no-parking signs in Manhattan: "Don't even think about it."

- **DON'T CLAM UP IN TOUGH TIMES.** When the going gets tough, the natural tendency is to withdraw from the market. Stop earnings guidance, shorten conference calls, send substitutes to shareholders meetings, file financial reports late, and reduce voluntary disclosure.[50] These reactions are not smart. There is absolutely nothing to be gained and much to lose from such market pullback. The evidence of companies in distress stopping quarterly guidance, for example, shows that stock prices drop sharply on the announcement of guidance cessation and analysts abandon the stoppers (see chapter 6). When performance stalls, shareholders—your principals—should be doubly engaged (see further details in chapters 6 through 8).

- **THE VIRTUES OF CONSERVATISM.** When the business deteriorates, exercise extra care with insider trading (yours, and those of other top executives) and avoid aggressive accounting procedures, such as understating loan loss reserves or switching from accelerated to straight-line depreciation, to increase reported earnings. Both insider trading and accounting trickery attract the attention of regulatory agencies, trial lawyers, and perceptive investors and reporters. A case in point: a *Wall Street Journal* article with the headline, "Is AIG on Slippery Slope?" discussing analysts' and investors' concerns with AIG's change of accounting technique amid continuing problems with its subprime-linked securities.[51]

- **AVOID ELEVATED EXPECTATIONS.** Manipulation is often "forced" on managers by overly optimistic investor expectations and inflated stock prices that have to be justified by ever-higher revenues and earnings. You have to nip such heightened expectations and overpriced shares in the bud by releasing realistic information to investors. If you procrastinate, you won't be able to safely dismount the price tiger; you will not survive the large price correction when investors finally realize it was all a dream. Chapter 5 deals with overvalued shares, their consequences, and how to avoid this predicament.

- **COME OUT WITH IT, QUICKLY.** If you or your predecessors engaged in misrepresentation, come out fully and cleanly as soon as possible. Spin, gloss, or half-truths about the manipulation—such as Coca-Cola's claim that the reversal of the gallon-pushing scheme was a planned move—are harmful to shareholders and ultimately to you. Don't hide the truth, like the "stealth restatement," which is changing previously reported earnings or sales *without* alerting investors to it. Glass Lewis & Co. reports that no less than

254 companies tried to hide their restatements from investors in 2006.[52] And don't delay the bad news. Research has shown that announcements of earnings restatements without numbers—postponing the grim magnitude of the restatement for later—trigger a sharper stock price decline than when all the details are disclosed at once.[53] Remember that the truth will come out sooner or later, so get it over with quickly. Referring to Mark Twain writing *The Adventures of Tom Sawyer*, Huckleberry Finn said that "he told the truth mainly." Just tell the truth.

## Chapter 4

# Kill All the Lawyers?

## How to Immunize Your Company from Class-Action Lawsuits

Shareholder lawsuits, many believe, are seriously harming the U.S. economy.[1] John Thain, former CEO of the New York Stock Exchange (NYSE) (later of Merrill Lynch, until his resignation in 2009) joined the chorus of U.S. business leaders blaming, in part, the prevalence of shareholder lawsuits for the increasing number of companies registering abroad. Thain told the *Financial Times*: "the high risk of litigation [in the United States] compared with other jurisdictions remained a disincentive for companies to list in the U.S."[2] And the chairman of a leading law firm is quoted in that article, saying: "The risk of litigation is seriously undermining New York's competitiveness as an international financial center." How onerous is this litigation risk and what can managers do to immunize their companies against litigation? Let's look at the data.

## Surprise, surprise . . .

How many times have you heard that in the United States, the number of shareholders' class-action lawsuits against companies, their managers, directors, and auditors is constantly on the rise and getting out of control? Have I got a surprise for you: figure 4-1, from an NERA (an economic consultancy) 2010 report, provides the year-by-year number of federal shareholder lawsuits filed against public companies from 1996 to 2010.[3] It covers the entire cycle of economic stability in the mid-1990s, the tumultuous tech bubble of the late 1990s, the subsequent burst of the bubble and the scandal-ridden years and recession of the early 2000s, through the economic and stock market growth period from 2002 to 2006, and ending with the financial crisis and recession from 2007 to 2010. A period of boom and bust such as this is surely fodder for trial lawyers.

The figure portrays some striking facts:

- The yearly number of lawsuits—typically around 220 to 230—is in fact quite small relative to the seven to six thousand public companies listed on U.S. exchanges during the examined period (roughly 3.5 percent annual litigation odds), considering that each of these companies releases four quarterly reports a year and other public filings as well as numerous press releases and conference calls all inviting snooping class-action lawyers.[4] To characterize such a modest number of lawsuits as posing a "high risk of litigation" (Thain's statement) is a stretch.

- Even more surprising, the number of lawsuits has declined since 2001, reaching a record low of 131 in 2006. The increases from 2007 to 2010 are mainly due to the financial crisis. Roughly half of the 2008–2010 cases were filed against financial institutions, up from 16 percent from 2005 to 2006. This spike should subside with the abatement of the crisis. Of note to foreign companies, the number of lawsuits filed against such companies listed in the United States also declined: from thirty in 2004, to twenty-five, fourteen, and nine in 2005, 2006, and 2007, respectively.[5] For foreign executives, there

FIGURE 4-1

**Federal filings, January 1, 1996–December 31, 2010**

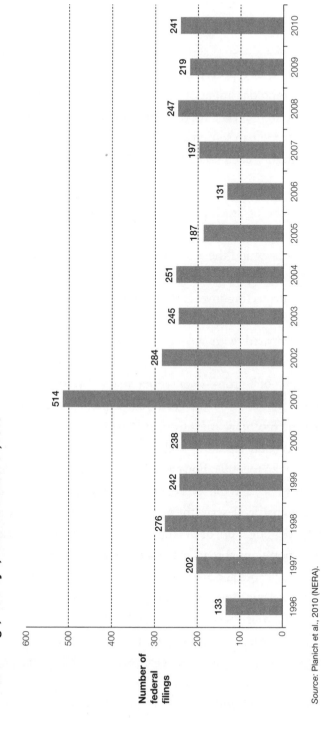

are obviously pros and cons to being listed in U.S. exchanges, but they should hardly count the risk of litigation among the latter.

- Since most lawsuits settle out of court, the typical settlement number (not reported in figure 4-1) provides another perspective on shareholder litigation. The median settlement increased from $7.8 million in 2005 to $11.1 million in 2010. These relatively modest median settlements do not reflect, however, several mega-settlements, each exceeding $1 billion.[6]

The decrease in litigation frequency in the early 2000 was mainly due to the general rise of stock prices until 2008; litigations follow large price declines. Of perhaps even greater relevance is the increased enforcement of securities laws and the Sarbanes-Oxley Act by the SEC and the DOJ. These public enforcers are arguably more effective than private shareholder litigators in protecting investors.[7] In 2006, for example, the DOJ investigated 490 corporate fraud cases, resulting in 171 indictments and 124 convictions, compared with 405 investigations, 497 indictments, and 317 convictions in 2005. Of the convictions, the longest sentence was given to Jeffrey Skilling of Enron—twenty-four years.[8] Investors' misfortunes, like the 2000 burst of the tech bubble, the subsequent accounting scandals, and the subprime mortgage mess from 2007 to 2008, generate ups and downs in the class-action statistics, both in lawsuit frequency and settlement amounts. Taken together, however, the frequency of shareholder lawsuits (220 to 230 a year) and the level of settlement amounts in the last fifteen to twenty years hardly deserve the alarmist claims of an American epidemic of shareholder litigation, or of a heightened risk of lawsuits allegedly driving U.S. corporations abroad and deterring foreign registrants.[9]

And, yet, statistics and averages tell only part of the story. You will soon see that for certain types of companies and economic circumstances—which may fit your specific case—the likelihood of being sued by shareholders or the SEC is substantially higher than the average across all corporations. Since this specific litigation risk is what matters to you most, I discuss the necessary and sufficient conditions for getting sued by shareholders or the SEC, followed by a research-based profile of the typical class-action targets, enabling managers to assess their company's likelihood of becoming a lawsuit defendant. I conclude by prescribing litigation immunization policies.

## Postcards from the Edge: Sharp Price Drops

Plaintiffs in shareholder lawsuits have to establish, among other things, that they were *damaged* by the alleged manipulation or misrepresentation of facts. The most straightforward way to do this is to document an investment loss by subtracting the stock price immediately following the public disclosure of the manipulation—presumably the true price—from the acquisition price—allegedly inflated by the manipulation.[10] For example, the lawsuit filed in 2003 against Ibis Technology was triggered by the company's announcement of large impairment charges (loss due to a decrease in asset value) made on Monday, December 15, 2003. Ibis's stock price dropped on the impairment announcement from $15.40 to $10.37—a whopping 33 percent decline. Accordingly, a shareholder who bought Ibis shares on, say, December 1, 2003, at $17.18 would allege a damage of $6.81 per share ($17.18 − $10.37). Thus, a substantial price drop upon disclosure of reporting improprieties, such as an earnings restatement or news about an SEC investigation, is obviously a *necessary condition* for a successful lawsuit. Large price drops, promising high damages and awards (settlements), also enhance the incentives for lawyers to file class-action suits.

However, contrary to the common wisdom, a large stock price decline is not a *sufficient condition* for litigation. That is, while lawsuits follow steep price drops, very few price drops trigger lawsuits. To demonstrate this, I identified all cases from 2002 to 2003—a period characterized by relatively high litigation frequency—in which the stock prices of public companies declined over a two-day period by 20 percent or more.[11] These sharp price decreases, generally in reaction to corporate disclosures of serious adverse information, obviously caused significant losses to shareholders. I identified 2,746 and 1,421 companies that, in 2002 and 2003, sustained two-day price drops of 20 percent or more. I then searched the Securities Class Action Clearinghouse database[12] for shareholder lawsuits that specifically identified those price drops in the allegations.[13] Surprisingly, and reassuringly, only a few lawsuits followed these price plunges. The 2,746 companies with a 20 percent or more price drop in 2002 triggered 113 lawsuits, and the 1,421 companies with a 20 percent or more price drop in 2003 resulted in 67 suits.[14] Thus, based on the 2002–2003 record, the litigation likelihood subsequent to a sharp price decline is 4–5 percent ($113/2,746 = 4.1$ percent, and $67/1,421 = 4.7$ percent). Stated positively, 95 percent of U.S. public companies experiencing sharp stock price declines escape unscathed by trial lawyers. If you find this unbelievable, recall that the total number of annual shareholder lawsuits was roughly 220–230 in the early 2000s (see figure 4-1), for about six to seven thousand companies listed in the United States. But, if a precipitous stock price decline is not an automatic trigger of a lawsuit, what is?

## Being in the Wrong Place

If your company is operating in litigation-prone industries, you are in the wrong place from a litigation point of view. The distribution of lawsuits across industries shows a marked concentration in high-tech, science-based, and other volatile sectors. A study by Lin Peng and Ailsa Röell, covering 479 class-action lawsuits filed from 1996 to 2002 against companies in the S&P 1500 index, identified the leading litigation-prone industries.[15]

It indicates that almost 40 percent of telecommunications companies, a third of computer and software producers, and a quarter of health-care and drug enterprises (where lawsuits often allege failure of management to alert investors to product development failures) were targets of shareholder lawsuits during the seven-year period from 1996 through 2002. In contrast, only 8.8 percent of manufacturing firms, 4.2 percent of oil, gas, and coal companies, and 8.6 percent of consumer durable goods manufacturers (cars, TV, appliances, furniture) were targets of shareholder lawsuits during the examined period. NERA's computation, at my request, confirms that the sectors with the largest number of lawsuits during the more recent period from 1997 to 2007 were electronic technology (15.1 percent of total lawsuits), technology services (15 percent), finance (13.5 percent),[16] health (8.9 percent), consumer services (5.8 percent), and communications (5.4 percent). Specific to the financial crisis, about half of shareholders lawsuits filed from 2008 to 2010 were against finance companies.

Thus, being in the wrong place—operating in high-tech, communications, finance, health-care, or science-based sectors—increases significantly your exposure to litigation risk. Even a stellar performer like Cisco Systems, with an enviable record of a single loss year (in 2001) from 1996 to 2010 and an eightfold rise in net income during that period, disclosed in its July 30, 2005, financial report a slew of pending class-action lawsuits: litigations related to the 1999–2001 tech-bubble period alleging "that defendants have made false and misleading statements"; derivative lawsuits that were settled in 2005; and a brand-new 2005 lawsuit claiming breach of fiduciary duty and unjust enrichment related to managerial stock options.

The prevalence of lawsuits among high-tech, telecom, health-care, and financial companies is undoubtedly related to the high volatility of their operations and, consequently, their stock prices. Competition, particularly in global markets, affects all economic sectors, but none more than high-tech, science-based, Internet, and telecom companies, due in particular to the fast pace of innovation (e.g., the ever-expanding services provided by wireless devices), the quick change in consumer tastes (for Internet services, for example), the virtual absence of barriers to entry, and the poor protection of intellectual property rights in many countries (the widespread copying of software programs, DVDs, and the manufacturing of drugs without license from patent holders). Consequently, the operations of companies in these industries—even those that are well established like IBM in the early 1990s and, more recently, Dell and Vodafone—are frequently disrupted, and sales and earnings growth grind to a halt, often leading to disappointing performance and share price declines. These setbacks serve as fodder for class-action lawyers.

But there is another, less appreciated attribute common to the frequently sued industries—they are rich in intangible (intellectual) assets: R&D, patents, trademarks, brands, franchises, alliances, and highly skilled employees. These assets, which are the major value drivers of high-tech, science-based, health-care, Internet, and telecom enterprises, are notoriously fickle. Competitors often infringe on patents, the majority of drug development programs come to naught, and key employees of software and biotech companies frequently shift employment, taking with them proprietary knowledge—all recipes for business setbacks, growth disruptions, and shareholder disappointments. Often, the hard-to-value intangible assets acquired in M&A transactions, and paid for dearly, turn sour and require an embarrassing write-off (loss), followed by lawsuits. AOL Time Warner's $100 billion (yes, billion) goodwill write-off in 2003, JDS Uniphase's $45 billion write-off in 2001, and eBay's 2007 $1.4 billion goodwill write-off from the acquisition of Skype are reminders of how quickly certain intangibles vanish or, alternatively, how excessive is the price often paid for these elusive assets.

But there is more to intangibles attracting lawsuits than the high uncertainty of their value. Many intangibles-intensive companies, such as biotech, software, and Internet-based enterprises, have few tangible assets and low income streams. Consequently, the share prices of these "conceptual" firms primarily reflect investors' growth expectations, rather than current earnings and asset values. These growth expectations, often stoked by managers' rosy forecasts, are particularly sensitive to bad news—earnings shortfalls or product failures—and to changes in investors' perceptions, frequently leading to disappointments and lawsuits. Furthermore, the compensation packages of managers of intangibles-intensive companies typically include a disproportionately large share of options and other stock-based incentives. Fraud (options backdating, for example) and reporting manipulations are often linked to stock-based compensation and lead to lawsuits.

Yet you aren't doomed even if your company operates in a high-litigation sector. There are many high-tech, science-based, Internet, and financial services companies that experience large price drops yet escape litigation. How do they do it? Safeguarding oneself from heart attacks requires familiarity with the causal risk factors (high cholesterol and blood pressure, sex, age, and family history). Similarly, effective immunization from litigation requires a comprehensive understanding of the multiple causes of this predicament.

## Meet the Risk Factors

Extensive research on the causes and consequences of shareholder lawsuits points out the following factors, in addition to large price drops and operating in suspect industries, as enhancing the risk of litigation.

- LARGE COMPANIES, typically having a large number of shareholders and a high share turnover, are frequent lawsuit targets, because the large number of shareholders assures class-action lawyers of big plaintiff classes and substantial damage estimates, leading to fat fees. Since plaintiff lawyers incur the costs of filing lawsuits—the research required to identify and substantiate with particularity the alleged wrongdoings as well as the legal filing costs—it is generally not cost effective for lawyers to target small companies with few shareholders. Equally important, large companies have deep pockets and substantial insurance coverage of executives and directors, all conducive to big settlements. And, yes, lawsuits against large companies receive media exposure, which lawyers crave.

- **GROWTH COMPANIES THAT SUSTAINED STOCK PRICE INCREASES.** Growth, as demonstrated in this book's introduction, is fickle, and sooner or later it comes to a screeching halt, causing significant losses to shareholders who bought at high prices. In many such cases, it is relatively easy to allege and even document that the growth was hyped by managers who failed to warn investors early on of the trend reversal. Making the situation worse, managers of growth companies are generally loaded with stock options, and the exercise of these options prior to the price decline provides plaintiff lawyers with the motive for the alleged hype and information manipulation: obscuring the deterioration of business and enabling managers to cash in on richly priced stock options. The lessons to growth companies' managers regarding the hazards of hype and option trickery are obvious.

- **COMPANIES WITH ACCOUNTING AND FINANCIAL REPORTING ISSUES,** such as those that restate their earnings or are investigated by the SEC, are frequent litigation targets. And as you'll see in the next section, even companies that use aggressive accounting techniques considerably enhance their litigation exposure.

- **COMPANIES WITH FREQUENT STOCK ISSUES AND SERIAL ACQUIRERS (M&A)** are also litigation prone, since business acquisitions often fail to live up to expectations, and it is relatively easy to allege that shareholders were not properly apprised of the risks involved and not alerted in time to the difficulties in merging the acquired enterprises.[17] Similarly, IPOs are also frequent litigation targets, since many IPOs disappoint investors.[18]

- **FINALLY, COMPANIES WITH LAVISH MANAGERIAL AND DIRECTORS' PAY AND PERKS,** particularly stock-based compensation, preferential loans, and platinum parachutes, are exposed to heightened litigation risk, alleging shareholder exploitation and manipulation of financial information to enhance bonuses and incentive pay (Fannie Mae comes once more to mind).

Echoing the counsel of cardiologists, if your company has two or more of the these risk factors, it is exposed to high shareholder litigation risk. Here are the actions you should take to mitigate this risk.

## Operating Instructions: Immunize Your Company

Being a middle-aged male heightens your risk of heart failure, but there isn't much you can do about that. Similarly, a high-growth telecom or software company or a financial institution will not intentionally slow growth or switch industry to reduce litigation exposure. However, like exercise and a proper diet to reduce coronary disease risk, there are important actions you can take to mitigate exposure when your company faces a high litigation risk.

### Warn Early On of Impending Disappointments

The J. Jill Group, a women's clothing retailer, expanded its operations in the late 1990s and early 2000s from a catalog-only retailer to mall-based stores and saw its revenues and stock price increase substantially. Then, in December 2002, the company issued a warning that it would substantially miss its fourth-quarter earnings target. On the warning, J. Jill's stock tumbled almost 30 percent and, surprise, a class-action lawsuit followed, alleging that executives and board members were aware of the downturn in operations well before they issued the warning, yet delayed it to cash out on $17 million of the company stock. Nevertheless, in June 2004, a U.S. District Court judge dismissed the lawsuit. While the judge did not elaborate on the reasons for dismissal, J. Jill's early public warning—nine weeks before the earnings release—was likely a major mitigating factor.

Similarly, in early 2002, Skechers USA, a sports and recreation shoe manufacturer, issued optimistic press releases about its earnings and revenues, followed by reported revenue increases for the first two quarters of 2002. The stock price followed suit, yet Skechers' growth was short-lived, and in September 2002, it warned of an earnings shortfall ahead of the end-of-year financial report release that confirmed the bad news. Skechers was nevertheless sued, alleging that executives were aware of the downturn before the warning, but in April 2005, a federal court in Los Angeles dismissed the lawsuit, likely due to the public warning.

There are good reasons why alerting investors to impending bad news as soon as possible deters litigation or mitigates its consequences, leading to suit dismissal or a reduced settlement figure. A warning generally decreases the stock price, thereby shortening the class-period (alleged fraud interval) and reducing the alleged "price inflation" due to misinformation, both factors decreasing investors' damage claims. The reduced potential damages also dampen lawyers' enthusiasm to file lawsuits. Most importantly, an early warning (and I mean *early*, not just two or three days before the release of bad news) removes or weakens a frequent plaintiffs' claim that managers "sat on the information," failing to alert investors in time to the adversity.

To be sure, as the previous cases indicate, a warning is not a foolproof deterrent of litigation. In fact, the record shows that litigated companies warn investors *more* frequently than similar, but nonlitigated ones, a finding that led some to suggest that warnings attract lawsuits. This, however, is like concluding that hospitals are a health hazard since more people die there than at home. In both cases, cause and effect are reversed. Clearly, companies with a high litigation exposure—experiencing a business downturn, or an earnings restatement—will issue more warnings *and* be sued more frequently than less exposed enterprises, much as seriously sick persons are rushed to hospitals and some unfortunately die there. It is, therefore, reassuring that research by Laura Field, Michelle Lowry, and Susan Shu, simultaneously accounting for the seriousness of litigation exposure *and* the release of a warning, shows that the latter indeed reduces the frequency of litigation.[19] Moreover, Douglas Skinner reports that early warnings, even when they do not prevent a lawsuit, result in a lower settlement figure (recall that most shareholder lawsuits settle out of court).[20] In chapter 6, I will return to warnings in the wider context of investor guidance, but, in the litigation setting, early warnings are an important component of a deterrent policy.

## Avoid Earnings Management and Aggressive Accounting

It is widely believed that shareholder lawsuits are largely frivolous, filed as a Pavlovian reaction to large drops in share price, alleging a boilerplate of complaints against managers, directors, and auditors. Indeed, the major objective of the Private Securities Litigation Reform Act (PSLRA) of 1995 was to curb meritless lawsuits by raising the evidence bar for pleading securities fraud cases. Examining the frivolity issue is important, because if shareholders' lawsuits are indeed meritless, there isn't much managers can do to immunize themselves from litigation. The research, briefly summarized next, lays to rest the frivolity myth.

Marilyn Johnson, Karen Nelson, and Adam Pritchard examine computer hardware and software companies—a favorite target of class-action lawyers—comparing sued companies with similar (same industry, close stock price drops) nonsued companies and report that litigation targets issued more earnings restatements and had higher accounting accruals than did nonsued companies.[21] Restatements often follow manipulations and misapplications of accounting principles, and accruals—the noncash earnings items, such as the bad-debt expense, or an inventory write-down—are largely based on managers' estimates, which are prone to manipulation.[22] Yvonne Lu confirms the association between large accruals and litigation frequency across many industries.[23] This evidence indicates that accounting shenanigans are at the core of most shareholder lawsuits. Stephen Choi, Karen Nelson, and Adam Pritchard, comparing the pre- and post-PSLRA periods, conclude that lawsuits lacking a "smoking gun," such as a restatement or an SEC investigation, face a greater likelihood of dismissal or low settlement amount after PSLRA than pre-PSLRA.[24] And Johnson et al. report that, whereas in the pre-PSLRA period one in four lawsuits contained accounting allegations (revenue recognition problems, improper estimates, or understatement of expenses), in the post-PSLRA period the share of accounting-based lawsuits mushroomed to 57.3 percent.[25] To survive in the present environment a lawsuit, therefore, must be based on solid allegations.

The message for managers of companies with high litigation risk is clear: stay away from earnings management and even aggressive accounting (see chapter 3 for more details). While this prescription may sound as helpful as "you'll avoid prison by not committing a crime," it's really not. In many cases, the fine-tuning of earnings via the multitude of estimates and projections (accruals) underlying financial information (a small decrease in, say, the bad debt or pension expenses) may not seem to you like an outright manipulation or fraud, since it often does not violate explicit GAAP, the evidence shows clearly that such aggressive accounting is the trigger for many shareholder lawsuits. Make sure that your accounting and financial reporting is pristine: conservative, consistent with previous years, and with a clean bill of health from auditors.

## Avoid Excessive Insider Trading and Stock Option Grants

Equity-based managerial compensation—the component of total executive pay granted in the form of company stocks and options—increased dramatically during the 1980s and 1990s, from a median of less than 1 percent of total CEO pay in 1984 to two-thirds of pay in 2001.[26] While equity-based compensation serves important objectives—enhancing goal congruence between shareholders and managers and attracting talent by young, cash-starved companies—the experience of the last ten to fifteen years showed its dark side: excessive option grants to poor-performing executives, manipulation of share prices around grant and exercise dates, backdating of stock options grants to enhance gains, and repricing of under-the-water options. All these self-serving schemes are fodder for class-action lawyers.

Empirical studies consistently document a significant association between the extent of equity-based compensation and the manipulation of financial information, leading in turn to lawsuits. Johnson et al., for example, examined forty-three companies targeted by the SEC for enforcement actions that relate to accounting and auditing fraud; they report that their managers had substantially larger equity-based compensation than did executives of a comparable group of companies that were not subject to SEC actions.[27] In a similar vein, Natasha Burns and Simi Kedia show that the CEOs of companies that restated their earnings—the usual manipulation suspects—had a substantially larger share of stock options in their compensation packages than similar, nonrestating companies.[28] Let me be clear: not all managers with a large equity-based compensation manipulate earnings or backdate options. Far from it. But the evidence indicates that most manipulators had large equity-based compensation. "I can resist everything except temptation," said Oscar Wilde, even though he was never granted a single option.[29]

Litigation alleging information manipulation is also related to managerial insider trading. For example, Johnson et al. document that corporate insiders (executives and directors) of lawsuit targets sold significantly more company shares during the lawsuit class (manipulation) period than did their counterparts in similar, nonsued companies.[30] Furthermore, the researchers report that, whereas in the pre-PSLRA period (up to 1995) the proportion of lawsuits alleging managers' insider trading was 33.3 percent, in the post-PSLRA period this proportion ballooned to 75 percent. And Mary Billings reports a positive correlation between managers' gains from insider trading and subsequent lawsuit settlement amounts.[31] Remember that insider trading prior to the disclosure of bad news provides plaintiff lawyers with the all-important *motive* for the manipulation and the often-delayed disclosure of improprieties.

So, if you receive generous equity-based grants, good for you. But keep in mind that such grants—and the manipulation temptation that they create—will attract the attention of the SEC, state attorneys, and class-action lawyers. Accordingly, and particularly when the going gets tough—a period of heightened litigation exposure—you and the board's compensation committee should exercise extra care in setting clear and reasonable criteria for incentive pay and apply them consistently. Unusually large option grants and exercises during the period of heightened litigation risk play into the hands of plaintiffs. The same goes for abnormal managerial insider trading during litigation-exposed periods. In one of the largest fraud settlements in U.S. history, Cendant Corporation agreed in 1999 to pay $2.85 billion (and its auditors Ernst & Young chipped in $335 million more) to settle charges of financial-reporting fraud. At center stage of the lawsuit were seven top executives, including the CEO, who sold Cendant shares worth $143 million prior to the public disclosure of the extensive accounting irregularities that caused the share price to crash by almost 50 percent and triggered the lawsuits.

### And Don't Detach Yourself from Investors

Finally, irrespective of legal advice, it's important that you don't let a heightened litigation risk dampen your interaction with investors. In particular, don't curb vital communications with capital markets or the disclosure of beyond-GAAP information (product pipeline, same-store sales, and the like) intended to improve transparency (see chapter 7) because you operate in a high litigation-risk industry. The various actions that I prescribed earlier are called for to reduce litigation risk. Clamming up isn't among them.

To recap, shareholder litigation is not a *force majeure*. You can do a lot to avoid, or at least substantially mitigate, litigation exposure and lawsuit consequences.

## Chapter 5

# Nothing in Excess

## The Hazards of Under- and Overpriced Shares,
## Particularly the Latter

My dictum, nothing in excess,[1] will test your patience with me. You surely believe that the higher the share price, the better. I will argue, based on solid evidence, that share overprice (price above fundamental, intrinsic value) is prevalent and—hard to believe—bad for you, leading managers to dysfunctional activities and ultimately to seriously disappointed investors. Share underpricing is detrimental too, but you surely knew that all along. So, bear with me as I develop the case against overpricing.

FIGURE 5-1

## Dell stock price versus the S&P 500 index, 2002–2007

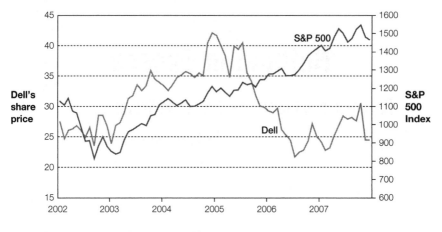

*Source:* Center for Research in Stock Prices (CRSP) database.

## Overpriced Shares 101

Figure 5-1 depicts the share price changes of Dell Inc. against the S&P 500 index, from 2002 through 2007 (thereafter, Dell's share crashed in the financial crisis, along with other stocks). Until mid-2005, Dell strongly outperformed the S&P 500 index, yet things abruptly turned ugly for the PC giant. Whereas the S&P 500 index continued its ascent, Dell's share price fell precipitously, by mid-2006 losing all the gain made from 2002 and then some. Not unexpectedly, Dell's CEO Kevin Rollins was replaced in January 2007 by founder Michael Dell in an attempt to reverse the slide.[2] Poor economic fundamentals, mainly a dated business model, triggered Dell's decline, but as I will argue in the next section, the price collapse was exacerbated because Dell shares were substantially overpriced from mid-2003 to mid-2005. When investors realized the overpricing, they reacted with vengeance—a typical overreaction to overpricing—driving the stock below its intrinsic value.

So what?, you may ask. Two years of overpriced shares gave Dell an opportunity to finance investments and business acquisitions with cheap currency (shares), provided managers and employees handsome gains from stock options, and benefited selling shareholders during the over-pricing period. No mean feat. Isn't the real problem share *underpricing*, rather than overpricing? And how prevalent and persistent is overpricing anyway?

To be sure, underpriced shares are detrimental to companies and their managers: They lead to excessive cost of capital, stunting corporate investment and growth.[3] Undervalued stocks also reduce employee compensation and deter key talent from joining the company. But managers know all this. In fact, I have yet to encounter a corporate executive who is not convinced (or at least professes) that his or her company's shares are seriously undervalued and indeed, in many cases, they are.[4] The means for closing the undervaluation gap—earnings and sales guidance, pro forma earnings, disclosure of beyond-GAAP information, executives' purchases of company shares, and so on—are thoroughly discussed in chapters 2, 6, 7, and 8. What will come as a surprise to managers is the finding that the shares of many companies and even entire sectors are occasionally overpriced and remain so for protracted periods of time. Historically, large and consistently profitable companies (the "nifty fifty") were substantially overpriced during the bear market of the 1970s, most biotech stocks were overvalued in the mid-1980s, and the values of tech stocks, particularly the dot-coms, were in the stratosphere during the bubble period of the late 1990s.

Managers, however, aren't overly concerned with inflated share prices.[5] They should be. I show later that the adverse consequences of seriously overpriced shares are as detrimental to companies' operations and managers' careers as are those of underpriced shares, arguably even more so. In both cases, a carefully planned and executed managerial intervention is required to get the stock price smoothly back to fundamentals (intrinsic value), before it's too late. I provide operating instructions for a safe return to fundamentals in this chapter (for overpricing) and the following one (for underpricing). But first, back to Dell and the hazards of overpricing.

## Dell's Price: Too Much of a Good Thing

The harmful consequences of overpriced shares are obscured, since in the short term, overpricing, like an elixir, seems to confer the converse of all the harms of underpricing mentioned earlier. An overpriced stock provides cheap financing for investment and acquisitions—recall the highly overvalued AOL acquiring of the larger Time Warner in 2000—and overpriced shares generate high managerial compensation and serve as a beacon for key talent and customers. But this in fact is a mirage, as Michael Jensen notes, *"by definition* if our equity is overvalued we will not, except by pure luck, be able to deliver the financial performance the market requires to justify that valuation."[6] And when this happens, all hell breaks loose. Share prices plummet, often overreacting to the disappointment, and customers and key employees bail out, soon to be followed involuntarily by managers. The "benefits" of overpricing are illusory, indeed.

If you doubt this gloomy scenario, consider the case of Dell once more. On December 13, 2004, Dell's share price hit a post-tech bubble high of $42.38, after hovering around $35 for most of the year. The price stayed around $40 until early August 2005, when it started sliding on a slippery slope, approaching $20 in July 2006, thereafter making up for some of the lost ground with the CEO change (see figure 5-1). Dell's stock performance from 2003 to 2004 and particularly in the first half of 2005 outstripped considerably the S&P 500 index, but was the stock inflated?

Obviously not for investors who willingly paid $40 or more for a Dell share. However, a dispassionate evaluation of the share price at the 2005 peak begs to differ. Dell's price/earnings (P/E) ratio—a widely used valuation indicator—was 31.3 in late January 2005 (share price $40.04 on January 21, 2005, divided by the consensus 2005 EPS of $1.28), substantially higher than those of competitors Hewlett-Packard (13.2) and

IBM (16.5), providing a strong presumption of Dell's overvaluation.[7] Why is the P/E ratio a value indicator? Consider hypothetical companies A and B, operating in the same industry.[8] Company A has a P/E ratio of 25, while B's is a meager 15. Why would investors pay $25 for one dollar of A's earnings and only $15 for B's? Simple. No one pays for past earnings, but for future profitability. So, paying 25-for-1 in A's case and only 15-for-1 in B's implies that investors expect a substantially higher earnings *growth* from A than from B. P/E ratios thus reflect investors' growth expectations, but if those expectations are unfounded—company B is gaining on A's product market share, or A's patents are soon to expire, for example—then A's share price is inflated. Thus, comparing a company's P/E ratio with those of similar companies (in risk and expected growth) suggests over- or undervaluation. Dell's 31.3 P/E ratio in January 2005 was roughly double those of icons Hewlett-Packard and IBM. Either Dell's growth prospects in 2005 were that much brighter than those of its stellar and innovative competitors—an unlikely event—or Dell's stock was overpriced.

An improved share valuation indicator is the price/earnings/growth (PEG) ratio, measured as the stock's P/E divided by the long-term earnings growth expectation (three to five years) for the company. Recall that the P/E ratio reflects, among other things, investors' aggregate growth expectations *implicit* in the stock price. If you adjust (divide) the P/E ratio by another, more reliable growth forecast, such as analysts' consensus long-term earnings estimate or managers' forecast, you get a stand-alone valuation measure that need not be compared with other companies. Thus, a PEG ratio of one suggests a fairly valued stock, because investors' growth expectations implicit in the P/E ratio match the explicit consensus growth forecast of financial analysts or managers'. In contrast, a PEG value greater than one indicates that investors' growth expectations *exceed* those of analysts', and given that analysts as a group tend to be optimistic, a greater-than-one PEG likely indicates an inflated stock. The converse holds for less-than-one PEGs.[9]

Back to Dell. In late January 2005, its P/E ratio was 31.3, and the consensus long-term annual earnings growth estimate for Dell was 19 percent, yielding a PEG value of 1.65 (31.3/19) and suggesting a healthy

65 percent share overvaluation. For comparison purposes, the PEGs of competitors Hewlett-Packard and IBM in early 2005 were 1.32 and 1.65, respectively. (Interestingly, IBM's stock price decreased by more than 20 percent during the first quarter of 2005, consistent with a 1.65 PEG overvaluation.) Thus, by both the P/E and PEG indicators, Dell's shares were substantially overpriced during 2004 and the beginning of 2005, and as Jensen warns, an overvalued company will not "be able to deliver the financial performance the market requires to justify that valuation."[10] Let's then compare Dell's financial performance expectations with reality.

In January 2005, analysts' consensus long-term annual earnings growth forecast for Dell was 19 percent. Since its PEG ratio was 1.65, investors obviously expected a substantially higher than 19 percent earnings growth from Dell. This was clearly too tall an order. Consider that in late 2004, industry experts predicted a 10 percent to 11 percent increase in PC shipments for the entire industry.[11] It stretches the imagination to think that Dell, the PC market leader at the time, would see its earnings grow by 20 percent or more annually when the industry PC shipments were predicted to rise by only 10 percent to 11 percent. Indeed, Dell's actual earnings growth rates in 2005 and 2006 were in the teens: 15 percent and 17.4 percent, respectively (the corresponding revenue growth rates were 18.7 percent and 13.6 percent). No mean feat, but clearly falling short of the over 20 percent investors' growth expectation built into Dell's obviously inflated share price.

When investors realize that their growth expectations are unattainable, they react with fury. Momentum, high-growth-seeking investors are first to bail out, leading others observing the price fall to dump the stock, resulting in a price cascade. Dell didn't escape this fate, and its stock price fell precipitously in late 2005 and most of 2006, to below $20 in July 2006, less than half of its beginning 2005 share price. Also typical of overpriced shares, disillusioned investors overreacted. Dell's PEG value in late July 2006 was 0.95, thus switching from a substantial overpricing to a slight underpricing.

Sharp share price drops are bad news for all. Frustrated key employees with useless stock options leave, top management is often replaced, as at Dell, and the SEC and trial lawyers circle over the prey. Indeed, in

2006, the SEC opened an investigation of accounting improprieties at Dell, and in August 2007, the company announced a massive restatement of four years of financial results, essentially admitting to a prolonged, systematic effort by Dell's executives to manage earnings in order to meet investors' inflated expectations. In a conference call, Dell's CFO, said, "This is not a happy story." Indeed.

## Meeting Expectations at All Costs

As Dell's case demonstrated, the major problem with a seriously overpriced stock is that the company will soon fall short of investors' sales and earnings expectations, an adversity in the making. This is a sure thing, mind you, because if the company is able to meet investor's expectations, then its stock is not overvalued. So, what's to be done when the day of reckoning arrives and the company's performance disappoints? The right thing to do, of course, is never to reach this predicament by avoiding increasing and protracted overvaluations—see the operating instructions later in the chapter. Satyam is a cautionary tale. On January 7, 2009, its CEO and founder, Ramalinga Raju, informed the board of a massive financial reporting manipulation perpetrated over several years. In his final letter to the board, Raju states that "the concern was that poor performance would result in a take-over." Thus, the multiyear manipulation was primarily intended to maintain the lofty, inflated share price to avoid takeover.

The only way to mitigate overpricing is to alert investors to a sales or earnings shortfall as soon as managers realize it's not temporary. This action should be followed by a truthful reporting of financial results and a credible plan to reverse the adversity. This, however, will not go unnoticed by investors. There is no way to dismount the overvaluation tiger unscathed, particularly when investors' inflated expectations are substantial and protracted, causing shareholders a very rude awakening. Sharp price decreases, analysts' and investors' ire, loss of managerial reputation, and sometimes even lawsuits and SEC investigations are sure to follow managers' warnings and the subsequent reporting of serious earnings shortfalls. No wonder, then, that executives often opt for alternative, less painful courses of action.

There are many ways to keep the growth facade going and investors content; alas, none are permanent. But, what the heck, managers are an optimistic breed, hoping for a miraculous recovery down the road. A frequent "temporary filling" of the expectations gap to maintain the appearance of growth is a hasty and expensive business acquisition aimed to lift dropping sales and earnings, sometimes without a compelling strategic motive. Cutting discretionary expenditures, such as on information technology, advertising, maintenance, or R&D, to boost reported earnings is another attempt to shore up investors' confidence when growth slacks off.[12] Such artificial supports of investors' expectations are clearly myopic, adversely affecting long-term survival and growth.[13] This is managerial myopia at its worst.

Sometimes, managers cross the line, bridging the expectations gap with manipulated earnings and sales figures. In chapter 3, I provided examples of SEC-sanctioned cases in which the manipulation motive was alleged to meet investors' inflated expectations (recall Gateway, i2 Technologies, and Coca-Cola). Dell's multiyear earnings restatement announced in August 2007 is also consistent with inflated earnings, originally reported, which were aimed at keeping the growth castles in the air. If you think these were isolated cases, here is my large-sample evidence linking overpriced shares to manipulation. I ranked companies within a large number of industries by their mean three-year P/E ratio—an indicator of share valuation—in the early 2000s. I then classified the companies in each industry to five equal-size groups of ascending P/E size. Finally, I recorded for each P/E group the frequency of subsequent earnings restatements—generally an indication of earnings manipulation or other accounting improprieties.[14] Figure 5-2 presents the earnings restatement frequency for each P/E group of high-tech companies (computers, software, electronic equipment) generally having a high restatement incidence.

It is evident that the frequency of restatements from P/E group 2 on increases monotonically with share valuation from 15 percent to 25 percent. Thus, a quarter of the mostly overpriced companies—the

FIGURE 5-2

**Mispricing and restatements**

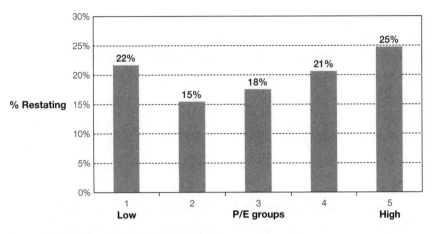

Source: CRSP, I/B/E/S, and GAO Restatements dataset.

highest P/E group is number 5—subsequently restated their earnings. So strong is the temptation to maintain the growth appearance and so thin is the manipulation veneer.

Some other notable findings: The highest P/E group, number 5, has the largest restatement frequency for all industries, not just high tech. The two highest P/E groups (4 and 5) also have the largest frequency of shareholder class-action lawsuits filed after restatements. And finally, look once more at the figure. The lowest P/E group, number 1—likely undervalued shares—also has a high frequency of restatements. Apparently, in their zeal to prop up lagging share prices, some managers of undervalued companies help themselves to accounting trickery.

## Going with the Grain

I know what you think. Yes, overpriced shares will end with a day of reckoning sometime in the future, but why not enjoy the immediate benefits, which might even prevent such reckoning? After all, overpriced shares reduce the cost of funding investments and acquiring businesses; both, if successful, rejuvenate corporate growth.[15] Indeed, during the tech bubble of the late 1990s, serial acquirers like Cisco, Tyco, and AOL financed multiple mergers and acquisitions with inflated equity. (In March 2000, for a short while at the height of the tech bubble, Cisco Systems became the most valuable company in the world by market capitalization; how about overpricing?) Overpriced shares also provide an opportunity to handsomely cash out on stock options and attract key talent. So, why not enjoy and even prolong share overpricing?

For starters, there is, of course, a serious ethical issue when managers *knowingly* use inflated shares for funding investments or corporate acquisitions. Such practice, which investment bankers and consultants often recommend, is in fact an unjust transfer of wealth from new shareholders—receiving the inflated shares—to current equity holders, including managers. Robbing Peter to pay Paul. Once the share overpricing is corrected, and sooner or later this is bound to happen, the consequent ill will of the new shareholders seriously damages the relationship between managers and investors, diminishing the effectiveness of the former and hurting the merger. Time Warner's acquisition paid for with highly inflated AOL shares is a cautionary tale:

*AOL's $112 billion purchase of Time Warner in January 2001 came to symbolize the boom and bust of the web bubble and the rise and fall of new media. The purchase led to a record $98.7 billion loss in 2002 and caused the shares to tumble as the promised profit and sales growth never emerged. Regulators then accused the company [AOL] of overstating advertising and subscriber numbers starting in mid-2000. Time Warner settled all charges with $510 million in payments this year.[16]*

And there was more bad news:

*If Richard D. Parsons, the new chief executive of AOL Time Warner, had any questions about the state of morale inside the company, he doesn't anymore ... What he has found is a company whose executives and shareholders are united in more or less open revolt ... AOL Time*

*Warner's stock has fallen by more than 60 percent, decimating the savings of many executives, since Time Warner sold itself to America Online ... Now the bitterness and resentment that employees on the Time Warner side have toward their sister division at AOL are straining the company's ability to cooperate, ... and the restive executives throughout the company have become a vocal stand-in for the company's unhappy shareholders.*[17]

Here you have the "benefits" of acquisitions financed by inflated shares: festering intracompany conflicts; disillusioned executives and shareholders, smarting from share losses, in open revolt; and the merger architects, Gerald Levine and Stephen Case, resigning. Huge asset write-offs and, to top it all, an SEC investigation and class-action lawsuits are the icing on the "merger cake." Such dire consequences, although not always so dramatic, are not restricted to AOL Time Warner, as my research with Feng Gu shows.

Gu and I address the question whether acquisitions made with over-priced shares save the day by rejuvenating growth and ultimately closing the expectations gap.[18] The short answer: they don't. How do we know? We devised a comprehensive measure of share overpricing and relate it to two key measures of merger success: the postacquisition stock returns of the acquiring firms and write-offs (loss recognition) of goodwill from acquisitions (generally, a large part of the acquisition price).[19] The results of our study covering twenty years of data and thousands of acquisitions are emphatic. First, there is a strong negative correlation between share overpricing at acquisition and subsequent shareholder returns: the higher the overpricing, the lower the returns (in fact, negative for substantial overpricing). Second, corporate acquisitions with overpriced shares tend to lead to substantial goodwill write-offs, a public admittance of merger failure.[20] Thus, for example, the 20 percent of the companies with the lowest share overpricing in our sample suffered only 2.2 percent of goodwill losses (relative to total assets), on average, whereas the 20 percent of firms with the highest overpricing had an almost seven times larger goodwill loss: 14 percent of total assets. And a whopping 44 percent of the latter were sued by shareholders for using inflated stock as the acquisition currency.[21]

How to explain these startling findings? Briefly, easy come, easy go. When shares are overpriced (easy come), buyers are less scrupulous about price and tend to substantially overpay for corporate acquisitions. Moreover, eager to justify investors' lofty expectations, managers rush to acquire businesses, some strategically ill advised. The day of reckoning, as with AOL–Time Warner, is soon to come, and both shareholders and managers (not investment bankers, though) pay the price.

## Prices Out of Kilter?

How prevalent is share mispricing, both over- and underpriced? Can stock prices in large and active capital markets deviate from business fundamentals over sustained periods? No, say ardent believers in capital market efficiency, a state in which securities prices essentially reflect all publicly available valuation-relevant information (earnings, growth potential, competitive position) without systematic biases or pronounced investor sentiments (optimism or pessimism). While individual investors may, of course, over- or underprice securities, such mispricings will be quickly identified and offset by sophisticated arbitrageurs in search of gains from investors' mistakes, thereby reverting prices to intrinsic values. If, say, certain investors get overly enamored with a biotech stock hyped by company founders and underwriters, then cool-headed, astute investors, seeing through the hype and sensing a profit opportunity, will sell the stock or even short it, thereby reverting its price to fundamentals. Mispricing, goes the efficient markets doctrine, is an isolated, temporary phenomenon.

This idyllic view of capital markets governed by rational and sophisticated investors is increasingly challenged by empirical evidence, showing that share prices frequently deviate from fundamentals over protracted time periods, often for years. Two examples of widespread, long-lasting mispricings—an overvaluation and an undervaluation—will make the point. Starting in 1996 with Richard Sloan, an accounting researcher, a large body of research on accounting accruals (items, such as depreciation and stock option expense, comprising the difference between earnings and cash flows) shows that investors become enamored with companies that report high earnings (due to large accruals), despite the fact that in many cases these earnings are of low quality (sustainability), as evidenced by the relatively low cash flows of these companies.[22] The evidence shows that investors systematically bid up—overprice—the stocks of such high-accruals companies, only to see their prices plummet over the following two years. While this accruals mirage abated recently, it persisted for decades, casting serious doubt about the ability and willingness of sophisticated arbitrageurs to quickly eliminate share overpricing.[23]

And now to a substantial undervaluation. Allan Eberhart, William Maxwell, and Akhtar Siddique show that the shares of companies with growing R&D (more than 5 percent annual growth in R&D-to-total assets) yield positive and significant risk-adjusted stock returns for up to five years following the R&D increase.[24] Since R&D data is clearly reported to investors in quarterly income statements, the fact that these companies generate abnormal *future* stock returns—almost 20 percent in the first two years—implies that investors *undervalued* their shares when the R&D information was reported (that is, investors failed to fully appreciate the growth potential of R&D), and it took several years for the undervaluation to be corrected. Stated differently, if investors properly price R&D information—assessing without bias the aggregate contribution of R&D to growth—there would be no way to profit from the R&D information years after its public release. I elaborate in chapter 7 on the reasons for such R&D-induced undervaluation, which, not surprisingly, is related to accounting deficiencies.

The evidence documenting protracted share mispricings—the result of investors' excessive sentiments—is voluminous and growing.[25] It points out that mispricing is prevalent among young and small companies, particularly those scantily followed by analysts ("orphan stocks") or shunned by institutions, for which investors have limited information. Companies with hard-to-value assets and prospects, such as intangibles-intensive businesses, are also frequently mispriced, as are companies in countries characterized by poor transparency or weak enforcement of securities laws.[26]

## Where Have All the Arbitrageurs Gone?

No one, even ardent believers in rational and efficient capital markets, disputes the existence of sentimental investors, hopeless optimists or pessimists, or the possibility that otherwise rational investors will occasionally act irrationally, like dumping a stock because its price has fallen sharply without an informed analysis of the reasons for the price decline or the prospects of reversals. But, claim the "rationalists," investors' sentiments will be *arbitraged away* by sophisticated, gain-motivated contrarians, which will quickly restore prices to fundamentals.[27] So, given the prevalence of share mispricings, where are the arbitrageurs?

A smooth back-to-fundamentals process will, of course, work only if a sufficient number of arbitrageurs are able to identify mispriced securities and are willing to invest or disinvest in these stocks. Such arbitrage, however, is both costly and risky; one never knows how long it will take other investors to realize the mispricing, at which point the arbitrageur makes money. Not only that, the stocks that are commonly mispriced are those that arbitrageurs generally shun. Consider once more the accruals mispricing I discussed earlier. High-accruals companies—reporting substantially higher earnings than cash flows—are generally overvalued by investors. For decades, an accruals arbitrage—investing in low-accruals companies and shorting those with high accruals—yielded a nifty gain in excess of 10 percent annually. The reason why the accruals mispricing persisted for so long is that high-accruals companies are typically small, low-profits, and no-dividend companies, with volatile stock.[28] And these are the companies that most well-funded institutional investors—the potential arbitrageurs—shy away from.

An example: Cabela's, a retailer of hunting, fishing, and camping gear, reported large accruals: $31 million on December 30, 2006 (net income of $86 million against cash from operations of $55 million), increasing to $108 million on June 30, 2007 (net income of $18 million and negative cash from operations of $90 million). Cabela's was thus an attractive candidate in 2006 and early 2007 for an accruals-arbitrage strategy—sell, or short its shares. This would have worked out nicely: typical of overpriced, high-accruals companies, Cabela's stock dropped 32 percent in the second half of 2007. Why didn't sophisticated investors sell Cabela's heavily in 2006 and early 2007 when the large-accruals information was publicly released? Simply because institutional investors didn't have many stocks to sell. Active institutions (nonmutual funds) held a relatively small equity position in Cabela's—only 17.5 percent of shares outstanding for the top-five holders, as of August 2007. Cabela's is a small, low-profit, and volatile stock, not a favorite of institutional investors—the potential arbitrageurs.[29]

Why are many institutions shying away from the likes of Cabela's? For several reasons. Such companies typically have low liquidity—meaning that trading in their shares has a large price impact—an obvious concern to institutions. Furthermore, large stock price volatility is an invitation to unpleasant surprises, which money managers abhor.[30] So here you have a major deterrent to mispricing arbitrage. Companies that are mainly affected by investor sentiments—medium-size to small, young, low-profitability, and high-volatility enterprises (biotech, high-tech, recent IPOs)—are those that most institutional and sophisticated investors shun. Share mispricing of such stocks—over- or underpricing—often persists for lack of effective contrarians. Occasionally, even large companies—like Dell from 2003 to 2005, or Cisco in the late 1990s—are overpriced. The lesson for managers is don't rely on "market forces" and rational investors to quickly correct mispricing. This is your job; see the operating instructions, next.

## Operating Instructions

Share underpricing is a no-brainer: it should be corrected as soon as possible, as I elaborate next and in chapters 6, 7, and 8. Overpricing poses a wrenching decision, though. Any active deflation by managers will obviously trigger a price decline with the usual consequences: despondent investors and employees, lower gains from exercising stock options, increased scrutiny by directors, and, worst of all, the possibility of an overreaction by investors—stock prices can rarely be fine-tuned—driving the price below intrinsic value. The reaction of disillusioned investors will be harsh. All these adverse consequences are, of course, mitigated or even avoided when the price deflation is done at an early stage of the overvaluation cycle, when the overpricing is low and few shareholders bought at inflated prices. So, the overriding operating instruction is as follows: don't procrastinate; nip the overpricing in the bud. But how to determine whether the shares are mispriced?

## Are Your Shares Mispriced?

Here is a practical, sequential process for assessing the extent of mispricing, above or below fundamentals. First, does your company fit the evidence-based profile of businesses whose shares are often overpriced? These are: (1) *Medium-size to small or immature companies* (typically, recent IPOs or emerging technologies companies, such as Internet, environmental, or nanotech), which are rarely or sparsely followed by financial analysts, resulting in scant public information, and have a short, often patchy history of performance, making it difficult for investors to adequately determine share value, predict growth, or assess risk. To make things worse, such companies are often hyped by founders, venture capitalists, and underwriters, making their shares prone to overpricing. (2) *High-growth, intangibles-intensive enterprises* (biotech, software, Internet, small telecommunication, and financial services companies), rich in hard-to-value assets, such as patents, brands, trademarks, and highly talented employees. Growth companies typically don't pay dividends but instead invest heavily in the future, thereby shifting a large part of their value considerably into the future and making their shares difficult to value. The valuation difficulties of such enterprises increase the likelihood that investors will considerably miss their intrinsic value, upward or downward. (3) *Media-hyped companies* (currently, environmental, green, alternative energy)—the "flavor of the day" sectors—where the buzz often leads to overpricing.

If your company fits the mispriced-shares profile, its shares are likely over- or undervalued. If it doesn't fit the profile—it's a large company and profitable—you are not off the hook yet (recall Dell), but the likelihood of serious mispricing is lower than that of the usual suspects. You obviously need more evidence. You can obtain a clue about mispricing from the dispersion of analysts' earnings forecasts. This is somewhat technical, but worth knowing. Forecast dispersion—the variability of the individual analysts' estimates of earnings around the consensus—has been shown as a reliable measure of uncertainty about the future earnings of your company. The higher the uncertainty, the larger the disagreement among analysts and investors concerning future earnings, and the more likely the stock is to be over- or underpriced.[31] So, if the dispersion of analysts' estimates concerning your company's earnings is high relative to competitors, your shares may well be mispriced.

### Estimating the Extent of Mispricing

After you establish a solid presumption of share mispricing, you proceed to the second stage—estimating its extent. Obviously, correcting minor mispricings is not worth the risk of investors' overreaction. There are several gauges of share mispricing; none are, however, perfect. The most reliable estimation of mispricing is to compare your internal forecasts of earnings and sales—the key components of the firm's budgeting/control process—with investors' estimates. Thus, for example, in August 2007, the average EPS estimate of the twenty-two analysts covering Coach Inc., a leading luxury-goods producer and retailer, for the year ending June 2008 was $2.08, and for the following year, $2.47.[32] The revenue estimates for the two years were $3.2 billion and $3.8 billion, respectively. This translates to expected annual earnings growth rates of 19 percent to 23 percent for the two years (18 percent to 22 percent for revenues). As Coach's CEO or CFO, if your internal growth estimates are substantially lower than investors' (around 20 percent annual growth), your shares are likely overpriced, and vice versa for underpriced shares. The difference between your estimates and investors' provides a pretty good idea about the magnitude of mispricing.

In addition to the use of internal estimates, a widely used indicator of mispricing is the company's P/E ratio relative to comparable companies. The devil lies, of course, in the details of "comparable." Comparable in what? Products, size, expected growth, or risk? Obviously, the more comparability criteria one uses, the smaller the group of comparable companies becomes, quickly diminishing to zero (no company is comparable to Intel or Walmart in *both* product mix and size). As a practical matter, for medium-size and small companies, the mean or median P/E ratio of the industry (three- or four-digit Standard Industrial Classification Code) is a reasonable benchmark for their own P/E. For dominant companies, choose two or three close competitors as benchmarks: Chevron, BP, and Royal Dutch Shell for evaluating Exxon's P/E, or Airbus for Boeing's.[33] Back to Coach; its August 2007 forward-looking P/E (using the June 2008 consensus earnings estimate in the denominator) was 21.2, only slightly higher than the industry mean P/E of 19.1. A minor overvaluation, if any.

The PEG ratio discussed earlier has the advantage of controlling for expected growth—a major determinant of the P/E ratio—thereby doing away with the need for comparables.[34] Coach's PEG ratio in August 2007 was 1.05 (a P/E of 21.2 divided by analysts' expected long-term earnings growth of 20.2), corroborating the presumption of reasonable valuation of Coach's stock. In contrast, for example, as of August 2007, AT&T and the much smaller logistics company, Expeditors International, had PEG ratios of 1.82 and 2.02, respectively, suggesting serious overpricing. So, once you establish overpricing, how should you deflate it safely?

## A Soft Landing

To be sure, there is a sometimes subtle difference between investors' optimism—a good thing—and delusion. Only the latter needs ameliorating. In case of excess optimism (delusion), don't make things worse by exploiting it. "Experts" will tell you to take advantage of overpriced shares by issuing stock or acquiring businesses on the cheap. This is, as I showed earlier, a sure recipe for discontented, sometimes rebellious shareholders once they realize they paid for—or were paid with—inflated shares. Lawsuits are likely to follow.

A soft landing or better yet preventing overpricing is achieved primarily by credible and measured guidance (more on guidance in chapter 6). The Internet auctioneer eBay did just that in late 2005 and early 2006. "Burnt" by an almost doubling of the stock price in 2004, which led to a 22 percent price drop in January 2005 upon a one-penny consensus miss (see chapter 1), the company took great care to cool investors' renewed optimism in response to good results. Specifically, eBay had a banner third-quarter 2005. Revenue and earnings rose 37 percent and 40 percent, respectively, from a year earlier, meeting analysts' consensus estimate. Yet, to prevent a rerun of 2004, eBay accompanied the third-quarter results (announced October 19, 2005) with a downer: the fourth-quarter 2005 EPS, said eBay, will be $.21 against a consensus of $.22, and 2006 operating earnings were guided to a lower range than the consensus. And for investors slow to get the message, eBay added that operating margin would decline by two percentage points in the fourth quarter of 2005. eBay's stock price decreased 3.1 percent on this guidance (the S&P 500 was essentially unchanged). The following fourth quarter of 2005 (announced January 18, 2006) was a repeat performance for eBay: revenue and earnings rose substantially, both beating the consensus, yet eBay continued to slow down its stock rise, predicting that its first-quarter 2006 EPS would miss the consensus by a penny and that its 2006 revenue would also come slightly below the consensus. The price deflation clearly worked, with the *Wall Street Journal* quoting an analyst saying that eBay's guidance "suggests they are either being more conservative than they could be, or there are other elements of the business where growth may be more challenging to come by."[35] The former—"more conservative than ... could be"—is what a measured price deflation is all about.

# Guiding the Misguided

## Chapter 6

## Why It's Beneficial to Assist Investors
## with Forward-Looking Information

The practice of earnings guidance—managers' public forecasts of earnings, and often additional performance measures—is a hotly debated issue. Both the reasons and consequences of guidance are contested. This obviously calls for a thorough examination of the evidence. But first, let's consider three cases.

- **THE GOOD.** On July 14, 2009, Intel, the chip giant, surprised investors and analysts with second-quarter results: while reporting a loss due to a one-time $1.45 billion antitrust fine by the European Union, its revenue and gross margin beat its own guidance given a quarter earlier, as well as analysts' forecasts. If this wasn't good enough, Intel projected that revenue would further increase in the rest of the year with additional improvement in margins. Investors definitely got it: Intel's stock advanced 9.5 percent on the news (the S&P 500 rose 3.5 percent).[1]

- **THE BAD.** Apple too had good news to impart. On January 18, 2006, it reported results for the peak 2005 holiday quarter. Net income almost doubled to $565 million, and revenues, at $5.8 billion, rose 65 percent. But then Apple sprung a downer—for the current quarter, ending March 31, 2006, the Macintosh and iPod producer decreased both earnings and revenue guidance. EPS, Apple said, would come in at $.38 (substantially below analysts' consensus of $.48) and revenues at $4.3 billion ($4.6 billion being the consensus). Apple's stock dropped 6.7 percent on the guidance (S&P 500 was unchanged).

- **AND THE MUM.** According to an article in *Forbes*, "The law of large numbers has caught up with Dell. Once worshipped for consistent performance, Dell has had seven quarters of declining revenue growth and missed its own revenue predictions in three of the last four quarters. It finally gave up giving quarterly guidance (arguing that its competitors don't do so either)."[2]

Why would Intel release upbeat forecasts of earnings and revenues on top of outstanding financial results, setting itself up for investor disappointment and price drops if performance failed to live up to the forecast?[3] All for a few percentage points of stock price? Even stranger, why did Apple spoil the 2005 holiday-quarter party of impressive sales and earnings with a downbeat forecast of current quarter results? Why not wait until the end of the quarter, when perhaps sales or earnings would pick up? (Indeed, for the March 31, 2006, quarter, Apple reported $.49 EPS and $4.6 billion sales, far exceeding its gloomy guidance.) And why did Dell guide investors in good times, yet drew a blank in a downturn? Don't Dell managers know that in capital markets "no news is bad news"?

And in general, why do thousands of companies, see figure 6-1, voluntarily guide investors about their future performance, ignoring Warren Buffett—the sage of Omaha—along with the U.S. Chamber of Commerce, Financial Executives International, and for good measure, the consulting firm McKinsey, all imploring companies to desist from guiding investors? Why is managerial guidance such a controversial issue, drawing influential organizations and individuals into a heated debate? Why not just let the guiders guide? And, most importantly, what are the benefits and costs of managerial guidance to investors and managers? And speaking about guidance, should managers intervene in the lively debate about their companies and themselves in cyberspace and chat rooms and guide the misguided? I will answer all these questions and more later. But first, what exactly is guidance?

## Anatomy of Guidance

Figure 6-1 shows the number of U.S. public companies providing *annual* and *quarterly* guidance about forthcoming earnings from 1995 through 2007.[4] Thus, in 2007, about eight hundred companies regularly provided quarterly earnings guidance (most also releasing annual guidance), and about fourteen hundred firms released annual earnings estimates (about half releasing quarterly estimates, too). Many of the guiders, like Intel, Boeing, and Apple, are large or medium-size companies. Earnings guidance is obviously a sustained and widespread communications practice.

The substantial increase in the frequency of quarterly and annual guidance from 2000 to 2001 was mainly triggered by the SEC's Regulation Fair Disclosure (RegFD), issued in October 2000 (see figures 6-1 and 6-2). RegFD requires managers who wish to disclose material nonpublic information on, say, forthcoming earnings, sales trends, or significant new

FIGURE 6-1

## U.S. firms providing quarterly and annual earnings guidance for fiscal years, 1995–2007

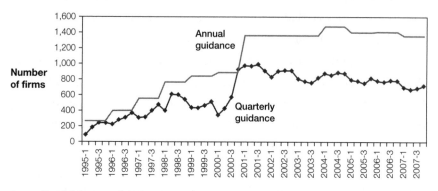

*Source:* First Call Company, Guidelines database.

contracts, to do so publicly to all investors at the same time, generally via press releases or conference calls. The regulation—very controversial at enactment time—was aimed at curtailing the widespread practice of managers privately communicating with select analysts and investors, often by reviewing their earnings estimates and underlying valuation models. Barring such privileged communications, the practice of *public guidance* took off from 2000 to 2001, indicated by the spikes in the two figures.

Figure 6-2 portrays the message mix of quarterly guidance: positive (about 20 percent in 2007), negative (40 percent), and in-line, confirmatory guidance (40 percent). Positive and negative guidance refers to managerial earnings forecasts exceeding or falling short of the recent analysts' consensus estimates or of the company's own previous guidance. Interestingly, the main decrease in quarterly guidance in recent years has been in the in-line guidance; some managers apparently doubt the usefulness of such confirmatory disclosure.

The two-to-one preponderance of negative over positive guidance in figure 6-2 is puzzling. What's the rush to impart bad news before it is legally required? Aren't managers known to exude optimism? Thwarting shareholder litigation by an early warning is a possible motive, as well as the belief of many executives that good news will take care of itself

FIGURE 6-2

## The type of quarterly earnings guidance issued by U.S. companies, 1995–2007

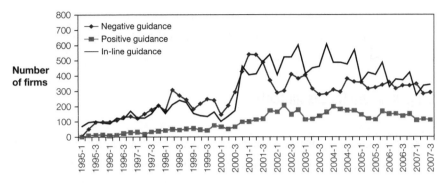

Source: First Call Company, Guidelines database.

when the financial reports are released, yet bad news calls for an early warning, because most investors are more concerned with prospective losses than gains.[5] This investors' sentiment is indeed supported by the well-known behavioral "prospect theory," which its founders, the Nobel Laureate Daniel Kahneman and the late Amos Tversky succinctly summarized as "losses loom larger than gains."[6] As to the form of guidance, a 2005 survey reveals the following distribution: 5 percent point estimates (e.g., EPS at $2.50), 83 percent range estimates (sales between $3.5 billion and $4 billion), 7 percent release of an earnings model, and 5 percent other disclosures.[7] Companies usually guide either during the fifty to seventy days prior to the end of the quarter or immediately after it (but, of course, before the earnings release). The former are truly in the spirit of guidance, whereas the latter, issued just a few days before the earnings report, are in fact last-minute red alerts, of lower value to investors.

Looking abroad, managerial prospective disclosures are found in most countries with active capital markets. Comparative analysis highlights systematic differences between guidance in the United States and in other countries, related to institutional and cultural differences. For example, Stephen Baginski, John Hassell, and Michael Kimbrough report a higher frequency of annual guidance in Canada than in the United

States.[8] However, the frequency of quarterly guidance, in contrast to annual forecasts, is higher in the United States than in Canada, and is particularly prevalent in companies with poor earnings, likely to thwart litigation. Canadian managers, however, release more guidance in good times and provide longer-term guidance than their U.S. counterparts.

## Guidance and Its Discontents

Managers clearly possess valuable up-to-date information about such topics as current trends in sales and input prices or product development progress and new contracts, but should they disclose this information via earnings or sales guidance?

Absolutely not, says the CFA Institute, which joined the Business Roundtable in a dramatic "Call to Action" emphatically recommending, "End the practice of providing quarterly earnings guidance."[9] Why? Because it entails:

> (1) unproductive and wasted efforts by corporations in preparing such guidance, (2) neglect of long-term business growth in order to meet short-term expectations, (3) a "quarterly results" financial culture characterized by disproportionate reactions among internal and external groups to the downside and upside of earnings surprises, and (4) macro-incentives for companies to avoid earnings guidance pressure altogether by moving to the private markets. Corroborating research identifies the most significant costs of issuing guidance to be management time.[10]

A mouthful of harms indeed. The influential U.S. Chamber of Commerce concurs,[11] and McKinsey adds:

> Most companies view the quarterly ritual of issuing earnings guidance as a necessary, if sometimes onerous, part of investor relations ... We believe that they are misguided. Our analysis of the perceived benefits of issuing frequent earnings guidance found no evidence that it affects valuation multiples, improves shareholder returns, or reduces share price volatility.[12]

One wonders why earnings guidance, a voluntary communication by managers, is drawing the ire of leading organizations and influential observers. Can't managers be trusted with the decision if and when to guide investors? Perhaps the practice of guidance is so controversial because it blatantly blurs the idyllic distinction between Wall Street and Main Street. Purists expect corporate managers to focus on running the business, for the long term, of course, leaving its analysis and valuation—primarily based on forecasted performance—to investors. Furthermore, say the critics, once managers invade investors' territory with guidance, they will be infected with the capital markets malady—the focus on short-term performance—forcing them to sacrifice long-term corporate growth to meet their own quarterly guidance and the similarly myopic analysts' estimates. These are good reasons indeed for a heated controversy, but as I show next, the guidance discontents are in fact misguided.

For starters, it's easy to counter each of the CFA–Business Roundtable anti-guidance arguments quoted. The "corroborating research," which presumably points at management time as the "most significant cost of issuing guidance," was in fact based on an online survey of executives that had 124 responses. Fifty-three percent said that the cost of guidance in time spent is high, versus 43 percent saying it is low. That's not exactly an overwhelming difference. As to the short-termism allegedly induced by guidance, in chapter 10 I debunk both investor myopia and the allegedly consequent managerial short-termism. But even on sheer practical grounds, the antiguidance short-termism argument defies logic. Abstaining from quarterly guidance will not deter analysts from issuing quarterly EPS estimates—as they currently do for the thousands of companies that don't issue guidance—and will therefore not relieve the pressure on managers to meet the consensus estimate, guidance or no guidance.[13] If at all, this "myopic" pressure is heavier on nonguiders because unguided analysts' forecasts, as the evidence shows, are more difficult to meet than those that are guided.

Finally, the CFA–Business Roundtable argument that the pressure to provide earnings guidance drives companies into the arms of private equity funds is the most far-fetched of all criticisms. Isn't it easier for managers to just abstain from issuing quarterly guidance, as thousands of public companies do, than to engineer a buyout? And what about all those companies that were taken private, allegedly to escape the tyranny of capital markets, yet were flipped back in short order to the public arena?[14] Thus, most of the antiguidance *a priori* arguments can easily be dismissed. But arguments and counterarguments aside, what does the empirical evidence say about the consequences of providing guidance as well as ceasing the practice?

## Parting the Mist

Earnings guidance, which a large number of companies practice regularly, is obviously fodder for researchers, yielding robust findings. Here is what you should know about the consequences of imparting forward-looking information.

### Guidance Benefits Both Investors and the Company

Critics sometimes assert that guidance is pure noise, since managers are no better prognosticators than are expert analysts or sophisticated investors. This argument is intriguing, but factually wrong. With my colleagues Joel Houston and Jenny Tucker, I examined a large sample of quarterly earnings forecasts issued by managers from 2002 to 2005 to evaluate the usefulness of such guidance. Predictive ability is, of course, relative and should therefore be evaluated against alternative predictions. We compared the accuracy of managers' quarterly guidance (regarding the subsequently reported earnings) with the accuracy of the most recent analyst estimates issued prior to the guidance. The results showed that managers were more accurate than analysts in 70 percent of the comparisons and less accurate in only 26 percent (the rest were ties)—a pretty impressive managerial performance. Our analysis also makes clear that financial analysts recognize the predictive edge of managers, since we found that in over 50 percent of the sample cases, analysts revise their earnings forecasts in the direction of the guidance within a scant two days of managers' guidance release, increasing to about 70 percent revisions within ten days of the guidance. The experts obviously recognize the usefulness of guidance. The company benefits too when its guidance disciplines off-the-mark analysts' estimates.

Our findings corroborate other studies indicating that management guidance enriches the information environment in capital markets. Improved information—increased transparency—has been shown to lead, in turn, to higher stock prices, lower stock volatility, and reduced cost of capital. Good things indeed. The guidance research, in addition, clarifies the means and extent of information enrichment, as well as the consequences of ceasing guidance. Thus, Amy Hutton examines the pre-Regulation Fair Disclosure (2000) period for 360 companies that reviewed analysts' earnings prediction models (commenting on underlying estimates—sales growth, for example—or simply providing management forecasts), a widespread but privileged information-sharing procedure abolished by RegFD.[15] Hutton documents, among other things, that many of the reviewing companies were complex organizations, as evidenced by the large number of industries they operated in. Thus, rather than being induced by investors' myopia, guidance was driven by their need for information about large and complex businesses. As for the consequences of guidance, Hutton shows that the quarterly earnings estimates made by analysts whose models were reviewed by managers were significantly more accurate than unguided estimates. Once more, managers improve investors' information. This is not shocking, but good to know.

Moving to the recent, post-RegFD period and examining the calls for stopping quarterly guidance, in 2010 I studied, with my colleagues Joel Houston and Jennifer Tucker, 222 companies that heeded the critics and stopped providing quarterly earnings guidance after doing so routinely, and compared them with 680 companies that maintained quarterly guidance throughout the corresponding period.[16] We recorded some surprising findings. First, regarding the motive for guidance cessation: it was not exactly an epiphany about the harms of guidance, rather the continuously deteriorating earnings and the failure to meet analysts' consensus estimates. As in the Dell example leading this chapter, guidance stoppers clammed up simply because they sat on bad news. And what happened after guidance cessation? More bad things: stoppers lost analysts' coverage—an undesirable result—and investors' uncertainty about their operations, as indicated by the errors of analysts' estimates, increased significantly.[17] The elimination of guidance obviously reduces transparency, and both the company and its shareholders are harmed. No wonder then that Shuping Chen, Dawn Matsumoto, and Shiva Rajgopal, focusing on companies that *publicly announced* their decisions to stop quarterly guidance from 2000 to 2006, recorded a mean 5 percent stock price drop upon the cessation announcement.[18] The upshot is that you aren't doing any favor to your investors or yourself by stopping quarterly guidance.

## Don't Embarrass Your Analysts

Several years ago, over lunch in San Francisco, the CEO of a successful pharmaceutical company told me that the gravest sin an executive could commit in capital markets was to embarrass the analysts following his or her company by springing surprises, particularly disappointments, on them. "They rarely forget and never forgive," said the CEO, "when you make them look incompetent. Your credibility with [the] analyst is lost." Earnings guidance, he continued, is an effective tool for minimizing surprises and analyst embarrassment. Indeed, Julie Cotter, Irem Tuna, and Peter Wysocki observed an interesting phenomenon: the frequency of issuing quarterly guidance increases with analysts' optimism regarding future earnings.[19] That is, when the consensus estimate early into the quarter is optimistic (relative to the subsequently reported earnings), managers tend to issue downbeat guidance, thereby drawing the consensus closer to reported earnings. Analysts' embarrassment from overshooting earnings is obviously minimized by such "downer" guidance.

But, of course, it is not only analyst embarrassment that guidance mitigates; it is primarily the large stock price drops upon earnings disappointments that are softened. Executives' surveys show, not unexpectedly, that managers are seriously concerned with the consequences of missing the consensus.[20] Credible and consistent guidance is an effective tool for avoiding consensus misses and minimizing stock volatility. It works on the upside too. When investors are downbeat about the stock and the consensus estimate is low, a positive, credible guidance, particularly about long-term earnings, will lift share prices, particularly when it's accompanied, for example, by managers and board members buying a substantial number of company shares.

There is a sting in the guidance tail, however. A fine line is drawn between *steering* investor expectations toward realistic future earnings or sales, and *manipulating*—"walking down"—the consensus so that subsequently reported earnings will comfortably exceed it. The road from steering to manipulating analysts' expectations is slippery, and no doubt some managers are practicing the latter, as indicated by research.[21] One hopes, though, that analysts will wise up to egregious manipulations of their views and adjust or ignore such "guidance" altogether.

## Helps with Litigation, Too

Guidance aimed at reducing investors' inflated expectations mitigates shareholder litigation and its consequences in several ways. First, the lower stock price in response to the guidance (warnings) decreases the subsequent price decline upon a disappointing earnings, or the revelation of improprieties, such as earnings restatements, which generally trigger lawsuits, thereby decreasing investor damage estimates that are based on the size of the price drop. Stated differently, the warning shrinks the "inflation band"—the difference between the inflated stock price and its intrinsic value—that proxies for shareholder losses. Lower damage estimates also decrease lawyers' incentives to file lawsuits. Second, the lower damage estimates lead to lower litigation settlement amounts (the large majority of shareholder lawsuits settle rather than go to court). And, third, judges generally consider the fact that managers warned investors about an earnings shortfall a mitigating factor.

### What Not to Expect from Guidance

Guidance will not increase share prices permanently without an improvement in the business fundamentals. Substantial and persistent increases in stock prices and shareholder returns are achieved primarily by unexpected improvement in corporate performance or by other positive developments, such as an FDA drug approval. It's obviously unrealistic to expect short-term earnings guidance to permanently improve share prices.

Nor do warnings of an impending earnings shortfall mitigate investors' negative reaction to the disappointment once earnings are announced. Ron Kasznik and I, and, in a separate study, Jenny Tucker showed that the combined price decline, upon the warning and the subsequent earnings release, is close to the price hit to companies with similar earnings disappointments that chose not to warn shareholders.[22] Investors clearly react to the substance of the news, rather than to its packaging—one versus two partial disappointments. Warnings, though, have other advantages: mitigating the consequences of litigation, discussed earlier, reducing the defection of financial analysts that often follows serious earnings disappointments, and enhancing the credibility of managers as being on top of things and straight shooters.

So, don't expect miracles—permanent price increases, for example—from sharing forward-looking information with investors a few weeks or even months before the earnings release. Short of miracles, however, guidance, under the right circumstances, is a potent communications tool (see the operating instructions at the end of the chapter).

## "Guiding" Short Sellers Is a Bad Idea

Short-selling—selling borrowed shares and expecting to buy them later at a lower price, thereby gaining from the price drop—is a controversial activity. Advocates believe that short-selling is highly beneficial to investors because sellers identify overvalued shares, and by selling the shares, they narrow the price inflation. Some even argue that short sellers identify serious issues, like operating difficulties and financial fraud, and alert investors to such problems by their actions. Detractors, many managers among them, view short-selling as preying on companies facing operating challenges and blame the sellers for undermining investors' confidence in the company and spreading false rumors to exacerbate the stock price fall. In the context of guiding investors and analysts, what should managers' stance be toward short sellers? Indifference, or active challenge? The research has two important lessons to impart:

- **DIRTY FIGHTING OF THE SHORT SELLERS IS FUTILE.** An examination of 266 companies that challenged their short sellers with accusations of spreading false rumors, threatening the sellers with lawsuits, complaining to the SEC, and even asking shareholders not to lend shares to the sellers found that by and large these efforts came to naught.[23] The performance of the companies' shares after the challenge to short sellers was dismal: roughly 25 percent below the corresponding market performance. And none of the individual measures taken against the sellers—threats, lawsuits, regulatory actions—was particularly effective. The lesson: don't waste time and money fighting short sellers. If your company's fundamentals are solid and its stock price justified, guide investors on earnings and sales and even on operating data, such as expected subscribers' growth. If the fundamentals are weak, focus all your efforts on fixing them.

- **PAY ATTENTION TO THE SELLERS' MESSAGE.** Research established a significant link between short-selling and subsequent revelations of reporting improprieties and fraud.[24] That is, the amount of short-selling in companies that were disciplined by the SEC for financial misrepresentation or that restated their earnings rose significantly over the two years prior to the public revelation of the misdeeds. Short-selling obviously is far from random; it is attracted to misreporting and operational weaknesses. Recall from an earlier discussion that financial misrepresentation is generally a symptom of serious operating difficulties, such as growth grinding to a halt. Accordingly, when you observe an increase in the short-selling position in your company (the "short interest"), rather than charging against the sellers, initiate serious internal soul-searching about the company's operations and the integrity of its financial reporting. There is often an important message in short-selling.

## Guidance in Cyberspace

The volume of Web messages on financial chat rooms and message boards is large and growing fast. For example, the 100 most-discussed message boards on Yahoo! in September 2009 had a median volume of 150,000 topics since inception. Much of this Web-circulated information is anonymous, repetitious, strongly opinionated, sometimes irresponsible, and even false. Yet early research shows that Web-based discussions generally focus on important issues. Research shows that message volume increases significantly around the release of companies' financial reports and decreases investors' uncertainty about the company (information asymmetry), as indicated by lower bid-ask spreads of stocks.[25] It's not all fluff or cyber-smear. The impact of Web discussions on stock prices and volumes is noticeable for medium-size and small companies whose shareholders are often information starved. And yet, most managers ignore the Internet discourse about their companies. It's not a smart attitude.

Managers' nonchalant attitude toward the Web is probably rooted in the widespread disregard for individual investors. The continually increasing role of institutional investors in capital markets in the 1980s and 1990s cast a large shadow on individual investors. Institutions are high-maintenance investors; they are in constant search for new information and draw considerable managerial attention because their investment decisions have a significant impact on stock prices. Individual investors, in contrast, are relatively passive; managers largely ignore them. Their financial means are generally modest, and they rarely demand face time with managers. Yet most individual investors crave information and affect share prices too.[26] They also possess a quality managers highly desire: they are much less trigger happy to events than institutions, as demonstrated by the relatively low turnover of the stocks they hold. The lethargy of most individual investors is a significant, yet unappreciated virtue from managers' point of view. Individuals—over 40 million of them directly own shares—are much more loyal to the company than institutional investors that are constantly concerned with their quarterly performance. Most individuals are truly long-term investors, so vaunted by managers. Smart managers, therefore, maintain a healthy share of individuals in their shareholder mix to assure stability and continuity.

Enter the Internet. It enables companies to reach, cost effectively, large numbers of individual investors and do so with increasing effectiveness by using multimedia visualization (unavailable in "flat" financial reports). The Internet also allows companies to gauge the mood and sentiment of investors and the effectiveness of corporate communications programs. Currently, though, corporate use of the Internet for disseminating financial information is in its infancy. It's time to rethink the corporate attitude toward financial Web discussions.

## Experts and Persuasion Bias on the Web

Unattended Web discussion can seriously hurt companies, particularly when led by experts, as the following ParkerVision case demonstrates. For over twenty years, ParkerVision promised to produce various revolutionary technological innovations, without delivering much on the promise. The company received generous venture capital financing and enjoyed a certain investor following. Its stock price reached $56 in 2000, but traded in the range of $10 to $15 in 2007. *Barron's* recounted a lively Web-based debate between supporters and detractors of ParkerVision.[27]

Foremost among the latter were a well-known Silicon Valley investor and entrepreneur, Mike Farmwald, and his wife Barb Paldus, a Stanford-trained engineer. The couple, who obviously had the training, experience, and industry contacts required to evaluate the potential of ParkerVision's innovations, spared no costs to substantiate their negative assertions. They engaged, for example, the leading experts on radio power amps to examine ParkerVision's patents and talked to experts at companies that ParkerVision pitched. This research led Farmwald and Paldus to conclude that "ParkerVision is just a bad joke that won't go away"—a typical comment in cyberspace. They backed this conclusion by shorting ParkerVison's stock and creating a Website, PV Notes, touting their opinion of the company. Investors who heeded the couple's advice saved themselves the agony of seeing ParkerVision stock price slide to one dollar in August 2011. Evidently, some of the Internet financial discussion is indeed first-rate expert opinion, on par with the best financial analyses.

Managers' intervention in Web discussions about their companies is particularly necessary because of the widely documented "persuasion bias" phenomenon, that is, individuals' failure to properly adjust for or avoid the impact of the *repetition* of a message, the failure to distinguish between new information and a rerun.[28] Suppose, for example, you read a glowing report about a company written by an analyst who maintained a "strong buy" recommendation on its stock for quite some time. The highly favorable report you just read is, in fact, a repetition of the strong-buy recommendation, but if the report sways you to buy the stock while the recommendation didn't, you are subject to a persuasion bias. Effective propaganda, the repeated exposure of people to a message, is a manifestation of persuasion bias, as are political spin and marketing campaigns where the endless repetition of an advertisement is aimed at creating a cumulative effect on customers. In capital markets, the persuasion bias was demonstrated by Brad Barber and Terrance Odean, who documented that individual investors tend to increase trading in stocks associated with repeated news items ("attention-based buying").[29] In cyberspace, blogs and chat rooms are rampant with repeated messages, particularly when initiated by "star bloggers." What may start as an opinion or conjecture soon becomes a "fact" by the weight of the repeated messages, affecting stock prices and volatilities. Managers' intervention to set the record straight, not to proliferate rumors, is of considerable importance in this environment to stabilize the individual shareholder base.

So, what should managers do? They should continuously monitor Web discussions about their company. They don't need to comment on every rumor or opinion, but they should correct factual falsehoods ("the company's sales have been decreasing lately," or "employees are defecting") with supporting data. They should pay special attention to well-regarded discussants—bloggers with a large following and well-substantiated opinions. Managers should engage such opinion makers when their comments steer off base. The Web provides a rare opportunity to speak directly to individual investors. Such investors rarely participate in conference calls, and only a few attend shareholders meetings, generally for food and entertainment. Directing simple but compelling messages about the company's strategy and the progress made to achieve its goals, via the Web, is an effective way of increasing the share of individual investors in a company's shareholder mix.

## Operating Instructions

Should you guide investors, or not? If so, by quarterly or annual earnings guidance? And how about predicting other key value drivers, like revenue, margins, or same-store sales? These decisions primarily rest on your predictive ability relative to analysts' and the investors' uncertainty about your company. (The decision process to guide or not is summarized in figure 6-3.)

- **ANALYZE THIS** . . . It's a no-brainer; you should regularly guide investors only if you are a better predictor of earnings or sales than the analysts are. How will you know? Start by measuring the quality of analysts' consensus estimate. Using quarterly data from the last three to five years, compute the percentage "forecast errors" of the *unguided* analysts' consensus earnings estimates

FIGURE 6-3

## Deciding whether to guide or not to guide

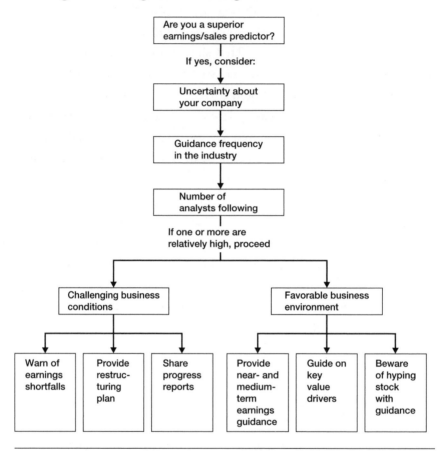

available soon after the release of previous-quarter earnings, but before your guidance. That is, compute the *percentage error* of the consensus estimate for each quarter as follows:

$$\frac{\text{(Actual quarterly EPS)} - \text{(Consensus estimate of EPS)}^{30}}{\text{(Actual quarterly EPS)}}$$

The average of the quarterly forecast errors (in the formula) over the past twelve to twenty quarters will give you the benchmark—

analysts' predictive ability—to compare with yours.[31] Use the average of the *absolute* quarterly forecast errors (eliminating the error's sign), since the quarterly errors may be positive or negative, largely canceling each other in the regular mean forecast error, giving the impression of superior predictive power.

Next, compute your forecast errors, based on the company's internal EPS quarterly forecasts, generated for the budgeting-control process, over the corresponding period. Alternatively, if you currently provide earnings guidance, compute the accuracy of your guidance, released soon after the consensus estimate, using the percentage error measure (replacing the consensus with your guidance), and average over the corresponding period. If your EPS internal predictions or guidance are consistently better than analysts' (say, in 75 percent or more of the individual quarters, and on average), you are a promising candidate for providing quarterly guidance. If not, repeat this test with *annual* earnings, evaluating the consensus annual earnings forecasts against your internal forecasts or your annual guidance. If you are a better predictor of annual earnings than analysts, although not of quarterly earnings, stick with the annuals. If you don't beat analysts in predicting quarterly or annual earnings, forget about guidance.

Once you establish your superior predictive ability, there are additional considerations for guidance provision. If the majority of companies in your sector or industry provide guidance, you don't want to stand out as having information to hide or as a manager who is not on top of things and uncertain about the future, even if you don't beat analysts handily. Also, if your company is followed by the same number or even a larger number of analysts as your close competitors—and analysts' demand for guidance is well known—this becomes another plus for providing guidance. Finally, if the dispersion or variance of individual analysts' forecasts around the consensus estimate of your company is high relative to competitors—an indicator of serious analysts' uncertainty about your company—chalk up another plus for guidance.[32] Having satisfied these conditions—superior predictive ability, guidance (quarterly or annual) practiced regularly in your industry, multiple analysts, and elevated investor uncertainty—you should provide earnings guidance regularly. What about additional, beyond-earnings guidance? Here are some key considerations.

- **POSTCARD FROM THE EDGE.** In challenging times, you should provide an early warning before the release of particularly bad news—a loss or a serious miss of the consensus—especially if you suspect that the stock price is inflated (see chapter 5 for gauges of overpriced shares) and all the more so if your company operates in a sector with a high risk of litigation (see chapter 4 for these factors). If your operations are complex (a diversified company or an intangibles-rich enterprise, for example) and when investors' uncertainty about your company is high (indicated, among other things, by highly volatile stock), you should consider guiding on key drivers of your business model, such as the number of subscribers (telecom, Internet), order backlog, same-store sales, or load factor (for transportation companies), in addition to earnings to improve transparency and reduce investors' uncertainty. Remember, though, that the larger the number of guided variables (earnings, sales, order backlog), the larger the likelihood of missing certain forecasts and disappointing investors.

- **THERE IS THERE, THERE.** What about profit-components guidance? A substantial number of companies, close to 40 percent of S&P 500 firms, provide guidance on key income statement items, such as sales, margins, and major operating costs. Benjamin Lansford, Jennifer Tucker, and I found that such profit-components guidance characterizes companies with an optimistic earnings view, large institutional ownership, and wide analyst coverage.[33] Thus, if the demand for guidance is high and you wish to convince investors of your favorable earnings prospects, it is a good idea to enhance the credibility of the earnings guidance by expanding it to the key drivers of earnings—sales, margins, or operating costs.

- **PRACTICE, PRACTICE.** The data shows that a substantial number of companies provide guidance in certain quarters or years and not in others. So, if you are unsure whether to guide or not—or whether to provide quarterly or annual guidance—why not experiment? Start with an annual guidance and check for investors' and analysts' reactions: Does the price move upon your guidance? A sign that investors take you seriously. Is the guidance moderating stock price gyrations around earnings announcements? If investors pay attention to your earnings guidance, you can experiment with guidance about the fundamentals, like sales or margins, to perfect this communication device. Always remember that it is easy to lose credibility, but hard to regain it, so don't manipulate investors' expectations with earnings guidance. Guide responsibly.

## Chapter 7

# Life Beyond GAAP

## Why Managers Should Disclose More Information
## Than Legally Required

Does the information provided in corporate financial reports fulfill investors' needs? Is the usefulness of this information increasing or decreasing over time? And should managers augment GAAP disclosures? For answers to these weighty questions, look at figure 7-1, spanning the thirty-two-year period from 1975 through 2006. Obviously, the yearly bars are quickly descending from the heights of 75 percent to 85 percent from 1975 to 1984, through 50 percent to 60 percent in the early 1990s, to the recent lows of 30 percent to 40 percent. What is this shrinking phenomenon, you ask? Hard to believe, it's the relevance of accounting information to investors. The figure's bars indicate how much of the difference in the capitalization (market value) of public companies is explained or accounted for

FIGURE 7-1

**Proportion of stock price differences across companies explained by reported earnings and net asset values, 1975–2006**

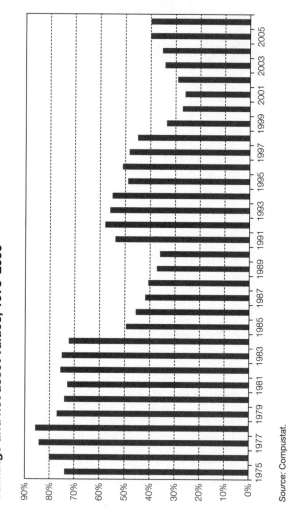

*Source:* Compustat.

by the key information items in corporate financial reports—annual earnings and equity (net asset) values. Obviously, if financial information is very relevant to investors' share valuation, corporate earnings and asset values will largely explain why some companies' capitalization is high, while others' is low. If, on the other hand, financial information is not particularly relevant, companies' values will not be strongly related to that information. The right-sloping bars clearly indicate that accounting information plays a decreasing role in investors' decisions.

How did I compute the bars? By a regression—sophisticated correlation analysis—of companies' share prices on their earnings and net asset values per share over a large sample of firms, for each of the years 1975–2006. The $R^2$ of this regression (ranges between 0 and 100 percent)—displayed for each year in the figure—indicates the extent to which earnings and asset values *account for* or *explain* stock price differences across companies.[1] Thus, in the 1970s and early 1980s, reported earnings and book values accounted for a whopping 75 percent to 85 percent of the differences in capitalization across companies, indicating that almost the entire difference in share values across companies was due to accounting data, whereas the same information variables explained only 30 percent to 40 percent of the differences in capitalization in recent years. That's a decline of 50 percent in the informativeness of reported earnings and asset values![2]

I document this dramatic fall from grace of accounting-based financial information to call managers' attention to the fact that they can no longer rely on the statutory financial reports (quarterly and annual statements) to provide all the information needs of investors. To avoid detrimental mispricing of shares and excessive price volatility, managers must voluntarily provide a substantial amount of high-quality information beyond the generally accepted accounting principles (GAAP) framework. Many companies do that. For example, pharmaceutical and biotech companies routinely disclose details of the product pipeline, retailers publish same-store sales data, airlines show customer and employee satisfaction scores, Internet companies give the number of eyeball visits, and many European companies supply sustainability or social responsibility indicators (the "triple bottom line"). Yet, most firms do so haphazardly, primarily when the information makes them look good. They don't fully understand what kinds of information and what circumstances will most effectively satisfy investors' needs and minimize adverse disclosure consequences, such as benefiting competitors or enhancing litigation exposure.

This chapter makes the case for beyond-GAAP disclosure and outlines a coherent framework of information release benefiting companies and their shareholders. But first I describe a brief case, courtesy of Home Depot, which demonstrates a misunderstanding of the fundamentals of effective information disclosure.

## Counterintuitively, No News Is Bad News

On May 16, 2006, during a routine conference call discussing second-quarter earnings that beat the consensus estimate, Home Depot—the nation's largest home-improvement retailer—surprised the market by announcing that it would no longer provide same-store sales data. Home Depot's stock price dropped 6.1 percent (S&P 500 decreased 1.9 percent) on the going-mum announcement, despite the positive earnings and sales news. Investors clearly disapproved of the retailer's decision to suppress same-store sales data (revenues of stores open for a least a year), a key indicator of the organic growth of the company, particularly when Home Depot's main competitors would continue to supply the information withheld. A sharply negative investor reaction to the suppression of information is a ubiquitous phenomenon. Shuping Chen, Dawn Matsumoto, and Shivaram Rajgopal, for example, reported a 5 percent mean stock price drop for companies that publicly announced they would no longer provide quarterly earnings guidance to investors.[3]

Why the negative reaction to the withholding of information that is not legally required? In part, because of investors' presumption that no news is bad news. Indeed, CNNMoney.com quoted a Goldman Sachs analyst saying, "We can only surmise that [Home Depot's decision] reflects a reality that this measure does—and will—reflect poorly on the firm vs. competitors."[4] But the main reason for investors' adverse reaction to information suppression is the consequent increase in uncertainty about the company's operations and future course. In the absence of monthly same-store sales data, Home Depot's shareholders are in the dark about the retailer's performance throughout the quarter. That no news is bad news for investors is a no-brainer, yet that it's bad news for managers too is surprising, as I will show you. To fully appreciate this profound insight, we must delve briefly into the fascinating world of Akerlof's lemons.

## Information Asymmetry: Gainers and Losers

Information asymmetry is the mysterious-sounding name economists gave to a ubiquitous phenomenon: one party to a contract or arrangement knows more about the object traded than the counterparty. Thus, for example, managers know more than investors and lenders about the company's recent sales trend, changes in competitive position, progress of products under development, and key employee turnover. Substantial information asymmetries are not limited to capital markets; they also prevail in used cars and existing home markets, among many others, because sellers generally know much more than buyers about the condition of their cars or houses (oil leaks and prior car accidents or the existence of termites and polluted grounds in houses). Information asymmetries are so prevalent and their consequences so profound that in 2001 the Nobel Prize committee awarded three economists, George Akerlof, Michael Spence, and Joseph Stiglitz, the highly coveted Nobel Prize for their work on this subject.

Is information asymmetry good or bad? I bet you'll say that it's good for the informationally advantaged and bad for the informationally challenged. Managers, for example, can exploit their inside information by selling shares before the disclosure of disappointing earnings, and owners can overcharge for defective cars or ground-polluted houses. Do managers exploit information asymmetries? You bet. My research with David Aboody revealed that managers of R&D-intensive companies—where the information asymmetry is particularly large, since hardly any information about the nature and consequences of ongoing R&D programs is included in GAAP-based financial reports—gain on trade in their companies' shares three times more than managers of companies with low or no R&D activities, where information asymmetry is relatively low.[5]

However, the gains of information exploiters are often ephemeral and generally self-defeating. Surprisingly and reassuringly, the research showed that the major losers from large information asymmetries are no other than the informationally advantaged. How can this be? George Akerlof, the Berkeley Nobel Laureate, provides the answer.

## The Market for Lemons

As everyone knows from experience, there are *good* and *bad* used cars (lemons)—"pre-owned" in the modern lingo—in the market. Sellers can obviously distinguish between the good and the bad, but suppose that buyers do not (they have no reliable facilities to check cars and no sellers' declaration)—an information asymmetry case. In such a market, said Akerlof in 1970, "good cars and bad cars must still sell at the same price—since it is impossible for a buyer to tell the difference"[6] This uniform price will obviously be relatively low, since buyers will assume the worst about car quality, namely, that all used cars released for sale are lemons. And now to the central question: what are the consequences—social and private—of the information asymmetry about used cars? First and foremost, says Akerlof, good cars will be driven, no pun intended, out of the market by the low price. Owners of these cars will postpone the sale, give the car to a relative, or donate it to charity, rather than sell at the prevailing low price. The better the car, the stronger the incentive of the seller to withdraw from the market. Information asymmetries will, therefore, cause the market to degrade to a "lemons market." Who loses? Everybody. Buyers are denied good cars, and the informationally advantaged—primarily owners of good cars—lose, too, because they cannot sell their cars for the right price. A profound lesson.

The lemons phenomenon applies to all markets characterized by substantial information asymmetries. For example, insurance companies offering unrestricted (no preconditions) health insurance—a prime objective of the recent health-care legislation in the U.S.—will naturally quote relatively high premiums to cover their unmitigated risk. Such premiums, however, will primarily attract sick persons, for whom the premium, though high, is still a bargain, if they can afford it. Young, healthy individuals will naturally avoid the pricey insurance, thereby causing the market for such unmitigated health insurance to degrade to "health lemons." Here, the information advantage is held by the buyers-customers, yet the outcome is the same: some of the informationally advantaged (i.e., healthy people) are priced out of the market, and insurance sellers are burdened with high-risk customers.[7] The consequences of information asymmetry are so adverse that various mechanisms have been developed over time to mitigate it: multiyear guarantees for used cars (one rarely hears the term "a lemon car" anymore), home sellers' declarations about defects, and mandatory insurance for young, healthy persons in the recent health-care legislation in the United States.

But what does all this have to do with corporate managers, whose cars, houses, and health insurance are often provided by the company anyway? Well, everything. In particular, a major implication of the lemons model, that the informationally advantaged are seriously harmed by information asymmetry, applies to companies and their managers, as we'll see next.


## Through a Glass Darkly

A fundamental tenet of capital markets is that investors require and receive compensation—excess return—for assuming risk. That's why stocks over the fifty-year period 1955–2004 yielded almost twice as much as the safer corporate bonds (12.25 percent versus 7.26 percent average annual return); corporate bonds, in turn, outperformed the safer government bonds (7.26 percent versus 6.96 percent average annual return); and stocks of small companies whose risk of failure is relatively high yielded substantially higher returns than those of large, stable enterprises (17.25 percent versus 12.25 percent average annual return).[8] These yield differentials reflect the well-known risk premium in capital markets.

An important component of securities' risk premium is "information risk," distinct from "business risk," which stems from the industry or line of business the company operates in. Just as uninformed used-car buyers in Akerlof's world discount car prices to protect themselves from mishap, investors with scant information about the company's operations and risk exposure will discount share prices by demanding an extra return as a safety against unpleasant surprises that could have been avoided by better transparency: a restructuring plan going awry while details are kept under wraps from investors, or an IPO sold at inflated prices.[9] So, the larger the information asymmetry between corporate insiders and investors, the higher the investors' uncertainty about the firm and the larger the information risk premium that they will demand for holding the stock. And here, the vicious cycle comes full circle: the

**FIGURE 7-2**

**The vicious information cycle: From information asymmetry to your compensation and tenure**

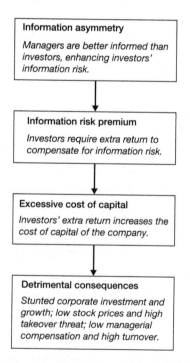

excess return investors demand as compensation for information risk increases the company's *cost of capital*—investors' expected return mirrors the company's cost of capital—stunting its growth and depressing its share price.[10] Lest you get confused by the cause and effects of the information asymmetry vicious cycle, figure 7-2 outlines the essence of this important capital markets phenomenon and its consequences.

## How Real Is All This?

Over the years, I have talked to many executives about information asymmetry and the merits of voluntary disclosure to increase transparency. Their frequent reaction was skepticism: all this talk about information asymmetry, risk, and cost of capital sounds like ivory-tower speak, of little consequence in reality. I will try to convince you otherwise. Consider the three biotech companies, Amgen, Novacea, and Targacept. (Don't be embarrassed if you haven't heard about the latter two; I hadn't either before searching for this example.) On September 6, 2007, the *bid-ask spreads* of the three stocks—the difference between prices offered by market makers (traders) for buying and selling the stocks—were 0.02 percent, 0.37 percent, and 0.62 percent of their stock prices, respectively.[11] Why the large differences in the spreads of the three stocks? You guessed it, it's primarily due to information asymmetry.

The market maker who sets securities' prices by offering to buy or sell the stock at fixed prices (up to a certain quantity, the "depth") runs the risk of overpaying when buying the stock (too high a "bid") and losing on a subsequent sale when the price falls, or quoting too low a price (a low "ask") when selling the stock, thereby losing on the round-trip (buying and then selling). Obviously, the market maker's risk of losing increases with the number of investors who are better informed about the company and its prospects and with the quality of their information (for example, buying shares from persons who know about the failure of a company's drug in a clinical test before the information becomes public). The better informed investors will sell to or buy from the market maker *only* if the quoted "bid" (the market maker's offer price to buy the stock) is high relative to the stock's true value or the quoted "ask" (the market maker's offer price to sell) is low relative to true value. To minimize losses to the better informed investors and increase gains from the less informed, the market maker increases the spread (buy at lower prices and sell at higher) to all investors when facing a larger information asymmetry.[12] Thus, a share's bid-ask spread reflects primarily the information asymmetry (lack of transparency) between those in the know and other investors.

Let's go back to the three biotech companies. The large differences in spreads—2 versus 37 and 62 basis points (a basis point = one-hundredth of one percent)—for Amgen, Novacea, and Targacept, respectively, reflect, in part, the large differences in investors' information about these companies. Amgen is a large, mature company followed by no less than thirty financial analysts (as of September 2007) who routinely research and disseminate information about the company and predict its performance. Novacea and Targacept are small, young biotech companies (2006 IPOs) with short financial histories and sparse analyst following (five analysts for Novacea and four for Targacept). Consequently, the information asymmetry between investors and managers is relatively low for Amgen and high for Novacea and Targacept, as indicated by the large difference in spreads. Here is the crucial point: a stock's bid-ask spread is a major component of investors' transaction costs, since the spread determines the cost of a round-trip to investors—buying and selling the stock. Targacept's spread, almost two-thirds of one percent of its share price, is a hefty cost for active investors, buying and selling the stock several times a year. Investors will naturally demand compensation for this information-induced cost in terms of a higher return, and a higher return to investors means a higher cost of capital to the company, as outlined in figure 7-2.[13] I admit this argument is a bit dense, yet important nevertheless.

For the yet unconvinced, still perceiving that the link between lack of transparency and excessive cost of capital is "theoretical," I performed the following analysis. I chose the dispersion of analyst' earnings forecasts around the consensus estimate—the disagreement among analysts concerning the company's future earnings—as a measure of transparency (information asymmetry): obviously, the higher the experts' disagreement about the firm's potential growth, the lower the transparency. I chose the firm-specific Value Line–based expected returns as an estimate of companies' cost of capital (recall that investors' expected return is the company's cost of capital).[14] I then correlated the two variables across 1,750 observations of transparency (analysts' disagreement) and cost of capital (expected returns), and found the correlation to be rather high: 0.40 (maximum: 1), implying that, on average, firms with high information asymmetry (low transparency) will also have a high cost of capital. Once more, excessive cost of capital means reduced investment (in R&D or acquisitions), stunted growth, and lower share prices. The relation between transparency and cost of capital is thus reality, not just theory. Given such substantial cost considerations, you obviously have to mitigate information asymmetry.

## Isn't GAAP Enough?

Aren't the accounting rules underlying corporate financial reports stretching literally over tens of thousands of pages sufficient to provide all investors' needs, and then some? No. A single number will demonstrate this. The average market-to-book (M/B) ratio (companies' total market value, or capitalization, divided by their balance sheet value of net assets, or book value) of the S&P 500 companies prior to the free fall of stock prices in 2008 was close to 3. This means that of every $3 of share value paid for or received by investors, only $1 was reported on the companies' balance sheets as net assets. So, why were investors paying a $2 premium for every a dollar of book value? A massive rip-off? Hardly. The $2 premium primarily reflects the presence of intangible (intellectual) assets as the dominant value creators of business enterprises.[15] The dramatic rise of intangibles was initiated by emerging key economic sectors that are almost entirely intangible—software, biotech, and, later, Internet enterprises—as well as by the increased use of intangibles (like patents, brands, or business processes) by traditional sectors using these value drivers to compete successfully. The increasingly competitive business environment makes continuous innovation of products, services, and business processes (supply chains, for example) a matter of life or death for companies in practically every economic sector. Innovation, in turn, is achieved by massive investment in intangibles: R&D, acquired technology, information systems, brands, and talented employees. It's no wonder, then, that over the past two to three decades, intangible assets rose to become the major value drivers of businesses, high- as well as low-tech, manufacturing and services alike. Physical assets are now, by and large, commodities, available to all.[16]

All this is hardly controversial, but if you examine companies' balance sheets, you will be justified in concluding that the remarkable worldwide intangibles–knowledge revolution has gone unnoticed by accountants. Coca-Cola's major asset, its unique brand, which surely accounts for most of its $147 billion capitalization, in March 2011 is nowhere to be seen on its balance sheet (yet "vital" Coke assets, such as the $150 million short-term investments or its $1.6 billion inventory are proudly exhibited on the asset list). Pfizer's multibillion-dollars worth of patents on leading, internally produced drugs are also AWOL from its balance sheet, as are Walmart's major value-driving supply-chain processes. Those, and many other intangibles overlooked by GAAP, yet recognized, albeit with considerable inexactitude by investors, account for the high M/B values of Coke (4.7), Pfizer (1.8), and Walmart (2.7).

You might ask, who cares about the balance sheet? Isn't it the income statement that really counts? Perhaps, but what is misreported on the balance sheet also distorts corporate earnings. For example, companies with increasing investment in intangibles, R&D, brands, or information technology have both their earnings depressed (by the immediate expensing of these investments) and their assets (and equity) understated by the unrecognized intangible assets. The absence from balance sheets of the major business value drivers and the consequent distorted earnings obviously detract from the informativeness of corporate financial reports. This is not just my claim. Listen to the CEOs of the world's six largest accounting firms who stated emphatically: "The large discrepancies between the 'book' and 'market' values of many, if not most, public companies . . . provide strong evidence of the limited usefulness of statements of assets and liabilities . . . Clearly, a range of 'intangibles' that are not well measured, or not measured at all, under current accounting conventions are driving company performance. Investors and other stakeholders . . . want to know what those intangibles are and how they might plausibly affect how businesses perform *in the future.*"[17] And that from the mouths of those who really know accounting.

The absence of internally generated intangibles from corporate balance sheets and the consequent distorted earnings are bad enough; no less detrimental to transparency and the quality of investors' information is the inconsistent and logic-defying GAAP treatment of intangibles. While the cost of *internally generated* patents, brands, trademarks or the set-up of Internet operations and business processes are immediately expensed, similar intangibles when acquired in M&As or other transactions are capitalized and considered as assets. This inconsistency impedes any attempt to compare the performance (earnings or ROE) of companies across time or within sectors. A company that switches, for example, from being primarily a developer of drugs to an acquirer, will boost significantly both its earnings and asset values, while performing essentially the same economic activity as before the switch. Furthermore, the absence of any systematic GAAP disclosure on the company's crucial value-creation chain—the progress of developing new products, services, or processes—denies investors (and often managers) of vital information needed to assess investments and production decisions.

Do all these accounting deficiencies have significant impact on investors and companies? You bet. Research clearly shows that investors systematically *undervalue* companies with substantial investment in R&D.[18] Why? Akerlof's lemons, of course. With patchy information on

R&D—how much R (basic research) and how much D (development of current technologies), for example—investors cannot be faulted for considering much of R&D a mystery, possibly a lemon, and discounting its prospects heavily. Indeed, Dennis Oswald and Paul Zarowin showed, using U.K. data, that when R&D is capitalized, the company's market valuation fully reflects its expected outcomes, whereas lower market values are accorded to companies that expense R&D.[19] And if such harmful consequences are documented for R&D, an activity whose total outlay is disclosed to investors, imagine the information asymmetries and related uncertainties created by other types of intangible investments that are totally obscured in financial reports.

GAAP efficiencies are by no means restricted to intangibles. The ever-increasing impact on earnings and asset values of *managerial estimates* (fair value accounting, stock option expense, or pension liabilities)—subject to considerable errors and frequent manipulation—diminishes too the reliability of accounting data, as demonstrated by the constant decline in the informativeness of earnings and book values, starkly shown by figure 7-1 at the opening of this chapter. Surely, one can't rely on GAAP to provide all of investors' information needs. Management has to supplement accounting information. But what exactly are the information needs of investors and what's the best way of providing these needs while minimizing competitive harm and litigation exposure?

## A Small Turn of the Dial

What information do investors want? The simple answer is that they want information to evaluate corporate performance and growth potential, that is, a measure of *location* showing where the business is currently and an indicator of *direction* pointing at where it is heading. The accounting system provides various, albeit noisy measures of location—current profits and assets or liabilities values (some at historical costs, others at current values)—but no reliable compass of direction.

Managers' task, accordingly, is to improve on the current location measures (a small turn of the dial) and design an information system to point out the future course of the business (a big turn). Let's start with the former.

## Resurrecting and Improving Pro Forma Earnings

What ails currently reported corporate earnings? Primarily three things: First, the hodge-podge nature of the income statement, mixing *recurring* items (core sales and cost of sales, for example) that point at the future course of the business with *nonrecurring*, one-time revenues and expenses (gains from asset sales and write-offs). Second, the presence in earnings of expenses (like R&D and software development costs) that are, in fact, investments. Third, imprecise estimates, such as stock options expense and fair values of assets. The amalgamation of all these varied items in a single earnings number blurs the message about business performance and its future course.[20] No wonder then that my recent research shows that reported earnings do not improve the prediction of companies' future performance beyond "naive" forecasts based on past cash flows.[21] What can managers do to improve the relevance of reported earnings? Enter *pro forma earnings*—managers' much maligned attempts to improve on GAAP income.

On May 9, 2006, Cisco Systems released its third-quarter results: a GAAP-based EPS of $.22, along with a 32 percent higher non-GAAP, or *pro forma* EPS of $.29. Interestingly, the consensus estimate just before the earnings release, according to Thomson Financial, was $.26. Thus, Cisco's GAAP earnings missed the consensus, whereas the pro forma EPS conveniently beat it by three pennies.[22] This and similar exploits of other companies led many to dismiss pro forma earnings as managerial wishful thinking or, worse, an attempt to manipulate investors. Surely, that's what the *Wall Street Journal* had in mind writing: "As they await companies' second-quarter results, investors may want to remind themselves that there is often a gulf between the profit figures that get trotted out in analysts' reports and the financial news media and the profit recorded under generally accepted accounting principles, or GAAP . . . many companies preferred that investors focus on what earnings might have looked like if the bad things hadn't happened."[23] Taking the pro forma ridicule to an extreme, cynics suggest that the ultimate pro forma construct is EBE—earnings before expenses (Luca Pacioli, the inventor of accounting, RIP).

I see nothing wrong in managers' honest attempts to improve on the deficiencies of GAAP earnings by releasing their own alternative number, particularly after the 2003 SEC requirement that non-GAAP measures included in statutory filings (like Cisco's) should be reconciled quantitatively with the relevant GAAP numbers.[24] Since pro forma earnings are disclosed along with, rather than in lieu of, GAAP earnings, and the differences between the two measures are highlighted, investors cannot be worse off with pro forma earnings. Rather, as the evidence shows, they are better off.

Cisco indeed reconciled the two EPS numbers ($.22 and $.29): the $.07 difference results from the exclusion of the following GAAP expenses from the pro forma EPS: employee stock option expense ($.04), amortization of intangibles ($.02), the expensing of in-process R&D ($.01), and a few additional smaller items. Obviously, Cisco's management believes or wants investors to believe that the excluded expenses blur the company's current and future performance. But is this really the case? It sure is. The value of employee stock options— the amount expensed in the income statement over the options' estimated benefit period—is notoriously difficult to ascertain. Option valuation formulas used by companies, like the Black-Scholes model, are based on multiple, difficult-to-estimate yet easy-to-manipulate assumptions, and the application of these models designed for *traded* options to the *illiquid* employee options is questionable. Consequently, the option expense is a highly unreliable number.[25] It's the same with the second excluded item: the amortization of intangibles, such as customer list, brands, or software. I spent over two decades researching and working in the intangibles area and, trust me, no one really knows how to reliably estimate the useful lives of intangibles required to compute amortization. As for the third excluded item—in-process R&D—the FASB itself recently realized the foolhardiness of this expensing requirement and abolished it.

Research clearly corroborates the usefulness of pro forma numbers to investors. It indicates, for example, that pro forma earnings are more strongly associated with stock returns as well as with the revisions of analysts' earnings forecasts, than GAAP earnings, indicating the pro formas' usefulness to investors and analysts.[26] Furthermore, Lawrence Brown and K. Sivakumar reported that pro forma earnings are better predictors of future earnings than GAAP earnings.[27] Interestingly, Daniel Collins, O. Li, and H. Xie noted that from the early 1990s—a period characterized by a substantial increase in intangibles and one-time restructuring charges, all detracting from the usefulness of GAAP earnings—the pro forma numbers triggered a substantially stronger trade volume—a measure of information usefulness—than GAAP earnings. All in all, the evidence clearly indicates that the pro forma numbers are important complements to the increasingly relevance-challenged GAAP earnings.

Finally, what is a useful pro forma earnings number to report? Essentially, one that improves the prediction of business performance over GAAP earnings.[28] Accordingly, one-time, transitory income or expense items, unlikely to recur in the foreseeable future, and GAAP expenses that are in fact investments expected to enhance future performance are legitimate candidates for exclusion in computing pro forma earnings. I also don't see anything wrong in alerting investors via pro forma earnings to highly unreliable expenses like stock options, or dubious gains or losses from fair-valuing nontraded assets or liabilities. In short, use pro forma numbers to convey your view about the performance and prospects of the enterprise.

Yet, while touting pro forma earnings, I am cognizant that not all pro forma numbers are paragons of truth. Some managers intend pro forma earnings to beat the consensus estimate or to enhance their compensation. So, to maintain credibility, refrain from manipulation and be consistent: if you exclude an expense item from pro forma one year, don't include it the next year; and if you exclude one-time expenses, be careful to exclude one-time gains too.

# A Big Turn of the Dial

Effective beyond-GAAP disclosures share two key attributes: they are *standardized*, well-defined measures that can be compared across time and peers, and they provide a *direct link to performance*, rendering them ready inputs to investors' and analysts' valuation models. An example of such a uniformly measured, linked-to-results indicator is the *product pipeline* of pharmaceutical and biotech companies informing on the location of products in various phases of drug development: exploratory tests, clinical (human) tests, and awaiting FDA approval. Such information can be compared across time (is the company's pipeline getting thinner?) and across industry peers, allowing investors to evaluate the growth potential of companies: the more advanced the products under development in the pipeline, the better the company's prospects and prospective cash flows. Another example is the *order backlog*, which is a leading indicator that can be compared across companies and informs about future sales.[29] Less useful are nonstandardized indicators such as Ericsson's, a Swedish telecom company, which reported in its May 2006 SEC Form 20-F that "every year an employee satisfaction survey is conducted … In 2005 over 92 percent of employees participated in the survey. The results show a marked improvement from last year … The Human Capital Index as well as the Empowerment Index improved by 7 points." Firms measure employee satisfaction, like customer satisfaction, differently, and its real meaning is often unclear (what exactly is Ericsson's Empowerment Index?). The link of satisfaction with operating results is obscure, too. (Do empowered employees enhance the bottom line or their paychecks?)

But even when the disclosed indicators are standardized and linked to results, more is often required to effectively shape investors' perceptions. Consider this example of effective disclosure: on April 21, 2008, Netflix Inc., an online movie rental company, released its first-quarter 2008 earnings and provided extensive beyond-GAAP information clearly depicting its business model (see table 7-1).

TABLE 7-1

## Netflix operating data, first-quarter, 2008

| Period | Acquisition cost per customer | Net subscriber increase | Monthly churn | Revenue from new subscribers | Customer lifetime value** |
|---|---|---|---|---|---|
| First quarter 2008 | $29.50 | 764,000 | 3.9% | $32.3 million (9.9%)* | $730 million |
| Fourth quarter 2007 | $34.60 | 451,000 | 4.1% | $19.2 million (6.3%) | $683 million |
| First quarter 2007 | $47.46 | 481,000 | 4.4% | $22.9 million (7.5%) | $696 million |

* Percent of total quarterly revenues.
** Not reported by Netflix.

Note that Netflix's disclosure, in contrast with the release of disparate operating measures, such as order backlog or same-store sales, provides an *integrated information system* of efforts and consequences, clearly outlining the company's *business model*: starting at the left of the table with the expenditures needed to acquire customers, through the impact of customer acquisition on subscribers' growth as well as the closely watched "churn rate"—monthly loss of customers—to the revenues from the new customers, and finally to total revenues (percent revenue in parentheses). This depiction of Netflix's business model provides a clear picture of the company's investment in growth, the success of growth efforts, and an indication of things to come. The steep decline in acquisition costs per customer from 2007 to 2008 (from $47.46 to $29.50) and the sharp increase in net subscribers, along with a slight but steady decrease in the churn rate, bode well for Netflix's future growth. The substantial growth of revenues from new subscribers (from $22.9 million to $32.3 million) explains the firm's top- and bottom-line improvements. Compare this with the meager information provided by the GAAP income statement: revenues and earnings without reference to the underlying factors (acquisition costs, customer growth, churn, and so on) generating these outcomes, and you'll realize the importance of enhanced disclosure.

The information Netflix provided also allows for my calculation of customer lifetime value, an innovative and revealing measure of the major intangible asset of the company.[30] Notably, the first-quarter 2008 customer value ($730 million) accounts for almost half of the difference between Netflix's market and book value, thereby substantially closing the gap between the relevance-challenged balance sheet and the real value of the enterprise. Finally, to further enhance usefulness, Netflix provided forward-looking *guidance* on subscribers, revenues, and earnings for the rest of 2008. That's what I mean by disclosing effective beyond-GAAP information, essentially reporting on the *path to growth*. Companies in every sector can similarly provide actionable information to investors. Here is how.

## The Path-to-Growth Report

Figure 7-3 presents my generalized template for path-to-growth disclosure, focusing on the major value drivers of modern businesses and informing on *inputs* or investments in growth (left column), followed by *intermediate outputs*, a necessity, given the usually lengthy time required for growth gestation. The *ultimate* outputs (right column) show the valuation fundamentals: sales, earnings, and cash flows. This template is an articulation of the business model of the enterprise—the essence of investors' information needs.

Don't let figure 7-3 intimidate you. No company can be expected to disclose all the information in the template, since very few businesses deploy all the value drivers shown (R&D, technology acquisition, alliances, brands, Internet activities, risk hedging, and so on). I've shown all those value drivers and their consequences in the figure for the sake of comprehensiveness, to make the template applicable to a broad range of industries. For your disclosure, just choose the major value drivers that best characterize your business model and develop the required information for these drivers.

If your company engages in R&D, consider figure 7-3's top line, which informs about investment in innovation—research and development, both organic (internal) and acquired—and its consequences.

FIGURE 7-3

## The path-to-growth template

| Inputs (value drivers) | | Intermediate outputs | | Ultimate outputs |
|---|---|---|---|---|
| Innovation: R&D and acquired technology | ⟶ | Patents, trademarks, product pipeline | ⟶ | Innovation revenues; cost savings |
| Customers: Brand creation and enhancement | ⟶ | Trademarks and brand values; customers' loyalty and lifetime value | ⟶ | Market share; price premium |
| Human capital: Workforce development, training, and incentives | ⟶ | Employee turnover and quality | ⟶ | Cost savings; enhanced productivity |
| Connectivity: Alliances and joint ventures | ⟶ | Patents, trademarks, new products | ⟶ | Innovation revenues, market share, cost savings |
| Internet activities | ⟶ | Site visits, number and size of transactions | ⟶ | Revenue increases; cost savings |
| Organization capital: Processes, supply chains | ⟶ | Nonfinancial efficiency indicators | ⟶ | Revenues generated; cost savings |
| Risk management: Hedging activities | ⟶ | Value at risk (VAR) | ⟶ | Cost savings |

The left column should report the inputs or investments in these items for the last three to five years, preferably with meaningful breakdowns, such as for product and process R&D (the latter aimed at reducing production costs), and for basic versus development research (the former is aimed at creating new technologies, whereas the latter focuses on improvements to available ones), as well as for organic versus acquired (in-process) R&D.[31] And what did the investment in innovation buy you? Moving to the right along the path-to-growth template, the middle column informs about the intermediate consequences of the investment: the number of patents and trademarks (applied for and granted) generated by the R&D in the last three to five years, as well as other innovation markers, such as products along the development stage (e.g., a pharmaceutical's product pipeline or software products that passed beta tests). To the extent available, indicators of patent value, such as the number of citations to these patents by subsequent patents of other companies ("forward citations"), can be provided.[32] The intermediate consequences of innovation investments thus allow for a preliminary assessment of the productivity of such investment. The path to growth culminates in the right column informing on the ultimate outcomes of innovation investments: "innovation revenues"—the percentage of total revenues generated by products or services introduced during the last three to five years, a key indicator of the ability to quickly bring new products to the market, as well as the cost savings from process R&D.[33] To be sure, that's a lot of disclosure. So start by disclosing just a part of the information and gauge investors' reaction.

What about companies without R&D? Next on the path-to-growth template are customers: brand creation and enhancement. Advertising and promotion expenditures are the inputs (currently, often "buried" in the income statement in general and administrative expenses), while trademarks granted and revenues from brands and trademarks sold are the intermediate outputs. The ultimate outputs of branding efforts are increased market share and the contribution to revenues of the price *premium* (company's product price relative to nearest competitor's price) enabled by the brand.[34] The latter—price premium—is obviously sensitive information and may therefore be reported for internal use only.

Next in the template is the investment in the workforce and its consequences, which management rarely reports and often does not even track: employee training (in-house and external), special recruiting efforts (signing bonuses, for example), and effective incentive or compensation schemes. These should lead to intermediate outputs, like low employee turnover rates and, of course, ultimate results—cost savings and increased productivity. If workforce investments fail to generate cost savings and/or higher productivity, investors and particularly managers should be made aware of that.

Down the template, we find the "connectivity" efforts of the firm: alliances and joint ventures that characterize many modern corporations. They enhance R&D productivity and share its risk, as well as further manufacturing or marketing activities. Such corporate connectivities are often extensive and costly in terms of investment and executive time, and sometimes even in loss (theft) of intellectual capital to alliance partners, and yet few companies systematically trace alliance investments and relate them to benefits, and even fewer publicly report any meaningful alliance information.[35] The template articulates the alliance value-creation chain, starting with the investment in alliances, through its intermediate outputs—patents, trademarks, and new products and services—ending up with the ultimate outputs: revenues from alliances, market share gained, and cost savings from marketing and manufacturing alliances. Such costs-to-benefits information allows for an assessment of investment productivities (ROI) in alliances and joint ventures.

Next on the template are the company's Internet activities and other strategic moves aimed at fostering growth, such as business acquisitions and restructuring. Such activities, if successful, lead to intermediate outcomes—site visits and transaction values for online activities or operating efficiencies from restructuring—and to ultimate outcomes: impact on revenues and costs. Next, the template informs on "organization capital"—a stealth intangible—reflecting unique business practices and models (Walmart's vaunted supply chains) and their consequences.

Finally, the template turns to an increasingly important corporate activity—risk management. There can be no sustainable growth without risk containment. Investors should therefore be informed about the essentials of the company's risk management, such as the costs of hedging raw materials and foreign exchange (prevalent in airlines, for example) and their consequences: cost savings and reduced exposure to input prices and interest rate fluctuations. In its financial reports, Southwest Airlines, for example, elaborates on its successful fuel-hedging activities and the consequent savings.

Note that the information in the figure conforms with my two criteria for effective disclosure: (1) standardized, well-defined measures—all of the indicators in the template are either defined by GAAP (R&D, capital expenditures, revenues)—or comparable measures across companies, such as the number of patents generated or Web site clicks; and (2) direct links between the indicators and financial results—revenues, earnings—posted in the right column of the template. Consequently, the path-to-growth information factors directly into investors' and analysts' valuation models, hence, its usefulness. Notably, managers do not currently use many of the proposed disclosures, particularly the linkages between inputs and outputs. So, start with developing and analyzing this vital information internally and gradually release segments of it for external use.

## Show Me the Money

I know what you think: aren't current disclosure requirements burdensome enough without my proposed disclosures? What will these new disclosures buy me? And what about the potential benefits to competitors of the proposed disclosures and will they enhance litigation risk? Frankly, benefiting competitors and attracting trial lawyers by information disclosure are worn-out arguments often raised to oppose disclosure proposals. Consider that most pharmaceutical, biotech, telecommunication, and Internet companies—all operating in fiercely competitive sectors—routinely disclose extensive product pipeline and customer-related information (Netflix, for example) without any apparent competitive harm. I am not advocating the disclosure of secret, future development plans, just recent relevant facts that are mostly known to your competitors.[36] As for litigation exposure, all the information in figure 7-3 is *factual*; there are no estimates, hype, or forecasts, fodder for the trial lawyers. So, unless the information you release is outright fraudulent, it will not enhance your litigation exposure.

And what will the path-to-growth disclosure buy you? Plenty, as the following brief survey of evidence indicates:

- Research has documented that the voluntary disclosure and improved quality of financial information reduce both the cost of equity capital and the cost of debt.[37] A striking quantification of the benefits of improved disclosure is provided by Luzi Hail, reporting that Swiss companies that follow a practice of enhanced disclosure enjoy a 2.5 percentage point lower cost of capital than their tight-lipped counterparts. Now we are talking real benefits.[38]

- Enhanced disclosure also decreases stock price volatility, so abhorred by managers. For example, Rejin Guo, Nan Zhou, and I reported that biotech IPOs' improved prospectus disclosure about the progress of their drug development program, patent protection, expected launch time of new products, and other key information for valuing these companies is associated with significantly lower stock price volatility and narrower bid-ask spreads (lower cost of capital) after the IPO.[39]

- Enhanced disclosure also increases the number of analysts following the company and the size of its institutional ownership, both positive outcomes from executives' perspective.[40]

- And improved disclosure decreases stocks' bid-ask spread (again decreasing cost of capital) and increase trading volume. Christian Leuz and Robert Verrecchia reported that German companies that switched from German accounting principles to the more stringent and transparent international reporting rules, or to U.S. GAAP, saw their stocks' bid-ask spreads shrink significantly and trade volume rise.[41]

- Finally, Irene Karamanoue and George Nishiotis reported that European companies voluntarily adopting the more transparent and comparable International Accounting Standards for financial reporting (before they became mandatory in 2005) saw their stock prices increase upon the announcement of the voluntary adoption and an upgrade in analyst stock recommendations after the announcement.[42] That's not a bad outcome for an accounting change.

The evidence for the benefits of voluntary disclosure is unanimous. CFOs, however, are split. A 2003 CFO survey revealed that 44 percent of respondents strongly agree that voluntary disclosure increases a stock's liquidity, while 17 percent strongly disagree; 39 percent strongly agree that voluntary disclosure reduces cost of capital, while 22 percent strongly disagree.[43] Given the evidence, the ayes should easily have it.

## Operating Instructions

- **ARE YOU A CANDIDATE FOR ENHANCED DISCLOSURE?** GAAP is particularly deficient in satisfying investors' information needs for "change" companies: innovative, intangibles-intensive enterprises, high-growth, and early life-cycle businesses, and those undergoing restructuring. If your company has one of these characteristics, you should seriously consider systematically releasing beyond-GAAP information as proposed.

- **USEFUL SIGNS.** If you are followed by a below-industry median number of analysts, or if the dispersion of analysts' earnings estimates of your company is above the industry median—clear signs of abnormal information asymmetry—your case for beyond-GAAP disclosure is further enhanced.

- **DEVELOPMENT COMPANIES.** If your company is engaged in the *development* of products or services (software, Internet, financial services, pharmaceutical or biotech, health care), you should definitely consider disclosing information along the path-to-growth template. Without such disclosure, investors will be in the dark during the development period, and any surprises, particularly disappointments (drug failure in tests) will rock the stock and create deep resentment among investors and analysts.

- **CONSISTENCY ABOVE ALL.** If you voluntarily disclose certain information when you have good news (a large number of patents granted, for example), don't refrain from disclosure in bad times, lest you condition investors to assume the worst when you don't disclose. Effective information sharing is a long-term commitment. It's the same with the procedures generating the information. If, for example, you report the percentage of revenues from new products (innovation revenues), don't include revenues from marginally improved products in lean years.

- **AND INTEGRITY.** Many a manager can't resist layering hype on voluntary disclosures. A deep product pipeline of a pharmaceutical company can be presented by the underlying data (number of drugs in phases I, II, and III clinical tests) or with wildly optimistic speculations about future profits and market share; a disclosure about a marketing alliance can be fact-based (related expenditures, consequent trademarks, and generated sales) or with a heavy dose of wishful thinking. Opt for the former. Gregory Miller reported that when earnings grow, managers provide lots of voluntary information to investors with a sprinkle of hype, but when the growth subsides, they restrict disclosure and fail to alert investors to the trend reversal.[44] That tendency is a sure recipe for the loss of credibility.

## Chapter 8

# Put Your Money Where Your Mouth Is

## Why Certain Financial Actions Affect Share Prices and Others Don't

➡ Actions (signals) speak louder than words.

➡ The message in dividends and stock splits.

➡ Share buybacks: the myth and reality.

➡ What do managers' share purchases and sales signal?

What is common to dividend increases or decreases, share buybacks, financial leverage changes, share purchases and sales by company executives, and stock splits? Not much, except that they are managerial actions, in contrast with the previously discussed communications, like conference calls, pro forma earnings, or guidance, in part aimed at changing investors' perceptions regarding the company's prospects. Such actions, which economists have dubbed *signals*, are supposed to deliver a heavier punch than just words, since managers are putting their (rather their company's) money where their mouth is. Thus, for example, a share buyback or repurchase is believed to signal to investors that the company shares are undervalued, given its intrinsic growth potential, and therefore a good investment for the company. Similarly, a divided increase is supposed to convey good news, since managers are believed to increase dividends only when they expect future cash flows to be sufficiently high to support the elevated dividends level. These and other financial actions speak louder than words.

"None of this makes sense to me," says Louis Lowenstein, a keen observer of companies and finance. He, among others, argues that financial decisions should be dictated by solid economic reasons—distributing funds to shareholders by buying back shares or increasing dividends only when the return on investments available to the company is lower than shareholders' alternative return in capital markets—rather than using financial decisions to signal managers' views to investors. Lowenstein commented, "But prophetic or not, if a company allocates capital intelligently and if it communicates those decisions with candor, dividend signals are irrelevant. Dividends are too important a *business* issue to be relegated to the role of (trivial) news carrier for the stock market."[1] This seemingly unassailable logic is, however, challenged occasionally by events, such as when Bank of America disclosed on July 21, 2008, a 41 percent quarterly earnings plunge amid a severe mortgage crisis, slowing the economy and causing serious difficulties in managing its just-acquired Countrywide Financial, one of the largest and most beleaguered U.S. mortgage lenders. Despite the dismal earnings, Bank of America insisted on maintaining its good-times dividend level. It's hard to believe that the bank's decision not to cut dividends in such dire times was aimed at optimally allocating capital, as Lowenstein propagates; Bank of America could surely have used the dividend money to buttress its depleting capital, rather than to calm investors by signaling its positive outlook of the future.[2]

Intending to signal future outcomes or not, managers should thoroughly understand the impact of corporate financial decisions and their own trading in company shares on investors' perceptions and share prices. Is a dividend increase or a CEO's share purchase, for example, more effective in raising investors' growth expectations and lifting stock prices than, say, a positive earnings guidance? Are actions, like share buybacks and stock splits, driven by solid economic motives or are they ploys to manipulate investors? And most importantly, which of these actions or signals is effective in fundamentally changing share prices?

## Signaling: On a Wink and a Prayer

Since my early student days, I aspired to be an academic. At the time, I didn't know the rewards and travails of research, but the privilege of teaching seemed to me on par with healing (body and soul) as the highest callings. A couple of years' experience as a teaching assistant convinced me that I could be an effective instructor (winning a teaching award at Berkeley lay far, far in the future). But how could I, holding a humble bachelor's degree, convince a top university to hire me? How could I credibly *signal* my capabilities and belief in my academic potential, differentiating myself from the pack coveting an academic career?

Get a PhD from a top university, says Michael Spence in the seminal paper, "Job Market Signaling" and a subsequent book *Market Signaling*, which won him the 2001 Nobel Prize in economics.[3] Spence's model, like that of another 2001 Nobel recipient, George Akerlof (whom we met in chapter 7), deals with the ubiquitous situation of *information asymmetry*, in which one party to a deal or an arrangement knows more about the product or service traded than the counterparty. In Spence's model, employers initially cannot distinguish between capable (high-productivity) and incapable employees when interviewing candidates. Consequently, employers will offer a relatively low wage (somewhere between the product value of capable and incapable employees) by "crowding out," that is, deterring the capable or talented ones who will look for other opportunities like self-employment in search of higher rewards (just as owners of good cars are driven out of a lemons market in Akerlof's model, discussed in chapter 7). How can such a degradation of labor markets be avoided? You guessed it: by capable employees signaling their high productivity through, say, demonstrated ability in previous occupations or by obtaining an advanced academic degree, preferably from a top university. Obviously, and this is key, for the signaling process to work the signal must be *costly* (an advanced university degree requires multiyear university tuition and loss of income), otherwise the low-productivity employees will mimic the signal to obtain employment. For the quality signal to work, it obviously must effectively differentiate the good from the bad.

I indeed followed Spence's advice (shortly before he gave it) and obtained a PhD from a top-notch school—the University of Chicago—although my motivation for higher education and the choice of school were not just to obtain an effective talent signal, but also to enhance my academic capabilities. But the advice I received from friends that "with a Chicago PhD every business school will hire you" was sufficient to overcome Chicago's weather (at the end, I was hired by the University of Chicago itself; talk about inbreeding).

Economists and finance scholars quickly applied Spence's signaling model to the capital markets arena where information asymmetries—between managers and shareholders or between informed (say, hedge funds) and uniformed investors—are rife and the need for signaling value acute. For example, Stewart Myers and Nicholas Majluf argued that managers signal to investors a higher corporate value by increasing the company's debt: how can borrowing enhance investors' valuation of shares?[4] Start with investors' inadequate information about the company's prospects, such as on the progress of products under development, or managers' plans and strategies. Such inadequate information—prevalent in capital markets—will naturally lead investors to overvalue some businesses and undervalue others. The managers of the latter companies, having better information than investors about intrinsic firm value and future prospects, will finance new investment projects with borrowed capital, rather than stock. The reason is that a stock financing of the new investment will require issuing an excessive number of the undervalued shares, thereby seriously diluting shareholders' value. Investors know that, so raising debt to finance investment will convey the message that, in managers' opinion, the company's shares are undervalued. Somewhat convoluted but makes sense nevertheless.

The effectiveness of this signal stems from the fact that a debt increase is costly—it commits the company to future interest and principal payments, constraining managers' flexibility relative to a stock issue—and therefore will not be mimicked by undervalued companies with insufficient earnings power.[5] The reverse reasoning holds for financing investment or acquisitions with stock when the company's shares are overvalued. If all this sounds theoretical to you, note that empirical evidence indeed confirms that share prices generally rise when companies increase debt (investors get the message that the stock is undervalued) and fall upon the announcement of a new stock issue.[6]

Researchers claimed that a host of other financial decisions—dividend changes, stock buybacks, and retained interest in IPOs[7]—also serve as signals to investors. At the time, it seemed that almost every financial decision is a signal. A dubious proposition. Yet, there are indeed effective and ineffective signals, and it's important for both managers and investors to understand thoroughly what managerial actions signal promising future performance and, among those signals, which is cost effective and which is not. Here are the main lessons from research in the financial signaling arena.

## Shareholder Distributions: Dividends and Share Buybacks

Why do corporations pay dividends? And why do investors pay attention to dividends? asks Fischer Black of Black-Scholes option-pricing formula fame.[8] After careful consideration of various possible explanations, Black succinctly concludes, "We don't know." What a letdown.

But wait, isn't shareholders' preference for dividends a no-brainer? Everyone knows that a bird in the hand is worth two in the bush. You are safer getting a dollar now via a cash dividend than leaving it for the company to invest in risky projects or sometimes for managers to just squander. So, what's the dividends dilemma? On close inspection, though, the dividend issue is not self-evident: since the stock price of a dividend-paying company drops on the ex-dividend day by roughly the amount of the dividend, shareholders of nondividend companies look-ing for the safety of cash could just sell shares for the amount of the dividends they wish and be as well off as shareholders of dividend-paying companies.[9] So why should shareholders care about dividends?[10] Some evidently don't. Cisco Systems, for example, has never paid divi-dends since its inception and even stated in its 2007 annual report (p. 79) that "The Company has never paid cash dividends on its common stock and has no present plans to do so." Yet Cisco's market capitalization in March 2011 approached $100 billion. There are quite a few takers for this and many other nondividend companies.[11] Many shareholders clearly like dividends, since roughly three-quarters of the S&P 500 com-panies regularly pay dividends. Does this explain managers' reluctance to cut dividends, even when experiencing a sharp earnings drop, as in the BofA case? Shareholders' mixed feelings about dividends perplexed Fisher Black.

## Burning a Hole in Their Pocket

Managers' primary use of funds, both internal and raised in capital markets, is for investment purposes: R&D, capital expenditures, technology acquisitions, and M&As. But attractive high-yielding investment opportunities aren't easy to come by, particularly in a com-petitive environment where everyone wants to invest in the new-new technology and make growth-generating acquisitions. And when the expected returns on available investments don't exceed the cost of capital—the return investors can get in the capital markets for a similar level of risk—the company should return its free cash flows to share-holders. This fundamental investment axiom is, however, easier to state in textbooks and finance courses than to implement in a corporate context. Distributing excess cash to shareholders, in the form of, say, a special dividend, seems to managers an admission of defeat in the race for growth. For years, Microsoft resisted shareholders' calls to distribute its huge hoard of cash, claiming it's intended for future investments, until it finally yielded in 2004 and paid a whopping special dividend of

$32 billion, coupled with a share buyback of $30 billion. Surely, it would have been better and more tax beneficial to shareholders to smooth out these payments over several years. Furthermore, managers, ever the optimists, likely overestimate the expected returns on prospective investments, particularly in new technologies (think investments in clean energy alternatives, nanotechnology, and biotechnology), leading them to overinvest company funds in inferior projects. The large number of goodwill write-offs—recently over a thousand a year—attests to the rampant optimism in acquisition decisions. A regular and generous dividend payment mitigates managers' temptation to hoard funds and invest excessively.

Thus, my version of the bird-in-the-hand (cash dividends) explanation focuses on preventing the waste of the birds in the bush on ill-advised or self-aggrandizing projects, such as the tallest headquarters building in town or a football stadium. This explanation of investors' demand for dividends obviously implies that mature, profitable companies operating in low-growth sectors, such as large banks and insurance companies, energy, and retail enterprises, should pay relatively high dividends, whereas companies with attractive investment opportunities, such as high-tech, biotech, or Internet companies, or companies operating in volatile sectors where ample cash reserves are needed for rainy days will refrain from dividend payment. Similarly, companies in the initial, high-growth phase of development will avoid dividends, but on reaching maturity will initiate dividend payments (as Microsoft did in 2003, after its exploding growth of the 1990s subsided, and Cisco, another maturing enterprise, in March 2011).

To empirically substantiate my claim that high-growth and/or volatile companies pay low (or no) dividends, while mature, profitable enterprises pay high dividends, I computed two corporate growth measures and a volatility indicator for the S&P 500 companies in 2007 (just before the financial crisis), and related them to the firms' dividend payout ratio (dividends over earnings). The M/B (market-to-book) ratio reflects investors' growth expectations: a high expected growth justifies paying more for the company's assets (a higher M/B ratio). Analysts' long-term (five years) earnings growth expectation is another growth indicator. The data in table 8-1 shows that, indeed, the mean and median growth expectations of dividend payers are substantially lower than those of nonpayers: payers' mean M/B ratio and analysts' growth forecasts are 4.75 and 11.35 percent, respectively, versus 5.27 and 16.17 percent for nonpayers. Turning to operational stability, I computed the companies' earnings volatility over the preceding twenty years by the EPS coefficient of variation (the variance of EPS divided by its mean). The data shows that the mean EPS volatility of nonpayers (13.59) is five times higher than that of dividend payers (2.77). Thus, the need for cash—for investment and/or rainy days—clearly differentiates dividend payers from nonpayers. So, the dividend decisions isn't such a mystery after all and is hardly intended to be a signal.

Why are managers so reluctant to cut dividends, as surveys indicate?[12] According to general wisdom, because of the negative message about future cash flows that such a cut conveys to investors. This is likely yet another of the many myths in capital markets. Consider, for example, Allegheny Technologies, a specialty materials producer, that cut its quarterly dividend by 70 percent on November 14, 2002, and saw its stock price unaffected by the announcement.[13] Not only that, from the cut date to the end of 2005, Allegheny's stock surged almost 700 percent while the S&P 500 index advanced over the corresponding period by only 38 percent. And, generalizing, the *Wall Street Journal* quoted a

TABLE 8-1

## Dividends at S&P 500 companies, 2007

|  | DIVIDEND PAYERS | | DIVIDEND NONPAYERS | |
|---|---|---|---|---|
|  | **Mean** | **Median** | **Mean** | **Median** |
| **Market-to-book ratio** | 4.75 | 2.68 | 5.27 | 3.13 |
| **Long-term growth forecast** | 11.35% | 11.10% | 16.17% | 15.00% |
| **Earnings volatility** | 2.77 | 0.73 | 13.59 | 1.30 |

Thomson Financial study of the S&P 500 companies that cut dividends by more than 10 percent from 1990 to 2004, finding that starting three months after the cut, the dividend-decreasing companies as a group comfortably beat the S&P 500 index.[14] So, dividend cuts are hardly an ominous signal.

The dividend bottom line: there are good economic reasons for paying high or low (or even no) dividends. Signaling to investors isn't among them.

### Hey, Big Spender: Share Buybacks

In nominal terms, aggregate corporate profits of the S&P 500 companies quadrupled over the last twenty years until the financial crisis, which disrupted almost everything, whereas the dividend yield (dividends-to-earnings) decreased continuously until 2001 (from 4.3 percent to 1.0 percent), rising modestly thereafter to about 2 percent, likely spurred by the 2003 dividend tax decrease.[15] Share buybacks from 1988 to 2001 also decreased (as a ratio of earnings) from 6 percent to 2 percent, yet came roaring all the way back to 6 percent by 2007. This different pattern isn't the only mystery about share buybacks.

Indeed, the plot about the motives and consequences of share buybacks is thick. The motives span the spectrum of distributing excess cash (no attractive investment opportunities) without having to raise the cash dividend rate, to the antidilution motive—repurchasing shares to offset large employee stock option exercises. And then there is the oft-heard undervaluation (signaling) motive: managers buy back shares when they are undervalued, both as an attractive investment and to signal investors about the share undervaluation (put your money where your mouth is). For the conspiracy theorists, there is always the sinister motive of manipulating investors by boosting earnings-per-share via the buyback without actually improving business performance. Which of the buyback motives holds true, you ask? All of the above, under different circumstances.

Consider Cisco Systems: during fiscal years 2005 through 2007 (July 30, 2004–July 28, 2007) it repurchased a cool 1.27 billion shares for $26.2 billion. During the same period, executives and employees exercised 538 million shares, so that the buyback (1.27 billion shares) offset more than twice the dilutive effect of stock options. Obviously, there was more to Cisco's massive buyback than preventing a shareholder dilution. What about cash distribution? Cisco's aggregate earnings during the three years from 2005 through 2007 were $18.7 billion, and expenditures on property and equipment as well as on business and technology acquisitions amounted to $12.7 billion. So the share buyback also served to distribute to investors the excess of earnings over investment balance of $6 billion. But the three-year aggregate buyback of $26.2 billion was still substantially larger than the stock options' offset and the excess earnings distribution. What else could account for Cisco's buybacks? Were Cisco's shares so deeply undervalued from 2005 through 2007 to warrant a strong buyback signal to investors? That's unlikely, since Cisco's P/E ratio on December 31, 2005 (the mid-period examined) was 19.7, roughly on par with technology bellwethers IBM (15.2) and Microsoft (20.8).

So, I suspect that Cisco's turbocharged buyback program was also aimed at enhancing its reported EPS to favorably affect investors' growth perceptions. Suggesting this calls for some detective work. In fiscal 2006, Cisco broke ranks with other technology companies and issued bonds to the tune of $6.5 billion. Volatile enterprises, like high-tech and biotech companies, generally refrain from debt financing to avoid the burden of fixed-interest and principle payments that have to be made in good and bad times. Cisco's motive for issuing the bonds was likely to take advantage of the low interest rates in 2006, thereby enhancing shareholders' returns by the difference between its high profitability and the low interest rates. A smart financial move to be sure, but with a sting in the tail: the interest payments on the bonds depress earnings and EPS growth. The solution: contemporaneous share buybacks to decrease the number of shares outstanding (the denominator of EPS), thereby boosting EPS. Indeed, the buybacks delivered the goods: Cisco's EPS grew from fiscal years 2005 to 2007 by 37.5 percent, while its ROE—unaffected by the number of shares outstanding—increased during the period by only a third of the EPS growth (13.2 percent) and its ROA—return on assets deployed—actually *decreased* by 8 percent. The buyback-driven decrease in the number of Cisco's shares used for the EPS computation, from 6.74 billion at the end of fiscal 2004 to 6.1 billion at end of 2007 (9.5 percent), did much of the EPS growth trick.[16] Thus, Cisco's EPS growth masked a rather anemic profitability, demonstrating once more the wonders of finance. Not for nothing are certain business schools now offering courses in "financial engineering" or better yet, "financial alchemy."[17] Finally, did all these maneuvers impress Cisco's shareholders? Not really; over the four profitable years, 2004 through 2007, Cisco's shares rose a trifling 15 percent, lagging the S&P 500 index. All those share buybacks were for naught, except for providing an important lesson to managers expecting wonders from share buybacks.

Cisco's case is consistent with the large sample evidence on share buybacks. Erick Lie examined 4,730 share buybacks made from 1981 to 2000, documenting the following:[18] First, investors react favorably, though not enthusiastically, to a buyback announcement (mean and median stock price increases of 3.0 percent and 1.9 percent, respectively). Second, companies generally repurchase shares during or following a period of successful operations. Alas, subsequent to the buyback, their performance tends to slow down (a "reversion to the mean" in the statistical parlance), but less so than a control group of non-buybackers with similar prior performance. Thus, the buyback announcement conveys good news of sorts.[19] Third, notably, the slower slowdown in the subsequent operating performance of the buybackers (relative to control firms) is evident only for those that actually buy back shares (some buyback announcers never deliver on the promise or repurchase substantially fewer shares than announced).

The main takeaway from Lie's study is that the timing of the buyback—following good performance—generally coincides with a transition from a growth period to maturity, where the limited investment opportunities free up resources for the buyback, as with Microsoft, mentioned earlier. Thus, signaling theories notwithstanding, most buybacks don't signal share undervaluation or particularly good things to come, but rather the existence of excess cash. Investors' mildly positive response to the buyback announcement apparently reflects their relief that all that excess cash from the end-of-growth period will not burn a hole in managers' pockets.

Finally, back to my conjecture that Cisco's $26 billion buyback was partially aimed at boosting EPS. This is not an outlandish accusation. Paul Hribar, Nicole Jenkins, and Bruce Johnson, examining buybacks from 1988 to 2001, reported that an unexpectedly large number of companies that would have missed analysts' consensus EPS estimates avoided the embarrassment by an accretive (EPS-enhancing) share buyback.[20] Surprisingly and reassuringly, the researchers also report that investors tend to see through the ploy, largely ignoring the companies' leap over the consensus hurdle with the help of the share buyback, consistent with the disappointing share performance of many buybackers.[21] Investors are not so gullible after all.

## Stock Splits: Where Is the There, There?

A vendor asked a person ordering a pizza, "Should I slice it to four or eight pieces?" The person answered, "Four is fine. I am not that hungry."[22] Ditto, a two-for-one stock split, for example, which slices the total value of the company—the "pizza"—from four million shares, say, to eight million without having an impact on its value.[23] So, stock splits and stock dividends (small stock splits) are, by definition, nonevents.[24] But why do hundreds of companies split their stock every year, and even more puzzling, why do investors react favorably to this apparent nonevent? Hanock Louis and Dahlia Robinson reported that the mean and median abnormal (above benchmark) stock price increases around split announcements are 2.5 percent and 1.6 percent, respectively.[25] That increase is not enough to catapult shareholders to the *Forbes* billionaires list, nevertheless, the price increase indicates a positive investor reaction to a split announcement.[26] So, what's going on here? How is a pizza (corporation) sliced into eight rather than four pieces worth more?

Once again, signaling comes to the rescue. Some finance scholars argue that what excites investors about a split is not the post-split larger number of shares, rather it is managers' use of the split to signal a forthcoming performance improvement. That's the reason a split announcement is sometimes accompanied by a cash dividend increase—a double whammy of a signal. Alas, this intriguing signaling story was slain by a study I performed years ago with Josef Lakonishok showing that, like share buybacks, companies tend to split their stock *after* a period of substantial earnings and sales growth, not before it.[27] Compared with similar growth companies, the stock splitters' post-split performance is indistinguishable from that of nonsplitters.[28] Thus, there isn't really good news behind the split signal.

So, what's in a split? I believe there are two reasons for stock splits; both, I admit, don't fit academic orthodoxy. The first explanation: keeping the stock price within a reasonable trading range. Shlomo Benartzi et al. calculated that without frequent stock splits, General Electric's stock price, which was $38.25 in December 31, 1935, would have been $10,094.40 on December 31, 2005.[29] In fact, GE's end-of-2005 stock price was $30, cheaper than seventy years earlier (substantially cheaper, if inflation is accounted for). Clearly, GE, like the majority of splitting companies, tries to keep its share prices in a reasonably constant *nominal* range. Benartzi et al. showed that from 1933 to 2005, the average annual stock price of all U.S. publicly traded companies moved within the $20-to-$30 range (the overall average: $25.74) most of the time, which may be considered "normal."[30] Maintaining these stable stock prices' range over seventy years took almost two hundred splits a year. Intriguingly, the almost constant nominal share price ranges are typical to the United States; in Japan and the United Kingdom, for example, stock prices tend to increase over time, though less than the inflation rate.

What's wrong with a GE stock price of $10,094, or Berkshire Hathaway, which, prior to 2009, never split its stock, having a Class A share price of $115,000 on August 1, 2008? After all, large stock prices save brokerage commissions and other transaction costs, which are usually paid on the *number* of shares traded. The answer lies in investors' psychology. Most managers believe that investors, particularly individuals, are afflicted by a price illusion: they regard high-priced shares as "expensive" and, therefore, risky, whereas very low share prices convey the impression of a failing company.[31] Accordingly, stocks priced "normally," in the $30 to $50 range, will be most attractive to investors. Even Warren Buffet, a celebrated contrarian, succumbed to the normal range logic and split Berkshire Hathaway's Class B shares 50-to-1 in late 2009.[32] That's why most splits follow an enhanced growth period, during which stock prices exceed the upper bound of the normal range. A reasonable explanation for stock splits indeed.

The second explanation for stock splits is "attention grabbing." I discussed in chapter 2 the well-documented phenomenon of investors' limited attention. With thousands of stocks available and a flood of information about them, there is obviously no way for even sophisticated investors, equipped with state-of-the-art technology, to keep abreast of the news avalanche. Cues get investors' attention, and there are few managerial cues as inexpensive and harmless as stock splits, which nevertheless are widely publicized in the business media and on Internet message boards.[33] A stock-split cue puts the company on every trader's and analyst's screen, reminding them to check it. This likely explains Patrick Dennis and Deon Strickland's finding that there is a post-split increase in institutional ownership, particularly for companies with low pre-split ownership.[34] Large companies, frequently in the news, may not need such a cue, yet medium-sized and small, attention-starved companies occasionally do.

## Finally, a Genuine Signal

In May 2006, Ronald Williams, Aetna's CEO, acquired a substantial number of Aetna shares (relative to his holding), as did Andrew Liveris, Dow Chemical's CEO, a couple of months later, buying a big chunk of Dow shares. What's common to these share purchases? You guessed it: very good timing. The stock prices of both Aetna and Dow increased substantially subsequent to the share purchases. During the twelve months following the purchases, Aetna's share price increase exceeded the S&P 500 index by 10 percent, whereas Dow's price increase beat the index by 14.5 percent. Money managers would kill for such a performance. Even more intriguing, both companies' stock performance prior to the CEOs' purchases were decidedly unimpressive: flat in Aetna's case, and decreasing for Dow. The CEOs share purchases thus signaled good things to come for investors (and themselves, of course). The large sample evidence clearly indicates that these cases weren't aberrations.

Josef Lakonishok and Inmoo Lee reported that insiders' trades during the 1980s and 1990s indeed foretold subsequent company performance: companies with large insider purchases during the prior six months outperformed companies with substantial insider sales by almost 8 percent during the year following the trade.[35] The researchers also reported that future stock price movements after insider trades are more pronounced for small rather than large companies; the trading signal is more potent in small companies because less information is available about them. Similarly, John McConnell, Henri Servaes, and Karl Lins examined stock price changes around insiders' share purchase announcements, documenting a positive investor reaction to the announcements—an indication of significant information conveyed by such purchases—but the strength of the reaction weakens with the increase in the size of managerial ownership.[36] Large ownership implies managerial entrenchment, which is generally detrimental to company performance and shareholder value. The researchers also reported that financial analysts revise upward their earnings forecasts following insiders' share purchases. So, the evidence clearly indicates that managers do provide relevant information with their share trades, explaining investors' and analysts' reaction to such trades. These studies, however, are from the 1980s and 1990s, and so much has transpired since then: the burst of the tech bubble, the wave of corporate scandals, the Sarbanes-Oxley Act of the early 2000s, and the substantial shortening of the time required to notify the SEC on insiders' trades. Therefore, I conducted my own examination of the signal in managerial share purchases in 2006, the last full normal year prior to the financial crisis.

To ascertain the message, intended or unintended, in managers' own purchases of firm stock, I collected data on such purchases made by the top corporate executives (CEO, COO, CFO, president) and the board chair—all presumably familiar with company affairs and therefore able to signal. To focus on information-driven purchases, I eliminated from the sample all share purchases from stock option exercises, since those may be motivated by other factors, like vesting period considerations. For the remaining open-market stock purchases, I computed the market-adjusted stock returns for two periods: two and four months before and after the purchases.[37] Table 8-2 presents the mean returns for all the stock purchases in my sample and shows that the companies' stock performance prior to the insiders' purchases was decidedly negative (–8.4 percent during two months, and –11.8 percent for four months prior to purchases) and positive thereafter: almost 2 percent for the two and four months examined (roughly 6 percent to 12 percent on an annualized basis). Managers (and the board chair) obviously time their stock purchases to coincide with the inflection of the stock price trend from negative to positive. Moreover, the positive stock performance subsequent to the purchases increases with the size of purchase (relative to the executives' share holding before the purchase): whereas the mean post-purchase stock return over the entire sample is 1.8 percent (see the table), for large purchases, exceeding 20 percent to 30 percent of the executives' prior share holding, the mean stock return over the two months after the purchase is almost three times larger (5.2 percent) and for purchases between 50 percent to 100 percent of prior share holdings the return is 6.0 percent, a rather sizable market-adjusted return for two months.

TABLE 8-2

## Managerial stock purchases, 2006

MEAN MARKET-ADJUSTED RETURNS FOR TWO AND FOUR MONTHS BEFORE AND AFTER THE PURCHASES

|  | Before | After |
| --- | --- | --- |
| Two months | −8.4% | 1.8% |
| Four months | −11.8% | 1.8% |

As always, there is a caveat. Managers can be wrong or just wish to portray unsubstantiated confidence in the business. In August 2008, for example, three top executives of Hologic Inc., a health diagnostic tests manufacturer, bought $1.7 million of company shares after the share prices dropped to a two-year low and analysts downgraded the company. The *Wall Street Journal* discussed these purchases, quoting an analyst saying that these purchases are "noteworthy" because the executives had a history of stock sales.[38] However, the Hologic stock price, which was in the $20 range in August 2008, further decreased to $15 in early November 2009, a 25 percent drop, while the S&P 500 Index dropped roughly 15 percent over the corresponding period. So much for the "positive signal" in Hologic purchases. In the majority of cases, though, managerial share purchases bode well for the future.

## Operating Instructions

- **DON'T HOARD SHAREHOLDERS' MONEY.** If your company is not cash strapped or doesn't have attractive investment opportunities, pay regular cash dividends and carefully increase these payments with the growth of the core business. Certain investors, particularly individuals, prefer getting dividends, and catering to these investors will diversify and stabilize your shareholder base. Cutting or eliminating dividends altogether is naturally viewed unfavorably by investors, but it's not the end of the world, as I have shown. If the reasons for the dividend cut are well articulated and credible, you may even avoid a temporary hit to the stock (recall the Allegheny example). There is no sense in hoarding cash; you just invite investors' pressure to pay out, cash-hungry hedge fund attacks, and hostile takeovers.

- **WHEN TO BUY BACK.** Share buybacks or special dividends should be primarily aimed at distributing surplus funds to shareholders when the expected returns on corporate uses of funds—new investments, business acquisitions, or R&D—don't exceed the investment returns available to shareholders (cost of capital). Investment bankers' and hedge funds' advice notwithstanding, buybacks are not a miracle cure for chronically lagging share prices. The buyback boost to the price when announced is relatively small and often temporary. Investors scoff at games, like beating the consensus earnings estimate by a buyback. Borrowing funds to finance buybacks doesn't make sense either. And, yes, announcing a buyback and not delivering on it later won't buy you anything, except a red face.

- **FIRM MATURITY AND CASH DISTRIBUTIONS.** The overriding consideration in dividends and buybacks is the "cold" economics of resource allocation. Investment in growth is paramount; shareholder distributions should be a derivative outcome of available cash in excess of attractive investments. There is nothing embarrassing in a company's natural transition from a growth phase to maturity (akin to midlife), and such transition generally creates excess cash (excess weight in humans), which should be distributed to owners. A transition from growth to maturity happens to all businesses; the smart (or lucky) avoid a worse outcome: decay.

- **SPLITTING HAIRS.** Stock splits and stock dividends are not heavy hitters and will not significantly affect investors' perceptions and stock prices. However, for reasons not entirely clear, there are advantages in keeping your share price within a normal range of $30 to $50, which you can achieve by stock splits.

- **SIGNAL CREDIBLY.** Of all the financial moves discussed in this chapter and hyped as signals in finance texts, managers' purchases or sales of company shares provide the most potent message to investors of things to come. When you wish to signal a turnaround in the company's operations, purchasing a substantial amount of shares will generally do the job. If the turnaround is genuine, you will also make money. Accordingly, when you decide to purchase unusual amounts of the company's shares, make sure it is backed by improving fundamentals. Importantly, avoid selling shares in a decreasing share-price situation. This will surely exacerbate the price decline and will draw the attention of the SEC and trial lawyers. Avoid suspicious-looking trades. The *Wall Street Journal* reported on insiders at Cutera Inc. and Power-One, Inc., selling shares between their initial earnings guidance and the subsequent failure to meet the guidance (the selling insiders insisted to the *Journal* that the share sales were planned before the guidance and they had done nothing wrong).[39] Remember, with share trading, your credibility is on the line.

## Chapter 9

# Is Doing Good, Good for Business?

## Which Corporate Social Responsibility (CSR) Activities Are Worth Pursuing and Which Are Not

In May 2005, GE unveiled with great fanfare and a multimillion-dollar advertising budget its awkwardly named "ecomagination" initiative, aimed "to help meet customers' demand for more energy-efficient products and to drive reliable growth for GE—growth that delivers for investors long term. Ecomagination also reflects GE's commitment to invest in a future that creates innovative solutions to environmental challenges and delivers valuable products and services to customers while generating profitable growth for the company."[1]

At launch and in subsequent reports, GE goes out of its way to assure investors that ecomagination is all about business: "simply put: ecomagination had to make money for our investors" (p. 4), and "the payoff for investors continues to increase" (p. 5). Rest assured, shareholders: the project experiences "tremendous progress that will translate to the Company's bottom line, rewarding investors" (p. 8).

And yet, the 2007 *Ecomagination Report* makes clear that this initiative, while purely for-profit, is very different from other GE business enterprises, like a new line of refrigerators, or new equipment leasing offers, which are routinely introduced by the various business units of the conglomerate. Ecomagination, says the 2007 report, aims "to help address some of the world's big challenges" (p. 1), an obviously ambitious objective for the provider of home appliances, jet engines, and financial products. Indeed, the third of five commitments made by the ecomagination initiative is "reducing its [GE's] GHG [greenhouse gases] emissions 1% by 2012, reducing the intensity of GE's GHG emissions by 30% by 2008, and improving energy efficiency 30% by the end of 2012 (all compared to 2004)"[2] (p. 2).

One wonders, will these voluntary and presumably significant GHG emission reductions also "make money for our investors" or just address "the world's big challenges"? Intriguingly, the 2007 report doesn't mention the expected costs of achieving the emission-reduction targets (forgone GHG-increasing investment projects, for example) or, for that matter, the costs of other ecomagination initiatives, such as "Green is Universal": "In May 2007, NBC Universal (NBCU) announced its 'Green is Universal' initiative, dedicated to effecting positive change for the environment by raising awareness and educating consumers as it substantially greens its own operations . . . NBCU launched its first 'green week' in November, during which 37 units across the television, theme park and film studio divisions participated in green-themed, on-air programming and digital content" [p. 22]. Is greening NBC programs what most viewers really want or what environmental zealots want them to watch? And, are green-themed programs best for making "money for our investors"?

There is more: with all the talk about "making money for our investors," the 2007 *Ecomagination Report* mentions various revenue targets, but is surprisingly silent about the costs and consequent profits of the sprawling initiatives. Is, for example, the Hamma Seawater Desalination Plant in Algeria, "designed, built, operated and financed by GE" (p. 9) a profit center? And what to make of the embarrassing fact that from May 2005—the launch date of ecomagination—to September 2008, the height of the financial crisis, GE's stock price lagged the S&P 500 by about 25 percent. Is that shareholders' gratitude for the "growth that delivers for investors long-term"?

It's not my intention to denigrate GE's ecomagination. Time will tell the extent to which this initiative delivered on its multiple promises to shareholders and society. Rather, I want to demonstrate the inevitable schizophrenia of most corporate social responsibility (CSR) programs. These are *corporate* activities—presumably done in the best interests of shareholders—and yet they are also *socially responsible*, aimed at advancing social, health, educational, and environmental objectives. But what if the two conflict, as often happens? What if GE's Hamma desalination project, for example, turns out to be good for Algerians but not for GE's shareholders? Will the project be canned? A highly socially irresponsible act, to be sure. And, more generally, what criteria should managers follow in resolving conflicting objectives? As Michael Jensen states: "It is logically impossible to maximize in more than one dimension at the same time ... whereas [shareholder] value maximization provides corporate managers with a single objective, stakeholder theory directs corporate managers to serve 'many masters.' And ... when there are many masters, all end up being shortchanged."[3] Well put.

## As If Managing the Business Isn't Hard Enough

Should managers engage in social engineering with other people's money and, frankly, without being particularly qualified to do so? And how should managers choose among all the worthy socially responsible projects? While the criterion for selecting business projects—comparing expected returns with company's cost of capital—is widely accepted, the ranking of the numerous health, environmental, educational, civic, and peace projects in terms of desirability and importance is highly subjective.[4] And if that's not onerous enough, what corporate governance mechanisms should oversee CSR activities? Another board committee (green directors)? And who audits the effectiveness of CSR programs (the environmental contribution of NBC's Green is Universal initiative, for example)? Thus, the title of this chapter—"Is Doing Good, Good for Business?"—is obviously a very complex, yet important issue facing every corporate executive. Presumably, doing CSR the right way will enhance the company's performance, mitigate its risk, and contribute to shareholder value. But what exactly is the right way?

It's easy to dismiss CSR by quoting the Nobel Laureate economist Milton Friedman (I heard him say this in class), "there is one and only one social responsibility of business—to use its resources and engage in activities designed to increase its profits."[5] But this is no longer an option for managers. In a 2008 special report on CSR, *The Economist* wrote: "Three years ago a special report in *The Economist* acknowledged, with regret, that the CSR movement had won the battle of ideas. In the survey by the Economist Intelligence Unit for this report, only 4% of respondents thought that CSR was 'a waste of time and money.' Clearly CSR has arrived."[6] Managers can't ignore CSR: to be ranked at the bottom of the widely watched sustainability rankings and indexes of companies (e.g., the Dow Jones Sustainability Index or FTSE4Good Index) is embarrassing and exposes executives to criticism and distracting shareholder proposals. And the incessant prodding by nongovernmental organizations (NGOs), local communities, and often employees to "do good" calls for a managerial response.

So what's a manager to do? What kinds of CSR activities are consistent with the company's fundamental objective of enhancing long-term growth? How much time and resources should you devote to CSR activities? And will shareholders support your CSR initiatives, helping to protect your job? In short, how can you navigate in the CSR maze of initiatives, consultants, NGOs, and activist shareholders? That's what this chapter is all about.

## Spot the CSR

What exactly is CSR? You'll be surprised to know that despite the ubiquity of the term, it's difficult to distinguish between CSR activities and regular business initiatives. Try to answer the following:

- Is Toyota's highly successful Prius hybrid model a smart business response to high gas prices and consumers' environmental awareness or a socially responsible move to reduce GHG emissions and fight climate change, or both?

- Is Whole Foods, a supermarket chain specializing in natural and organic foods, a response to an increasing consumer demand for such products, akin to Apple's pure business-driven response to iPad demand, or a social initiative aimed at improving people's health and the environment?

Perhaps selling green cars and organic produce is just smart business, so what about the following?

- CompartamosBanco, a Mexican microfinance bank, offers loans (average size, $450) at eye-popping interest rates of about 80 percent a year, according to *The Economist*.[7] Such "loan sharking" obviously troubles traditional microfinance enthusiasts, calling Compartamos's interest rates usurious. Yet, said *The Economist*, by generating profits, Compartamos was able to increase its client base from sixty-one thousand in 2000, after operating for a decade as a nonprofit microfinancing bank, to close to a million customers in 2008. The profits generated by the high interest rates attract investors and new capital, enabling the bank to reach more cash-strapped entrepreneurs. Seven new microfinance banks recently followed Compartamos's business model. So, is such for-profit microfinance a mere business or a socially responsible activity? Does one have to operate at a loss to qualify as CSR?

- Hewlett-Packard initiated its *e-inclusion* strategy to narrow the digital gap in Brazil, India, and South Africa, among other countries. HP partnered with community groups and NGOs to provide Web-based services for agriculture, health-care, and educational projects. Was this primarily a socially responsible activity or a smart strategy to push HP's products and services to new markets, or both? (HP terminated the program in 2006; apparently the digital gap had closed.)

- Renato Orsato reported on Ecolean, a Swedish packaging materials manufacturer, which developed new filling systems and stand-up pouches for soft and liquid foodstuff.[8] The company's impressive growth is attributable to a unique, environmentally friendly cost strategy, substituting the low-environmental-impact raw material, calcium carbonate (chalk or lime), for the traditional and still widely used plastic (polyethylene and polypropylene) products. In addition to being more environmentally friendly than plastics, calcium carbonate doesn't raise toxicity issues. To top it all, Ecolean's packaging materials cost 25 percent less than traditional ones; hence, the company's growth. By now you know the drill: is this CSR or good business?

- What about the large civic, health, and education philanthropic contributions of U.S. companies, amounting to $14 billion in 2009? Surely CSR, you say. But wait. In a comprehensive study I conducted with Christine Petrovits and Suresh Radhakrishnan, summarized later, we show that such philanthropy increases sales and profit growth through enhanced customer satisfaction and awareness.[9] So, is such cause-related giving just successful marketing or an advancement of social causes?

- Finally, a simple case, an activity that will surely seem to you pure social responsibility: KPMG, a large accounting firm, allows its U.K. employees to spend half a day a month of paid time on community work, adding up to tens of thousands of hours a year for the firm. Surely a laudable CSR. But even this initiative furthers an important business objective: enhancing employee morale and attracting socially conscious recruits.

So, what exactly is CSR, and how does it differ from smart, for-profit corporate initiatives? Must CSR always provide a business benefit to the company (CSR à la Milton Friedman), or can it operate at a loss? Interestingly, I couldn't find an *operational definition* of CSR in the sprawling CSR literature. The bewildering array of social responsibility concepts, terms, and descriptions advanced by consultants, writers, and NGOs—like the purple economy, green capital, TBL (triple bottom line) reporting, total net value added (in contrast with shareholder value added), social return on investment, live the brand, companies with conscience, cause companies, and national capitalism, to mention a few, putting business consultants' speak to shame—is not helpful in delineating CSR activities.[10] So, rather than trying to define and identify CSR initiatives, a futile task, I will develop the more important operating criterion for selecting worthy CSR initiatives in a world expecting businesses to be *both* socially responsible and create shareholder value.

## Anything You Can Do, I Can Do Better

What's a CSR initiative that's worth doing? My succinct answer: that which the company can do substantially better, in benefit-to-cost terms, than its shareholders ("Anything you can do, I ...").[11] I derive this maxim directly from Friedman's rejection of CSR, which rests on two arguments: managers have no special expertise in prioritizing and fixing social, health, or environmental ills, and shareholders should be the arbiters of what to do with their money (corporate profits). It's obviously very hard to object to Friedman's logic, except where managers bring unique *corporate capabilities* to bear on CSR—functions in which they clearly have expertise and supporting assets—and which individual investors, lacking such capabilities, cannot, of course, match.[12]

The main advantage of my CSR maxim is that, in contrast to the oft-suggested innocuous slogans—CSR should be an integral part of the company's strategy, CSR should be embedded in the corporate genes, doing good while doing well, and the like—my "anything you, the shareholder, can do, I can do better" criterion is *operational*. It provides managers with a workable decision rule for selecting CSR projects: In essence, follow your unique, specialized capabilities. Consider the following cases:

Michael Porter and Mark Kramer described Cisco's initiation of the Networking Academy project in 1997. Cisco realized that its initial CSR program for designing and installing computer networks for schools was impeded by the lack of qualified personnel to maintain the networks.[13] Hiring network experts for schools was constrained by the general shortage of these professionals in both the public and private sectors. Using its *specialized capabilities* as the leading worldwide provider of network equipment, Cisco's engineers developed Web-based, distance learning curricula to train and certify secondary and postsecondary-school students in networking administration. By 2008, the fast-expanding Network Academy trained nine hundred thousand students a year in more than a hundred sixty countries.[14] As Porter and Kramer note: "Because the social goal of the program was tightly linked to Cisco's specialized expertise, the company was able to create a high-quality curriculum rapidly and cost-effectively, creating far more social and economic value than if it had merely contributed cash and equipment to a worthy cause."[15] This laudable program, training a large number of young people all over the world in a highly demanded, high-paying skill, obviously cannot be conducted by Cisco shareholders. Moreover, as is often the case when managers use specialized capabilities in pursuing CSR, the company and its shareholders benefit too—a win-win situation. Cisco, as the industry leader, has a large number of academy graduates who enable IT users around the world and boost demand for Cisco's products. This program obviously meets my criterion for worthy CSR.

Another case that meets my CSR maxim is recounted by John Peloza: Home Depot partnered with KaBOOM!, Inc., a nonprofit outfit that builds playgrounds in U.S. inner cities.[16] Home Depot contributes the program cash, products, and employee volunteers, as well as access to the company's accounting and legal staff. The fact that Home Depot's operations are spread nationally allows local stores to maintain close relationships with KaBOOM!'s playgrounds and provide specific needs on an ongoing basis. Thus, several of Home Depot's unique capabilities are central to this CSR. The local reputational benefit to the retailer is a sweetener to the deal.

A questionable case of worthy CSR, from Porter and Kramer, is American Express's funding of travel and tourism academies in secondary schools aimed at training students for careers in travel agencies, airlines, hotels, and restaurants.[17] The case for this CSR is less straightforward than Cisco's and Home Depot's, since unlike networking administration, the tourism, hotel, and restaurant businesses are not emerging, high-growth areas in short supply, and hence the social need for philanthropic support of such training is not self-evident. Nor are American Express's specialized capabilities in *training* such personnel obvious. True, the company has widespread travel operations, but its core business is finance and credit cards, not training. Furthermore, tourism and hotel management training and education are widely provided by colleges and trade schools, so the need for another provider isn't clear. My "I can do better" maxim is less compelling here.

Clearly inconsistent with my worthy CSR maxim are corporate contributions to charities and NGOs, unrelated to their core business and specialized capabilities, such as AT&T's $100 million gift (in 2008, spread over four years) to address the problem of high school dropouts. "We view it like any other investment we make," said the president of AT&T

Mobility, the company's wireless operations, according to the *New York Times*.[18] Really? Are high school dropouts using cell phones less intensely than graduates? Or, consider Freddie Mac, the government-sponsored mortgage company that essentially collapsed in the 2007 to 2008 financial crisis. Freddie contributed in 2006 over $3 million to foster care and adoption agencies, $1.3 million to public awareness/education causes, $6.1 million for stable homes and stable families, and a further $2.3 million for strengthening families (already stable? or still unstable?), as well as $5.3 million for youth development, for a total 2006 contribution of close to $18 million.[19] One wonders whether channeling that $18 million to hire a few top-notch risk analysts to monitor Freddie's risk that had spiraled out of control would have prevented its financial collapse and megabillion bailout at taxpayers' expense.

Finally, an intriguing question: should CSR activities always benefit the bottom line in addition to furthering social goals? Porter and Kramer, among others, seem to think so: "The essential test that should guide CSR is not whether a cause is worthy but whether it presents an opportunity to create shared value—that is, a meaningful benefit for society that is also valuable to the business."[20] It's undoubtedly laudable to create such "shared value," such as Walmart's campaign to slash 5 percent of its packaging materials by 2013, saving trees and energy along with shareholders' money. I expect that my maxim—conduct those CSR initiatives that are enabled by the company's specialized capabilities—will in most cases generate a shared benefit, particularly for leading companies, such as Cisco and Home Depot, that can capture much of the social benefit. Yet I don't believe that a company should rule out occasional CSR initiatives where using its specialized capabilities creates significant social value, even without a direct benefit to earnings and shareholder value, as long as such initiatives will not prevent the company from achieving its strategic targets. For example, TNT NV, a Dutch delivery and logistics company, has a task force of some fifty employees ready to intervene in emergencies around the world, such as the 2004 Asian tsunami or the 2007 Bangladesh floods.[21] Such a CSR initiative, while obviously "doing good," using TNT's specialized logistical expertise, isn't a revenue generator, yet it doesn't seem to hurt TNT's financials: from 2004 to 2007, its revenues grew 25 percent and its net income rose 31 percent. Doing good *and* doing well is great, but occasionally doing good, period, is fine too.[22]

## The Bad Rap of Cause-Related Philanthropy

CSR purists dismiss cause-related corporate philanthropy—companies' support of social causes or venerated organizations (the Olympics, operas, museums)—as mere or phony publicity. Everyone recounts Philip Morris's $75 million charitable contributions in 1999, accompanied by a lavish publicity campaign about the contributions, and similar "contributions" by others as examples of inefficient, even offensive social activity ("cause-related marketing falls far short of truly strategic philanthropy," say Porter and Kramer[23]).

However, in a comprehensive study of corporate philanthropy from 1989 through 2000, which I conducted with colleagues Christine Petrovits and Suresh Radhakrishanan, we established that cause-related philanthropy can be a very potent marketing device while benefiting society.[24] (This was the first corporate-giving study to distinguish causation—does philanthropy enhance sales or earnings growth?—from mere association—are the two related?) We estimated that for our sample companies, a half-million-dollar contribution increased future sales by a whopping $3 million, on average, and enhanced earnings by almost $800,000—a very respectable return on investment in "doing good." Advertising agencies eat your heart out.

But for corporate philanthropy to be an effective revenue generator, the contributions should favorably affect customer attitudes (we indeed documented the positive impact of contributions on customer satisfaction). When this customer satisfaction conduit is missing—generally in companies such as Boeing that sell to governments or other corporations, whose demand is less affected by philanthropy than individuals—corporate giving doesn't enhance revenues materially.

For such businesses, unless it clearly affects other objectives—corporate lobbying, or employee morale—such CSR is better left to shareholders. So I don't see anything wrong with cause-related philanthropy. Done well, it's good for business and society. Even Friedman would not object (though it's hard to confirm now).

## Looking over the Precipice: CSR as Insurance

I have so far dealt with the business *upside* of CSR: the aspect of doing well by doing good. This business upside, however, is at best modest—I have yet to encounter a company whose main revenue generator is CSR—and generally pales against the potential downside resulting from corporate social misbehavior or environmental mishaps. Union Carbide's December 1984 Bhopal, India, gas-leak disaster, which killed thousands and seriously hurt tens of thousands of people, is still—a quarter-century later—not fully resolved.[25] A large area in Bhopal is yet to be cleaned up, and Dow Chemical, which acquired Union Carbide in 2001, is still haunted by claims and ill will dating back to the 1984 tragedy.

Not just disasters on the scale of Union Carbide in Bhopal, the Exxon Valdez oil spill in Alaska's Prince William Sound, and, of course, the most recent 2010 BP deep-sea oil spill in the Gulf of Mexico seriously disrupt companies' operations, adversely affect their shareholders, and often devastate entire communities. Even indirect company involvement in mishaps can be very damaging, as in the case of the New Zealand cooperative Fonterra Group, a large dairy products company, which owned 43 percent of the Sanlu Group, a Chinese dairy company. Sanlu, along with other Chinese dairy producers, was exposed in autumn 2008 as producing and marketing milk and dairy products contaminated with the industrial chemical melanin, causing several infants' death and hospitalizing close to fifty thousand children. Fonterra had to write off its investment in the Chinese company due to its fast-vanishing brand value after the scandal. But this was the least of

Fonterra's problems. The New Zealand company, with three representatives on Sanlu's board, was widely criticized for waiting six weeks before alerting government officials in Wellington to the milk contamination at Sanlu, thereby prolonging the harm to children.[26] The damage to Fonterra's reputation has been serious.

Managers often pay a heavy price for social misbehavior. (Who will forget BP CEO Tony Hayward's memorable line before being shown the door, "I'd like my life back," in the midst of the Gulf disaster?) The widespread corruption scandal at Siemens, surfacing in 2006, cost its highly successful CEO Klaus Kleinfeld his job in April 2007, despite Siemens' stock beating the S&P 500 handily during his tenure. Kleinfeld got off relatively lightly; soon after his firing from Siemens, he became Alcoa's CEO. On the other hand, Richard Ness, head of Newmont's mining operations in Indonesia, was put on trial in Jakarta for criminal negligence in an alleged water-pollution case around Newmont's gold mine, facing a ten-year prison sentence (Newmont and Ness were exonerated in 2007 after a twenty-one-month trial).

Thus, while the *business* case of CSR as creating shareholder value is modest, at best, the case of CSR as insurance, avoiding or mitigating the consequences of social or environmental mishaps, is compelling. This *value-preserving* role of CSR, which often lies in the shadow of the glamorous and widely publicized "shared value creation"—like GE's ecomagination, which presumably addresses "some of the world's big challenges, while making money for shareholders"—deserves much of managers' attention.

Leveraging CSR for risk mitigation can be a powerful component of a company's strategy. CSR functions here on two levels. First, companies that routinely engage in CSR activities generally consider the impact of social or environmental mishaps on their operations more carefully than non-CSR firms and will therefore attempt to prevent such mishaps. Second, CSR also functions as a signal to outsiders of reliability and forthrightness, of good corporate citizenship, and of ethical behavior. When mishaps happen, such as human rights violations, contaminated products, or corrupt corporate behavior, companies with substantial social capital—trust and networks, built on CSR—will likely weather the storm better than others. Their mishap will often be considered an aberration, giving the business the benefit of the doubt and precious time to manage the scandal.[27]

## Sounds Good, but Does It Really Work?

Specific cases of successful CSR as insurance are difficult to come by because one never knows what would have happened without the CSR. Would the repercussions of Mattel's massive lead-contaminated toy recall in 2007 or Gap's child labor problems in India in the same year have been more serious were these companies not involved in extensive CSR activities? We will never know. However, large sample studies, controlling for the extent and type of company CSR, provide a clue. Thus, for example, Walter Blacconiere and Dennis Patten measured the impact of the news of Union Carbide's Bhopal tragedy on the stocks of *other* chemical companies (Union Carbide's own capitalization fell by almost 30 percent on the news).[28] Their evidence shows that while the overall impact of the Bhopal news on chemical stocks was negative, reflecting the expected costs of post-Bhopal increased regulation of the industry and the negative reaction of local communities around the world to chemical operations and facility expansion in their midst, the extent of the impact on the individual company price depended on its disclosure in financial reports of environmental policies and procedures. An extensive disclosure generally correlates with environmentally responsive corporate behavior: companies making public commitments to cut pollution or to increase investment in environmental control facilities, for example, will usually disclose these commitments publicly. The researchers' evidence thus indicates that the negative price reaction to the Bhopal news was *mitigated* by the extent of environmental disclosure by the company, suggesting that investors expected a higher level of CSR activity to shield the company to some extent from the public wrath of Union Carbide's mishap.[29]

A recent study by Paul Godfrey, Craig Merrill, and Jared Hansen examines whether the share price impact of corporate negative events, such as customer or competitor lawsuits or investigations by government regulatory entities, is tempered by their CSR activities.[30] The extent of these activities was measured by the Socrates ratings of companies, reflecting such CSR aspects as community involvement, corporate governance, employee relations, environmental stewardship, diversity, and product quality (published by KLD Research & Analytics, Inc.). The statistical findings of the study indicate that higher levels of CSR activities *moderated* the stock price impact of news about negative corporate events. CSR thus seems to confer a certain insurance affect on companies against social and environmental setbacks. Investors apparently believe that regulators and customers will be more forgiving of the misbehavior of companies doing good, giving them the benefit of the doubt. This evidence is obviously preliminary and lacking in specificity (What types of CSR activities are effective insurers? How long into a scandal does CSR protection last?), but it lends support for the CSR as insurance argument. Summarized succinctly by *The Economist*: "Most of the rhetoric on CSR may be about doing the right thing and trumping competitors, but much of the reality is plain risk management. It involves limiting the damage to the brand and the bottom line that can be inflicted by a bad press and consumer boycotts, as well as dealing with the threat of legal action."[31]

Recall that CSR operates as insurance in two ways: First, *mishap mitigation*—firms actively engaged in CSR likely consider the impact of social or environmental misdeeds on various constituencies more carefully than those unfamiliar with CSR, and will therefore have appropriate processes and internal control systems to prevent mishaps and react quickly when they occur. CSR awareness mitigates negative events.[32] Second, *social capital*—CSR builds social capital which, once a negative social or environmental event occurs, shields the company to some extent from public sanctions and other adverse consequences, such as customer desertion. Social capital—networks, norms, and trust that enable participants to act jointly more effectively[33]—is created and maintained by well-targeted and executed CSR activities. These activities include involvement in social programs in the communities the company operates in; partnerships with local governments to advance health and education causes (such as Merck's partnership with the Bill & Melinda Gates Foundation and the government of Botswana to battle AIDS); and companies getting together with industry peers, governments, and NGOs to establish codes of conduct. One such code is the Extractive Industries Transparency Initiative, launched in 2002 by Tony Blair, to tackle government corruption in resource-rich nations.[34] Such efforts to forge multistakeholder networks—create social capital—foster CSR as insurance.

### Social Capital: The Devil They Know

We often forgive or give the benefit of the doubt to relatives, close friends, and trusted colleagues, even for committing serious offenses. For the offender, this forgiveness or benefit of the doubt is the return on investment in *social capital*. The social capital built by CSR includes the networks and relationships with local governments, NGOs, and charities, as well as the norms and codes of conduct established with industry peers, regulators, and organizations, such as the UN (the Kimberley Process, a certification procedure to prevent trade in blood diamonds, for example), and the *trust* built among members of the CSR network. That social capital and trust enable companies, it is often argued, to mitigate the consequences of social and environmental mishaps. Sounds good, but how exactly does it work?

Trust among network members—the essence of social capital—is, surprisingly, at the core of most business activities. The Nobel Laureate economist Kenneth Arrow, known for his rigorous, formal (namely, mathematical) approach to economics, ventured into the marshy field of trust and cooperative behavior, concluding: "Virtually every commercial transaction has within itself an element of trust, certainly any transaction conducted over a period of time."[35] Thus, when you buy a car with a five-year warranty, you trust the manufacturer to be there when prob-lems arise and abide by the warranty terms; or, when you pay a premium price for organic food, you trust the retailer that the items you bought were indeed organically grown. These and many other transactions will obviously not take place, or have their terms radically changed, without the trust between the parties to the deal. Arrow went further, conjectur-ing that much of the economic backwardness worldwide can be attrib-uted to the lack of mutual confidence. The low participation of individuals in the stock markets of many developing countries, believing that stock prices are rigged and that minority shareholders are often exploited, is an example of economic backwardness due to lack of trust.

How is business trust created and maintained? You guessed it—by devel-oping social capital. People in high social-capital communities act together more effectively because they trust each other due to the ability of the community (network) to punish deviants effectively or as a result of moral attitudes imprinted by education, such as the virtues of charitable contri-butions.[36] Thus, social capital enhances personal trust, which in turn increases economic efficiency and development, mostly by avoiding costly legal mechanisms and cumbersome contracts.[37] Indeed, researchers docu-ment that social capital in Italy plays an important role in the degree of financial development across different regions of the country (increasing the likelihood of people using checks, investing in stocks, and increasing the level of bank deposits, all enhancing economic development).[38] Using the World Values Survey for measuring cross-country trust, Stephen Knack and Philip Keefer show that trust and civic cooperation (social capital) are positively associated with stronger national economic performance.[39]

That's the raison d'être of CSR initiatives as insurance against the repercussions of social or environmental mishaps. The social capital created by CSR, building trust among members of the network—businesses, regulators, local governments, and NGOs—creates a strong shared interest in the continued success of the entire enterprise of educational, health, or environmental programs, motivating network members to support each other in time of need to continue deriving the benefits of organizational success.

# Parting the Mist: Reputation, Brand, Image

The CSR literature is replete with claims that companies "risk their reputation"—their most valuable asset—ignoring CSR; that CSR is critical to the "company's image," which is key to its survival; that CSR builds a reservoir of *goodwill* that comes in handy during crisis; and that causing social or environmental harms threatens the *credibility* of a company and its *license to operate*. Lurking in the background are strong business motives. CSR consultancies promise to protect and enhance a company's reputation, image, and goodwill, and obtaining a social performance certification (SA 8000, ISO 14000, ISO 14001, or similarly helpful names) protects the company's *brand*. Don't feel guilty for being bewildered; reputation, image, goodwill, credibility, and the like are ill-defined, largely vacuous concepts. As far as the company's "license to operate" is concerned, who exactly grants such licenses? Greenpeace? PETA? However, when dealing with CSR, you are bound to get entangled sooner or later in discussions involving these concepts, so let me part the mist and inject substance into the cloud.

## The Economist's View of Corporate Reputation

Kia Motors, a South Korean car manufacturer, offers a ten-year warranty on its cars in the United States, whereas Honda gets away with a three-year warranty on similar vehicles. Is Honda stingy? No, its reputation for car quality is impeccable, while Kia, a relative newcomer, has yet to establish a solid reputation for quality. In lieu of such a reputation, Kia offers a seven-year warranty edge over Honda.

So, this is reputation. It is the seller's guarantee for the quality or more generally for contractual performance regarding a product or a service, when buyers cannot perfectly observe quality at time of purchase. At the end of a cab ride in New York City, you can perfectly observe the "quality" of the ride: arrival in time at stated location, attitude of driver, tidiness of car, and so on, and compensate the cabbie accordingly (no, low, or a large tip). Therefore, you couldn't care less about the reputation of the driver (nor does he care about yours). It's the same with restaurant waiters or booksellers. In contrast, when you purchase a car, sign a contract for house renovation, visit a doctor, or hire an IT consultant, you cannot perfectly observe the quality (contractual performance) of the ordered product or service at the time of purchase or even delivery (computer systems crashing the day after they were installed). In such cases of incomplete observability, the seller's reputation serves as a *quality guarantee*. That's when reputation really matters. You will not hire just any house renovator or IT consultant, or visit the first doctor in the Yellow Pages list. You will spend time investigating their reputation. Accordingly, lacking Honda's reputation for quality, Kia has to compensate car buyers with a seven-year-longer car warranty.[40]

This economic concept of reputation as a quality guarantee has important implications. Primarily, it establishes reputation as a corporate asset—a source of future revenues or cost savings. Reputation allows its owners to charge higher prices; Harvard's and Wharton's business school tuitions are substantially higher than those of less reputable business schools, and Amazon charges higher prices for the same book than less known online booksellers, reflecting Amazon's solid reputation for on-time delivery and credit card security. Reputation also saves costs by allowing sellers to offer shorter and restricted warranties and by avoiding the expensive practices of less reputable retailers, such as offering unlimited returns with full refunds. Reputation is obviously worth maintaining and enhancing by a commitment to quality—delivering on the promise—and by a credible disclosure, certified by a third party, of quality records, such as hospitals and doctors disclosing success or failure rates of medical practices, professional schools revealing graduate salaries, airlines publishing records of on-time arrival and lost baggage, and restaurants proclaiming "under same ownership since 1950." Reputation for quality is indeed among the most important assets a business has.

In this sense, the economic concept of reputation is synonymous with that of a *brand*. Many confuse brands with name recognition. Most people still identify Polaroid with an innovative instant camera, but the company is long gone and so is its brand. Everyone recognizes Yahoo!, but this search engine struggles to compete. Not much of a brand there either. What characterizes a brand is the ability of its owner to charge a *premium price* over competitors—Bayer aspirin, for example—and/or to consistently command a leading market share, like Google. This is very different and much harder to maintain than name recognition. A brand is primarily enabled by the product's reputation for quality. The price premium on branded products is the buyers' payment for the quality guarantee, given unobserved product quality at time of purchase. In contrast to these clearly defined and quantifiable concepts, image, and stature—popular terms in the CSR vocabulary—are just vacuous phrases in relation to business. And yes, goodwill in a business context is an accounting term, indicating the difference between the price paid for a business entity and the fair value of its net assets.

## CSR to the Rescue?

So, what do reputation or brand have to do with CSR? Not much really, despite activists' claims to the contrary. Reputation is determined by customers, the quality arbiters of the company's products or services, and is rarely affected by the company's social and environmental policies. Exxon, the largest and most successful oil company in the world, obviously has an impressive reputation among its customers (and investors, for that matter), yet is a pariah among environmentalists. Walmart, with $422 billion sales in 2010, obviously enjoys a commanding reputation among its customers, yet "socially responsible funds" shun it because it sells firearms and has objectionable labor practices, or because of the harm it causes small store owners in its vicinity. In contrast, BP has for a long time been the darling of environmentalists and social activists, not the least for effectively changing its name from British Petroleum—so "out"—to the politically correct Beyond Petroleum.[41] Yet, all its "do gooding," or talk about it, didn't prevent BP from suffering serious setbacks to its reputation, profitability, and stock performance when it got mired in serious refinery accidents in Texas and criminal probes of corrosion and oil spills in Alaska in 2005 and 2007, as well as involved in various energy price manipulation schemes, not to speak of the disastrous 2010 oil spill in the Gulf of Mexico.[42]

Does a company have a reputation or image independent of its products' quality, as often claimed in the CSR literature? I doubt it. Dell Computers had a long-standing reputation as a leading-edge, innovative company, but in 2005 when its products became a commodity—indistinguishable from competitors'—gone was the company's innovator reputation. Kodak's reputation diminished due to its struggling products. The dependence of a company's reputation on the quality of its products is also clear from the fact that even serious social or environmental scandals don't permanently impair a company with high-quality products. Nike, which was widely ostracized in the early 1990s for its suppliers' abusive labor practices, weathered the storm without permanent scars, and McDonald's continuous skirmishes with animal rights activists ("scalding chickens alive is the wrong way to prepare meat for a McNugget," says PETA) didn't slow its relentless growth worldwide.

Corporate reputation or brand is indeed a very important asset, but it is not enhanced or detracted in a major way by CSR activities or the lack thereof. Keep delivering the contractual promise—high product quality and service at reasonable prices—and your reputation among customers and investors will be intact, while your "license to operate," whatever this means, will not be seriously questioned. CSR or reputation consultants cannot repair the damage done by faulty products and poor service.

## Operating Instructions

- **DON'T FEEL GUILTY.** First and foremost, don't be defensive if you are not a CSR leader. As long as you conduct your business well—earn more on shareholders' investment than they can on their own (cost of capital) and avoid product recalls, serious employee and safety issues, or corrupt business practices—you create a very substantial value for shareholders and society. Unilever, an Anglo-Dutch consumer-goods company, documented with

Oxfam, a poverty relief agency, that in Indonesia, its normal business activity supports three hundred thousand equivalent full-time jobs, creates a total economic value of $630 million a year, and pays $130 million annually in taxes to the Indonesian government.[43] How many NGOs or charities create this level of social value in one country in a year or even a decade?

- **THE BENEFITS OF CSR AS INSURANCE.** Ignoring CSR altogether is no longer an option for managers, even those running a successful business. You have to do something. The biggest bang for the CSR buck is obtained from the creation of social capital—a network of trust—for risk mitigation. This is crucial for companies vulnerable to social and environmental mishaps, particularly businesses having long supply chains with important links outside the home country, as well as companies having high environmental impact, such as utilities, oil and gas, mining, and chemical enterprises. Consumer products companies susceptible to product contamination and safety issues are particularly vulnerable to consumer boycotts and negative media coverage. Large firms and particularly industry leaders are also vulnerable since activists often single them out because they have much to lose from scandals and therefore are expected to yield quickly to pressure. (No wonder that in recent years the social activists' hit list was led by Nike, Nestlé, Coca-Cola, McDonald's, Walmart, and Exxon, all sector leaders.) Intangibles-intensive companies whose major assets are specific to the firm (e.g., R&D, patents, brands, or trademarks) are also vulnerable to scandals and bad press (you can't sell your R&D) and therefore could also use CSR insurance. Setting up cooperative CSR projects with local governments and NGOs, establishing industry standards of conduct and codes, and obtaining good-conduct certification from reputable organizations is the essence of the social capital underlying the CSR-as-insurance practices.

- **DO GOOD.** Beyond insurance, look for opportunities to employ the company's specialized capabilities in furthering social and environmental causes. If such initiatives contribute to the bottom line (Porter and Kramer's "shared value")—great. If not, don't rule them out, as long as they don't seriously detract from your ability to meet the company's strategic targets. Doing good even without doing well for oneself is meritorious.

- **CHEAP TALK WON'T GET YOU LOVE.** Analyzing the management presentations in quarterly conference calls of companies with analysts and investors, I found an interesting behavior: managers of "sin companies"—gambling, tobacco, arms producers, oil and coal—mention CSR terms, like social responsibility, sustainability, stakeholders, climate change, and philanthropy, much more frequently than managers of other companies. While managers of so-called virtuous companies mentioned CSR terms in 28 percent of the calls I examined, managers of defense companies talked about CSR in 57 percent of the calls; utilities' executives, in 56 percent of the calls; and oil and coal managers, in 31.3 percent of the calls. Yet all this CSR speak didn't change the stigma of sin stocks among socially responsible funds and "conscientious" investors. Don't waste time on cheap talk.

- **THE BUSINESS ALWAYS COMES FIRST.** When confronted by social or environmental activists, be flexible and responsive, but never compromise core business assets or plans. Remember, if you don't create economic value from your business, you won't be socially responsible for long.

- **BEWARE THE GLASS HOUSE SYNDROME.** Finally, before you embark on correcting the world and making a social or environmental difference, make sure your house is in order. There is nothing worse than a phony "world repairer." Enron was a large civic and charitable contributor in the Houston area. BP's pipeline corrosion, lax refinery safety measures, manipulation of energy prices, and massive oil spills made a mockery of its strong commitment to environmental and social causes. Royal Dutch Shell, another major oil company committed to sustainability, overstated its publicly reported oil reserves data. U.S. utilities Duke Energy and Dominion asked customers to pay a little extra for electricity to foster renewable energy, yet spent only a fraction of the money collected furthering this cause, and were accordingly labeled as selling "bragging rights."[44]

## Chapter 10

# In the Long Run, We're All Dead

## Why the Much-Maligned Investor Short-Termism and Managerial Myopia Are Myths

➡ Surprise: long-term investors dominate capital markets.

➡ Investors' myopia is often an excuse for ill-advised managerial decisions.

➡ Monitoring long-term projects requires short-term benchmarks, but that's not myopia.

➡ Successful managers manage both the short and the long term.

"Breaking the Short-Term Cycle" is the dramatic banner of a joint call for action by the influential Business Roundtable and the CFA Institute aimed at freeing managers from the shackles of all those pesky short-term investors:

> *The Panel agrees that an obsession with meeting short-term expectations of varying constituencies too often hinders corporate managers and all types of investors from focusing on long-term value creation.*[1]

Not to be outdone, a high-level commission established by the U.S. Chamber of Commerce in 2007 joined the chorus:

*The Commission believes that there is too much focus on the short-term performance of U.S. companies. The pressure for businesses to "hit" their targets can be overwhelming and creates adverse incentives to forgo value-added investments in long-term projects.*[2]

Many managers' too believe in the myopia affliction. Daniel Vasella, while CEO of the major pharmaceutical company Novartis, stated:

*The men and women running public companies often think of little else [than meeting quarterly targets]. They become preoccupied with short-term "success," a mindset that can hamper or even destroy long-term performance.*[3]

And what exactly is this deleterious myopia? The Business Roundtable / CFA Institute Panel clarified:

*Short-termism refers to the excessive focus of some corporate leaders, investors, and analysts on short-term, quarterly earnings and a lack of attention to the strategy, fundamentals, and conventional approaches to long-term value creation.*[4]

So, here is the vicious cycle: investors' "obsession" with corporate quarterly earnings meeting or exceeding predetermined targets—consensus analysts' estimates or last year's same quarter earnings—forces managers to comply by sacrificing corporate long-term growth for meeting short-term targets, to the detriment of patient investors and the economy at large. And why are investors so shortsighted? Presumably because most institutional investors report on a quarterly basis to their shareholders on their performance and therefore insist that the companies they invest in meet stringent short-term profitability targets.

"The tragedy of science," Thomas Huxley famously said, "is the slaying of a beautiful theory by an ugly fact." Consider Amazon: on October 24, 2006, the company disclosed that its third-quarter 2006 earnings had slid 37 percent from the previous year. How did myopic investors "obsessed" with quarterly earnings react to this calamity? They bid Amazon's stock price *up* by 14.6 percent (the S&P 500 advanced 0.4 percent). How come? Amazon's modest revenue growth in the third quarter may have sweetened the earnings drop, but the main reason for the stock price rise was the explanation the company gave for the profit slide: it had made heavy investments in technology and Web content, aimed at future growth. So much for investors' indifference to long-term growth. Undeterred by investors' alleged myopia, Amazon continued to enhance long-term investment in technology and content—$451 million, $662 million, and $818 million in 2005, 2006, and 2007, respectively—despite the considerable hits to quarterly earnings, while investors drove up Amazon's stock price from $37.68 on October 25, 2006, to $92.64 at end of 2007, 150 percent growth! Some short-termism.

Perhaps Internet companies, like Amazon, play by different rules and investors are more patient with them. The bricks-and-mortar Toyota, on August 3, 2005, reported a disappointing 6.9 percent fall in quarterly earnings and an even larger 9.7 percent decline in operating income. Analysts were caught sleeping at the wheel; their consensus estimate of Toyota's operating income for the quarter ended June 30, 2005, was $3.98 billion, compared with the reported $3.64 billion profit. If this was not sufficiently alarming for short-term-oriented investors, the reasons Toyota gave for the profit disappointment should have been. The world's second-largest car manufacturer at the time decided to do the opposite of short-termism—to accelerate long-term investments: it increased R&D by 13 percent and capital expenditures by a whopping 23 percent, depressing quarterly earnings in the process. Myopic investors would have reacted swiftly and harshly to the sacrifice of short-term profits for future, uncertain growth, but here is what happened. Toyota's American depositary receipt (ADR) stock price in the United States decreased from $76.95 on August 2, 2005 (the day preceding the earnings announcement) to $76.13 on August 4, 2005 (the S&P 500 dropped 0.7 percent)—a measly 1 percent price decline for an almost 10 percent drop in operating income. But a week later, on August 12, 2005, Toyota's stock price gingerly bounced back to $80. Where had all the myopic investors gone?

As I show next, backed by "ugly facts," Amazon and Toyota are by no means aberrations. Investors by and large are far from myopic, obsessed with quarterly earnings. In fact, they are often surprisingly tolerant of disappointments and stick with companies, such as the dot.coms of the late 1990s and more recently biotech companies, despite their losses, while investing for the long term. Investors' myopia is, like so many other things in capital markets, a myth. In fact, a harmful myth.

My concern with the widespread belief in short-termism goes far beyond slaying a myth. The widely held perception of short-term investors dominating capital markets seriously distorts the decisions of the many managers who believe they have to cater to investors' myopic whims by beating analysts' consensus estimates by any means and continuously reporting increasing EPS. Such beliefs in myopic investors trigger most of the manipulations of financial reports and often lead to detrimental decisions, such as cutting R&D and maintenance, making ill-advised acquisitions, or repurchasing shares in order to make the numbers. It is, therefore, of considerable importance to examine the investors' myopia allegation rigorously and to properly inform managers how best to satisfy their shareholders' needs.

## Whence Myopia?

Where did the pervasive and persistent belief in myopic capital markets come from? I trace the emergence of the belief in myopia to the sharp and protracted decline in U.S. productivity (output per hour) in the 1970s and 1980s, which triggered a serious soul-searching among academics, policy makers, and think tanks to identify the causes of the productivity decline and prescribe remedial policies. The data was indeed disturbing. From annual productivity growth rates of 2.5 percent to 2.7 percent during the 1950s and 1960s, U.S. annual productivity rates plunged to 1.7 percent, on average, from 1972 to 1978, further dropping to 1.2 percent from 1978 to 1987, and improving only slightly to 1.5 percent from 1987 to 1994.[5] This lingering productivity slump—slowing economic growth—seemed particularly ominous at the time when compared with Japan's astounding 6 percent annual growth of productivity from 1970 to 1986.[6] Thus, Japan and, to a somewhat lesser extent, Germany demonstrated that productivity declines and the consequent hits to the standard of living are not a force majeure. There must be, therefore, systemic reasons, unique to the U.S. economy, causing the decline. But what are these reasons?

The culprit, almost by acclaim of think tanks and pundits, was the U.S. capital market, which differed substantially by size, structure, and impact on the corporate sector from the capital markets of Japan and Germany, the major outperforming economies at the time. During the productivity slump, U.S. capital markets were increasingly dominated by institutional investors whose performance was and still is reported quarterly to their shareholders and the public at large. Such frequent reporting, went the argument, drove financial institutions to invest for short-term performance; they achieved that by pressuring corporate managers to focus on meeting strict quarterly and annual earnings targets, with the threat of sharp price declines for targets missed. And if long-term corporate growth opportunities, such as by investing in R&D, brands, or technology, have to be sacrificed at the quarterly EPS altar, so be it.[7]

The argument for investor-induced managerial myopia seems particularly compelling when comparing American managers in the 1980s with their Japanese counterparts, largely immune to investors' pressure because of the interlocking ownership of Japanese corporations within cozy, mutually supportive business groups (*keiretsu*). Free from the need to meet quarterly targets, Japanese and German managers could focus on long-term growth and global market-share expansion, driving the impressive performance of their companies and national economies in the process. The increasing prowess of foreign companies in the 1980s and early 1990s—the likes of Toyota, Sony, Mitsubishi, and Daimler-Benz, often at the expense of their American competitors—lend considerable credence to the myopia argument about U.S. investors and managers.

Thus, in a 1995 report to the Competitiveness Policy Council, aptly titled "Lifting All Boats," Robert Denham and the strategy pioneer Michael Porter wrote:

> *Today's managers fear that institutional investors are too quick to divest, generating pressure on firms to underfund certain long-term or intangible investments in order to maintain growth in short-term earnings … Increasingly, the issue is whether the Continental European and East Asian systems of corporate governance, characterized by stable, sizable, and active institutional shareholders, provide an advantage to foreign firms in terms of greater support for long-term investment.* [8]

The scenario of short-term-oriented investors, particularly the fast-growing institutional ones, driving corporate managers to myopic decisions that harm their companies and the economy at large quickly gained traction and popularity. Management guru Peter Drucker reported that 82 percent of U.S. CEOs blamed the stock market's focus on short-term accounting earnings for the drop in long-term investment. [9] And the American Business Conference emphatically stated in 1991:

> *There is almost universal agreement that the competitiveness of U.S. industry has slipped dramatically in the past two decades. This slippage in part has been attributed to the "short-term" focus of investors, CEOs, and Boards of Directors. Our failure to invest for the long term has manifested itself in a reduced tendency to put capital at risk unless it is accompanied by a strong prospect for near-term profits.* [10]

Among the proposed remedies for this vicious investors–managers myopia cycle were: educate investors, particularly institutions, about the merits of long-term investment; impose new regulations and taxes (on short-term capital gains, for example); increase managerial incentives for corporate long-term investments; and change accounting rules (capitalize—recognize as assets—R&D, brands, and IT investments) to avoid the managerial disincentives from the hits to earnings from the expensing of these investments. Thus, a 1992 report on three roundtables on financing technology, sponsored jointly by the U.S. departments of Commerce and Treasury, opened with the question: "Are U.S. investors and capital markets providing adequate funds for the long-term investments in technology needed by U.S. companies to meet global competition?"[11] Answering the question in the negative, the report highlights the accounting aspect of the problem:

*The long-term health of the company may require extensive expenditures for technology, which accounting standards require to be charged to expense, and which will reduce quarterly earnings. If the earnings are less than projected by the securities analysts, speculators often will sell and the market price will fall. Thus, actions to enhance the long-term earnings capacity of the company can result in short-term loss of stock value.*[12]

Short-termism thus became the "usual suspect" of the productivity and economic woes in the 1970s and 1980s.

## The End of Short-Termism? You Wish.

The claim of a capital market-driven managerial myopia was advanced as a major cause of the U.S. economic stagnation of the 1970s and 1980s. One would therefore expect this claim to fade away with the robust economic performance and particularly the resurgent productivity growth of the U.S. economy, which started in the mid-1990s. Fueled primarily by the corporate sector's heavy investment in information technology, R&D, brands, human resources, and physical assets, the U.S. economy embarked on a growth path unprecedented since World War II, surpassing the records of the 1950s and 1960s, and those of many other developed nations. During the ten-year period 1997 through 2006, the business sector's average annual productivity gain was 3.1 percent, and the manufacturing sector had a blazing annual gain of 4.7 percent over that period.[13] As for international comparisons, the U.S. average annual growth rate of GDP from 1996 to 2006 was 3.2 percent, compared with 1.1 percent and 1.5 percent for the presumed long-termers, Japan and Germany, respectively.[14] These sustained economic gains, primarily generated by the business sector, should have given pause to believers in managerial short-termism. They did not.

Nor did the technology bubble of the late 1990s—stoked by millions of investors pouring untold billions of dollars into upstart dot. com, telecom, and biotech companies racking up massive losses while offering, at best, a vague promise of far-distant profits—change people's minds about the prevalence of short-term investors focused on quarterly profits. Even investors in Amazon, one of the few survivors of the 1990s dot.com debacle, endured eight years of losses before seeing the company report its first, albeit slim, net income (before extraordinary items) of $35.3 million in 2003. Massive investments in chronically losing enterprises, heavily spending on R&D, brands, information technology, and other long-term investments, are not exactly a behavior typical of short-term, earnings-obsessed investors.

But unlike General Douglas MacArthur's "old soldiers" who "just fade away," the belief in myopic investors forcing short-termism on corporate managers refuses to comply, as made recently clear by the proclamations of the influential business organizations that lead this chapter and the writings of commentators and experts, such as the highly respected Vanguard founder John Bogle, who devoted considerable space in his 2005 book, *The Battle for the Soul of Capitalism*, to investors' and managers' myopia:

> *The emphasis on short-term price came to overwhelm the reality of long-term value, as investors failed to honor the distinction between investment and speculation... Owners and managers must unite in the task of returning the focus of corporate strategy and corporate information alike to long-term financial goals... Quarterly earnings guidance, pernicious yet still omnipresent, should be eliminated.*[15]

And in 2007, Peer Steinbrück, then German finance minister, told the *Financial Times* that "German companies should resist the short-termism of Anglo-American corporate reporting... The German model—medium to long-term industrial planning—worked even if that was not compatible with short-term aims of hedge funds."[16]

True, pundits may not do much economic harm, but corporate managers' apparent conviction that investors are myopic and that corporate strategy has to accommodate their short-termism has serious consequences indeed. A 2003 CFO survey found that "80% of survey participants report that they would decrease discretionary spending on R&D, advertising and maintenance to meet an earnings target. More than half (55.3%) state that they would delay starting a new project to meet an earnings target, even when such a delay entails a small sacrifice in value."[17] This is serious stuff, and that's why I devote considerable space to the myopia argument. The belief in investors' myopia, whether founded or not, affects managerial long-term decisions—to the detriment of investors and the economy at large.[18] It's time to consider the evidence.

## What's in a Stock Price?

Economic theory tells us that stock prices primarily reflect the current value of the company's net assets and its earnings growth potential. For no-growth companies, share value equals asset value, whereas the prices of growth stocks primarily reflect the companies' growth potential. This provides a unique opportunity to empirically test the investor myopia claim: if investors are predominantly short-term oriented, then stock prices should primarily reflect current asset values and *near-term* earnings. Myopic investors, by definition, heavily discount or ignore altogether the long-term earnings prospects of companies. That's what myopia is: nearsightedness regarding longer-term earnings. Here then is a powerful test of investors' myopia: do investors largely ignore the long-term earnings prospects of companies?

As if made to order, Tom Copeland, Aaron Dolgoff, and Alberto Moel performed such a comprehensive test for the S&P 500 companies during the 1992–1998 period.[19] Specifically, the researchers (partners in two major consultancies) estimated the effect on stock prices of revisions in near-term (one and two years ahead) earnings forecasts by analysts and the changes in long-term (three to five years) analysts' earnings forecasts. Such forecast revisions are ubiquitous and when announced trigger share price changes. To recap: if myopic investors dominate markets, they will largely ignore revisions of analysts' long-term earnings forecasts, whereas short-term forecast revisions will dominate investors' attention. The research findings were striking, as summarized by the authors:

> *This research is consistent with an interpretation that shareholder returns [stock price changes] in the current year are* primarily *related to expectations about long-term performance [earnings]. Our results run counter to the "conventional wisdom" that all the market cares about is that a company hits or exceeds its quarterly earnings target, and suggest that share prices respond to changes in short-term earnings only insofar that they are signals of long-term earnings potential (emphasis mine).*[20]

I couldn't have said it better.[21]

For the still unconvinced, I took a different approach to examine the myopia issue and computed the portion of the stock price reflecting the short term: the value of the enterprise net assets (owners' equity) and next year's expected earnings—the presumed focus of myopic investors—and by default the portion of the stock price reflecting the corporate long-term growth potential. Once more, myopic investors should largely ignore the latter. This analysis was done by regressing (relating statistically) the market value (capitalization) of companies on their balance-sheet value of net assets and analysts' consensus forecast of earnings next year. This regression yields an estimate of the portion of the stock price reflecting the short term: current asset values and near-term earnings.[22] The remaining portion of the stock price, by default, primarily reflects the value investors place on the long-term growth prospects of the company, a lowly value for myopic investors.

Figure 10-1 presents, for a broad range of major industries, the average portion of stock prices *unrelated* to short-term drivers (asset values and next-year expected earnings), that is, the portion of the share price reflecting long-term growth prospects. The results are, once more, striking. For most industries, more than half of the share value reflects long-term growth! For some industries—oil and gas, measuring and medical equipment, and computers—the long-term portion of the stock price reaches 60 percent to 70 percent. Naturally, sectors with significant growth potential occupy the top half of the figure, whereas low-growth sectors—insurance, retail, and financial trading—populate the bottom half, where stock prices reflect primarily short-term value drivers.[23] Overall, the message of figure 10-1—a large portion of the stock price of U.S. companies reflects long-term growth potential—is clearly inconsistent with myopic capital markets.

You don't have to be an econometrician (a person like me, obsessed with statistical analysis) to appreciate these findings. Stripped of statistical jargon, they strongly indicate that investors *highly value* the long-term growth prospects of companies, clearly supporting managers' investment in long-term growth. Managers who cater to the alleged myopic whims of investors shoot themselves (and their shareholders) in the foot. The figure also explains the two cases leading this chapter—Amazon and Toyota—in which investors shrugged off dismal quarterly results and reacted enthusiastically to the improved long-term prospects promised by the increased R&D and capital expenditures of these companies.

FIGURE 10-1

## Long-term-driven market value (%)

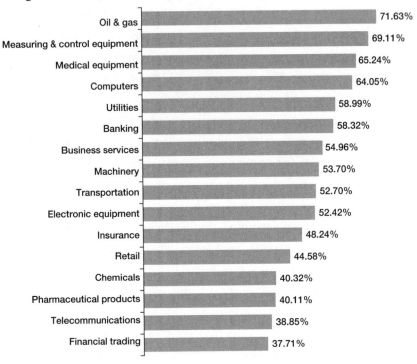

| | |
|---|---|
| Oil & gas | 71.63% |
| Measuring & control equipment | 69.11% |
| Medical equipment | 65.24% |
| Computers | 64.05% |
| Utilities | 58.99% |
| Banking | 58.32% |
| Business services | 54.96% |
| Machinery | 53.70% |
| Transportation | 52.70% |
| Electronic equipment | 52.42% |
| Insurance | 48.24% |
| Retail | 44.58% |
| Chemicals | 40.32% |
| Pharmaceutical products | 40.11% |
| Telecommunications | 38.85% |
| Financial trading | 37.71% |

*Source:* Compustat and I/B/E/S.

Finally, the clincher: if investors' short-termism forces managers to sacrifice future growth for meeting quarterly targets, then privately held companies, unbeholden to myopic investors, should outperform operationally, over the long-term, similar publicly held companies whose managers are subject to the "tyranny of capital markets." Such a straightforward test was conducted by Jeffrey Coles, Michael Lemmon, and Lalitha Naveen, and its findings will disappoint the myopia crowd: both the mean operating-profit-to-sales ratio and the mean net-profit-to-sales—key profitability measures—of publicly held companies are more than double the profits of their privately held brethren.[24] There are undoubtedly several reasons for this surprising finding, but let me suggest a major one: investors', particularly institutional ones', monitoring of managers and their decisions enhances the long-term efficiency and productivity of public companies, whereas the absence of capital markets' discipline in private companies allows certain laxity and waste. Capital markets are hardly a hindrance to corporate performance.

## The Perils of Myopic Management

Are some investors myopic, focusing on next quarter's earnings? Sure, and there is absolutely nothing wrong with such activity, ethically or economically. In fact, frequent traders contribute to market liquidity. If all investors were long-termers, who would sell you shares when you wish to invest? But, as the evidence I've presented clearly shows, long-term investors *dominate* capital markets. Since I don't expect all executives who have read the preceding section and glanced at the figure to immediately convert to becoming long-term value pursuers, here is a cautionary tale.

On September 1, 2003, *Barron's* featured 3M and its new CEO, James McNerney Jr., a Jack Welch disciple at GE. Among the praises heaped on the chief for deep cost cutting and instilling a sharp strategic focus at 3M, *Barron's* raised concerns about the CEO's decision to cut 3M's R&D intensity (R&D as a percentage of sales): "spending on R&D as a percentage of sales is declining... McNerney's critics argue that he is mortgaging 3M's future."[25] Of particular rancor to critics was the disappearance of "the '15% Rule' that let scientists spend 15% of their time 'fiddling' on projects with no immediately foreseeable return." Interviewing Art Fry, a retired 3M scientist who developed the highly profitable Post-it Notes, *Barron's* recounts: "Fry questions whether he could have developed Post-it in 3M's current stringent atmosphere." And what did investors have to say about this short-term-oriented move at 3M, an innovation icon? Myopic investors would have rejoiced, of course, at the earnings boost from the R&D slowdown, yet 3M shareholders obviously shared *Barron's* concerns about the threat to innovation and growth potential of 3M, evidenced by the company's stagnating stock price, which seriously lagged the S&P 500 from 2004 to 2006. Two and a half years later, a February 20, 2006, article in *Barron's* revisited R&D at 3M: "Investors have been concerned that 3M's former CEO,

James McNerney (who left to head Boeing in 2005), had focused more on cost-cutting than new products." Catering to the elusive myopic investors is clearly hazardous to the company's health.

3M is not an aberration. Investors not only reject managerial short-termism, but also applaud long-term investments, even though these expenditures lower current earnings. John Doukas and Lorne Switzer, for example, examined stock price reactions surrounding corporate announcements of substantial increases in R&D budgets.[26] Such R&D boosts lower current earnings yet enhance future growth prospects. Whereas the average investor reaction to all the R&D announcements was mute, investors' reaction to R&D increases made by companies operating in concentrated industries where few enterprises command a large market share was decidedly positive. As argued by Joseph Schumpeter, the Austrian-born economist who was first among academics to realize the important role of technology and innovation in economic growth, companies with considerable market power have a significant financing and marketing edge over firms operating in highly competitive industries in turning R&D projects into value-creating products and services.[27] Thus, investors reacted positively to R&D boosts by companies with good prospects of creating value from R&D. This attitude is remarkably perceptive and long-term oriented. More recent studies all document a strong and positive association between stock price changes, or returns, and advertising and R&D expenditures.[28] Investors evidently welcome corporate long-term investments.

## Why the "Obsession" with Quarterly EPS?

At this stage, you cannot be faulted for bewilderment: how to reconcile the considerable weight investors place on the long-term growth prospects of companies with their similarly obvious concern with businesses missing quarterly and annual earnings targets? If the latter isn't myopia, what exactly is it? The same issue on the corporate level is, how to reconcile managers' pervasive long-term growth strategies and actions—evidenced, among other things, by the substantial and rising corporate investment in R&D (roughly $250 billion a year in the first decade of the twenty-first century), information technology, brand creation, employee training, alliances, and joint ventures, all aimed at fostering long-term growth—with their obvious preoccupation with meeting quarterly EPS targets. An epidemic of schizophrenia affecting both investors and managers? Hardly. The answer to both questions lies in realizing that framing investors' and managers' decisions in the simplistic terms of short versus long term, so often done, is a misconception. In fact, there is no short-term–long-term contradiction or contest in business strategy (remember Keynes: "in the long run, we're all dead"[29]). Successful investors as well as managers don't sacrifice one at the altar of the other. Rather, they satisfy *both*, as I make clear in the following cases.

Consider two remarkable turnaround stories: IBM in the 1990s and Deere & Company in the early 2000s. IBM's case is told in numerous media reports, business school case studies, and a best-seller book by its implementer Louis Gerstner.[30] Following years of dismal performance— IBM's stock price during the pre-Gerstner five-year period, 1989–1993, decreased from $22 to $10—Lou Gerstner, a technology novice, took the helm in April 1993 and completely revamped IBM's strategies and product lines, moving decisively out of heavy hardware production and into IT services and software development. This obviously long-term strategic shift raised IBM's stock price from $10 in 1993 to $94.60 upon Gerstner's retirement as CEO in March 2002 (the S&P 500 index increased 2.5 times during that period).

Deere & Company's turnaround is less publicized yet equally dramatic. Farm equipment is after all far less glamorous than computers. During the five years before Robert Lane assumed its chairmanship in August 2000, Deere's stock price hovered around $10, inching up to $13.70 in August 2000. An uninspiring stock performance to be sure. From $13.70 per share upon Lane's assuming the leadership of Deere, its stock price reached $81 in April 2008 (the S&P 500 retreated 8.7 percent during corresponding period), before getting hit by the financial crisis market meltdown.[31] CEO Lane executed this remarkable turnaround by substantially overhauling Deere's manufacturing and marketing processes, trimming costs, revamping control and compensation systems (implementing, for example, performance evaluation by economic value-added measurement throughout the organization), and introducing new technology, such as global positioning systems (GPS), to Deere's farm equipment.

Why do I recount these two turnarounds? Because, while the extensive restructuring of both IBM and Deere was obviously aimed at rejuvenating long-term growth, neither Gerstner nor Lane sacrificed the short term. As figures 10-2 and 10-3 make clear, during the process of restructuring IBM (starting in 1994) and Deere (from 2000), the widely maligned quarterly earnings of both companies (dotted line) steadily rose, beating the consensus analyst earnings forecasts (continuous line) in the process with but few hiccups. Stock prices (broken line) naturally followed suit. Neither Gerstner nor Lane asked their shareholders to be patient and tolerate declining earnings and sales for a while, as they fixed the companies for the long term. They, like other successful managers, didn't sacrifice the short- for the long term. They catered simultaneously to both. Come to think of it, isn't the long term just a succession of short terms?[32]

And what about investors' myopia? Their ostensible obsession with quarterly earnings is a misconception too. This analogy will be helpful. The space agency NASA is obviously concerned with achieving the long-term objectives of its various space missions, reaching the moon, Mars, or other explorations. Yet, while a shuttle is making its way in space, NASA's control engineers are preoccupied with its second-by-second progress. Indeed, an observer of the scores of NASA's mission control engineers glued to computer monitors, continuously tracking in real time the path of the shuttle, may conclude that they are "obsessed" with the short-term progress of the mission, rather than a focus on the long term. Such an absurd conclusion is no different, in principle, from characterizing investors' concern with companies' meeting periodic performance targets as a short-term fixation.

In fact, the effective management and control of any project or a portfolio of projects—such as a business enterprise—entail a *simultaneous* concern with the end-of-project outcome (defined by the strategy) as

FIGURE 10-2

## IBM: Quarterly EPS, consensus earnings estimates, and stock prices (all split-adjusted), 1994–2002

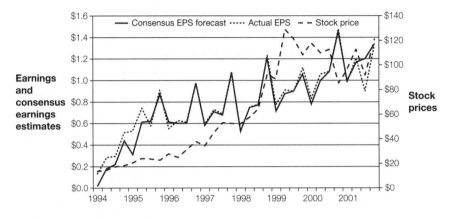

*Source:* CRSP and I/B/E/S.

FIGURE 10-3

## Deere and Company: Quarterly EPS, consensus earnings estimates, and stock prices (all split-adjusted), 2000–2008

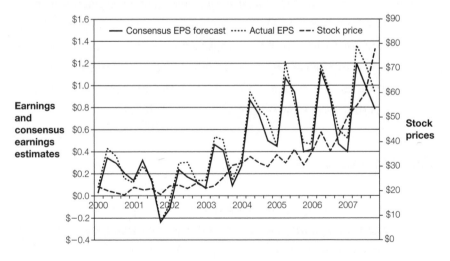

*Source:* CRSP and I/B/E/S.

well as with the day-to-day trajectory and progress of the project (monitoring and control). The same applies to the owners of the projects—investors—most of whom obviously care about the long-term prospects of companies, as evidenced by their support of massive and prolonged corporate investments in R&D, brands, corporate acquisitions, and other long-term projects, while at the same time monitoring the firm's progress toward those distant goals against predetermined benchmarks, such as analyst forecasts of earnings or past performance. Put differently, a long-term investor orientation does not imply sitting idle all the way to the elusive long term (though some managers wish they were). Whether it's a drug under development, a multiyear loan provided by a bank, or the evaluation of a business start-up, the long-term strategies and considerations cannot be separated from the continuous monitoring of the projects' progress toward the ultimate goal. Which brings to my mind the title of an old hit song, "Let forever begin tonight."

Clearly, there are some short-term-oriented investors. I reject, however, the assertion that those short-termers *dominate* capital markets to the extent that managers have to shape corporate strategies and decisions (sacrifice future value) to accommodate them. The evidence I've presented clearly supports my view. Still, some managers who are reluctant to bear the risks and hazards of long-term investments in basic (paradigm-changing) R&D and technology, risky foreign market penetration, or serious restructurings, which all might turn out badly, use investors' myopia as an excuse to refrain from bold moves. Investors will tolerate and even encourage taking the risks of investment in growth, as they have shown time and again. Will you?

## Operating Instructions

- **FORGET MYOPIA.** Don't be swayed by the widespread and vociferous allegations that myopic investors dominate capital markets. By no means let the myopia misconception lead you to dysfunctional decisions, such as cutting R&D, advertising, or other long-term investments for the sake of meeting quarterly earnings targets. For the still wavering, revisit the Amazon and Toyota cases leading the chapter. Also, don't follow the myopia believers' advice to refrain from guiding investors (see chapter 6). To entrepreneurs and managers of private companies or non-U.S. businesses, don't let the alleged "tyranny" of American capital markets affect your decision to go public or list your shares in U.S. stock exchanges. To be sure, there are weighty considerations in these decisions to go public—the Sarbanes-Oxley burden on small companies, for one—but investors' myopia isn't among them. And, certainly, don't engage in financial reporting manipulation to placate investors' alleged obsession with quarterly earnings (see chapter 3). Rather than waste time and energy on pondering the short-term versus long-term issue, focus on good versus bad decisions. You should embark on value-creating projects—investments having positive net-present-value cash flows fully accounting for risk—whether the outcomes are expected to materialize in the near or the long term. And if this causes you to miss a few quarterly earnings targets, rest assured that you will survive and prosper, as I showed in chapter 1.

- **THE LONG TERM IS A SUCCESSION OF SHORT TERMS.** The fact that most investors are not myopic doesn't give you license to destroy shareholder value in the process of building for the long term. Corporate graveyards are littered with companies that pursued so-called long-term growth without tight control of costs and effective monitoring of the progress of the investments generating the growth—without specifying interim benchmarks and meeting them. Good management, demonstrated by the IBM and Deere cases, caters *simultaneously* to the short and long term. While pursuing growth opportunities, don't remove your eyes from quarterly and annual results. Missing a couple of quarterly targets is OK; making a habit of it signals flawed strategies and loss of control.

- **THE LIFE CYCLE MATTERS.** Investors' concerns with the short and long hauls shift along the life cycle of the enterprise. In the early growth stage of the business cycle, investors are tolerant of slim margins, low earnings, even losses. They primarily look for promising investment in growth, consistent execution, and some top-line (sales) activity. Don't waste time on managing earnings and margins in these early development stages. In the mature stage of the life cycle, earnings, margins, and cash flows loom large. Accordingly, executives' stories about managing for the long term to justify poor performance will not be tolerated, even by long-term investors. Your interaction with investors and the message conveyed to capital markets should, therefore, fit your company's life-cycle stage.

- **KEEP INVESTORS ENGAGED.** The crucial issue for managers is how to systematically pursue value-enhancing strategies, particularly those requiring large upfront investments with protracted, uncertain payoffs (new product development, fundamental restructuring of the enterprise), while garnering the full and continuous support of capital markets. This involves the complex issues of how to engage investors with the affairs of the company (e.g., continuous communication of the progress of the development program) without benefiting competitors, what financial information to disclose when GAAP rules distort reality (such as the expensing of R&D and brand enhancement), and how to fend off disruptive activist investors and trial lawyers. These, and similarly nuanced issues, discussed in chapters 7 and 11, are the essence of a successful capital-market-oriented management.

- **INTEGRITY ABOVE ALL.** The difference between NASA's mission control engineers and down-to-earth investors has important implications. NASA's engineers are not concerned with getting *intentionally misleading* information about the shuttle's position and astronauts' condition. They have only to deal with facts.

In contrast, investors are generally poorly informed about the fundamentals of the business (e.g., the success or failure of products under development, or the progress of a restructuring plan), and they are justifiably concerned about the integrity of the information disclosed to them. Under these circumstances, it's not surprising that investors latch on to a few easily understood and comparably computed performance indicators, such as earnings, sales, and gross margins, and actively look for managers' guidance. The oft-recommended "strategic information" disclosure about the company's long-term plans and goals, in lieu of quarterly earnings guidance, is too soft and vague and sometimes self-serving to be useful to investors. In such an environment of uncertainty and even skepticism, establishing credibility as a straight-shooter is of the utmost importance. Once shattered, such credibility is very difficult to restore.

## Chapter 11

# Breathing Down Your Neck

## How to Handle Activist Investors and
## Hedge Funds Intruding on Your Turf

We have come a long way since the 1932 annual shareholder meeting of the New York City Consolidated Gas Company, where the "chairman read through the company's annual report and then, without recognizing stockholders who raised their hands to ask questions from the floor, adjourned the meeting and invited everyone present to proceed to another room for lunch."[1] Who said there is no free lunch? In 2011, the J.C. Penney Company announced that, to keep the peace, it would add the chiefs of two activist funds that had amassed 27 percent of the retailer's equity to its board. Penney's shareholders reacted enthusiastically to the prospects of activists shaking things up: its stock rose 7 percent. In the eighty years spanning these events, shareholder activism rose and ebbed with the changing landscape of players and regulators. Recently, gathering unusual steam, hedge-fund-led activists emerged as a potent force for corporate change—a force that every manager and board member must take seriously. In the wake of the 2007–2008 financial wreck and subsequent recession, the notion that shareholders should have a direct say in company affairs and managers' compensation gained considerable public currency, particularly among policy makers.

How did shareholder activism, which started on a low key a century ago and gathered steam slowly in the 1930s due to the tenacity of a few individuals—Lewis Gilbert, in particular—develop in the early 2000s into a serious agent of change in corporate America and abroad?[2] What are the economic and social needs that shareholder activism fills, and what are its consequences in terms of benefiting shareholders and creating or destroying economic value? And above all, what should managers' policy be toward corporate activism? Passive? Largely ignore it? Aggressive? Try to forestall it? Or passive/aggressive, act only when they come calling? I give specific operating instructions at the end of the chapter. But first things first: why corporate activism?

## From Adam Smith to Hedge Funds: Why Activism?

In 1776, that critical year for the American Revolution, Adam Smith, the Scottish founder of modern economics, drew attention to a growing problem: the separation of ownership of businesses (investors) from their control (managers), and its adverse consequences. Among those consequences are the waste of resources, enrichment of a few at the expense of many, and the trickling down of the lax moral behavior at the top of business enterprises:

> The directors of such [joint stock] companies, however, being the managers rather of other people's money than of their own, it cannot well be expected, that they should watch over it with the same anxious vigilance with which the partners in a private copartnery frequently watch over their own ... Negligence and profusion, therefore, must always prevail, more or less, in the management of the affairs of such a company.[3]

How prophetic of the massive savings and loan debacle of the 1980s, the corporate scandals of the 1990s and the early 2000s, and the 2007–2008 implosion of financial institutions.

Fast-forward 150 years from Adam Smith to the 1932 Adolf Berle and Gardiner Means classic, *The Modern Corporation and Private Property*, which argued forcefully that not just the separation of ownership from control, but primarily the *atomized* shareholding—where investors' stakes in large companies are typically too small to justify their involvement in corporate affairs—transfers to managers practically all the powers and control over corporate resources, allowing certain managerial laxity, abuse of power, and self-serving behavior. In 1976, the inherent conflicts between owners and managers and the means to alleviate them were formalized by Michael Jensen and William Meckling in a rigorous and influential body of economic research dubbed *agency costs* theory. Various means and mechanisms, says the theory—such as the board of directors, the monitoring of managers by large investors, the dissemination of audited financial reports to shareholders, and a substantial shareholding by managers and directors—can alleviate these agency costs arising from conflicts between shareholders and managers, but never completely resolve the agency problem. Thus, a door opens to direct involvement of shareholders in company's affairs: enter investor activism.

But who wants to be an activist? Who can overcome the debilitating problem economists dub "free riding"? Simply put, if you own 1 percent of a company's shares and wish to be active—dispose of complacent, incompetent directors or challenge managers' excessive compensation—you will bear all the costs of your activism, which will be substantial if you are to succeed: waging a public campaign to rally shareholders to your cause, obtaining supporting expert opinion, and the like. Yet, and this is the crux of the problem, you will receive only 1 percent of the benefits of activism if you prevail, while holders of the remaining 99 percent of equity will *free ride* on your efforts. Viewed from a monetary angle, with 1 percent equity, you must expect an activism benefit of $100 for every dollar you spend, just to break even, a return even Bernie Madoff didn't promise to his investors. And 1 percent equity in medium-size and large companies is quite a substantial investment. As reported by Brad Barber in 2006, the giant and active pension fund CalPERS, for example, holds, on average, half of one percent in its portfolio companies. Obviously, the incentives to engage in such lopsided cost–benefit activity are rather low, unless you are the J.C. Penney activists, holding a 27 percent ownership stake. Add to the free-riding problem the activists' concerns with antagonizing managers and board members—a major worry for financial institutions offering banking, underwriting, or insurance services to corporations—and the reasons for the scarcity of activist shareholders become clear. So, who really steps up to the shareholder activism plate?

## Activism: A Brief History

Activism started with mission-driven individuals, such as the 1930s social activist Lewis Gilbert, who were oblivious to the rational free-rider considerations, and continued into the 1960s and 1970s, primarily focusing on social, political, and environmental issues.[4] A 1966–1967 campaign that aimed at getting Eastman Kodak to adopt preferential hiring of unskilled minority employees, a 1969–1970 Dow Chemical shareholder proposal that tried to stop the production of napalm used in the Vietnam War, and a 1970–1971 proxy that attempted to get General Motors to adopt various product safety and environmental resolutions are examples of the early activism.[5] Social and environmental activism persists to this day in the United States and even more so in Europe, yet most proposals fail to gain significant shareholder support, and they surely contribute little to resolving the fundamental conflicts between shareholders and managers.

Shareholder activism in the late 1970s and 1980s was largely overshadowed by the wave of hostile takeovers that was ushered in by junk bond financing, courtesy of Michael Milken. Hostile takeovers did alleviate, albeit unintentionally, some of the conflicts between shareholders and managers. "Raiders" took over undervalued businesses due to inefficient, lax, or self-serving management, yet with value-enhancing potential.

They paid shareholders considerable premiums, often 40 percent to 50 percent above the current, depressed share price. The high takeover premiums thus redressed shareholders' undervaluation misery, and the mere threat of takeover, summarily followed by the dismissal of the incumbent management team, did wonders to focus the minds of managers on enhancing shareholder value. The 1980s takeover predators thus served as effective shareholder activists in disciplining managers. Alas, the hostile takeover wave waned in the late 1980s due to the effective antitakeover devices (poison pills, staggered boards) that companies implemented, as well as the drying up of junk bond financing after Drexel Burnham's demise and Milken's incarceration, renewing the search for effective shareholder activists.

A few institutional investors, notably CalPERS and TIAA-CREF, as well as certain state pension funds, joined the activists' ranks by challenging the performance, governance, and managerial compensation of companies they invested in, but very few institutional investors followed. Free riding and reluctance to alienate corporate managers kept hindering institutions' activism, aggravated by various restrictions and regulations, such as the diversification requirement of many mutual funds, preventing them from holding the substantial equity in companies that is required for effective activism.

However, the absence of robust activism in the late 1990s went largely unnoticed. The euphoria of the tech bubble and the all-consuming dot-com era provided ample excitement to investors, diverting attention from corporate governance and managerial compensation issues. Not for long, though. The burst of the tech bubble and the widespread corporate scandals surfacing in the early 2000s changed the nonchalant attitude toward activism. The scandals demonstrated once more the ineffectiveness of the presumed guardians of investors—corporate boards, public accountants, and regulators—as well as the fallibility of financial report information, resurrecting the call for effective regulation like Sarbanes-Oxley and shareholder activism. Enter hedge funds and private equity firms.

As activists, hedge funds differ from other institutional investors. While most active institutions are *reluctant* activists, forced into it to comply with regulations (voting on shareholder proposals) or because they see their investment values sagging, hedge funds *choose* corporate activism as a strategy to enhance returns in a highly competitive industry. They execute their activism with ample funds and financial acumen, and are not deterred by the free-rider issue, given their often considerable stake in the target companies: Barrington Capital and Mark Cuban, for example, owned almost 30 percent of Register.com when they campaigned in 2005 for a board change, and K Capital Partners owned almost 15 percent of Office Max when it demanded board representation and a strategic change in 2005. Hedge fund activists are, therefore, tougher nuts for managers to crack and shake off than erstwhile activists. Confronting them requires sophistication and tenacity, as you will see later. So, in brief, this is the raison d'être and history of corporate activism, leading to the main questions: How is activism conducted? What are its consequences?

## A Road Map to Shareholder Activism

Who are the activists? What are their aims? How do they conduct their activities and what do they achieve? Figure 11-1—the activism road map—summarizes the complex answers to these questions.

### Who Are They?

Almost everybody is an activist these days, as figure 11-1 indicates (in the box on the top left). Individual investors, starting with Gilbert in the 1930s and leading to today's gadflies,[6] are still raising questions in annual shareholder meetings and advancing a broad spectrum of shareholder proposals. Overall though, the impact of individual activists on corporate governance and conduct is limited. More consequential are financial institutions—public and private pension funds, mutual funds, and hedge funds—whose fast growth in the 1980s and 1990s made it

FIGURE 11-1

## Shareholder activism: A road map

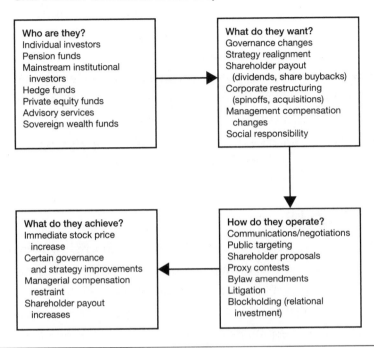

**Who are they?**
Individual investors
Pension funds
Mainstream institutional
  investors
Hedge funds
Private equity funds
Advisory services
Sovereign wealth funds

**What do they want?**
Governance changes
Strategy realignment
Shareholder payout
  (dividends, share buybacks)
Corporate restructuring
  (spinoffs, acquisitions)
Management compensation
  changes
Social responsibility

**What do they achieve?**
Immediate stock price
  increase
Certain governance
  and strategy improvements
Managerial compensation
  restraint
Shareholder payout
  increases

**How do they operate?**
Communications/negotiations
Public targeting
Shareholder proposals
Proxy contests
Bylaw amendments
Litigation
Blockholding (relational
  investment)

inevitable that some would join the activist ranks. Among the most committed are several large, publicly minded pension funds, CalPERS, the California state employees fund, and TIAA-CREF, the educators' fund, in particular.[7] However, with but few exceptions, the activism of mainstream financial institutions is rare and generally conducted on the cheap, primarily by voting on shareholder proposals. Most institutional investors are ill suited for effective activism: their investments in individual companies are small and they would rather sell than confront management. Hedge funds are different; they bring to bear a substantially higher level of focus, financial commitment, and sophistication than other institutions do. They focus on altering corporate strategy and structure, generally by changing the board composition; on increasing financial leverage and shareholder payouts (dividends, share buybacks); and sometimes even aiming at a change of control—a corporate sale or a merger—as do private equity firms. Hedge funds and private equity firms are clearly high-impact activists.

Since most mainstream institutional investors refrain from direct involvement in company affairs, yet are expected by various regulations to vote on managers' and shareholders' proposals and in proxy contests, a need has arisen for advisory services to guide institutions' on shareholder voting. Firms like Institutional Shareholder Services (ISS) fill this need by providing voting recommendations and other governance assistance.[8] A 2008 study of ISS recommendations in proxy contests found that the recommendations are almost evenly split between favoring the dissidents and management.[9] Nevertheless, business groups often decry what they see as a dissident bent in ISS and other advisers.

## What Do They Want?

As figure 11-1 indicates (in the box on the top right), shareholder activism aims at a broad range of objectives: corporate governance changes—director replacement, the elimination of antitakeover devices and staggered boards, and bylaw reforms; changes of corporate strategy and structure—spinning off subsidiaries, restructuring operations, changing the focus of product development, and marketing activities; and enhancing shareholder payouts (dividends or share buybacks) and arresting managerial compensation. William Bratton noted in 2006 that a third of his sample of activist hedge funds call for an outright sale of the target, a third urge specific policy changes or asset sales (of a division or real estate), and the remaining activists primarily call for large cash distributions to shareholders.[10] Undoubtedly, reversing the lagging performance of the target company and the undervaluation of its stock is the primary motive of most activists.[11] Indeed, in 2008, Alon Brav and colleagues documented that hedge fund targets tend to have lower market valuations (market-to-book ratios) than do similar nontargeted companies.[12]

Finally, a considerable activism effort, in terms of the number of shareholder proposals, though not financial backing, is aimed at fostering corporate environmental and social responsibility, along with advancing various political causes (e.g., unionization of employees at

Walmart) and lifestyle causes (e.g., strengthening gay rights at Exxon in 2006). Shareholders' support in the United States for social and environmental proposals is generally mild.[13]

## How Do They Operate?

Here's a typical example: in March 2006, Trian Fund Management delivered a letter to the venerable H.J. Heinz Company informing it of Trian's intention to nominate, at the forthcoming annual shareholders meeting, five new board candidates, including ace golfer Greg Norman (the golf course being an obvious training ground for the food business). A meeting between Trian's chief Nelson Peltz—a veteran of the 1980s hostile takeovers—and Heinz's CEO William Johnson followed, in which Peltz proposed certain operational improvements and strategy changes intended to enhance Heinz's lagging stock price, in addition to the demanded board changes. A second meeting followed, yet the hedge fund was subsequently informed that Heinz's board rejected both its strategic and board change proposals. Not easily rebuffed, Peltz reacted by filing a Schedule 13D with the SEC in April 2006 declaring the intention to initiate a proxy solicitation to elect the five board nominees. A publicly acrimonious war of words ensued between Heinz's management and Peltz, culminating in a shareholder vote in which two of the hedge fund nominees, Peltz and Michael Weinstein, won seats on the twelve-member board (apparently, for the sake of golf, Norman was spared the board distraction). A stock price analysis of the episode reveals that Heinz's shareholders reacted positively to the various moves by Trian; shareholders obviously welcomed the intruders, expecting them to stir things up. Such shareholder disillusionment with the status quo and expectations of change are a clear challenge to managers.

As the Peltz-Heinz imbroglio demonstrates, hedge fund activists often fire the first salvo by acquiring an investment foothold and communicating their demands to management. Some activists, notably CalPERS, publicly target a group of underperforming or governance-challenged companies—the "focus list"—as a prelude to negotiations or actions. Michael Smith noted in 1996 that 72 percent of CalPERS's targets either adopted the change proposals or settled their disagreements with the pension fund. Stuart Gilan and Laura Starks reported in 2000 that, when TIAA-CREF approached firms to eliminate "dead-hand provisions"—allowing only the directors who put a poison pill in place to remove it, thereby delaying a control change—fifty-six of the sixty target corporations have removed the provisions or their poison pills.[14] Thus, an all-out war with activists is often avoided.

When they fail, as in the Peltz-Heinz case, the activists typically increase their investment in the target company and formally advance shareholder proposals or engage in proxy contests to achieve their demands.[15] Such proposals, however, are not binding even if they win a majority, but they often catch the board's and management's attention, leading to change. A low-cost, increasingly popular variant of the proxy contest is the "vote no" campaign, in which shareholders withhold their support of the nomination of certain directors. A study documents that vote-no campaigns are correlated with abnormally high CEO and director turnover, indicating a certain effectiveness of this procedure.[16]

Bylaw amendments—a relatively new venue for shareholder activism—complete the "how they operate" road map. Bylaws are the rules governing the affairs of the corporation, stating the rights and powers of executives, directors, and shareholders. A bylaw change is often preferable from the activist point of view to a nonbinding shareholder proposal, since if it wins shareholder vote, it is binding. The *Wall Street Journal*, for example, reported on a pension fund–induced bylaw change at United Technologies preventing directors from being elected if a majority of the shares voted were cast against the nomination, rather than a majority of the larger share outstanding.[17]

So, here is all you want to know (perhaps even more) about shareholder activism: the players, their objectives, and the means they use. But what are the consequences of all this flurry of activity? Should managers and directors resist all interference in their domain, or should they welcome certain activism? I now turn to this key question.

## What Do They Achieve?

Who benefits from shareholder activism? The company? Shareholders? Does shareholder activism substantially improve governance, managerial compensation systems, and firms' social conduct, or is activism by and large a nuisance and a distraction to managers, benefiting primarily the activists? These are important questions for managers and society at large, because if shareholder activism generates a significant improvement in business performance and conduct, managers should not resist it—as they often do—and society should encourage rules and regulations aimed at facilitating activism and decreasing its costs (such as reimbursing the activists from company coffers). Potential activists and their sponsors should also understand the consequences of activism. So, what's the bottom line of shareholder activism?

## Activism in the 1980s and 1990s

The findings of twenty large-scale empirical studies on the consequences of shareholder activism in the 1980s and 1990s present a mixed bag.[18] Whereas activists had moderate success in changing the governance structure of targets, particularly weakening or eliminating antitakeover devices, their impact on the performance of companies—enhancing earnings or sales growth—has been at best marginal. Nor has the impact of activism on shareholder value been significant. For example, an examination of the 115 companies that were publicly targeted from 1992 to 2005 by CalPERS,[19] the most persistent of the pension fund activists, for lagging performance and governance deficiencies indicates that, upon the public release of CalPERS annual focus list of target companies, the mean market value of these companies increased by 0.25 percent (adjusted for the overall market movement).

This marginal value enhancement is not exactly a resounding vote of trust in CalPERS's ability to improve business performance.[20] Over the long term, the operations of the targeted companies improved significantly, although not by much more than other large, underperforming companies, and the long-term postintervention stock performance of CalPERS's targets, accounting for risk, was also on par with that of similar nontargeted companies. On the bright side, the targeted companies adopted many of CalPERS's specific governance proposals. In summary, good vibrations, but not much economic substance.[21]

## Activism in the 2000s

Investors' massive losses from the collapse of the 1990s tech bubble and the corporate scandals of the early 2000s resuscitated corporate activism, focusing attention on corporate governance and particularly on managers' compensation, the presumed culprits of the business mishaps. Shareholder proposals once more became a major venue for the activists. A study of mutual funds' voting records, which, since 2004, are required to be publicly disclosed, shows that while management proposals—which were often of routine nature, such as auditor ratification and director election—received more than 90 percent mutual fund support, shareholders' proposals to eliminate antitakeover devices also received an overwhelming 93 percent fund support.[22] Other shareholder proposals received weaker, though still substantial support: those targeting directors' election won mutual fund support 49 percent of the time, and proposals targeting executive compensation got the funds' support about one-third of the time. Social and environmental shareholder proposals were largely out of favor, garnering only 15 percent of mutual fund support.

Even though shareholder proposals are not binding and often fail to win a majority, they do capture the attention of management and the board. A 1999 study of 168 *defeated* shareholder proposals to cap directors' pay found that, despite the defeat, directors' pay in these companies increased the following year by only 2 percent, on average, compared with a 23 percent pay increase in similar companies without shareholder proposals.[23] More recent studies corroborate the general responsiveness of boards to shareholder proposals, pass or fail.[24]

Managers' compensation was a fast-growing target of shareholder activism in the early 2000s, mainly driven by accounting scandals that revealed egregious cases of financial report manipulation to enhance executives' pay (at Fannie Mae, among others), numerous stock options shenanigans, and otherwise excessive compensation and perks. The 2007–2008 financial crisis displayed yet another ugly face of executive compensation: the excessive risk taken by financial institutions' executives—a major contributor to the crisis—to boost their bonuses. It's no wonder that the number of shareholder proposals to curb and rationalize executive pay is constantly increasing.[25] But, how effective is this recent compensation-focused shareholder activism?

A 2011 study of 1,332 shareholder proposals and vote-no campaigns documented that activists generally target companies with high executive pay relative to similar, nontargeted companies, and particularly firms with *excessive* pay—unjustified by the company's performance.[26] Accordingly, when your compensation is targeted by shareholders, examine your pay package carefully, as most pay-related proposals aren't frivolous. The researchers further examined the specific pay aspects that raise shareholders' ire and report that proposals requesting shareholder approval for specific compensation items, such as pensions or golden parachutes, receive the highest vote-no support, followed by proposals aiming at equity grants to managers. In a rebuke to social activists, proposals for linking managers' pay to social criteria or environmental targets received scant shareholder support. Most importantly, shareholder pay proposals, though nonbinding, were quite consequential. Although the overall frequency of proposal implementation is very low—just 5.3 percent—implementation increases substantially to 32.2 percent when the proposals receive a majority of shareholder vote. In monetary terms, the mean executive pay cut following the proposals is $2.3 million for shareholder proposals and an impressive $7.3 million (an almost 40 percent cut in pay!) for vote-no campaigns. Recent pay-related shareholder proposals are thus a potent activist weapon that should get your full attention; see chapter 13 on managers' compensation.

## The hedge fund era

Ascertaining the consequences of hedge fund activism, both in terms of share value increases upon the fund's intervention and in terms of the extent to which activists' demands are being met, is straightforward. In contrast, separating the long-term improvement in the target's performance due to hedge funds (e.g., the contribution of the two new directors at J.C. Penney) from the continuous efforts of management to advance operations is much harder.

For the record, the stock price reaction to the initiation of hedge fund activism—the filing of Schedule 13D (acquisition of 5 percent or more of the target's outstanding shares)—reflecting investors' expectations of the activists' impact, was a 2.5 percent mean share price increase (market adjusted) upon the 13D filing and a sizable 7 percent to 10 percent target price increase for a wider window of thirty days before and thirty days after the filing.[27] These substantial shareholder value gains in anticipation of the activists' impact, clearly trumping investors' general indifference to the 1980s and 1990s shareholder activism, reflect the positive expected outcomes of hedge funds' intervention backed by substantial investment commitment, financial heft, and sophistication.[28] It is obviously difficult for managers to ignore the dissatisfaction of investors with the status quo, implied by the strong reaction to hedge fund intervention. SEC take note: the target companies' stock prices started to rise weeks *prior* to the 13D filings, clearly indicating that those in the know beat other investors to the activism game.

Investors' enthusiasm upon the hedge funds' announcement of threshold investment seems justified. The researchers document a surprisingly high success rate of activist demands. Activists gained board representation in 73 percent of the cases in which they demanded it; and practically all the calls for share buybacks—a relatively painless request—were met.

In about 50 percent of the cases where hedge funds demanded strategic changes, the target company responded positively. These findings in the United States are consistent with the U.K. experience. The Hermès pension fund—a longtime activist investor—achieved significant changes in board composition and asset restructuring of the companies it targeted for change.[29] Overall, impressive stuff.

## Short-Termism and Other Downers

Notwithstanding the evidence that recent shareholder activism restrains compensation excesses, improves governance, and creates shareholder value, detractors—particularly of hedge funds—abound. Consider these quotes: "In view of their incentive structure, hedge funds are the archetypical short-term investor ... what is good for a quick trade is not always good for longer-term interests."[30] And "instead of greenmail, their [hedge funds] goal is usually to get a quick return on their capital. But hedge funds have more money and a shorter time horizon than the hostile raiders of the 1980s."[31] There are, of course, cases of brief hedge fund interventions, but each such case can easily be matched with one or more long-term hedge fund investments. A comparison of 13D filings by hedge funds against the subsequent 13D/A filings—required when the investment falls below the 5 percent mark, an indication of the unwinding of investment—indicated that 87 percent of the 374 investments examined, made from 2004 through 2005, were intact as of September 2006 (the end date of the study).[32] This is an average hedge fund investment duration of over a year, hardly short term. Many of these investments likely continued beyond the study's end date. Even for the cases that dropped below the 5 percent investment level, the median duration between investment and liquidation was close to a year.[33]

So much for hedge fund short-termism. It is also often claimed that social and environmental activists, as well as labor unions negatively disposed to free-markets and corporate managers, hijack shareholder activism. However, the evidence on the weak endorsement of social and environmental proposals by shareholders, mentioned earlier, doesn't support the hijacking allegation. More serious are the concerns about hedge funds' and other large investors' conflicts of interest with regular shareholders. These sophisticated activists often use financial schemes unavailable to other investors, putting the latter at a disadvantage. Bear with me as you read the following case, which vividly demonstrates these conflicts.[34]

In July 2004, Mylan Laboratories, a generic drug manufacturer, announced its intent to merge with King Pharmaceuticals by an exchange of shares. Investors' reaction was swift: Mylan's shares dropped 16 percent on the announcement, whereas King's shares rose by 24 percent. Both price changes reflected the hefty premium offered in the exchange. The ensuing drama pitted two hedge funds against Mylan's management and against each other. Soon after Mylan's announcement, Carl Icahn disclosed that his Mylan holding exceeded 5 percent and subsequently increased to almost 9 percent. Icahn voiced strong opposition to the proposed merger, viewing it as strategically wrong and value decreasing, a position supported by UBS. Throughout Icahn's stock acquisitions, and undoubtedly affected by them, Mylan's share price recouped a substantial portion of the loss sustained on the merger announcement. However, in October 2004, Mylan's investors were surprised to learn that Icahn, while sharing with them a substantial investment in Mylan, sold short the stock of King, the intended merger partner (Icahn claimed that the short position was relatively small). This created a subtle conflict of interest between Icahn and other Mylan shareholders. Icahn may have opposed the merger not because it was misguided, but rather to gain from the fall in King's shares (his short position), if the merger were to fail.

And that wasn't all. The Perry Corporation, a New York-based hedge fund, which owned 7 million shares of King, obviously had a strong interest in the merger consummation. But Perry also acquired 9.9 percent of Mylan shares and hedged this position with investment banks, thereby limiting or eliminating its risk exposure to Mylan.

This posed yet another conflict with Mylan's shareholders. Perry, with a substantial ownership in both Mylan and King, might have chosen to vote in favor of the merger, expecting a hefty gain on its King shares, even if the merger were detrimental to Mylan's shareholders. Perry's hedged position in Mylan immunized it from the risk that the merger might turn out to be a dud. Happily, all these layers of conflicts unwound when, in February 2005, both Mylan and King announced the termination of the merger plan due to King's operating difficulties.

Thus, while the evidence on the consequences of hedge fund activism is largely positive, the potential for conflicts of interest with regular shareholders is definitely of concern. A strict requirement for full disclosure of all the financial relations and arrangements of the activists will go a long way in alleviating the conflicts.

## The Recent Financial Crisis: The End of Activism?

Thomson Reuters notes that in the fourth quarter of 2008, there were only two new hedge fund campaigns in the United States, down from thirty-two in the preceding nine months, and sixty-one in 2007.[35] Is hedge fund activism another victim of the financial crisis? The dismal performance of hedge funds during the crisis and their consequent dwindling resources, coupled with investors' flight to quality (U.S. Treasurys), led most hedge funds to abandon the activists' ranks. This occurred not just in the United States. In 2009, the Children's Investment Fund (TCI), a British activist investor, abandoned its drive to force a strategic change in Deutsche Boerse, a German stock exchange, and practically liquidated its investment in the exchange. TCI also sold its investment in J-Power, a Japanese energy wholesaler in 2008. And in France, shares of venerable Saint-Gobain, a building materials producer, sank following an investment in the company by activist fund Wendel, in contrast to the usual favorable price reaction to activism.[36] Surely this indicates a lull in activism.

Is this a crisis-specific hiatus of hedge fund activism or the end of an affair? Can managers of cash-rich but underperforming firms relax now or just catch their breath? My money is on a hiatus of hedge fund activism, although it may last a few years. True, some hedge funds liquidated during the financial crisis, but the bulk of them survived and most generated respectable returns from 2009 through 2010, reversing the outflow of money from hedge funds. Most importantly, the financial crisis left a large number of businesses across all sectors seriously undervalued, making them alluring targets for activist investors. Activist hedge funds were never numerous, and it won't take a lot to resuscitate the movement. I would therefore not prescribe relaxation to managers of underperforming, undervalued companies.

## Passive-Aggressive Sovereign Funds: The New Kid on the Block?

Sovereign funds are financial entities controlled by foreign governments, whose number and, particularly, assets surged in the early 2000s due primarily to the exporting boom of Asian countries and the steep increases in oil prices. The massive foreign currency reserves accumulated by exporting Asian and oil-producing Middle Eastern countries used to be conservatively invested, primarily in U.S. government bonds, but the continuous decrease in the value of the U.S. dollar and the desire to enhance return on investment led sovereign wealth funds (SWFs) to diversify their holdings across currencies, equities, and other investments like gold. The depressed stock prices from 2007 through 2009, particularly in the United States and Britain, offered attractive equity investment opportunities to SWFs.

The largest investments of SWFs are typically in private equity funds, but they also invest substantial amounts directly in cross-border private and public companies, although rarely seeking a controlling position. The reason is that the motives of these investors, controlled by foreign governments, are frequently suspect, perceived to be political rather than strategic, and threatening the national interests of the home countries of the investee companies. The 2005 flap over the bid by China National Offshore Oil Corporation (CNOOC) for the U.S. oil company Unocal (the bid was subsequently withdrawn), and the more recent (2007) public concerns about the Abu Dhabi SWF investment in Advanced Micro Devices (AMD)—raising the specter of industrial espionage—demonstrate vividly the sensitivity of SWF cross-border investments. Thus, SWFs are rarely corporate activists. Indeed, the reaction of investors worldwide to the announcement of investments by SWFs in their companies was found to be a rather muted 1 percent stock price increase, compared with the 7 percent to 10 percent price rise to corporate investments by hedge funds, mentioned earlier.[37] Obviously, investors don't expect much of an improvement in the course of business or managerial conduct as a result of an SWF investment.

Will SWFs ever join the corporate activists' ranks? They are likely to, albeit cautiously. Given their growing financial heft, widening world-wide acceptability, and the increasing sophistication of their fund managers, it seems unrealistic to expect SWFs to continue to be timid, passive investors in the face of the deteriorating business performance and lagging shareholder prices of many of their investee companies.[38] Sooner or later, some SWFs are bound to tip-toe into the activist fray.

## Operating Instructions

- HOW VULNERABLE ARE YOU TO HEDGE FUND ACTIVISM? Target companies are rarely among the industry's largest, because it is difficult to amass a sizable foothold position in giant companies to embark on serious activism. Target companies tend to be undervalued (low market-to-book or price/earnings ratios) relative to their industry peers. But, as Alon Brav and colleagues noted in 2008, despite the targets' undervaluation, their operating performance (sales growth, return on assets) was generally on par with industry peers, so that the likely reason for the undervaluation isn't necessarily inferior performance, but rather the easier-to-fix governance deficiencies or low shareholder payouts, making such companies attractive to hedge funds.[39] Finally, target companies tend to have above-average cash and below-average debt, signaling to the activist an opportunity to siphon liquidity from them. So, to avoid being targeted by activists, eliminate share undervaluation. That's easier said than done, I admit, but earlier in the book I provided guidance for closing the valuation gap. Improving governance deficiencies and avoiding holding idle cash will also make your company less attractive to activists.

- **WHEN TARGETED** ... When the activists strike, the worst reaction is no reaction. The record shows that hedge funds, in particular, will not simply go away, since they have a lot at stake. Rather, they will dig in: increase their investment, wage a public campaign, and attempt to create a "pack" by recruiting other activists to the cause. It's better to have an informal meeting with the activists to air their demands. Bring a board member or two with you, preferably with capital market experience and stature. If you are lucky, you may compromise with the activists relatively painlessly, such as declaring a share buyback, as in the Icahn–Time Warner 2006 agreement to distribute a special dividend, or agreeing to a debt repurchase, as in the case of Saks Inc., which was targeted in 2005 by Highbridge Capital Management. Although these are mild concessions, you should not grant them easily. Quickly conceding to the activists will only invite further demands. Try to strike a long-term ceasefire agreement, as in the Icahn–Time Warner case. In short, extract a stiff price for your concessions.

- **WHEN MONEY ISN'T ENOUGH.** Higher on the pain scale are activists' demands for governance changes: board representation, termination of antitakeover devices (poison pills, classified boards), or the separation of the CEO and board chair positions. Such demands deserve careful consideration and an open mind. In many cases, they make good business sense from your shareholders' point of view, as I note later. So, it may not be a bad idea to concede to the activists' demands by adding one or two independent directors, or the activist representatives, as J.C. Penney did in 2011, or weaken antitakeover defenses. You should weigh these concessions against a bruising proxy contest, where the likelihood of defeat is not insignificant. BKF Capital Group, targeted in 2005 by hedge fund Steel Partners, ended up after a proxy contest conceding three board seats and a board that was no longer staggered. And in 2008, Icahn, using the proxy tool, won three board members at Yahoo! You should carefully consider governance changes, of course, since you will have to live with them for a long time.

- **NOT FOR BARGAIN.** Ascending the pain scale, one reaches activist demands for significant changes in corporate strategy and structure, such as the 2005 TCI Fund Management and Atticus Capital's demand that Deutsche Boerse cease its attempt to acquire the London Stock Exchange (activists prevailed), or Icahn's opposition to the Mylan-King merger recounted earlier.[40] Such "strategic" demands are clearly a serious matter, not the subject of routine negotiations. If the activists' demands are inconsistent with your corporate strategy, you should vigorously oppose them. A public relations campaign, supported by expert opinion, will shore up management's position, particularly with institutional investors.

- **WHEN THEY GO FOR YOUR PURSE OR YOUR HEAD.** Finally, at the top of the pain scale are activist demands to constrain your pay or that you, the CEO, will resign or at least relinquish the board chairmanship. A well-known example was the 2004 vote-no campaign of the company's 401K participants demanding that Michael Eisner, Disney CEO, quit (he first lost the chairman title and subsequently resigned). Pay-related shareholder proposals shouldn't be summarily dismissed. The evidence I've discussed indicates that many such proposals aren't frivolous and should, therefore, lead to soul searching on compensation (more on this in chapter 13 on managers' pay). As to the ultimate demand for your resignation, I will not presume to suggest how you act (hara-kiri is no longer fashionable).

- **REMEMBER, YOU ARE NOT POWERLESS.** In 2008, Pfizer, Monsanto, and Sara Lee, among others, changed their bylaws to require that activists that nominate directors or propose resolutions in annual meetings disclose their complex transactions in the company's shares, like borrowing shares for the purpose of voting or hedging against share price declines.[41] Such public exposure of activist transactions may reveal conflicts of interest with the company and its shareholders, thereby weakening the activists' bargaining position and damaging their public image. Making public the track record of the activists and their relevant experience is another arrow in your quiver, as well as a thorough investigation of the activists' war chest, particularly in a credit crunch, to determine the strength of their bargaining position. Publishing expert opinion about the company's true performance and your pay, if favorable, will solidify your position. You definitely shouldn't lie prostrate before the activists.

## Chapter 12

# Looking Out for You, Dear Shareholder

## Why Corporate Governance Often Fails and How to Fix It

The two media giants Time Warner and News Corporation can be compared on many dimensions—market capitalization, profitability, number of employees, or customer reach—but can you tell which aspect of these companies is revealed by the indicators shown in table 12-1?[1]

It's the strength of corporate governance, of course. Consider each indicator: neither company has poison pills or a staggered (classified) board. This is considered a governance strength, since poison pills and staggered boards entrench managers and board members by deterring potential acquirers who often replace ineffective executives and directors.[2]

TABLE 12-1

## Governance attributes scoreboard

| Indicator | Time Warner | News Corp. |
|---|---|---|
| Has poison pill? | No | No |
| Has staggered board? | No | No |
| Dual stock? | No | Yes |
| CEO–chair duality? | Yes | Yes |
| Outside directors* | 75% | 47% |
| Outside/related directors* | 17% | 20% |
| Institutional holding | 86% | 61% |
| TCL governance risk rating (A = low; F = high) | D | F |
| Earnings restatements (since 2002) | 2 | None |

*Relative to all directors.

Next on the indicator list is dual stocks (like common shares A and B), which News Corporation has, but Time Warner doesn't. Dual stocks restrict the say and control of the majority shareholders in company affairs, a clear governance weakness.[3] This raises the score to 3:2 in favor of Time Warner. CEO–board chair duality (one person holding both jobs) has in recent years been considered a governance weakness; conventional wisdom suggests that a nonexecutive board chairperson would more effectively monitor managers on behalf of shareholders (you will be surprised by the evidence later on). Both companies have a dual CEO–chair position. As a benchmark, The Corporate Library reports that 41 percent of the S&P 500 companies had separate CEO and board chair roles in 2010. Duality is more prevalent among large rather than small companies.

Returning to the Time Warner–News Corporation governance scoreboard, a relatively high ratio of independent (or outside) to total directors is a positive sign for governance, since nonexecutive, independent directors are generally seen as more effective at monitoring management. Indeed, under NYSE rules, public companies must have a majority of independent directors. Here, too, Time Warner has the edge: 75 percent versus 47 percent are independent directors. It also has a slightly lower percentage of related directors (related directors are a governance minus): 17 percent versus 20 percent.[4] Finally, Time Warner has a larger share of institutional, presumably sophisticated, investors than does News Corporation (86 percent versus 61 percent), which is believed to enhance governance via institutions' effective monitoring of management. So, the final governance score is 7:3 in favor of Time Warner. When it comes to governance, Time Warner is obviously the "fairest" of the two media giants.

"So what?" you ask. What do all those governance attributes really mean in terms of corporate performance and shareholder value? Does effective governance lead to superior company performance, fewer improprieties and scandals (earnings manipulations, restatements, lawsuits, or SEC investigations), or perhaps enlightened and socially responsible corporate behavior?

At Time Warner and News Corporation, apparently not so much. News Corporation beat Time Warner by better than 2:1 in shareholder return—71 percent versus 30 percent over the five-year period 2003–2007—and had a 33 percent higher ROE (I abstract from the years 2008–2009, due to abnormal market conditions). Time Warner also had two embarrassing earnings restatements from 2002 through 2008 (where were all its independent directors?), while News Corporation had none.[5]

The lesson is that corporate governance—both its consequences and how it should be measured—is far more complex than pundits and vendors of governance services want you to believe. This chapter will attempt to clarify by explaining the real attributes and consequences of corporate governance, and how to measure it. I end with a call for a substantial overhaul of corporate boards to maintain a healthy balance between monitoring and advising managers.

Be warned, it's impossible to completely clarify all aspects of corporate governance. In recent years, we have seen a huge amount of academic research on the link between governance and performance, and the lessons from it aren't always clear or consistent. But ignoring the debate on corporate governance isn't an option for managers; it's constantly in their face. Highly visible commercial scoreboards rank most U.S. companies and many in Europe and Asia on governance strength, and to lag your competitors in governance quality is embarrassing. Moreover, perceived governance weaknesses invite distracting shareholder proposals and proxy contests to rectify the alleged weaknesses, such as the 2008, highly publicized campaign of the Rockefeller descendants to strip Exxon's chief of the board chairmanship. Furthermore, low governance ratings often affect the recommendations of proxy advisers to mutual funds and other institutional investors on how to vote on proxies and shareholder proposals, and they may even affect the investment decisions of some institutions. And pesky hedge funds often use perceived governance deficiencies as a justification for intervention in company affairs and demand for board and strategic changes.

## What's All the Fuss About?

What is corporate governance for? Can't managers be trusted with shareholders' money? Well, some can't. As discussed in the previous chapter, managers' objectives and preferences often diverge from those of shareholders. Managers, being mortals—although some are convinced otherwise—naturally wish to maximize their compensation and perks, which come out of shareholders' pockets.[6] They strive to secure their position by engaging in risk-reducing conglomerate (beyond-the-core) mergers, which rarely benefit owners[7] and endeavor to build an empire of large, diversified, and global mega-businesses, which often underperform more focused and nimble companies. They frequently engage in self-aggrandizing activities, spending shareholders' money on sport stadiums, opera houses, and glamorous, star-studded charities. And, yes, quite a few corporate leaders stick to their jobs long past their prime, devouring shareholder capital in the process. Corporate governance is aimed at minimizing these costs to investors—dubbed by economists "agency costs" and shown in figure 12-1—without effective, direct means for diffused, widely scattered shareholders to discipline

FIGURE 12-1

## Corporate governance: What is it all about?

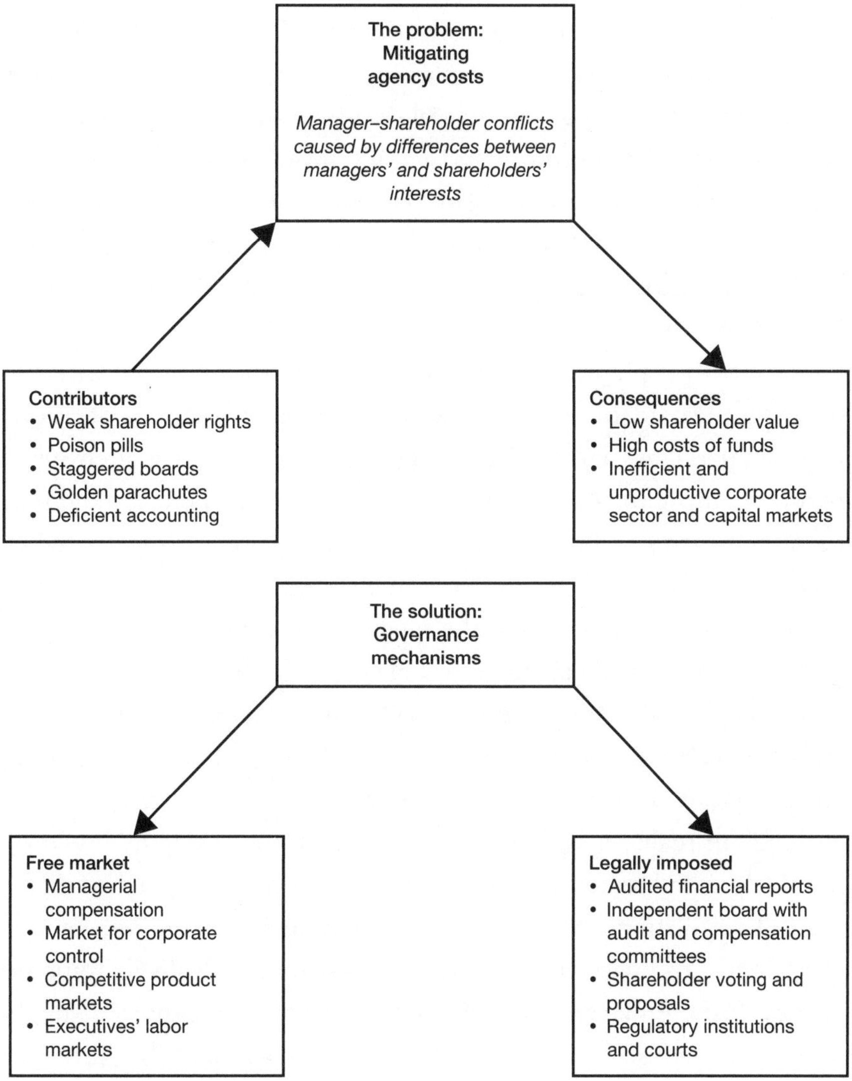

```
The problem:
Mitigating
agency costs

Manager–shareholder conflicts
caused by differences between
managers' and shareholders'
interests
```

**Contributors**
- Weak shareholder rights
- Poison pills
- Staggered boards
- Golden parachutes
- Deficient accounting

**Consequences**
- Low shareholder value
- High costs of funds
- Inefficient and unproductive corporate sector and capital markets

```
The solution:
Governance
mechanisms
```

**Free market**
- Managerial compensation
- Market for corporate control
- Competitive product markets
- Executives' labor markets

**Legally imposed**
- Audited financial reports
- Independent board with audit and compensation committees
- Shareholder voting and proposals
- Regulatory institutions and courts

wayward managers. But how exactly does corporate governance mitigate agency costs?

A large number of governance mechanisms (see lower part of figure 12-1)—some legally imposed, others resulting from competitive forces and market conditions—are aimed at monitoring and disciplining managers, thereby aligning their interests with shareholders'. Prime among the legally imposed governance mechanisms are the corporate *information disclosure* laws and regulations (IPO prospectuses, quarterly and annual financial reports, various required filings with the SEC, and annual disclosure about managers' compensation) that enable investors to continuously monitor managerial decisions and their outcomes and shape shareholder proposals and voting attitudes. Transparency is a powerful governance mechanism. The mandatory audit of financial reports by independent accountants aims to enhance investors' confidence in their integrity, although, in practice, the audit process leaves a lot to be desired.[8]

For most people, though, corporate governance equates with the company's board of directors, which oversees managers' decisions and conduct. Laws and stock exchange regulations in the United States require that the majority of board members be independent and that both the board's audit and compensation committees be restricted to independent directors. These committees oversee managers' conduct and compensation, as well as the quality of their financial reporting. Corporate bylaws, specifying internal corporate rules, serve as governance mechanisms too. And can shareholders voice their grievances and advance suggestions for change? Yes, through shareholder voting and proposals, as well as proxy contests. These allow owners a direct, although in reality a fairly restricted, venue to intervene in directors' nomination and certain important managerial decisions, such as mergers and acquisitions.[9] By and large, though, investors on their own— except for those with large equity stakes—cannot effectively mitigate agency costs. Enhancing shareholders' power is a perennial struggle with occasional successes, such as the recent "say on pay" legislation, allowing shareholders a nonbinding vote on managers' compensation.

The *legally imposed* governance mechanisms outlined are not the sole guardians against excessive agency costs. Various free-market governance mechanisms—often overlooked or dismissed in the corporate governance debate—complement those imposed by law (see the bottom-left box in figure 12-1). A *competitive product market*, forcing companies to continuously innovate and operate efficiently, obviously deters managers from gross waste and misallocation of resources (empire-building acquisitions that don't enhance competitive position, for example). The *corporate control market* (takeovers, M&As) is another governance mechanism, focusing managers' attention on enhancing shareholder value, lest the company be taken over and incumbent managers become history. Some even consider the *market for corporate executives* as a governance mechanism. Lax, incapable, highly paid executives will be pushed aside by higher skilled leaders eager to take the helm, although in reality the market for capable executives might not be as deep as desired. Finally, an effective and equitable *managerial compensation system*, outlined in chapter 13, contributes significantly to mitigating agency costs.

This edifice of governance mechanisms, buttressed by regulatory institutions (SEC, FASB, Public Company Accounting Oversight Board [PCAOB], and the courts) seems almost overkill in mitigating agency costs and aligning the interests of managers with shareholders'. Appearance, alas, deceives. In reality, financial reports suffer from major measurement deficiencies and are occasionally manipulated by managers, manipulations that auditors rarely detect. Directors' independence doesn't preclude incompetent and lax board members who are sometimes subservient to managers.[10] Proxy contests are expensive, and most shareholders' resolutions fail to garner a majority. And the overseeing regulatory institutions, even the SEC, are sometimes asleep at the wheel.[11] Unconvinced? Enron had a majority of independent directors on its board and nationally recognized financial experts on its audit committee, as did Satyam. The manipulated financial statements of Parmalat, Xerox, WorldCom, and Satyam were published over several years without raising auditors' and regulators' alarms. Let's not leave out the supposedly sophisticated financial analysts and institutional investors who pored over these reports without having a clue of the rot.

Are these "usual suspects" just aberrations or an indication of the serious, systemic failure of corporate governance? Let's consider the evidence on the impact of governance on corporate operations and conduct.

## Where's the Beef? The Impact of Effective Governance

The impact of effective governance is an important issue for managers. The numerous laws and regulations concerning corporate governance give the impression that managers have no leeway regarding the scope and quality of governance, that governance is a given and not actionable. That's wrong. Managers have considerable maneuverability in the governance arena. They obviously have a say in the selection of directors and the size of the board, whether the CEO should also occupy the board chair, whether to have poison pills and staggered boards, or whether to be more or less responsive to shareholder proposals. And, of course, managers make numerous financial reporting decisions and determine whether to disclose nonrequired but useful information to shareholders. And in extreme cases, managers might decide to list the company in a country with less-restrictive securities and governance rules (the no-Sarbanes-Oxley havens). In short, corporate governance should be managed. Audra Boone et al. document, for example, that successful CEOs "bargain" for less independent and intrusive boards.[12] To successfully manage governance, executives should know what works and doesn't work—which governance mechanisms matter and ideally what costs and benefits are involved.[13] Primarily, does effective governance enhance corporate performance, increase shareholder value, or improve company and managers' conduct? So, what's the verdict of the research?

Verifying the benefits of corporate governance is easier said than done. First, how should effective governance be measured? By the ratio of independent-to-total directors, the number of other boards company directors serve on ("busy directors"), the CEO–board chair duality, or by the absence of poison pills and staggered boards, to name just a few governance indicators? If you say, by all of the above—an aggregate governance score or index combining several governance attributes, such as those provided commercially—how should the individual indicators be weighed? Is separating the CEO and board chair positions more or less important than eliminating a poison pill?[14] Once you settle on the relevant governance attributes, a second question rears its head: how should you evaluate the impact (effectiveness) of governance mechanisms? By surveying investors or governance experts, or by hard measures, such as company ROA, ROE, share performance; or perhaps by good company conduct as measured by the number of SEC investigations, shareholder lawsuits, or earnings restatements?

Why do I bother you with these research issues? Because the thriving field of corporate governance consultancies and advisory services offers managers a plethora of products—governance scores, ratings, reports, and certifications—all backed by "research," of course. Understanding the challenges of such research should lead you to a healthy skepticism. So, don't panic if your company isn't at the top of a specific governance ranking. Worse things can happen.

Back to the evidence on the benefits of good governance:

- GOVERNANCE AND COMPANY PERFORMANCE. John Core, Wayne Guay, and Tjomme Rusticus measure governance quality by a company-specific index of shareholder rights.[15] Poison pills and staggered boards, shares with inferior voting rights, golden parachutes, and the like entrench managers and board members, thereby weakening shareholder rights. To be sure, shareholder rights are but one—albeit important—aspect of governance. Nevertheless, the researchers document that the operating profits (ROA) of companies with weak shareholder rights are lower than those with stronger rights, presumably because weak shareholder rights allow lax and incompetent management and tolerate the misuse of company resources by, say, excessive compensation and perks.[16]

  Sanjai Bhagat and Brian Bolton expand the governance measures, examining, in addition to shareholder rights, various board characteristics, such as the percentage of independent directors on the board and the separation of the CEO and board chair functions.[17] The researchers document that not only strong shareholder rights but also the amount of company stock that board members own is positively related to business performance. Moreover, the extent of board independence and directors' stock ownership is correlated with a higher turnover rate of executives when the company performs poorly. The bottom line: effective corporate governance does contribute to corporate performance.

- GOVERNANCE AND COMPANY CONDUCT. Effective directors, claim the experts, discipline managers' excesses and mitigate fraudulent financial reporting. To examine this assertion, I matched data on SEC settlements with public companies concerning accounting improprieties from 2002 to 2007 with three widely used measures of directors' effectiveness: the ratio of independent to total directors, CEO–chair duality, and whether the board is staggered or not.[18]

Comparing the companies that settled with the SEC with the much larger population that wasn't investigated, I found, counterintuitively, that settlers had a slightly higher mean ratio of independent directors than did the control group (0.694 versus 0.674) and a substantially lower frequency of staggered boards (0.472 versus 0.574). Settlers, though, had a higher frequency of CEO–chair duality (0.681 versus 0.646), a presumed governance weakness. Overall, the manipulators (SEC settlers) were not significantly inferior to the straight-shooters in the governance attributes examined. I also examined the *change* in the three governance measures, from two years before the settlement (the approximate period of misconduct) through one year after it, and compared it with the nonviolators. Given that the post-Enron and Sarbanes-Oxley period saw significant governance improvements at most companies, it's not surprising that both groups increased the proportion of independent directors and reduced the incidence of CEO–chair duality, but the settlers improved governance somewhat more vigorously than nonsettlers. Overall, however, firms that ran afoul of the SEC on financial reporting issues and other improprieties were not significantly different than others in terms of key governance attributes.

- **GOVERNANCE AND STOCK PERFORMANCE.** The research I discussed earlier indicates that effective governance is associated with improved operating performance and, in turn, with higher shareholder value. Does this mean that shareholders of good-governance companies will continuously make more money (higher stock returns) than those with weaker governance? Not necessarily. The reason: to have higher share *returns* (share price changes), investors have to be continuously and positively surprised by the companies' performance.[19] But why would companies with good or poor governance attributes, which are fairly stable over time, generate profitability that keeps surprising investors? They don't. And indeed, both Core et al. and Bhagat and Bolton show that companies with effective governance have, on average, similar stock returns to those with weaker governance.[20] Sorry for the bad news, but reaping gains from buying the stocks of companies with good governance—as advertised by some governance consultants—is questionable. Whatever the operational benefits of effective governance, they are already factored into the share price you pay.

- **OTHER COSTS OR BENEFITS OF EFFECTIVE GOVERNANCE.** Improved operating performance and higher shareholder value aren't the only outcomes of effective governance. Craig Doidge, Andrew Karolyi, and René Stulz show that better governance enables companies to raise capital at favorable terms, indicating that effective governance decreases a company's risk.[21] April Klein reports that companies whose boards and audit committees have fewer independent directors (post-Sarbanes-Oxley, all members of the audit committee have to be independent) have a higher tendency to manipulate earnings, presumably because independent directors monitor the quality of financial reports better.[22] And Olubunmi Faleye shows that the existence of a staggered board detracts from shareholder value, apparently by entrenching ineffective managers and directors, insulating them from a change in corporate control.[23] Indeed, Lucian Bebchuk, John Coates, and

Guhan Subramanian report that a staggered board doubles the odds that a company will deter a hostile takeover,[24] and when a company "destaggers" its board, its market value increases.[25]

Overall, the evidence indicates that effective corporate governance enhances operating performance and shareholder value, lowers somewhat the cost of funds, and improves transparency, whereas entrenched managers and directors detract from shareholder value. These positive effects of good governance were documented in the United States and the United Kingdom, where governance levels are relatively high. In other countries, which generally have a lower level of governance, improvements have a bigger bang. Bernard Black and Vikramaditya Khanna report, for example, that the May 1999 announcement by the Indian securities regulators of the intent to adopt a significant governance reform (requiring an audit committee, a minimum number of independent directors, and CEO or CFO certification of financial reports, among others) triggered a 4 percent to 7 percent increase in the share prices of the affected companies—a sizable shareholder value boost in anticipation of the benefits of improved governance.[26] A similar positive investor reaction to the 2001 governance reform in Korea is reported by Bernard Black, Hasung Jang, and Woochan Kim, as was the reaction to improved governance in Brazil.[27] In general, researchers find that countries with strong investor rights enjoy larger and more active capital markets.[28] The bottom line: there is much to be said for effective governance and investor protection.

## Owners in the Saddle

The agency conflicts between those who manage and those whose funds are managed are typical to the U.S., U.K., and Japanese corporations characterized by professional managers and diffused share ownership. In most other countries, the real conflict of interest is between minority (in terms of control) shareholders and the owners, frequently also the managers of companies, who are often members of the social and political elites. In these countries, prominent families and sometimes the state control, through complex pyramid structures, multiple public companies, which each in turn control other companies.[29] Founding family members and their descendants are often the key executives of these complex economic structures, retaining control by owning special classes of stocks that endow them with superior voting rights. Minority shareholders, who provide most of the capital, are deprived of real influence and are sometimes exploited by the diversion of corporate funds to family-related businesses and the appointment of inept, hereditary managers.[30] Such a corporate structure with its unique tensions and agency costs is prevalent outside the United States. Randall Morck, Daniel Wolfenzon, and Bernard Yeung reported that in Germany, for example, 65 percent of large corporations in the early 2000s were family controlled; in Mexico, a whopping 100 percent; and in France and Argentina, 65 percent; compared with 20 percent family-controlled companies in the United Kingdom and 6 percent in the United States.[31] Obviously, the main objective of corporate governance in this situation has to be the protection of minority shareholders against exploitation by the majority in terms of control.

Given the potential risks that control-deprived shareholders face, are they compensated by better corporate performance? The empirical record is somewhat slim and mixed. Ronald Anderson and David Reeb, for example, reported that the U.S. S&P 500 companies in which families or individuals have substantial ownership (large blockholding) have, on average, higher market valuations than their diffused-ownership counterparts, and Yakov Amihud and I documented that companies directly controlled by owners engage in fewer diversifying acquisitions—often detracting from value—than do manager-controlled companies.[32] Surprisingly, despite the bad rap, some of the pyramid groups perform well. For example, Investor, the large Swedish Wallenberg-led holding company, suffered a substantially lower market value decline than other Swedish companies did in the sharply down year 2008.[33] On the other hand, certain evidence suggests that family-controlled companies, apparently, beyond the first generation of founders, perform worse than widely held companies do; being shielded from control change via acquisition breeds complacency and inefficiency.[34] Indeed, Randall Morck, David Stangeland, and Bernard Yeung reported that family-controlled companies in Canada spend less on R&D than do other Canadian and U.S. companies, apparently believing they are immune to competition or takeover.[35] Importantly, in many countries where social or political elites control significant shares of the corporate sector and the national economy, capital markets are underdeveloped, financial resources are often used inefficiently, and innovation languishes, all retarding economic growth and social progress.[36] Effective corporate governance, protecting minority shareholders and enabling the revitalization of companies, is obviously called for in companies controlled by families or the state.

## The Scorekeepers' Score

Concern with corporate governance goes back at least to Adam Smith's 1776 warning that the corporate structure invites "negligence and profusion." Concern with corporate governance, however, was elevated in the early 2000s by the spate of corporate scandals and the massive investors' losses from the implosion of the tech bubble.[37] The *New York Times*, which in 2000 ran only 69 stories mentioning "corporate governance," increased the governance-related stories to 426 in the post-Enron year, 2002, and kept that high level of attention thereafter.[38] Such intense concern with governance naturally created a need for information on firm-specific governance quality worldwide, and the provision of such information soon followed.

Various commercial outfits, like The Corporate Library (TCL), GovernanceMetrics International (GMI), and Institutional Shareholder Services (ISS) rate companies around the world on governance attributes. The Web sites of the raters often claim that their governance indexes reflect the risk of governance failure and may even predict the future performance and stock returns of the rated companies. Not surprisingly, with such lofty promises, the raters' business is good. But how successful are their deliverables? This is an important question for managers who are often blamed by shareholders and activists for failing to make the governance grade.

So-so is the empirical verdict on the governance ratings. A 2010 comprehensive study of four major governance ratings—the Corporate Governance Quotient (CGQ) of the ISS, GMI, TCL, and the Audit Integrity Rating (AGR)—found that overall the predictive power of the ratings with respect to corporate performance and conduct is modest.[39] The AGR and TCL ratings predict to some extent improvement in company ROA and stock returns, whereas the other contenders don't. Higher AGR and GMI scores are modestly associated with a lower frequency of earnings restatements—primarily indicating corporate disclosure misconduct— and higher AGR scores are associated with fewer subsequent class-action lawsuits.[40] Overall, however, the predictive power of the governance ratings didn't impress the researchers. Interestingly, the AGR score, the relative winner among the examined ratings, focuses primarily on the quality of financial reporting, highlighting the importance of financial information disclosure—transparency—as a governance mechanism.

Until we have further research on the issue, the lesson for managers and directors is clear: if your company doesn't score high on a governance scale, you should definitely search for the reasons. Often there are straightforward things you can do to improve the rating; see the operating instructions at the end of the chapter. However, if a rating improvement requires changes you feel strongly are unwarranted—separating the CEO and board chair positions, or scuttling a staggered board, for example—don't do them. You should make governance changes for substantive reasons, not just to placate the raters.

## A Team of Rivals or a Kitchen Cabinet?

In 2007, Jeffrey Gordon, a legal scholar, vividly described the dramatic shift in corporate board structure over the past half-century. In the 1950s, boards of large U.S. public companies consisted mainly of senior executives; certain outside directors often related to the company, such as bankers and lawyers; and a few independent directors handpicked by the CEO. Today, the overwhelming majority of directors are independent, leaving the executives on boards endangered species. Sometimes only the CEO is a director, and company lawyers and bankers on the board are virtually extinct. Consider that the mean share of independent to nonindependent (inside and related) directors shifted from 20:80 in the 1950s to 75:25 in the early 2000s, and in more than 90 percent of large companies there are now only one or two executives on the board.[41] The lonely CEO now often faces a "team of rivals,"[42] sometimes adversaries (I don't propose a special compensation for loneliness). These developments shifted the role of the board from primarily *advising* managers about key decisions and strategies (M&A, restructuring) to *monitoring* their conduct, financial disclosure, and compensation, a shift hastened by the corporate scandals in the early 2000s.[43] A manifestation of this shift is the frequent practice of directors meeting in "executive sessions"—without senior management—chaired by the independent "lead director."[44] Obviously, not much advising goes on in sessions absent of executives.

The beginning of the shift to independent boards in the 1970s and 1980s wasn't all bad for managers. A robustly independent board shielded them from certain external pressures, primarily those from the market for corporate control, which was dominated in the 1980s by hostile takeovers. Those were scary times for managers; almost a quarter of large U.S. corporations received hostile bids.[45] But "[t]he blessing of takeover resistance by independent directors who would, in theory, independently evaluate the adequacy of the hostile bid against the firm's 'intrinsic value,' was an indispensible part of the legitimating mechanism [for resisting a hostile bid] ... The price of the power to 'just say no' to a hostile bidder was a board that consisted of a majority of independent directors."[46]

Entrenching managers is not the reason independent directors sit on corporate boards; they are there to create value for shareholders or prevent value destruction by monitoring and advising managers on tactical and strategic issues. And how successful are independent directors in this mission? The evidence will disappoint the legions of pundits and governance advocates pushing for ever more independence on the board: there is hardly any relation between the increased presence of independent directors and shareholder value.[47]

How can this be? It's elementary. Being independent is no guarantee for business acumen, diligence, and courage to stand for one's principles. If you doubt that, just think of the dismal performance of the scores of independent directors on the boards of Bear Stearns, Lehman Brothers, AIG, Merrill Lynch, Citigroup, Bank of America, and the smaller financial services firms that have gone bust or required massive public resuscitation in the 2007–2008 financial crisis. Furthermore, a strictly monitoring, sometimes confrontational board loses certain effectiveness because it is often deprived of the sensitive information executives have. One is naturally less forthcoming and candid (say, about investment projects that failed, or the state of the restructuring efforts) when facing monitors than with counselors and advisers. It's time to rethink the relentless drive toward an independent monitoring board.

I'm not saying that the typical boards of yore were truly advisory. Myles Mace, studying U.S. boards in the 1960s, concluded that directors of most companies didn't set strategies, select CEOs, or even ask penetrating questions in board meetings.[48] I am not calling for a return to the good old days, but rather for a reshaping of boards to perform *both* the monitoring and advising functions effectively, for a renewed emphasis on expertise of directors in the company's business, technology, and risk management.[49] The evidence in support of expertise, not necessarily independence, is overwhelming. Research showed, for example, that while the ratio of independent directors on the board is unrelated to the number of earnings restatements, the number of independent directors with financial expertise is negatively related to restatements.[50] April Klein's 1998 research indicates that insiders on the board's strategic development committee enhance company performance.[51] Complementing and enhancing the capabilities of top management should be the prime guideline for selecting "advising" directors. People with impressive titles and star quality but no specialized business capabilities, such as certain academics, prominent civic leaders, or retired executives from unrelated industries, are often an inefficient use of scarce board seats.[52]

## Operating Instructions

- **NO ONE SIZE FITS ALL.** Corporate governance should fit the specific circumstances of the company. Businesses in frequent need of external financing—particularly early-stage or high-growth firms—should strive to enhance governance quality and even maintain a high governance rating to address fund providers' governance concerns. Companies with specialized assets or technologies—biotech, high-tech, Internet-based services, and financial services—should particularly emphasize industry expertise in the selection of directors and may even tolerate certain barriers to takeover (staggered boards) to allow managers uninterrupted time to fully execute their long-term strategies. The complexity of the business model of such enterprises calls for particular clarity of financial reports and disclosure of key value drivers. In contrast, mature companies with nonspecialized assets or technologies—retailers, transportation companies, durable goods manufacturers—should put a premium on directors monitoring managers and remove barriers to control changes. Family-controlled companies with dual stocks, prevalent in many non–U.S. and U.K. countries, need to empower minority shareholders by effective financial disclosure and auditing, along with strict internal rules to prevent self-dealing and transactions with family-related businesses.

- **IMPERIAL CEOS.** Under activists' pressure to relinquish the board chairmanship—a popular demand in recent years—CEOs should know that the jury on the detrimental effects of CEO–chair duality is still out. A recent study on CEO–chair duality reported that executives holding both positions do not receive higher compensation and aren't involved in more earnings manipulation than non-chair CEOs, and that investors' valuation of companies with CEO–chair duality is not lower than that of similar companies with separate top positions.[53] What's telling is that the researchers found no negative investor reaction to companies' announcements of CEOs taking on the board chairmanship. This evidence is consistent with other studies showing that companies with independent (non-CEO) board chairs do not outperform those with dual positions, don't replace poorly performing CEOs more frequently, nor spend less on frivolous investments.[54] And during the 2007–2008 crisis, financial institutions with separate CEO and board chair positions didn't fare better than those with CEO–board chair duality.[55] So if you feel strongly that holding on to the twin top positions is justified because a unified command streamlines information and decisions better, go for it.[56] On the other hand, companies with demonstrated governance weaknesses, such as those that restated earnings or are subject to SEC investigation, should seriously consider separating the top positions to allow for power sharing and better monitoring of the CEO. Here are some instructive statistics: according to The Corporate Library, in 2010, 59 percent of S&P 500 companies had a dual CEO–chair position, down from 78 percent in 2002.

- SIZE ISN'T EVERYTHING. Bank of America's massive eighteen-member board didn't prevent its stumbling in the 2007–2008 financial crisis, nor its problematic acquisition of Countrywide. Large, unwieldy boards slow the decision-making process and are more difficult to get behind a concerted strategy. Research, albeit on somewhat old data, documented an inverse relation between board size and company market value.[57] Studies also documented a positive relation between board size and managers' compensation. Governance experts recommend a board size of no more than ten (the U.S. average range, ten to twelve). Private equity firms usually have slim six- to seven-person boards for investee companies. Here as elsewhere, go for quality, not quantity.

- **FRIENDS COME, BUT SHOULD ALSO GO.** CEOs should, of course, work closely with board members, keeping them informed and unified behind the company's strategy. But board loyalty and harmony should not come at the price of director entrenchment and staleness. Too many board members outlast their prime and overstay their usefulness, mainly because no one wants to dismiss old warriors and friends. But boards should be periodically refreshed, not just in the wake of scandals and business failures. The change initiative should come from within the board, nudged by the CEO.[58] Others will rarely do this unpleasant job. From 1996 through 2005, there were only 118 proxies in the United States proposing an alternate slate of directors (52 percent of them in very small companies), of which only 45 proxies were successful, and only 8 of them in companies with a capitalization larger than $200 million.[59]

- **OTHER PEOPLE'S MONEY.** It's easy to get bogged down by the details of corporate governance—directors' independence, CEO–board chair duality, poison pills, and internal controls—and forget what all these governance mechanisms are about. They are, of course, about the fundamental fiduciary duties of managers to shareholders, whose hard-earned money they are entrusted with. Accordingly, it is as important for managers to focus on being investors' trustees and guardians as it is for them to navigate within the complex web of legal governance requirements. To paraphrase Adam Smith, managers and directors should watch shareholders' money—corporate resources—"with the same anxious vigilance" with which they watch their own. This means, among other things, being attentive to shareholders' proposals even if they don't win a majority vote, refraining from blocking a change of corporate control when it is in the best interest of shareholders (recall Yahoo!'s chairman and the board rebuffing Microsoft's 2008 bid at $33 per share, leaving shareholders in mid-2011with half that value), linking managers' compensation closely to long-term company growth, and under no circumstances tampering with the information disclosed to shareholders.

## Chapter 13

# Excess or Excellence?

## How to Clean Up the Managerial Compensation Mess

What is the major problem with executive compensation and the primary source of the persistent public resentment of corporate managers? A look at figures 13-1 and 13-2 will help you grasp the problem immediately. Figure 13-1 presents the mean *total* annual compensation of S&P 500 CEOs from 1992 through 2008 (top line) and their mean *cash* compensation (bottom line)—salary and bonuses. The difference between the two is largely the result of the equity-based compensation: stock options, restricted and performance shares, and stock appreciation rights (SARs). Stock options constitute the bulk of equity-based compensation and will therefore feature prominently, warts and all, in this chapter. The data in figure 13-1, adjusted for inflation, shows a considerable growth in real executive pay: increasing spectacularly during the 1990s, from a mean of $4 million to $18 million (reflecting the tech bubble), followed by a retreat in 2001 to 2002 due to the sharp decreases in stock prices (the burst of the bubble, recession) affecting equity-based compensation,

FIGURE 13-1

## S&P 500 mean CEO cash and total compensation (CPI-adjusted) in $million, 1992–2008

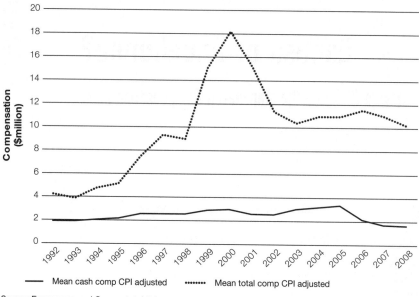

Source: Execucomp and Compustat databases.

FIGURE 13-2

## S&P 500 company-specific CEO total annual compensation (in $million) versus ROA (in %), averaged over 2003–2008

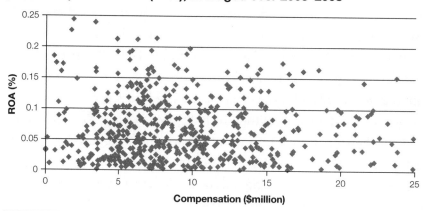

rising moderately thereafter and dipping again in 2008, mainly due to the sharp share price decreases in the financial crisis. No doubt, despite the mild retreats, executives fared very well during the past two decades.[1]

So what?, ask defenders of executive compensation; managers' pay is often dwarfed by the shareholder value they create. So, why begrudge them? Look at figure 13-2, which pits the mean 2003–2008 total CEO compensation (horizontal axis) for *each* S&P 500 company against the company's same-period mean performance, measured by the return-on-assets (ROA) on the vertical axis (negative ROA companies are eliminated). If executive compensation really incentivizes and rewards performance, as advertised, then the dots in the figure, representing mostly large enterprises, should be located closely around a steep, upward-sloping line: the higher the company's ROA, the larger the compensation. But that's clearly not the case. In fact, figure 13-2 is a mess, with no discernable trend. The multiple dots on the lower right side of the graph represent highly paid CEOs who generated meager, if any, return on assets, whereas on the upper left side of the graph are the many low-paid CEOs who delivered handsome asset returns. In between are the expected high-pay-for-high-performance and low-pay-for-low-performance managers, but they are swamped by the outliers, as indicated by the overall statistical correlation of executive compensation and ROA, which is an unbelievable zero! The inescapable conclusion: for too many companies, there is only a tenuous relation between managerial reward and performance; in essence—pay for no performance. Investors and the public cannot be faulted for being irked by that.

So, why is executive compensation so often detached from performance? Where are the directors representing shareholders' interests? And, most importantly, how should companies restructure executive compensation to overcome its systemic deficiencies? These have all been hotly debated issues for decades, yet, paraphrasing Mark Twain, everyone speaks about executive pay [the weather for Twain], but no one does anything about it. Proposals for change and for new regulations abound, particularly for managers of financial institutions in the wake of the 2007–2008 crisis, yet companies have taken scant action so far. Since the disconnect between managerial pay and performance is a major cause of investors' resentment and the driver for much of corporate activism ("say on pay"), the time has come for each company to seriously reform its managerial pay system, as I outline later. But first, how to explain the high and often increasing managerial pay, frequently out of sync with corporate performance? Welcome to the hot compensation debate.

## Witnesses for the Prosecution

Lucian Bebchuk, a Harvard Law School professor, is the most ardent and rigorous critic of U.S. executive compensation and governance systems.[2] With various coauthors and based on extensive research, Bebchuk essentially claims that managers' compensation system is broken. Rather than being based on an arm's-length pay-for-performance contract between shareholders—faithfully represented by the board—and managers, executive compensation is a "power grab" by managers who dominate corporate boards and distort the system to enrich and empower themselves at the expense of shareholders, resulting in a colossal governance failure. Here are the main building blocks of the prosecution's case against executive compensation (and my tempering comments).

- EXECUTIVE COMPENSATION BITES A BIG CHUNK OF SHAREHOLDER VALUE. In a 2005 paper, Bebchuk and Yaniv Grinstein responded to those who dismissed the brouhaha about executive compensation, saying that, even if it's sometimes excessive, it is negligible relative to managers' deliverables: corporate earnings and shareholder value—mere millions against billions.[3] The researchers report that aggregate compensation of the top-five executives in the United States averaged 8 percent of their companies' net income during the 1999–2003 period. Certainly not an insignificant amount of money, but it doesn't necessarily imply that executive compensation is *excessive*. Perhaps managers deserve the high pay?

- "INDEPENDENT DIRECTORS" AREN'T REALLY INDEPENDENT. Whether pay is deserved or not is a notoriously difficult question (did Alex

Rodriguez "deserve" $33 million in 2010? The Yankees didn't win the 2010 pennant). To determine "deservedness," one has to compare executive compensation to managers' contribution to shareholder value, distinct from other contributing factors, such as firm size, industry effects, the state of the economy, and sheer luck—a particularly challenging task. Given the difficulties proving that managers' pay is excessive, Bebchuk and Fried resorted to circumstantial evidence, claiming that directors, the presumed guardians against excessive pay, are beholden to the CEO.[4] Since managers obviously have a say in directors' appointment and renewal, vigorous opposition to executive pay and perk increases is hazardous to directors' tenure, and therefore directors will often go along with managers' demands for substantial pay increases, say the critics. But how prevalent is such director misconduct? Hard to say.

- **POWER BEGETS PAY.** Weak, complacent directors create a vacuum that empowers managers, a power they often use to enhance their pay. Indeed, several studies from the 1990s (quoted in Bebchuk and Jesse Fried's 2004 book) document a positive correlation between weak boards (generally large boards, with many directors appointed by the CEO and directors who sit on many other boards) and the amount of CEO pay.[5] Conversely, studies showed that the presence of large shareholders or institutional investors, presumably checking the CEO's power, is associated with lower pay. Furthermore, the existence of antitakeover provisions, entrenching and empowering managers, is also related to higher pay. It remains to be seen, however, whether these research findings relating governance weakness to higher executive compensation hold in the current, post–Enron and Sarbanes-Oxley environment of heightened awareness of the importance of effective governance.

- **CLOAK AND DAGGER.** Finally, say the critics, if executive compensation is not a power grab, why is so much of it made under stealth and disguise? Why do managers have to be "forced" by successive SEC regulations to clearly disclose to investors major components of their ever-more-intricate compensation packages? And why the seemingly endless array of embarrassing revelations of secret managerial payments and perks, sometimes from dubious, even macabre sources, such as the bonuses of bank executives paid from the proceeds of life insurance policies written on their employees who passed on.[6] Why all the cloak-and-dagger intrigue if their pay is legit? So, here is an explanation for the disconnect between executive compensation and managers' performance: a power grab.

## In Defense of Pay

Not so fast, say pay defenders. At the end of the day, what should really matter to shareholders and the public at large is not whether executives get lots of money and perks, but rather whether the pay is related to managers' skills and their performance. Few begrudge the prodigious earnings of star athletes—for example, Yankee's shortstop Derek Jeter's 2010 $22.6 million salary—because people feel they "earned it," as evidenced by objective, publicly available performance measures (Jeter's consistently high batting average, though down in 2010, and multiple Most Valuable Player awards). It's the same with movie and television stars' mega-size purses backed by high attendance and TV shows' ratings. The same test of the skill–performance–pay linkage should apply to managers. So, let's have another look at the pay–performance divide.

First, from a bird's eye view, Bengt Holmstrom and Steven Kaplan, well-known economists, asked in 2003, if it's so bad, why is it that good? If, as critics claim, managers' compensation doesn't reward skill and performance, but rather is the outcome of a power grab, how can we explain the remarkable U.S. economic performance and productivity gains of the private sector in the late 1980s and 1990s, when executive compensation hit all-time records (see figure 13-1)? And if managers' pay appropriates exorbitant shareholder value, why did the returns on U.S. stocks over that period outstrip other major exchanges? Shouldn't the captains of American industry and commerce and the governance system within which they operate get part of the credit for this outstanding economic and share performance? They should, say the researchers: whatever the compensation excesses, they were clearly outweighed by the benefits that managers generated.

Yet, while corporate managers clearly deserve certain credit for the outstanding economic performance of U.S. companies, a nagging question remains: does the national and corporate economic performance justify the *two-and-a-half-fold* rise in mean CEO pay over the past twenty years (figure 13-1), easily outstripping economic and shareholder value growth and the rather stagnant pay of private-sector employees? Isn't this executive compensation surge an outcome of managerial power plays and governance failure? Trust economists to provide an explanation to even this question (economists, always seeking to rationalize social phenomena, are more sympathetic to managers than legal scholars): executive compensation should rise with corporate size. As businesses grow, the complexity of their operations increases—large multidivision businesses operating globally are surely harder to manage than a local printing shop—and so should their managers' compensation. Indeed, look at figure 13-3, which recasts figure 13-1 with the addition of the mean total assets of the S&P 500 companies (the dashed line), also adjusted for inflation. (The scale of total assets is to the right of the graph, since it differs from that of compensation, on the left.) What's striking is that the rate of companies' size increased from 1992 through 2008 similarly to managers' compensation.[7] So, if corporate size and complexity are rewarded, the increase in executive compensation may not be that outlandish. But remember that we are talking here about corporate performance, not size, and asset growth does not necessarily imply performance improvement; lots of companies grow by acquisitions, many of which harm shareholders, as clearly shown in my 2011 study with Feng Gu.[8]

This finally brings us to a direct test of the relation between managers' skill, their performance, and their pay. In 2005, Robert Daines, Vinay Nair, and Lewis Kornhauser empirically addressed this critical question with a simple, yet intuitive skill measure: skillful managers reverse poor corporate performance (decreasing earnings) and maintain good

FIGURE 13-3

**S&P 500 mean CEO cash and total compensation (in $million) versus mean total assets (in $billion), all CPI-adjusted, 1992–2008**

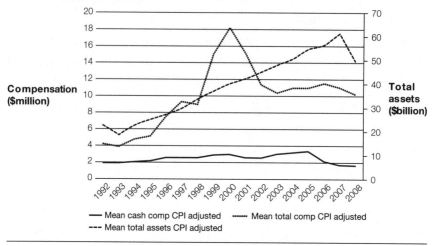

performance, whereas unskilled managers undo favorable corporate performance.[9] Having measured skill, the researchers then related it to pay for a large sample of public companies and reported that there is, on average, a positive relation between executive pay, on the one had, and skill and performance, particularly in small companies and in the presence of large shareholders (blockholders) who often monitor both managers' performance and pay effectively. In contrast, the pay of many CEOs of large companies is only weakly related to their performance, if at all. Herein lies the main problem with executive compensation: the fragile link between pay and performance.

## The Weak Performance–Pay Link

Obviously, we need more nuanced research to substantiate as serious a claim as the tenuous relation between managers' pay and performance, underlying my proposal later for pay reform.[10] To do that, I joined with colleagues Peter Demerjian and Sarah McVay to develop a unique managerial skill score and relate it to both company performance and

CEO total pay (salary, bonuses, stocks, and stock options) for various industries and time periods.[11]

Since our CEO skill score is new, here is a brief description: we start with the fundamentals—what exactly is expected of managers? Cutting through the political correctness cloud of "catering to all stakeholders" or "enhancing corporate sustainability," managers are essentially expected to enhance long-term corporate value by generating the largest benefit (sales or earnings) from employed resources: long-term assets (tangible and intangible), labor, and innovation activities, like R&D and branding. This is the essence of our managerial skill score: we measure each company's efficiency rate in generating revenues or containing costs from the multiple resources employed by the company *relative* to industry peers. That is, we measure the relative ratio of outputs to aggregate inputs. We attribute this overall efficiency measure to managerial talent or skill (skillful managers, for example, will derive higher revenues and earnings from a given number of employees or plant and machinery stock). We use a powerful computational methodology—data envelop analysis (DEA)—to generate the efficiency score for a large number of companies. Finally, we eliminate from the score the effect of factors like industry and company size, which affect business performance independent of managers (large R&D labs, for example, are more efficient than small ones, irrespective of managers), to focus on executives' unique contribution to company performance.[12]

Armed with a managerial skill score, I ranked companies in several major industries by their CEO's skill in the years 2003 to 2007 and classified those companies to the *top* (high skill) 20 percent of the industry, *middle* (medium skill) 60 percent of the industry, and the *bottom* (low skill) 20 percent of the industry peers. I then computed the mean annual ROA (company performance) and the mean total CEO pay of the companies in the skill group. The results for 2007, presented in table 13-1, speak loud and clear: there is indeed a strong positive relation between CEO skill and company performance. For each industry, the mean ROA increases from left (low CEO skill) to right (high skill). For example, in the energy sector, the mean ROA of low, medium, and high skill-led companies was 8 percent, 11 percent, and 15 percent, respectively, and in software, it was 0 percent, 5 percent, and 10 percent.[13] As to the central question—is skill and performance related to pay?—the answer is: only weakly. While mean CEO pay generally increases from left (low skill) to right (high skill and performance), there are numerous aberrations. In pharmaceuticals, machinery, telecommunications, and computers, CEOs with medium skill and performance make more, on average, than their high-skill counterparts. In software, low skill and performance is compensated more richly than medium skill, and in machinery, low skill is better compensated than high skill. And this occurred not just in 2007: the performance–pay relation from 2003 through 2006 was even weaker than in 2007.

TABLE 13-1

### Skill–performance–pay in major industries: Means of ROA and total pay in 2007

| Industry | | CEO SKILL RANKING | | |
| --- | --- | --- | --- | --- |
| | | Low | Medium | High |
| Pharmaceuticals | ROA | −34% | 8% | 13% |
| | Pay | $2.2 million | $10.6 million | $9.3 million |
| Machinery | ROA | 2% | 11% | 11% |
| | Pay | 5.4 million | 7.0 million | 4.5 million |
| Energy | ROA | 8% | 11% | 15% |
| | Pay | 3.9 million | 12.8 million | 14.5 million |
| Telecommunications | ROA | −5% | 2% | 5% |
| | Pay | 5.0 million | 18.2 million | 16.1 million |
| Software | ROA | 0% | 5% | 10% |
| | Pay | 5.0 million | 3.8 million | 7.2 million |
| Computers | ROA | 5% | 6% | 9% |
| | Pay | 2.7 million | 7.3 million | 4.0 million |

Here, then, lies the main problem with executive compensation: in many companies, but by no means all, executives' pay is largely unrelated (sometimes even negatively related) to their skill and performance, undermining shareholder value and economic growth.

If you thought that the 2007–2008 financial crisis changed executive compensation, think again: nine major U.S. banks, including Citigroup, Bank of America, Goldman Sachs, and JPMorgan Chase, which received a total of $175 billion in government relief paid $33 billion in employee bonuses in 2008, while racking up $100 billion in losses. No fewer than five thousand bank employees (many nonexecutives, though) each received a bonus of more than $1 million.[14] How's that for pay for no performance or, rather, chutzpah? The disconnect between managerial pay and performance is, in my opinion, the most serious stumbling block to restoring investors' and the public's trust in corporate executives. No amount of managerial do-gooding, public relations, or government regulation (to cap salaries, restrict stock options, or outlaw perks) will alleviate the fundamental problem of substantial pay for meager performance, which is too prevalent in corporate America and around the world. A thorough overhaul of the compensation system is obviously required, starting with fundamentals: if company performance is to drive pay, what exactly is the performance that should determine managers' compensation? You will be surprised how complex this question is.

## The Corporate Purpose

What *performance* is expected of corporate managers? Maximize share prices? Hit predetermined financial targets, such as ROA or ROE? Or perhaps consistently beat the analysts' consensus forecasts of earnings? To some, these shareholder-focused objectives are not enlightened enough. Managers, they say, should be motivated to advance the interests of all stakeholders—employees, suppliers, customers, and communities—and act responsibly, both ethically and environmentally, to enhance the much-hyped "triple bottom line" (people, planet, and profits). This is a bewildering array of corporate objectives, to be sure, some in conflict with others (pursuing social causes may detract from shareholder value, for example). And yet, an effective compensation system should clearly be based on an unambiguous, quantitative performance target for managers. So, what is that target?

To John D. Rockefeller, undoubtedly among the most successful entrepreneurs and managers of all time, as well as one of the greatest social benefactors, the answer to the question of corporate purpose was obvious. According to his biographer, Ron Chernow, Rockefeller often admonished Standard Oil executives not to do things that others can do, but rather to go back to the office and think how to make money for the Standard Oil Company.[15] Rockefeller paid a heavy personal price for relentlessly driving profits. Critics, particularly Ida Tarbell, doggedly pursued him with allegations that, in this profit drive, the oil magnate destroyed competitors, laid waste to communities (a forerunner of BP?), exploited employees, and ripped off customers with monopolistic prices. Rockefeller could never shake off the cloud of suspicion and mistrust that surrounded him.

The narrow, profit-focused corporate purpose fell into disrepute in the second half of the twentieth century. Critics argued that it ignores important corporate stakeholders—employees, customers, and suppliers—who are as vital to the enterprise's success as are its shareholders. But even that expansion wasn't satisfactory to those who argued for broadening the company's mission to include addressing social and environmental needs, as well as advancing the welfare of the communities in which the company operates. Indeed, a 1961 *Harvard Business Review* survey of seventeen hundred executives found that more than 80 percent of the respondents agreed that "for corporation executives to act in the interests of shareholders alone, and not also in the interests of employees and consumers, is unethical."[16]

The Nobel Laureate economist Milton Friedman would have none of this "enlightenment." His idea of the corporate purpose was succinctly summarized in the title of his September 13, 1970, *New York Times*

*Magazine* essay: "The Social Responsibility of Business Is to Increase Its Profits." Such reorientation of the corporate purpose and managers' mission toward profits and shareholder value fell in the 1980s on the fertile ground of hostile takeovers. Under a raiders' siege, managers and their boards quickly got the message that an effective defense against takeover and job loss is to maximize shareholder value, thereby making an acquisition prohibitively expensive. Finally, the rapid rise of institutional ownership of public companies in the 1990s cemented the focus on profits and shareholder value as the prime corporate purpose, since the performance of institutional investors and fund managers was primarily measured—often on a quarterly basis—by the change in the value of the shares they owned. Shareholder value enhancement regained its footing.[17]

## Managers' Mission

Operationally, of course, managers should be held responsible for pursuing a unique, clearly defined target. Advancing the interests of all stakeholders and perhaps even communities is not an operational yardstick by which to evaluate and compensate managers, since managing by multiple objectives often ends up as managing by none.[18] Multiple objectives often conflict with each other, raising a pesky and intractable trade-offs problem. Employee satisfaction will surely rise by slashing the number of working hours, by increasing pay, or by providing subsidized meals and child care to workers, but these generous benefits will surely cut into the company's profits and shareholder value.[19] Similarly, customer satisfaction will soar by decreasing prices and increasing the number and quality of customer-support personnel, but these too will cut into profits. And the outsourcing of company operations generally comes at the expense of local jobs. Given such conflicts, whose interests should managers advance? Shareholders? Employees? Customers? Decisions about such trade-offs require difficult value judgments, for which managers aren't qualified (and who is?).

Operationally, the corporate purpose that should drive managers' decisions and their compensation is the creation of *long-term corporate value*.[20] Note the emphasis on the *long term*, to exclude short-term opportunistic gains, such as from the pre-crisis securitization of toxic mortgages or the temporary profit boosts by such means as cutting R&D or inflating revenues. This objective also emphasizes *total corporate value* to include all fund providers, shareholders, suppliers, and bondholders, thereby excluding schemes aimed at increasing shareholder value at the expense of bondholders or undermining the safety of employee pensions by raiding pension assets. What's important is that the enhancement of a company's long-term value doesn't mean ignoring its constituencies. On the contrary, corporate value cannot be enhanced with frustrated employees or disgruntled customers and suppliers, or by seriously hurting communities. However, in considering measures that enhance the benefits of nonshareholder constituents, the impact on long-term corporate value should be paramount.

Finally, to those who think that in the wake of the 2007–2009 financial crisis and recession, advocating the pursuit of long-term shareholder value is "so 1990s," I would like to say that none of the major perpetrators of the crisis actually followed this dictum. Check the postcrisis market values of Lehman Brothers, Countrywide, Bear Stearns, Merrill Lynch, Citigroup, AIG, Britain's Northern Rock, Germany's Hippo Bank, and the rest of the "usual suspects." They are all gone or greatly diminished. No pursuit of long-term value was part of their strategies. An opportunistic, reckless, often silly strategy, lacking effective risk controls and encouraged by complacent, largely incompetent boards and ineffective regulators, as was the case with the major perpetrators of the crisis, shouldn't be confused with the persistent, disciplined pursuit of long-term corporate value, as I advocate here. Those who actually pursue this objective, like the managers of JPMorgan Chase, Deere & Company, Google, Exxon, Intel, Oracle, SAP, and Walmart, as well as many medium-sized and small companies in the United States and around the world, are doing just fine despite the financial crisis and the recession. So there is absolutely no reason to be defensive about value enhancement as the corporate purpose and the major performance yardstick for managers.

Having defined managers' mission, how can we ensure that executive compensation will indeed drive managers to consistently pursue it?

## Operating Instructions: Reforming Executive Compensation

A managerial compensation system based on the following instructions will ensure that managers doggedly pursue long-term growth and will do wonders to restore the trust of investors and the public in managers.

### Remunerate Performance Only

The surest means to achieve long-term growth is to remunerate executives strictly for performance. Except for the fixed-salary component of pay—a safety net—all other compensation elements should be linked to the company's performance.[21] This sounds like a no-brainer, yet too many companies grant executives substantial compensation irrespective of performance. There is no justification, for example, for fixed annual grants of stocks or stock options independent of the company's earnings or sales growth, nor is there justification for bonuses awarded to managers when the company's performance lags industry peers.

The most effective benchmark against which to evaluate managers' performance is the mean or median of a peer group, preferably an international cohort of comparable firms, because such a benchmark eliminates performance drivers over which managers have no control, such as a recession or legislation (subsidizing biofuels or windmills, for example), from pay. Too many companies, however, do not determine pay relative to peers. To mitigate managers' risk—an important issue, see later—which increases with the requirement to outperform peers, incentive compensation should not be limited to "super," above-average performance, which could lead to years with no incentive pay. A mixed strategy, such as a small amount of performance pay for surpassing the lower quartile (bottom 25 percent) of the peer group and a larger bonus for besting the group mean or median, should be applied. A special "superstar" bonus can be awarded for reaching the top decile (10 percent) of the peer group.

Once you set performance targets, stick to them. Any "flexibility" impairs shareholders' trust in executive compensation. For example, performance-based share grants to Royal Dutch Shell's executives were predicated on the company's ranking among the top three in peer shareholder return. Shell, however, placed fourth in 2008, yet directors granted managers the shares anyway.[22] No wonder Shell shareholders overwhelmingly voted no on executive pay. Importantly, to enhance managers' concentration on long-term value creation, their pay should be based on multiyear performance, as in a moving three- to five-year average. In this way, a short-term boost to earnings or sales by an acquisition with no long-term benefits or a cost shift to next year will be smoothed out (neutralized) in the multiyear average.

## Measure Performance Effectively

There is a bewildering array of performance measures: sales, operating income, EPS, economic value added, share return, and the like. Two considerations for the choice of measure are: (1) it should be closely linked to, namely predict, long-term company growth, and (2) it should be least amenable to managers' manipulation (a "hard" measure). Revenue growth is a fundamental performance indicator, shown to predict future corporate growth and should therefore be a prime performance measure. Earnings, however—by far the most popular performance measure—should be used selectively. Due to deficient accounting rules mandating the immediate expensing of most investments in growth (R&D, brand creation, employee training), the reported earnings of early-stage, high-growth, intangibles-intensive companies understate their true profitability and growth potential. Managers shouldn't be penalized for deficient accounting rules. When earnings fail to properly reflect performance, they should be augmented or even replaced by indicators of the company's fundamental value drivers: for example, progress in the product pipeline of drug and biotech companies (drugs advancing from phase I to phase II clinical tests), decreases in the churn rate (customer turnover) and cost of customer acquisition of subscription-based companies, or increases in the order backlog of manufacturers (see chapter 7 for elaboration).

As for resistance of measures to manipulation, *organic revenue growth* (net of revenues from recent acquisitions) is a harder to manipulate measure than total revenue growth because the latter rewards managers even for value-destroying acquisitions. The measurement of *residual earnings* (net income minus a charge for equity capital), popularly known as economic value added, is superior to net income because it provides strong disincentives to invest in projects that fail to return the cost of capital.[23] *Operating income* better reflects corporate performance and value creation than does net income, because operating income focuses directly on the inputs and outputs of the business (the terms of trade). EPS growth—a popular compensation driver—should be avoided as a performance measure altogether because it rewards earnings retention rather than just operating performance (the earnings that are not paid as dividends are added to capital and thereby boost subsequent EPS even when yielding inferior return). Cash flow measures (operating and free cash flows) are harder to manipulate than earnings, and in many circumstances they do a better job of reflecting and predicting the company's performance[24] Popular stakeholder measures, such as customer or employee satisfaction, workforce diversity, and the like, are too soft (every company I know has 94.5 percent employee satisfaction) and remote from the value-creation process of the business to serve as managerial performance measures.

### Align Managers' Responsibility with Controllability

Despite the superficial appeal of stock returns as a performance measure, seemingly aligning managers' interests with shareholders', they should be used sparingly as determinants of executive compensation.

TABLE 13-2

## Managerial Skill and mean Stock returns

| Managerial skill | 2006 STOCK RETURN | | |
| --- | --- | --- | --- |
| | Energy | Computers | Drugs |
| Low | 5.1% | 7.5% | 39.4% |
| Medium | 10.5% | 22.8% | 7.3% |
| High | 6.8% | 13.3% | 9.7% |

The reason: stock performance is largely beyond managers' control. Surprised? Here is the proof: I ranked managers in three key industries by skill (described earlier) and computed the mean 2006 stock return (intentionally avoiding the financial crisis and recession years, 2007–2009) for the companies in each skill group and industry (see table 13-2).

It is evident that there is no relation between managerial skill and stock returns. In particular, the highest-skilled CEOs (bottom line) don't generate the highest stock returns in any of the industries I examined. The reason is that they can't. Stock returns are affected by multiple factors beyond managers' control: industry- and economywide events such as the recent recession, energy price changes, and sweeping technological innovations (the dot-com craze of the 1990s). Moreover, stock returns primarily reflect changes in investors' *expectations*, rather than past performance. Since managers shouldn't be compensated or penalized for events beyond their control, share performance should not be a major determinant of executive compensation. An added benefit is that managers will be less inclined to manipulate share prices.

### Contain Managers' Risk Exposure

I bet you didn't encounter this important issue in the ongoing debate on managers' compensation. Its relevance derives from the fact that practically all the proposed "solutions" to the executive compensation problems enhance managers' risk exposure with no consideration for their potential counterreactions. Such proposed solutions include lengthening the vesting period of stock options, allowing clawback of "undeserved" pay, or capping executives' bonuses; each of these enhance managers' risk exposure. This enhanced managerial compensation risk comes, of course, on top of an increasing employment (termination) risk: a Booz Allen Hamilton study of twenty-five hundred companies worldwide reported a substantial shortening of mean CEO tenure from 9.5 years in 1995 to 7.3 years in 2001, and a study on more recent data by Steven Kaplan and Bernadette Minton reported that, from 1998 to 2005, the expected tenure of CEOs fell from eight to six years—a clip of CEO tenure by a quarter.[25] (A consolation: termination risk is not gender-sensitive; the tenure lengths of male and female CEOs are virtually identical.[26])

So, what's wrong with enhancing executives' risk, you ask? Doesn't it come with the territory? At moderate levels, yes, but an executive, like any person exposed to increased risk, will demand compensation for bearing additional risk, just as investors will expect a higher return from equities than from Treasurys. This will further boost executive compensation, to the consternation of shareholders. Even more damaging, managers will strive to mitigate their increased exposure to risk by reducing the riskiness of the company and thereby their job and shun, for example, uncertain, basic research (paradigm-changing), despite the substantial profit potential of such R&D, or engage in risk-reducing diversifying acquisitions, which rarely benefit shareholders.[27] Such counterproductive managerial risk-reducing actions should be avoided by a careful risk assessment of the proposed changes to managers' compensation, which is rarely performed in practice.

### Grant Stock Options Smartly

Talk about containing managers' risk inevitably leads to stock options, a major staple of management compensation. What makes an option attractive to managers vis-à-vis a straight grant of shares is the potential for unlimited upside gain from company share price increases, without the downside of share price decreases (if the company's share price falls below the exercise price, the options will not be exercised).[28] This unlimited potential gain without the risk of loss—a kind of insurance—was believed to mitigate managers' risk exposure, aligning managers' with shareholders' risk, which can be easily reduced by portfolio diversification. The real reasons for the popularity of stock options in the 1990s and early 2000s (see figure 13-1) had less to do with the conceptual niceties of options and more with the widely held belief among directors and managers that, since option grants don't involve cash payments and until 2005 were not considered an accounting expense hitting the bottom line, they were essentially free.[29] What's more, in addition to being cash neutral when granted, upon the exercise of the options by employees, the company in fact receives cash: a tax deduction equal to the difference between the exercise and the share price at the time of exercise. This options-as-manna-from-heaven belief is, of course, an illusion. The cost of options to the company and its shareholders is real and substantial: it is the value given away to managers and employees; that is, the price of these options if they were traded in capital markets.[30] This value, although difficult to estimate, is real indeed and is reflected by the *dilution* of shareholders' wealth when the options are exercised.[31]

Another heavy cost of stock options surfaced in the early 2000s with the unending and embarrassing revelations of widespread managers' manipulations to enhance their option gains. The list of documented manipulations to enhance gains from stock options is long and varied. For example, managing earnings to boost share prices around exercise dates (e.g., Efendi et al., 2007);[32] the backdating of options—choosing a day with a particularly low share price to designate as the options grant date, thereby lowering the exercise price and increasing the gain from the subsequent exercise of the options; and, when the company's stock price falls off the cliff and managers' stock options sink deep underwater, the options are often re-priced (reducing the exercise price) by the board, or reissued with a lower exercise price, with the lame excuse that underwater options no longer motivate managers. This widespread trickery to enhance managers' pay did considerable harm to their image and investors' trust.

It's easy to dismiss managerial stock options as a scam. They are not. They do provide strong incentive to employees and managers at a low risk level and should therefore be an important part of managerial compensation packages, particularly in early-stage, cash-strapped companies wishing to attract talent and in high-growth enterprises needing all their cash for investment. But boards should realize that options aren't free and explicitly factor their full costs into managers' pay, and they should exercise great care to mitigate option abuses.

## Shareholders' Say on Pay

The increasing public concern with executive compensation in the late 1990s and early 2000s, turning into a simmering rage against the handsomely compensated managers of bailed-out financial institutions before and during the financial crisis, led to various legislative proposals to grant investors stronger oversight of managerial pay. The result: the 2010 say-on-pay legislation, providing shareholders of public companies a nonbinding vote on the compensation of top executives (investors will decide whether the vote will be held every year, or once in two or three years). Since the vote is not binding, who cares? You should.

True, it's easy to dismiss say-on-pay. Given the mind-numbing complexity of managerial pay packages, described in fifteen to twenty pages of mostly gibberish in proxy statements, how can shareholders vote in an informed manner on executive compensation? Will they blindly follow the recommendations of compensation advisers? Worse yet, will say-on-pay be hijacked by politically motivated unions and public pension funds trying to advance their agendas? Early research on the U.K. experience, where say-on-pay has been mandatory since 2002, doesn't support the skeptics.[33] The researchers report that dissenting say-on-pay votes were generally aimed at poorly performing companies with excessive executive compensation, and that the vote had a significant dampening effect on pay. This effect was particularly pronounced where voters dissented in large numbers. Reassuringly, the researchers didn't find undue influence of labor unions or NGOs on pay votes.[34] While preliminary, this evidence bodes well for say-on-pay in America. So, while these votes are nonbinding, managers and boards should pay close attention to them.

## Finally, Apply the Embarrassment Test

Fred Goodwin, who led the Royal Bank of Scotland until its insolvency in 2008, mainly due to the ill-fated partial acquisition of the Dutch bank ABM Amro, nevertheless obtained a cushy retirement package. Sir Fred (yes, the Sir remains), who was fifty when leaving in 2008 from Royal Bank, negotiated a $1.1 million annual pension payment. The public revelation of such a large pension, particularly in light of the fact that Goodwin was given credit for ten years of work he didn't serve, caused a public outcry, driving Goodwin into seclusion. After resisting the public pressure for a while, Goodwin blinked and agreed to cut his pension by half.[35] Boards and executives should study this affair. When negotiating compensation and retirement terms, always apply the "embarrassment test": imagine your shareholders' and the public's reaction if the *full details* of the compensation plan are made public (in most cases, they will be), and avoid anything that will embarrass you or the company (such as the fat, long-term consulting contracts for retired CEOs, when everyone knows that new CEOs never consult their predecessors). It's not worth it. Executive compensation needs to be *perceived* as fair and well deserved, in both good and bad times. A good example is Daniel Vasella, the former boss of Novartis, a pharmaceutical leader, whose 2007 pay was down 33 percent from 2006 because of missed targets (he still made $14 million in 2007, poor thing).[36]

# What Then Must We Do?

## Chapter 14

## Meta-instructions

Warren Buffett, in his celebrated annual letters to Berkshire Hathaway's shareholders, imparted profound business acumen.[1] Some major Buffett principles are: the best managers think like and "walk in the shoes of owners." Forthrightness and candor in managers' communications with shareholders is of the utmost importance. Stock markets are not efficient, and both undervalued and overvalued shares exist and are dysfunctional, and they therefore have to be adjusted to intrinsic values. Most corporate acquisitions are value decreasing. Accounting information can be easily manipulated, and even when not, doesn't inform much about business value; therefore, extensive adjustments are needed to make this information useful to investors. Widely used managerial compensation schemes are inadequate. Managers shouldn't designate the charities to which the corporation contributes. Earning the trust of social communities enhances business performance. Finally, says Buffett, it's possible to attract and maintain a base of shareholders supporting long-term strategies.

I wholeheartedly concur and have provided in the thirteen chapters you just read breathlessly, I am sure, the detailed means to translate these principles into reality. What then must we do?[2] I now offer a meta-analysis and distillation of the main operating lessons and instructions I advanced in the preceding chapters, classified by the three major concerns of shareholders, or what shareholders really want: the pursuit of long-term corporate growth, sharing of relevant and truthful information, and avoidance of misconduct and embarrassments by the company and its managers.

## The Pursuit of Long-Term Growth

Contrary to widespread beliefs, ceaselessly repeated in the media, most investors are not myopic and obsessed with quarterly earnings. Rather, as I show in chapter 10, backed by extensive evidence, the majority of investors are surprisingly patient, "tolerating" huge corporate investments in long-term growth in the form of R&D (over $250 billion annually), technology acquisitions, brand creation, information technology, and employee training. Investors' "long-termness" is confirmed by my finding that over half of a company's capitalization or share price reflects its long-term growth potential, rather than short-term profits. Why is this important? So that you won't get hung up on the need to cater to the market's short-term tyranny. You are free and, in fact, encouraged by shareholders to pursue long-term, sustainable growth strategies.

This, however, does not give you license to ignore short-term performance benchmarks, such as the dreaded analysts' quarterly consensus forecasts of earnings or your own earnings guidance. You can't expect shareholders to sit idly waiting for the long term to materialize. Shareholders don't have to be myopic to insist on being periodically assured that the enterprise is indeed on a sustainable growth path and that you are taking the proper corrective actions when deviating from the path. Constant monitoring of the development of children doesn't mean that parents aren't primarily concerned with their long-term welfare; the same holds true for business enterprises. So, meeting periodic performance benchmarks, internal—set by the board—as well as external, is an integral part of pursuing long-term growth strategies. Same with informing investors about forthcoming earnings (guidance), not the least to prevent analysts' forecasts from going off the chart. The oft-mentioned argument that earnings guidance yields to investors' myopia is also a myth.

Yet occasionally missing the quarterly consensus forecast is not the end of the world, as I show in chapter 1. It happens to the best of companies and managers, and both survive the ordeal and often prosper. The specter of missing the consensus by no means justifies panicked actions to make the numbers, such as a last-minute deep-discount sales blitz or cutting R&D, advertising, or maintenance expenses. Such reactive tactics just worsen the situation down the road. Above all, don't even think of managing earnings to meet the consensus. To avoid that temptation, keep this statistic handy: nine in ten of the top executives whose companies were subject to SEC or Department of Justice accounting enforcement actions were dismissed by the end of the regulatory proceedings. That's truly alarming.

A successful pursuit of long-term growth is reflected, of course, in increasing stock prices, a good thing. But rising prices often create a buzz among analysts and Internet chat rooms and, when peppered with managerial hype—an often irresistible urge—can easily slide into overvaluation. Here is another myth: overvalued shares are good; they provide cheap currency for acquisitions and boost stock option gains. In fact, as I show in chapter 5, overvalued shares are a calamity in the making. An inflated stock is bound to drop to earth; otherwise it's not inflated. When this happens, few managers survive investors' wrath, trial lawyers' pursuit, and the board's search for culprits. The advisability of acquiring businesses with inflated shares—propagated by investment bankers in search of a buck—is a fairy tale, too. Recall the happy ending of the Time Warner acquisition with highly inflated AOL shares. Always remember the evidence: the hit you get upon missing the consensus earnings is generally mild and temporary, except when the stock was overvalued prior to the miss, in which case all hell breaks loose. Therefore, be on the alert—I discuss indicators of share mispricing in chapter 5—and nip the inflation bud early by realistic earnings guidance and truthful conference calls. The cure for the other peril—share undervaluation—also lies in smart disclosure.

The pursuit of long-term growth has a depressing effect—literally and figuratively—on current financial information. Most investments in growth—R&D, brand enhancement, software, employee training—are immediately expensed in the income statement, thereby understating corporate earnings and asset values. Not just growth investments are expensed; the value of stock options, a staple of growth companies, is expensed too. And the intangible assets built up during the growth process—patents, trademarks, unique business processes—are absent from the balance sheet. Investors are, therefore, in the dark regarding much of the value creation of growth companies, until it's finally reflected in sales and earnings. This adversely affects the fund-raising required to finance the growth, as well as suppliers' and customers' confidence in the long-term viability of the company. It is, therefore, incumbent on managers to augment the largely deficient GAAP-based financial reporting with targeted information disclosure prescribed in chapter 7: pro forma earnings, credible performance guidance, and, in particular, information on the path to growth—efforts and consequences—like the product pipeline of pharmaceutical and biotech companies, or data on customer acquisition, churn, and customer value of subscription-based enterprises. All this is depicted in the path-to-growth template in chapter 7.

Finally, achieving sustained growth and separating from the competition require a supportive, knowledgeable board of directors. So, while the independence and diversity of the board are laudable, companies should emphasize expertise and specialized connections, particularly abroad, when searching for directors. The monitoring and advising functions of the board should go hand in hand, rather than the former trumping the latter, as is currently fashionable. Effective management also requires a stable environment uninterrupted by trial lawyers, politically motivated activists, and hedge funds aiming to make a quick buck. I offer specific strategies to deal with "intruders" in chapters 4 and 11.

Companies cannot sustain growth without the continuous support of investors, suppliers, and customers, which is predicated on the dissemination of credible information; I deal with that next.

# Effective Information Sharing

Many managers propagate the myth that the company already provides too much information to investors. They believe that additional disclosure will only increase costs, benefit competitors, and could even enhance litigation risk exposure. This myth is wrong on all counts. For sure, the disclosure of lots of information is currently required, but much of it is dated and irrelevant. (Who is interested, for example, in what you paid for the plant and equipment fifteen years ago or in the arcane distinction between operating and financial leases?) Remember that information sharing isn't just a legal duty and a burden; it's in the best interests of the company and its managers. Information-challenged investors are skeptical, often discontented, and therefore discount the company's shares heavily. The consequent excessive cost of capital hinders investment and growth, hurting shareholders, as well as managers' compensation and careers. Undervalued shares also attract hedge funds and other corporate raiders. So, the question is not whether to augment the deficient GAAP information, but how and when. I dealt with these key questions in chapters 2, 3, 6, 7, and 8. Here are the essential instructions.

## Strategic Reporting

The accounting system provides information on the consequences of *past* decisions and actions: sales, earnings, and assets and liabilities values. It is mum, however, on the all-important *current state* of the business process. Amazon's earnings might be growing, but if its customer acquisition costs are increasing or if customer churn is rising (hypotheticals), the earnings growth will soon subside. Pfizer's sales might be declining, but if its product pipeline is rich, its sales growth will soon pick up. Amazon's customer acquisition costs and churn, Pfizer's product pipeline, Boeing's order backlog, and Macy's same-store-sales are examples of key business process indicators, crucial for evaluating the prospects of companies, yet not among the disclosures that GAAP requires. These key indicators—linking inputs (like customer acquisition costs) to outputs (revenues)—are the essence of the strategic disclosure elaborated in chapter 7.

Why disclose this information? Because it will narrow the deleterious gap between share value and intrinsic (fundamental) value, and because some of your competitors disclose this information already. If you don't, investors will suspect the worst and analysts' will hound you in conference calls for such strategic information. How long will you be able to say "we don't reveal this information" before you lose credibility? The many companies that routinely provide elements of strategic reporting—few, if any, provide a comprehensive portrayal of the business model, such as the "path-to-growth" template of chapter 7—attest to its usefulness to both investors and the information providers. But, remember, if you provide enhanced information in good times—when the order backlog is up or the cost of acquiring new customers is down—don't clam up when the trend turns against you. If you practice selective disclosure, you quickly lose credibility.

As to the competitive threat from enhanced disclosure, it's often overblown. Many of the companies that routinely practice such disclosure—drugmakers (product pipeline), manufacturers (order backlog), Internet-based service providers (customer churn), and retailers (same-store sales)—are operating in highly competitive industries and evidently aren't harmed by such disclosure. And what about litigation exposure? That's another ruse: as long as the information you disclose is fact based, rather than hype or speculation, class-action lawyers will find it useless for litigation.

## Integrity and Immediacy

Whenever the evaluated (taxpayers, job-seekers, or managers) provide the information used to evaluate them (self-reporting), you will find biases, selective disclosure, and manipulation. There are two things to keep in mind: First, investors and regulatory agencies are aware of the self-reporting hazards and apply increasingly sophisticated tools to detect financial information trickery. Second, the penalties for public information manipulation are very high. Research consistently documents abnormally high managerial turnover rates following earnings restatements or SEC Accounting Enforcement Actions, and shareholders' lawsuits are not far behind. If this doesn't deter you, remember that financial information manipulation is often a multi-person activity, with the weakest link sooner or later turning into a whistle-blower. So, don't even think about meddling in the information disclosure process: if you "borrow" $.02 per share from next quarter's earnings to make the numbers, you will need to "borrow" $.04 next quarter. The situation will soon spin out of control. Since manipulations are often perpetrated at the divisional level, make sure your subordinates are fully aware of the risks and apply adequate controls.

The immediacy—or timeliness—of disclosure is an important aspect of information integrity. Stale information is almost as bad as managed information. Don't drip bad news (a form of Chinese torture inflicted on investors). Earnings restatements that were preceded by "dripping" announcements like "the company is in the process of investigating certain accounting practices that might result in an earnings restatement" led to larger stock price drops (over all announcements) than a straightforward restatement. Accordingly, conclude all accounting investigations quickly and thoroughly, and disclose the truth promptly and fully. And, yes, refrain from playing games, such as "stealth restatement" (not publicly reported), or postponing the disclosure of bad news to coincide with positive information (a consensus miss coupled with the signing of a large sales contract).

No one, least of all investors, likes disappointments. A successful CEO told me: "Don't surprise your analysts; they will never forgive you." Even positive surprises—an earnings rise—will embarrass analysts, with customers complaining that they missed a buying opportunity. So warn investors of impending earnings shortfalls or drug-test failures and provide routine earnings guidance, particularly when your investors are deprived of fundamental information, as when the business operations are complex or when the company is followed by few analysts (see chapter 6 for details). Early warnings and guidance were shown to mitigate the risk of shareholder lawsuits, as is "conservative" financial reporting—an accounting, not a political persuasion—that is, choosing those procedures that minimize reported earnings and asset values from among accepted measurement procedures (LIFO or FIFO inventory valuation, or fair value methods).

## Actions, When Words Aren't Enough

"Put your money where your mouth is" is a forceful reminder to managers of what to do when words and data do not sufficiently convince investors. When performance is lagging, the stock is in a funk, and short sellers are circling the company, a positive earnings guidance might not be sufficient to resuscitate the shares. Real actions are called for, but which actions? Finance scholars tend to ascribe almost every financial decision—dividend increases, share buybacks, or stock splits—to managers signaling future earnings increases or undervalued shares. But the empirical evidence on the association between such financial decisions and future events is weak, at best, as I show in chapter 8, rendering these actions ineffective means of permanently changing investors' perceptions.

The only financial action that provides a convincing signal to shareholders is when managers buy or sell their companies' shares. Investors watch such trades closely, and they are shown to have a significant effect on share prices, particularly when their volume is high relative to managers' holdings. Accordingly, when you deem that the company's fundamentals warrant a higher share price, a positive earnings or sales guidance accompanied by top managers and even board members making a substantial share acquisition will often do the trick. On the downside, beware of selling shares when the price is in decline, which sends a particularly ominous signal and is sure to exacerbate the drop in price.

## Avoiding Company and Manager Misconduct

Two areas, managerial compensation and corporate social activities (or lack thereof), are rife with misconduct and often result in unintended consequences. Accordingly, I thoroughly discussed both in chapters 9 and 13. Next I discuss the essentials.

### Equitable Compensation

There is nothing that rankles shareholders and the public more than underserved managers' pay: increases in managerial compensation, bonuses, or perks while the company's performance and its shares stall, or rich retirement pay disproportionate with the executive's contribution. Just recall the public's revulsion at the large bonuses granted in 2008 to 2009 to managers of bailed-out financial institutions, or the embarrassing spectacle of car manufacturers' executives flying to Washington, D.C., in corporate jets, hats in hand, pleading for rescue. The major problem with executive compensation, as I have shown in chapter 13, is that in too many companies there is a weak relation—or even no relation—between managers' performance and their pay, an intolerable pay-for-no-performance situation. This has to change. All compensation components, except for the fixed cash salary—bonuses, stock, and options grants, even certain post-retirement benefits—should be linked to the firm's long-term financial performance. To reward managers' contribution, net of industry- and economywide effects over which managers have no control, their pay should be based on performance relative to peers. And boards should measure performance by indicators that are both hard to manipulate and closely linked to value creation.

Be attentive to what outsiders say about pay. A shareholders' say-on-pay vote, despite being nonbinding, generally signals compensation deficiencies that require mending. Hedge funds' demands, despite their often aggressive tone, might also convey an important message about serious compensation issues. So, pay attention and keep to a minimum, if at all, redressing managers' equity losses—options repricing, for example—when shareholder losses cannot be similarly rectified. Remember that investors don't begrudge high managerial compensation; it's the undeserved pay that infuriates them.

## Do Good, Effectively

Despite the fashionable rhetoric that businesses need to pay society for their "license to operate" or that the corporation is responsible to all its constituents, the environment, and the community, I will dare to say (what the heck, you have already read the book) that I fundamentally agree with Milton Friedman: the purpose of a business enterprise is to make money for its owners. Luckily, I am not alone. A recent survey, presented at Davos 2011, found that over 60 percent of the informed public in India, Japan, and South Korea, and over 50 percent in the United States, Canada, and Australia, among other countries, also agree with Friedman.[3] So, don't be guilt ridden if you are not a CSR leader; as long as your company earns more than owners' alternative return (cost of capital), provides steady employment, and doesn't violate the laws and regulations of the countries it operates in, you are doing fine. You create considerable social value. This, however, doesn't mean that you couldn't do more. But what exactly?

First, look for charitable activities that benefit both society and your company. Do such activities exist? You bet. In an extensive empirical study (details in chapter 9), separating causation from mere association, I have shown that under certain circumstances—particularly when your customers are individuals, rather than other companies or governments—cause-related community, social, and environmental contributions substantially enhance the donor's revenues and earnings. Individual customers frequently reward companies for well-targeted social contributions. But there is no need to restrict CSR activities to those that benefit the company directly. When a firm has specialized capabilities to advance health, education, or other social projects—examples abound in chapter 9—it should definitely use them, even without a direct monetary benefit, as long as these activities are not a major distraction from the company's core business. Walmart's use of its extensive supply-chain capabilities to assist Hurricane Katrina victims is a case in point.

Pay attention to a potentially important benefit of CSR that flies under the radar: risk mitigation. Working with charities and NGOs to create a network of trust and goodwill sometimes provides a safety net against public rage and governmental action when mishaps occur. This is important to companies vulnerable to social and environmental mishaps: businesses with direct environmental impact, such as oil, mining, and chemical enterprises; firms with long supply chains outside the home country, exposed to child labor abuse and other kinds of misconduct; and consumer product companies susceptible to product contamination and safety issues. A supportive network of charities, NGOs, and UN bodies can mitigate the consequences of social or environmental setbacks. Short of catastrophes, of course. All of BP's do-gooding over the years didn't come in handy during the recent Gulf of Mexico oil spill. Yet, in lesser mishaps, a network of trust nourished by CSR can provide effective relief.

## A Final Postscript

If you have gotten this far, you surely realize that this book is all about action: dealing with the consequences of missing the consensus forecast, conducting effective conference calls to alter investors' perceptions, immunizing your company from shareholder lawsuits, disclosing beyond-GAAP information when warranted, guiding investors about future performance, dealing with hedge funds and corporate activists, and structuring an equitable managerial compensation system, among other capital markets-oriented actions and policies. All these actions, reactive as well as proactive, blend into a systematic capital markets strategy, crucial for the successful pursuit of long-term growth, sufficiently funded and free of outside disruptions.

# Notes

## INTRODUCTION

1. Marcel Kahan and Edward Rock, "Embattled CEOs," *Texas Law Review* 88 (2010): 987–1051.

2. "Changes in stock prices have substantial explanatory power for U.S. investment, . . . " concludes Robert Barro, based on an empirical study. See Robert Barro, "The stock market and investment," *The Review of Financial Studies* 3 (1990): 115–131. For a survey of the evidence on the significant impact of capital markets on corporate investment and growth, see Ross Levine, "Finance and Growth: Theory and Evidence," *Handbook of Economic Growth*, vol. 1, part 1 (NY: Elsevier Publishing, 2005), pp. 865–934.

3. For evidence worldwide, see Mark Defond and Mingyi Hung, "Investor protection and corporate governance: Evidence from worldwide CEO turnover," *Journal of Accounting Research* 42 (2004): 269–312.

4. CalPERS specifically mentioned on its Web site the stock underperformance of the targeted companies as a prime reason for inclusion in its "Focus List."

5. Baker et al. document the important effect of capital markets on the investment and growth of equity-dependent firms. See Malcolm Baker, Jeremy Stein, and Jeffrey Wurgler, "When does the market matter? Stock prices and the investment of equity-dependent firms," *Quarterly Journal of Economics* (August 2003): 969–1005.

6. *Barron's*, February 6, 2006, p. 9.

7. See Louis Chan, Jason Karceski, and Josef Lakonishok, "The level and persistence of growth rates," *The Journal of Finance* LVIII (2003): 643–684.

8. In another sign of how precarious companies' stature is, only three of the ten most-admired companies in 2006 made it to the 2007 *Fortune* list.

9. Eugene Fama and Kenneth French, "Financing decisions: Who issues stock?" *Journal of Financial Economics* 76 (2004): 549–582.

10. A case in point: Thornburg Mortgage restated in March 2008 its 2007 results released not long before, turning a fourth-quarter $0.33 profit-per-share to a $4.74 EPS loss.

11. For example, several securities firms, such as Bear Stearns, provided their clients with corporate earnings adjusted for employees' stock options expense, long before such expensing became mandatory in 2005. Similar adjustments of financial data are made routinely by analysts for off-balance-sheet leases, pension obligations, and in-process R&D.

12. See Michael Mikhail, Beverly Walther, and Richard Willis, "When security analysts talk, who listens?" *The Accounting Review* 82 (2007): 1227–1253.

13. And not just in developed countries. In fact, capital markets drive corporate growth even in emerging economies. Chari and Henry document an increase in corporate investment (capital stock) in various emerging economies after the liberalization of local stock markets.

See Anusha Chari and Peter Henry, "Firm-specific information and the efficiency of investment," *Journal of Financial Economics* 87 (2008): 636–655.

14. Rene Stulz, "The limits of financial globalization," *The Journal of Finance* LX (2005): 1595–1638.

15. This data on diffused shareholding is for 2002. Given the rapid growth of capital markets throughout the world, current diffused ownership is surely higher.

16. Woojin Kim and Michael Weisbach, "Motivations for public equity offers: An international perspective," *Journal of Financial Economics* 87 (2008): 281–307.

## CHAPTER 1

1. Unless otherwise stated, all stock price changes in reaction to company announcements or events mentioned in this book are from the close of the day before the announcement (June 25, 2007, in Kroger's case) to the close of the day after the announcement (June 27, 2007). The change of the S&P 500 index, provided for comparison, spans the same period.

2. Sometimes the one-penny miss comes with a humorous twist, as when Ford reported on October 23, 2006, a third-quarter loss of 62¢ a share, against the consensus of a 61¢ loss. The relevance of the one-penny miss was, of course, dwarfed by Ford's total loss for the quarter of $5.8 billion ("a billion here, a billion there, pretty soon it adds up to real money," Senator Everett Dirksen said famously).

3. A survey of CFOs concludes: "the common belief is that a well-run and stable firm should be able to 'produce the dollars' necessary to hit the earnings target, even in a year that is otherwise somewhat down. Because the market expects firms to be able to hit or slightly exceed earnings targets . . . the market might assume that not delivering earnings means that there are potentially serious problems at the firm." See John Graham, Harvey Campbell, and Shivaram Rajgopal, "The economic implications of corporate financial reporting," *Journal of Accounting and Economics* 40 (2005): 29.

4. A case in point: The *Wall Street Journal* (February 16–17, 2008, p. B2) reports about a Citigroup analyst who issued, in November 2007, a warning about mortgage woes at E*Trade Financial, prompting E*Trade's CEO to publicly claim that the analyst's statement was reckless, liking it to yelling "Fire!" in a crowded hall.

5. From one who knows: "You can always hit the earnings target, just sell part of the business," said former Enron president and convicted felon Jeffrey Skilling in his trial testimony (*Wall Street Journal*, April 14, 2006, p. C3). In Ken Lay (Enron's last CEO) and Skilling's 2006 trial, the prosecution presented an e-mail written by an Enron accountant two weeks after a quarter had closed, saying: "it looks like we may be looking to beat the Street by 2 cents instead of 1 cent. I understand [former chief accounting officer Rick Causey] spoke to Skilling today, and this was his preference" (*Fortune*, February 20, 2006, p. 32). Now you know what is meant by the "earnings game."

6. Emre Karaoglu, Tatiana Sandino, and Ranolph Beatty, "Benchmarking against the performance of high profile 'scandal' firms," working paper, Leventhal School of Accounting, University of Southern California, 2006.

7. Louis Chan, David Ikenberry, Josef Lakonishok, and Sangwoo Lee, "Are all analysts alike? Identifying earnings forecasting ability," *Journal of Investment Management* 6 (2008): 1–19; Brad Barber, Reuven Lehavy, Maureen McNichols, and Brett Trueman, "Can investors profit from the prophets? Security analyst recommendations and stock returns," *The Journal of Finance* LVI (2001): 531–563.

8. Sarah Azzi, Ron Bird, Paolo Ghiringhelli, and Emanuele Rossi, "Biases and information in analysts' recommendations: The European experience," *Journal of Asset Management* 6 (2006): 345–380.

9. The fact that Walmart's explanation for the earnings shortfall—increase in gasoline prices and cool weather—seems transitory may have also tamed investor disappointment. Sometimes the reasons given by companies for missing the numbers stretch credulity: "[Overstock.com, the] online closeout retailer, in its recent conference call with analysts, speculated that weakness in late March and early April [2005] may have been related to Pope John Paul II's illness in March and his death on April 2." *CNNMoney,* May 12, 2005.

10. So do margins (the difference between sales and cost-of-sales, divided by sales). Intel reported, July 19, 2005, stellar second-quarter results: earnings growth of 22% from a year earlier, beating the consensus by a penny, and sales at $9.2 billion—a quarterly record—in line with the consensus. Intel even boosted its revenue guidance for the third-quarter. The stock, however, dropped 2.8% (S&P 500 rose 1.2%), because the gross margin ratio at 56.4% came below Intel's own forecast of 57%.

11. *CNNMoney,* October 25, 2006.

12. These stock price changes or returns are *abnormal,* that is, adjusted for a corresponding benchmark; in this case, the returns of similar-size companies. The average price decrease a couple of days around the earnings miss is generally less than 1%. See Sanjeev Bhojraj, Paul Hribar, Marc Picconi, and John McInnis, "Making sense of cents: An examination of firms that marginally miss or beat analyst forecasts," *The Journal of Finance* LXIV (2009): 2361–2388.

13. Douglas Skinner and Richard Sloan, "Earnings surprises, growth expectations, and stock returns or don't let an earnings torpedo sink your portfolio," *Review of Accounting Studies* 7 (2002): 289–312.

14. Here are several price / earnings (P / E) examples of value and glamour biotech stocks (based on Yahoo! Finance computation as of August 11, 2009): Value stocks: PDL biopharma (P/E of 6.9), OSI Pharmaceuticals (4.8). Growth (Glamour) Stocks: Celgene (P/E of 83.4), Genzyme (23.5), Gilead Sciences (19.2).

15. Assuming, of course, that A and B will not significantly change their investment and financial policies in the future.

16. An efficient capital market is one in which securities' prices fully reflect the value implications of publicly available information, such as earnings, asset values, and managers' communications.

17. There were a few exceptions to this rule, such as during the tech bubble period of the late 1990s.

18. This data on the returns of low vs. high market-to-book ratio stocks is from http://mba.tuck.dartmouth.edu/pages/faculty/ken.french/Data_Library/det_form_btm.html.

19. See Josef Lakonishok, Andrei Shleifer, and Robert Vishny, "Contrarian investment, extrapolation, and risk," *The Journal of Finance* XLIX (1994): 1541–1578. Value strategy—investing in value stocks—is widely used. A large number of value funds sprang up in the late 1980s and 1990s, offering a host of value investing opportunities to investors. My Google search for "value stocks" produced hundreds of sites and investment services catering to value investors.

20. Behavioral researchers notice in experiments this tendency of people to extrapolate past trends, without due consideration to "mean reversion," that is, the fact that for many social and economic phenomena—economic cycles or clothes fashion—past patterns of growth or decline are sooner or later reversed. See Daniel Kahneman and Amos Tversky, "Intuitive prediction: Biases and corrective procedures," in *Judgement Under Uncertainty: Heuristics and Biases,* eds. D. Kahneman, P. Slovic, and A. Tversky (Cambridge, U.K.: Cambridge University Press, 1982).

21. Skinner and Sloan, "Earnings surprises, growth expectations, and stock returns or don't let an earnings torpedo sink your portfolio."

22. Graham et al., "The economic implications of corporate financial reporting."

23. On October 18, 2006, Advanced Micro Devices (AMD) reported third-quarter earnings and sales that topped analyst expectations (earnings jumped 77%). AMD's shares, however, fell 14.2% (S&P 500 advanced slightly) because its gross margin narrowed significantly from the price war with Intel.

24. A widely used technique to "make the numbers" is to sell assets or securities that generate accounting gains (sales prices higher than cost). See (*Financial Times*, April 17, 2008, p. 21) article on GE.

25. Arthur Levitt, "The earnings game," 1998, p. 4, http://www.sec.gov/news/speech/speecharchive/1998/spch220.txt.

26. Beazer Homes, a home builder, disclosed to the SEC in August 2007 that it recorded excessive "reserves and other accrued liabilities," and that such excessive reserves could have been used, when reversed, to reduce expenses and inflate earnings.

27. Sarah McVay, "Earnings management using classification shifting: An examination of core earnings and special items," *The Accounting Review* 81 (2006): 501–531.

28. The pharmaceutical company Bristol-Myers Squibb's "channel stuffing" during 1999–2002—offering its wholesalers unusually large incentives to purchase its products in order to inflate reported sales and earnings; the former by $2.5 billion and the latter by $900 million—cost its CEO the board chairmanship and later his job, got two senior executives indicted on federal charges, and depleted the company's coffers by more than a billion dollars in settlements of SEC and shareholder lawsuits.

29. Vodafone's sharp price decline also reflected a substantial impairment charge of goodwill ($40 billion to $50 billion) announced with the lower growth warning.

30. Bhojraj et al., "Making sense of cents: An examination of firms that marginally miss or beat analyst forecasts."

31. Koh et al. indicate that in the post-Sarbanes-Oxley period, investors are less enamored than before with companies meeting/beating the consensus by a penny. The positive price reaction to these companies has all but disappeared. See Kevin Koh, Dawn Matsumoto, and Shivaram Rajgopal, "Meeting or beating analyst expectations in the post-scandal world: Changes in stock market rewards and managerial actions," *Contemporary Accounting Research* 25 (2008): 1067–1098.

32. The large software company Computer Associates (now CA) engaged in the late 1990s and early 2000s in a massive manipulation of financial information, leading in 2006 to a sixteen-year prison term for its CEO at the time. One of the manipulation devices used by Computer Associates came to be known as "the thirty-five-days month," in which sales during the first few days of next month were included in the current month's sales, to boost revenues and income. But this, of course, causes the next month to have only twenty-five days of sales, requiring more than five sale days in the following month to keep the growth façade. Such exponential manipulation soon gets out of control.

## CHAPTER 2

1. You will see later on that managers' increased emphasis on the future, at the expense of dwelling on the past, and the scarcity of quantitative data are typical of conference calls after disappointing results.

2. The Children's Place is far from a failing operation. In fact, in recent years, its stock outperformed the S&P 500 Index. My focus here is on a specific, dysfunctional, in my opinion, conference call following a dismal quarter.

3. See Harry Frankfurt, 2005, *On Bullshit* (Princeton, NJ: Princeton University Press, 2005), 42–43. Frankfurt would have surely relished the following, from Coca-Cola's 2006 annual report: "We remain fresh, relevant and original by knowing what to change without changing what we know."

4. Ibid., 56.

5. Gur Huberman and Tomer Regev, "Contagious speculation and a cure for cancer: A nonevent that made stock prices soar," *Journal of Finance* 56 (2001): 387.

6. Robert Bowen, Angela Davis, and Dawn Matsumoto, "Emphasis on proforma versus GAAP earnings in quarterly press releases: Determinants, SEC intervention, and market reactions," *The Accounting Review*, 80 (2005): 1011–1038. Similar evidence was documented for earnings *restatements*: investors' negative reaction to restatements that were prominently disclosed (in the headline of a press release) was double the reaction to restatements that were just discussed in the body of the press release. See Edward Swanson, Senyo Tse, and Rebecca Files, "Does the format of a press release announcing a restatement affect the market response and litigation?" working paper, Texas A&M University, 2007.

7. Indeed, for years, a Bear Stearns accounting expert provided investors with corporate earnings data adjusted for stock option expense, using companies' footnote disclosure, until the option expensing became mandatory in 2005.

8. Angela Davis and Isho Tama-Sweet, "Managers use of pessimistic tone across alternative disclosure outlets: Earnings press releases versus MD&A," working paper, Lundquist School of Business, University of Oregon, 2008.

9. Stefano DellaVigna and Joshua Pollet, "Investor inattention and Friday earnings announcements," *Journal of Finance* 64 (2009):709–749.

10. Similarly, good financial news tends to be disclosed early in the trading day, when investors are presumably alert, while bad news is deferred to later in the day, mostly after trade. See Jennifer Francis, Donalt Pagach, and Jens Stephan, "The stock market response to earnings announcements released during trading versus nontrading periods," *Journal of Accounting Research* 30 (1992): 165–184.

11. Herbert Simon, *Administrative Behavior*, 3rd ed. (New York: Free Press, 1976).

12. Paul Slovic, "Psychological study of human judgement: Implications for investment decision making," *Journal of Finance* 27 (1972): 779–799.

13. Libby et al. conclude from experimental research that "placement, categorization, and labeling [of information] all play a role in the simplification that even professional analysts apply when evaluating accounting information." See Robert Libby, Robert Bloomfield, and Mark Nelson, "Experimental research in financial accounting," *Accounting, Organizations and Society* 27 (2002): 786.

14. A striking example: while companies that publicly *announce* the cessation of quarterly guidance suffer 5% stock price decline on the announcement (Chen et al.), the majority that stop guidance without announcement don't suffer a similar decline (test conducted with Jennifer Tucker on data in Houston et al., 2010). See Shuping Chen, Dawn Matsumoto, and Shivaram Rajgopal, 2011, "Is silence golden? An empirical analysis of firms that stop giving quarterly earnings guidance," *Journal of Accounting and Economics* 51 (2011): 134–150; Joel Houston, Baruch Lev, and Jennifer Tucker, "To guide or not to guide? Causes and consequences of stopping quarterly earnings guidance," *Contemporary Accounting Research* 27 (2010): 143–185. The absence of serious penalty to the omission of information explains why companies frequently stop and later resume earnings guidance, unconcerned that stopping guidance will raise investors' suspicion about the reasons for stopping.

15. Scott Hensley and Peter Landers, "If drug firm's star falls, does anyone hear it?" *Wall Street Journal*, February 24, 2004.

16. On investors' limited attention and its relation to accounting choices, see David Hirshleifer and Siew Hong Teoh, "Limited attention, information disclosure, and financial reporting," *Journal of Accounting and Economics* 36 (2003): 337–386; and David Hirshleifer, Sonya Lim, and Siew Hong Teoh, "Disclosure to an audience with limited attention," working paper, Ohio State University, 2004.

17. Mitchell Petersen, "Information: Hard and soft," working paper, Kellogg School of Management, Northwestern University, 2004.

18. Ibid.

19. Ibid., 7.

20. A statement made by Time Warner CEO during a July 31, 2007, conference call.

21. Returning to the book-to-bill ratio, mentioned earlier, the "book"—orders for future delivery—usually differs across companies. Some orders are final and paid for, others can be canceled under certain circumstances. The "hard" book-to-bill ratio thus abstracts from such important nuances, causing a loss of information.

22. A fascinating example of the importance of soft relative to hard information is provided in Carruthers and Cohen, discussing the development of credit rating in the U.S. in the nineteenth century. The credit agencies transformed the extensive soft customer information they collected to hard credit score that was sold to merchants. However, for an additional fee, subscribers could view a detailed report (soft information) on the customer. It turns out that the information in those detailed reports was a better predictor of business failures than the hard credit score. See Bruce Carruthers and Barry Cohen, "Predicting failure but failing to predict: A sociology of knowledge of credit rating in post-bellum America," working paper, Department of Sociology, Northwestern University, 2001.

23. Baruch Lev, "On the usefulness of earnings and earnings research: Lessons and directions from two decades of accounting research," *Journal of Accounting Research*, Supplement (1989): 153–192; Ray Ball and Lakshmanan Shivakumar, "How much new information is there in earnings?" *Journal of Accounting Research* 46 (2008): 975–1016.

24. Brian Bushee, Dawn Matsumoto, and Gregory Miller, "Open versus closed conference calls: The determinants and effects of broadening access to disclosure," *Journal of Accounting and Economics*, 34 (2003):149–180.

25. Dawn Matsumoto, Maarten Pronk, and Erick Roelofsen, "Conference call disclosure and firm performance: An empirical analysis of the length and content of earnings-related conference calls," working paper, University of Washington, 2007.

26. To quantify these attributes, the researchers' linguistic algorithm uses "dictionaries" of the examined attributes, such as all financially related words in companies' reports, and computes the ratios of the attribute-related words (e.g., financial words) to the total number of words in the conference call.

27. Information (communications) theory measures the content of a message by the extent of change in the receiver's perceptions (more accurately, prior probability) regarding the event dealt with by the message. See Claude Shannon and Warren Weaver, *The Mathematical Theory of Communication* (Urbana, IL: The University of Illinois Press, 1964). Accordingly, uninformative conference calls will leave investors unmoved, while informative calls will generate stock trade.

28. Since earnings are sometime released after the end of trade, followed by a conference call early the next morning (so that the price change during the call reflects also the earnings announcement), we excluded such calls from our sample.

29. Our measure of the stock price change during the call is adjusted for the company's average stock price changes during the call time span (e.g., 10:00–12:00 a.m) in previous days, and the volume of trade measure (total shares traded) is similarly adjusted for the company's average volume during the call period in previous days, to identify abnormal investor reaction to the calls.

30. Our findings are consistent with Tetlock et al., who examine the impact of negative words in all *Wall Street Journal* and *Dow Jones News Service* articles about S&P 500 companies from 1980 to 2004. See Paul Tetlock, Maytal Saar-Tsechansky, and Sofus Macskassy, "More than words: A study of decision-making in administrative organization quantifying language to measure firms' fundamentals," *Journal of Finance* 63 (2008): 1437–1467. As an example, the authors quote a 1999 article about Microsoft allegedly overcharging customers for its software. The article's second sentence is: "The alleged 'pricing abuse will only get worse if Microsoft is not disciplined sternly by the antitrust court', said ..." There are five negative words here (alleged, abuse, worse, sternly, antitrust) of 29 total words in the sentence—a

17.2% ratio. Similar to our conference call findings, the authors' tests confirm that negative words convey additional (negative) information beyond the hard data on earnings decreases and consensus estimate misses, as reflected by the stock price response to the article, and furthermore, negative words predict future low earnings. Negative words, in particular, capture certain hard-to-quantify business aspects.

31. More on guidance in chapter 6.

32. Cheap talk is the economic term for unbinding, costless messages that cannot be verified by subsequent events ("we are on the right track") and are, therefore, often meaningless. See Vijay Krishna and John Morgan, "Cheap talk," in *The New Palgrave Dictionary of Economics*, eds. Steven Durlauf and Lawrence Blum (Houndmills, UK: Palgrave, Macmillan, 2008).

33. Elizabeth Demers and Clara Vega, "Soft information in earnings announcements: News or noise?" working paper, INSEAD, France, 2010.

34. A clarification: the finding that managerial optimism in earnings announcements is contagious may seem to contradict my earlier result about the special impact of negative words in conference calls. Recall, however, that my conference call study discussed earlier focused on "bad news companies." For that subsample, negative words connote honesty and signal managers coming to terms with adversity and trying to do something about it. Demers and Vega's study deals with both good and bad news companies.

35. Similar findings are reported by Davis and Tama-Sweet: levels of optimism and pessimism in earnings releases help predict future company performance beyond the hard data. See Davis and Tama-Sweet, "Managers use of pessimistic tone across alternative disclosure outlets: Earnings press releases versus MD&A."

36. For those who still waver on the merits of wavering in managerial communications, here is the Sage of Omaha, Warren Buffett, in his 2007 letter to the shareholders of Berkshire Hathaway: "That party is over. It's a *certainty* that insurance-industry profit margins, including ours, will fall significantly in 2008." (p. 3, emphasis in the original). You surely know where Buffet stands.

37. IR activities don't come cheap. Hong and Huang report that, in addition to the direct expenses, the IR programs of small or newly public companies requires 20%–25% of the CEO time and about 50% of the CFO's time. See Harrison Hong and Ming Huang, "Talking up liquidity: Insider trading and investor relations," *Journal of Financial Intermediation* 14 (2005): 1–31.

38. The National Investor Relations Institute (NIRI), the IR professional organization, defines investor relations as: "A corporate marketing activity, combining the disciplines of communications and finance, providing current and potential investors with an accurate portrayal of a firm's performance and prospects, therefore having a positive effect on total value relative to the overall market and the firm's cost of capital."

39. Harrison Hong, Jeffrey Kubik, and Jeremy Stein, "The only game in town: Stock-price consequences of local bias," *Journal of Financial Economics*, 90 (2008): 20–37.

40. Brian Bushee and Gregory Miller, "Investor relations, firm visibility, and investor following," working paper, Wharton school, University of Pennsylvania, 2006.

41. Ibid., 3–4.

42. Vineet Agarwal, Angel Liao, Elly Nash, and Richard Taffler, "The impact of effective investor relations on market value," working paper, University of Edinburgh Business School, 2008.

43. Much of this research and the underlying reasoning is provided in Brennan and Tamarowski, and Lehavy and Sloan. See Michael Brennan and Claudia Tamarowski, "Investor relations, liquidity, and stock prices," *Journal of Applied Corporate Finance* 12 (2000): 26–37; and Reuven Lehavy and Richard Sloan, "Investor recognition and stock returns," *Review of Accounting Studies* 13 (2008): 327–361.

44. Liquidity is, of course, fundamentally affected by information asymmetry—the knowledge gap between corporate insiders and outsiders (investors). The larger the gap, the more investors, concerned with being exploited by those in the know, will shy away from the company. A larger number of analysts and a higher quality of their product (earnings forecasts, company analyses) decrease information asymmetry that, in turn, increases stock liquidity and decreases cost of capital.

45. Li, using a "Fog Index" from computational linguistics (lots of syllables per word, many words per sentence, and lots of sentences in the text create "fog") reports that "foggy" (difficult to read) annual reports characterize firms with low earnings and low persistence of earnings (current level of earnings, even if high, isn't likely to be maintained in the future). See Feng Li, "Annual report readability, current earnings, and earning persistence," *Journal of Accounting and Economics* 45 (2008): 221–247.

46. TCF conference call, January 15, 2004.

47. Molly Mercer, "How do investors assess the credibility of management disclosures?" *Accounting Horizons* 18 (2004): 185–196.

48. G. Grullon, George Kanatas, and James Weston, "Advertising, breadth of ownership, and liquidity," *Review of Financial Studies* 17 (2004): 439–461 and Brad Barber and Terrance Odean, "All that glitters: The effect of attention and news on the buying behavior of individual and institutional investors," *Review of Financial Studies* 21 (2008): 785–818.

49. Davis and Tama-Sweet, "Managers use of pessimistic tone across alternative disclosure outlets: Earnings press releases versus MD&A."

## CHAPTER 3

1. U.S. Securities and Exchange Commission, Accounting and Auditing Enforcement Release No. 2676, September 12, 2007. This is only one of several fraud allegations against Nortel.

2. The data on restatements is from *Audit Analytics*, 2009 Financial Restatements, February 2010. It remains to be seen whether the restatement decreases in 2007–2009 are crisis-related or the reversals of a trend.

3. The St. Augustine and Kant quotes are from Evelin Sullivan, *The Concise Book of Lying* (New York: Farrar, Straus and Giroux, 2001), 58, 63). Lies for good causes are problematic, notwithstanding Kant's emphatic stand. Some appear clear cut, like the Allies' deceptions in World War II, which helped win the war; others are questionable, like physicians giving misleading statements to insurance companies so that patients will get reimbursement for treatments the physicians believe necessary. See Jeremy Campbell, *The Liar's Tale: A History of Falsehood* (New York: W.W. Norton & Co., 2001), 11.

4. Ibid., 128. Campbell's book is a particularly enlightening and entertaining treatise on lying.

5. Ibid., 58.

6. The butterfly *Thecla togarna* has a fake head painted on the tip of its rear wing. An attacker, intending to kill the butterfly by nipping its head, will harmlessly pinch the wing instead. Sullivan, *The Concise Book of Lying*, 276–277.

7. Campbell, *The Liar's Tale*, 18.

8. The annual decrease in the market value of machinery may be factually determined, but this is not accounting depreciation. Accounting depreciation is an allocation of the original cost of an asset (minus salvage) over its useful life.

9. See, for elaboration, Baruch Lev, "Corporate earnings: Facts and fiction," *Journal of Economic Perspectives* 17 (2003): 27–50.

10. Securities and Exchange Commission, Accounting and Auditing Enforcement Release No. 2033, June 9, 2004.

11. i2 indeed restated, on July 21, 2003, its previously reported revenues, decreasing 1999–2001 revenues by $750 million, and increasing 2002 revenues by $386 million.

12. Patricia Dechow and Catherine Schrand, *Earnings Quality* (Charlottesville, VA: The Research Foundation of the CFA Institute2004), ch. 5.

13. The vagueness of GAAP is a major reason for the frequent requests by companies and accountants for *rulings* by the FASB or the SEC on accounting for specific transactions and events, rendering GAAP increasingly detailed and complex (rules-based, in the accounting jargon).

14. David Aboody and Baruch Lev, "The value-relevance of intangibles: The case of software capitalization," *Journal of Accounting Research* (Supplement), 36 (1998): 161–191.

15. Dan Fisher, "Accounting tricks catch up with GE," *Forbes.com*, August 4, 2009, and U.S. Securities and Exchange Commission, Accounting and Auditing Enforcement Release No. 3029, August 4, 2009.

16. U.S. Securities and Exchange Commission, Accounting and Auditing Enforcement Release No. 1911, November 13, 2003.

17. This high-risk sales program was aptly dubbed internally the "DDS program," standing for "deep, deep, shit."

18. Following several largely unsuccessful revitalization attempts, Gateway was acquired in 2007 by Taiwan-based Acer.

19. Based on Securities and Exchange Commission, Accounting and Auditing Enforcement Release No. 2232, April 18, 2005.

20. Ibid.

21. Based on Securities and Exchange Commission, Accounting and Auditing Enforcement Release No. 2064, July 27, 2004.

22. Ibid.

23. This case led to an important legal issue. In shareholder lawsuits against Charter and its executives, the set-top box vendors, Motorola and Scientific-Atlanta, were named as codefendants. The broad legal issue is as follows: Are suppliers or customers responsible for inappropriate accounting of their trade counterparts? See Ted Frank, "Arbitrary and unfair," *Wall Street Journal*, May 31, 2007, A14.

24. Based on Securities and Exchange Commission, Accounting and Auditing Enhancement Release No. 1978, March 17, 2004.

25. Oil reserve overstatement isn't uncommon. This key information was, for example, overstated by Royal Dutch Shell in the early 2000s.

26. Based on Securities and Exchange Commission, Accounting and Auditing Enforcement Release No. 8525, January 24, 2005.

27. Rebates and allowance are generally given by vendors for purchasing large quantities, particularly of slow-moving products, or for buyers' promotional efforts to create a market for the products.

28. Indeed, a CFO survey suggests that, post-Sarbanes-Oxley, CFOs prefer to manage earnings by changing operating decisions (e.g., defer advertising) rather than mess with accounting techniques. See Don Durfee, "Management or manipulation?" *CFO Magazine*, December 1, 2006.

29. Christian Leuz, Dhananjay Nanda, and Peter Wysocki, "Earnings management and investor protection: An international comparison," working paper, Wharton School, University of Pennsylvania, 2002.

30. The 2006 findings of an investigation into Fannie Mae's manipulations headed by Senator Warren Rudman indicated, among other things, that in 1998 a $199 million amortization expense was not recorded so that reported earnings would meet managers' bonus target.

31. Sometimes managers manipulate reported earnings *downward*. This often occurs when earnings exceed the compensation cap or limit, and the manipulation creates a reserve for future boosts to reported earnings and compensation. Sometimes understated earnings are intended to decrease the stock price before a stock option grant (lowering thereby the exercise price and increasing subsequent gains on options). Or, as in Microsoft's case in the late 1990s, earnings were understated to divert public attention from its eye-popping profitability. It even happens that earnings are understated without an obvious reason, as by the perennial loss-maker General Motors (until its 2009–2010 reorganization), which inflated in 2006 its *losses* by $200 million.

32. Not always "true ones." Some companies are serial restaters, so that the initial restatement has to be corrected later on. Glass Lewis reports, for example, that Industrial Enterprises of America, a small chemicals company, restated its financials six times, three in 2005 and three in 2006. Arguably, a world record. See Glass Lewis & Co., "The errors of their ways," February 27, 2007.

33. Florian Englmaier, "A brief survey of overconfidence," ICFAI *Journal of Behavioral Finance*, 2006; and Catherine Schrand and Sarah Zechman, "Executive overconfidence and the slippery slope to fraud," working paper, University of Pennsylvania, 2010.

34. WATBlog.com, January 7, 2009.

35. CNNMoney.com, June 15, 2006.

36. Jonathan Karpoff, Scott Lee, and Gerald Martin, "The cost to firms of cooking the books," *Journal of Financial and Quantitative Analysis* 43 (2008): 581–611.

37. The mean one-day price drop (adjusted for the overall market change) upon the initial announcement of accounting problems by itself is 25.2%.

38. The average $400 million market value loss per company is substantial, considering that many enforcement targets are small firms.

39. A case in point: "Fannie Mae said it expects to hire 1,500 consultants and spend more than $420 million this year on its earnings restatement and legal costs stemming from the widespread accounting problems." (*Wall Street Journal*, August 10, 2005, A4.) On May 23, 2006, it was announced that Fannie Mae was fined $400 million by its regulator (OFHEO) and the SEC to settle matters related to its $10.6 billion income overstatement.

40. Nicholas Varchaver, "CA: America's most dysfunctional company," *Fortune*, November 16, 2006.

41. Mark Heinzl, "Nortel to restate several years' results to fix revenue-booking flub," *Wall Street Journal*, March 11–12, 2006, A3.

42. Simi Kedia and Thomas Philippon, "The economics of fraudulent accounting," *Review of Financial Studies* 22 (2009): 2169–2199.

43. Similar evidence of overinvestment by manipulating companies is provided by McNichols and Stubben. See Maureen McNichols and Stephen Stubben, "Does earnings management affect firms' investment decisions?" *The Accounting Review* 83 (2008): 1571–1603.

44. Jonathan Karpoff, Scott Lee, and Gerald Martin, "The consequences to managers of financial misrepresentation," *Journal of Financial Economics* 88 (2008): 193–205.

45. Given that these proceedings are quite long, typically stretching over several years, the researchers document that the targeted executives' turnover rates are significantly higher than the normal turnover rates of executives in nontargeted companies over similar time spans.

46. Quoted by the *Wall Street Journal*, May 26, 2006, 1.

47. Securities and Exchange Commission, Accounting and Auditing Enforcement Release No. 2033, June 9, 2004.

48. Kedia and Philippon, "The economics of fraudulent accounting."

49. Dyck et al. examine corporate misrepresentations and fraud, concluding (p. 35): "The table [of fraud detectors] shows a stunning increase in the role of auditors (a four-fold increase

in the relative frequency of detections) and of the SEC (a doubling of their importance, albeit from a very low level)." Alexander Dyck, Adair Morse, and Luigi Zingales, "Who blows the whistle on corporate fraud?" working paper 12882, NBER, Cambridge, MA, 2007.

50. Home Depot stopped providing the all-important "same-store sales" data, and Dell ceased providing quarterly guidance when facing operating challenges in the early 2000s.

51. *Wall Street Journal*, February 13, 2008, C1.

52. Glass Lewis & Co., "The errors of their ways," February 27, 2007.

53. Baruch Lev, Stephen Ryan, and Min Wu, "Rewriting earnings history," *Review of Accounting Studies* 13 (2008): 419–451.

## CHAPTER 4

1. This chapter deals only with shareholder lawsuits generally filed under Rule 10b-5 of the Securities and Exchange Act of 1934, which prohibits the release of materially fraudulent information to investors and the withholding of material information from investors. Other lawsuits, such as product or employee litigation, are not included here. Also, the lawsuit statistics provided here refer to federal lawsuits, excluding the generally smaller state lawsuits.

2. *Financial Times*, April 5, 2007, 21.

3. Stephanie Plancich and Svetlana Starykh, "Recent trends in securities class action litigation: 2010 year-end update," National Economic Research Associates, Inc., New York, December 2010.

4. I focus on "standard, or core filings," namely, the plain vanilla securities lawsuits. Occasionally, there are specific issues generating an unusual number of litigations, such as the spike in 2001 shown in figure 4-1, which is due to 315 "laddering" cases, alleging that companies and underwriters engaged in unfair allocations of IPO shares and price manipulation. The smaller spike in 2002 is due to 44 cases filed against analysts, and 27 cases in 2006 refer to options backdating. Those lawsuits appear to be one-time phenomena.

5. In 2010, ten lawsuits were filed against Chinese companies alleging accounting and internal control improprieties.

6. The largest were Enron ($7.2 billion), WorldCom ($6.2 billion), Cendant ($3.6 billion), Tyco ($3.0 billion), and AOL Time Warner ($2.7 billion). In addition to these private shareholder lawsuit settlements, there are many settlements with the SEC and DOJ. Notable among such settlements in 2006 were the following: AIG ($1.6 billion), Bawag ($675 million), Fannie Mae ($400 million), and Bear Stearns ($250 million). See PwC (Pricewater-houseCoopers) Advisory, *Securities Litigation Studies*, 2007, 32. A few of the settlements with foreign companies were also large: Nortel Networks (Canada), $2.2 billion in 2006; Royal Ahold (Netherlands), $1.1 billion in 2005; and Global Crossing (Bermuda), $444 million in 2004.

7. See Joseph Grundfest, "The class-action market," *Wall Street Journal*, February 7, 2007, A15. The Sarbanes-Oxley Act authorizes the SEC to collect funds for distribution to shareholders damaged by fraud. The SEC doesn't deduct from such funds the customary one-third or more taken by plaintiff lawyers in shareholder lawsuits.

8. PwC, *Securities Litigation Studies*, 25.

9. Managers of non-U.S. companies delude themselves in believing that they are immune to class-action lawsuits. It may only be a matter of time. England, Sweden, Spain, Germany, and the Netherlands already experience some class-action litigation, and the Irish and Italian governments are currently considering legislation to allow litigation by multiple parties (PwC, *Securities Litigation Studies*, 75). And, of course, in the United States, there is always the possibility of suing large foreign companies that do business in the U.S, such as the lawsuits against Parmalat (Italy) and British Petroleum (U.K.).

10. The court in *Dura Pharmaceuticals* affirmed the important role of the price decline upon disclosure of improprieties in the damage calculation. See James Spindler, "Why shareholders want their CEOs to lie more after *Dura Pharmaceuticals*," *The Georgetown Law Journal* 95 (2007): 653–692.

11. I chose the 20% cutoff based on studies showing that the average price decline preceding the filing of class-action (Rule 10b-5) lawsuits range within 20%–30%. See Michael Perino, " What we know and don't know about the Private Securities Litigation Reform Act of 1995," Testimony before the subcommittee of Finance and Hazardous Materials of the Committee on Commerce, United States House of Representatives on October 21, 1997; and Marilyn Johnson, Karen Nelson, and Adam Pritchard, "Do the merits matter more? The impact of the Private Securities Litigation Reform Act," *The Journal of Law, Economics & Organization* 23 (2007): 627–652. The two-day interval is necessary because often a price drop in reaction to adverse information spills over to the next day.

12. See http://securities.stanford.edu/.

13. The price drop following adverse corporate disclosure is generally considered the end of the "class period" during which the fraud or misrepresentation is alleged to have occurred. As such, the triggering price drop is often explicitly identified in the complaint.

14. The 2,746 and 1,421 companies were involved in a larger number of shareholder lawsuits—218 and 111, respectively—filed from 2002 to 2004. The additional lawsuits (over the 113 and 67 mentioned), however, appear unrelated to the identified stock price drops in 2002 and 2003.

15. Lin Peng and Ailsa Röell, "Executive pay, earnings manipulation and shareholder litigation," *Review of Finance* 12 (2008): 141–184.

16. The Peng and Roell data is relative to number of firms in the industry, while the NERA percentages are relative to total number of lawsuits.

17. Research has shown that companies engaged in substantial business acquisitions *underperform* similar nonacquirers during the three to five years subsequent to the acquisitions. See, for example, Tim Loughran and Anand Vijh, "Do long-term shareholders benefit from corporate acquisitions?" *The Journal of Finance* LII (1997): 1765–1790. This sobering experience underlies the frequent negative investor reaction to the announcement of plans to acquire companies.

18. See Ritter on the frequent underperformance of IPOs. John Ritter, "The long-run performance of initial public offerings," *Journal of Finance* 46 (1991): 3–27.

19. Laura Field, Michelle Lowry, and Susan Shu, "Does disclosure deter or trigger litigation?" *Journal of Accounting and Economics* 39 (2005): 487–507.

20. Douglas Skinner, "Earnings disclosures and stockholder lawsuits," *Journal of Accounting and Economics* 23 (1997): 249–282.

21. Johnson et al., "Do the merits matter more?"

22. A large number of SEC-sanctioned accounting manipulations were indeed done by "managing" accrual estimates. See Patricia Dechow and Catherine Schrand, *Earnings Quality*, The Research Foundation of CFA Institute, 2004, ch. 5.

23. Yvonne Lu, "Have defendant firms of shareholder securities litigation manipulated earnings?" working paper, University of Southern California, 2006.

24. Stephen Choi, Karen Nelson, and Adam Pritchard, "The screening effect of the Private Securities Litigation Reform Act," *Journal of Empirical Legal Studies* 6 (2009): 35–68.

25. Johnson et al., "Do the merits matter more?"

26. Brian Hall, "Six challenges in designing equity-based pay," *Journal of Applies Corporate Finance* 15 (2003): 21–33.

27. Johnson et al., Do the merits matter more?

28. Natasha Burns and Simi Kedia, "The impact of performance-based compensation on misreporting," *Journal of Financial Economics* 79 (2006): 35–67.

29. In Oscar Wilde, *Lady Windermere's Fan*, 1892, 1.

30. Johnson et al., Do the merits matter more?

31. Mary Billings, "Disclosure timeliness, insider trading opportunities and litigation consequences," working paper, New York University, 2009.

## CHAPTER 5

1. The motto *meden agan*, nothing in excess, greeted visitors to the Temple of Apollo at Delphi.

2. The change at Dell's top indeed inspired certain hope in capital markets, evidenced by the price increase in 2007, but this recovery didn't go anywhere.

3. The undervaluation of shares increases cost of capital in several ways. Fund-raising by issuing new stock requires an excessive number of shares (compared with a properly valued stock), thereby diluting existing shareholders' value. Such wealth transfer from current to new shareholders is a serious cost and often a deterrent to the use of stock to finance investment and growth by undervalued companies. Regarding borrowed capital, an undervalued stock, manifested by low P/E relative to competitors, for example, informs lenders of investors' concerns about the company's growth, and perhaps even solvency, leading them to charge higher interest rates and demand restrictive loan covenants, again increasing the cost of capital.

4. In the raging bull market of 1999, when overvaluations were rampant, a survey of 200 CFOs of large U.S. companies found that 61% believed their companies' shares were *undervalued*, while only 5% felt the stock was overvalued. See Robert Eccles, Robert Herz, Mary Keegan, and David Phillips, *The Value Reporting Revolution* (New York: John Wiley & Sons, 2001), 48.

5. Well, not all managers. Warren Buffett in his 1988 letter to shareholders wrote: "Charlie Munger [Berkshire Hathaway's vice chairman] and I are bothered as much by significant overvaluation as significant undervaluation."

6. Michael Jensen, "The agency costs of overvalued equity and the current state of corporate finance," *European Financial Management Journal* 10 (2004): 552.

7. These are forward-looking P/Es, based on next-year expected earnings. A trailing P/E is based on the prior-year's earnings. Empirical evidence indicates that forward-looking P/Es are better predictors of share value than trailing PEs. See J. Liu, Doron Nissim, and Jacob Thomas, "Equity valuation using multiples," *Journal of Accounting Research* 40 (2002): 135–172.

8. A within-industry P/E comparison is called for because it controls to some extent for business risk, which affects the P/E ratio.

9. Note that neither the P/E nor the PEG indicator assesses the share value against its intrinsic (fundamental) worth, which is the right way of identifying mispricing. Intrinsic values, however, are not available to investors, and rarely known by managers.

10. Jensen, "The agency costs of overvalued equity and the current state of corporate finance," 552.

11. International Data Corp. predicted an 11.5% PC shipment increase, while Gartner Inc. predicted a 10% increase. *eWeek*, October 19, 2004.

12. Cutting advertising or R&D for growth pretense is distinct, of course, from cutting expenses as a result of a carefully thought-through efficiency plan. Thus, for example, Amgen, a leading biotech company experiencing slumping sales of its leading anemia drug Aranesp in 2007, reported in its August 2007 10-Q quarterly filing that it would slow down spending on R&D and capital expenditures in order to reduce costs. Clearly a strategic, planned move rather than an earnings manipulation.

13. Gu and Lev document that companies with overpriced shares tend to engage in ill-advised acquisitions (overpaid for, or strategic misfits), leading to large goodwill write-offs

(losses). See Feng Gu and Baruch Lev, 2011, "Overpriced shares, ill-advised acquisitions and goodwill impairment," *The Accounting Review*, forthcoming.

14. See U.S. General Accounting Office, Restatement Database.

15. Cost of financing is reduced when equity is overpriced because fewer shares have to be issued to raise capital or acquire a business, compared with the equity that is given up when shares are properly priced.

16. Cecile Durant, "Time Warner may consider AOL spinoff," *Washington Post*, May 21, 2005.

17. David D. Kirkpatrick and David Carr, "A media giant needs a script," *New York Times*, July 7, 2002.

18. Gu and Lev, "Overpriced shares, ill-advised acquisitions and goodwill impairment."

19. Goodwill is the difference between the price paid for a corporate acquisition and the fair value of the net assets acquired. Accounting rules require that goodwill be examined annually for impairment, that is, loss of value, and when impairment is determined, the goodwill has to be written down to its fair value and the write-off recognized as a loss.

20. Three examples from our sample:

| | Relative P/E in 1997 | Ratio of Goodwill Write-off to Assets, 2001–2005 |
|---|---|---|
| Walt Disney | 3.9 | 1.9% |
| Gateway | 25.0 | 4.7% |
| Lucent Technologies | 67.3 | 12.1% |

Thus, Lucent, with a substantial share overvaluation in 1997 (difference between its P/E and the industry median was 67.3) suffered staggering goodwill losses of 12.1% of total assets, whereas Walt Disney, with a negligible share overvaluation (P/E exceeding industry median by 3.9 only), sustained subsequent goodwill losses of 1.9% of assets only.

21. Negative consequences were also documented for regular investments (not just acquisitions) by overvalued companies. See Christopher Polk and Paola Sapienza, "The stock market and corporate investment: A test of catering theory," *The Review of Financial Studies* 22 (2009): 187–217.

22. Richard Sloan, "Do stock prices fully reflect information in cash flows and accruals about future earnings?" *The Accounting Review* 71 (1996): 289–315.

23. For additional evidence challenging capital market efficiency, see Andrei Shleifer, *Inefficient Markets: An Introduction to Behavioral Finance* (Oxford, U.K.: Oxford University Press, 2000), ch. 1.

24. Allan Eberhart, William Maxwell, and Akhtar Siddique, "Returns and operating performance following R&D increases," *Journal of Finance* 59 (2004): 623–650.

25. Baker and Wurgler define investor sentiment as a view about firms' growth prospects and risk that is not justified by facts. See Malcolm Baker and Jeffrey Wurgler, "Investor sentiment in the stock market," *Journal of Economic Perspectives* 21 (2007): 129–151.

26. Importantly, share overpricing is more likely to arise and be sustained than is underpricing. Suppose investors A and B differ about the prospects of a certain company— A is very bullish about its growth prospects, whereas B believes it's an over-the-hill enterprise. What will they do? Investor A will buy as many shares as he or she desires, but B doesn't have enough shares to sell to back the negative view. Investor B could sell short (sell borrowed shares), but, for various cost and institutional reasons, most individuals and many institutions (mutual funds in particular) do not engage in short sales. Thus, if buying shares

on optimistic views is unconstrained and selling short is limited, the perceptions of optimistic investors will be reflected in stock prices more forcefully and persistently than will those of the pessimists, and share prices will tend to be overvalued, even if investors' opinions about the prospects of companies are equally distributed between optimists and pessimists. For empirical evidence supporting this scenario, see Joseph Chen, Harrison Hong, and Jeremy Stein, "Breadth of ownership and stock returns," *Journal of Financial Economics* 66 (2002): 171–205.

27. A representative view: "In fact, significant deviations from intrinsic value are rare, and markets usually revert rapidly to share prices commensurate with economic fundamentals." See Marc Goedhart, Timothy Koller, and David Vessels, "Do fundamentals—or emotions—drive the stock market?" *McKinsey on Finance* 15 (2005): 1.

28. Baruch Lev and Doron Nissim, "The persistence of the accruals anomaly," *Contemporary Accounting Research* 23 (2006): 193–226.

29. Cabela's had a market capitalization of $1.6 billion only in August 2007, a return-on-asset of 4.9% in 2006, and a beta value of 1.23, indicating an above-average stock return volatility (risk). It also abstained from paying dividends. All this does not mean that Cabela's is a poorly run or unpromising company. On the contrary, *Barron's* presented a positive view of Cabela's prospects. *Barron's*, August 20, 2007, 18–19.

30. Another reason for institutional reluctance to invest in small, volatile companies is the "prudent-man" law applied in lawsuits filed by investors seeking compensation from fund managers. Courts often ruled that if the defendant invested "prudently," generally in large, mature, and profitable companies (Walmart, IBM, and Exxon come to mind), they cannot be held liable for investment losses, short of fraud. See D. Del Guercio, "The distorting effect of the prudent-man laws on institutional equity investment," *Journal of Financial Economics* 40 (1996): 31–62. Many overpriced companies cannot be considered "prudent" investment and therefore pose a high risk to fund managers.

31. The dispersion of analysts' forecasts is widely available from the vendors of the forecasts, such as I/B/E/S, along with the consensus estimates. (Yahoo! Finance provides the "high and low" of earnings estimates, a measure of dispersion.) For example, on June 14, 2007, the dispersion of the current and following year's EPS forecasts (from I/B/E/S) for Dell, Hewlett-Packard, and IBM were, as follows:

| | **DELL** | | **HP** | | **IBM** | |
|---|---|---|---|---|---|---|
| | **Current** | **Following** | **Current** | **Following** | **Current** | **Following** |
| **EPS Consensus** | $1.35 | $1.60 | $2.78 | $3.11 | $6.85 | $7.72 |
| **Dispersion (CV)** | 0.060 | 0.101 | 0.007 | 0.022 | 0.010 | 0.025 |

The dispersion data is the standard deviation of the individual analyst forecasts, divided, to enable comparability, by the mean of the forecasts (the resulting measure is known as the coefficient of variation, cv). It is striking that Dell's forecast dispersions (0.060 and 0.101, for the earnings in the current and following year, respectively) are orders of magnitude higher than those of HP and IBM. Evidently, as of June 2007, investors' uncertainty about the future operating performance of Dell and the likelihood of share mispricing were substantially higher than those of its competitors.

32. Coach's analyst forecasts, as well as its P/E and PEG ratios, were obtained from Yahoo!Finance, http://finance.yahoo.com/q/ac.

33. For a practicable discussion of the P/E ratio and other valuation multiples, see Goedhart et al., "Do fundamentals—or emotions—drive the stock market?"

34. Recall, the PEG ratio is the ratio of P/E to expected growth, such as analysts' consensus long-term estimate.

35. *Wall Street Journal*, January 19, 2006, A11.

## CHAPTER 6

1. Not only in America: Nintendo, the Japanese video game producer, while still compiling its 2006 results, hastened on April 5, 2007, to raise its 2007 sales forecast to 966 billion yen ($8.1 billion) from 900 billion yen projected just three months prior. Nintendo's stock rose 2.1% on the news in the Osaka Exchange.

2. *Forbes*, June 19, 2006, 44.

3. In February 2006, Boeing, for example, raised its earnings guidance for 2006 and 2007, yet got mired in 2007 in serious delays in the production and tests of its innovative and fast-selling 787 Dreamliner, continuing well into 2011.

4. Figures 6-1 and 6-2 are based on First Call Company, Guidelines data.

5. Interestingly, Tucker and Zarowin document that large companies tend to warn investors about impending bad news *earlier* than small companies. The higher litigation exposure of large companies—see chapter 4—has clearly a lot to do with this disclosure trait. See Jennifer Tucker and Paul Zarowin, "Timeliness of firms' voluntary disclosure of good and bad news," working paper, University of Florida, 2006.

6. Daniel Kahneman and Amos Tversky, "Prospect theory: An analysis of decision under risk," *Econometrica* 47 (1979): 263–291.

7. National Investor Relations Institute (NIRI), news release, Executive Alert: *NIRI issues 2006 survey results on earnings guidance practices*, Vienna, VA, 2006.

8. The higher frequency of guidance abroad is corroborated by Frost comparing the guidance practice in several European countries with that in the United States. Carol Frost, "Characteristics and information value of corporate disclosures of forward-looking information in global equity markets," working paper, Dartmouth College, Dartmouth, NH, 2003. See, also, Stephen Baginski, John Hassell, and Michael Kimbrough, "The effect of legal environment on voluntary disclosure: Evidence from management earnings forecasts issued in U.S. and Canadian markets," *The Accounting Review* 77 (2002): 25–50.

9. CFA Institute and the Business Roundtable, *Breaking the short-term cycle* (New York: CFA Institute, 2006), 2.

10. Ibid., 5.

11. U. S. Chamber of Commerce, Commission on the Regulation of U.S. Capital Markets in the 21st Century: Report and Recommendations, 2007.

12. McKinsey & Co., "The misguided practice of earnings guidance," *McKinsey on Finance* 19 (Spring 2006): 1–5.

13. Indeed, analysts regularly issue quarterly earnings forecasts even for the most ardent guidance refuseniks—Warren Buffett's Berkshire Hathaway and Google.

14. Not to mention the private equity funds themselves, such as the Blackstone Group in the United States, the 3i Group in the U.K., and Canada's Onex Group, which take businesses private but are themselves public companies.

15. Amy Hutton, "Determinants of managerial earnings guidance prior to regulation Fair Disclosure and bias in analysts' earnings forecasts," *Contemporary Accounting Research* 22 (2005): 867–914.

16. Joel Houston, Baruch Lev, and Jennifer Tucker, "To guide or not to guide? Causes and consequences of stopping quarterly earnings guidance," *Contemporary Accounting Research* 27 (2010): 143–185.

17. Also increasing was the disagreement among analysts—the variance of their forecasts—about the future earnings of guidance stoppers.

18. Shuping Chen, Dawn Matsumoto, and Shiva Rajgopal, "Is silence golden? An empirical analysis of firms that stop giving quarterly guidance," *Journal of Accounting and Economics* 51 (2011): 134–150.

19. Julie Cotter, Irem Tuna, and Peter Wysocki, "Expectations management and beatable targets: How do analysts react to explicit earnings guidance?" *Contemporary Accounting Research* 23 (2006): 593–624.

20. See, for example, John Graham, Harvey Campbell, and Shiva Rajgopal, "The economic implications of corporate financial reporting," *Journal of Accounting and Economics* 40 (2005): 3–73.

21. See, for example, Dawn Matsumoto, "Management's incentives to avoid negative earnings surprises," *The Accounting Review* 77 (2002): 483–514.

22. Ron Kasznik and Baruch Lev, "To warn or not to warn: Management disclosures in the face of an earnings surprise," *The Accounting Review* 70 (1995): 113–134; and Jenny Tucker, "Is openness penalized? Stock returns around earnings warnings," *The Accounting Review* 82 (2007): 1055–1087.

23. Owen Lamont, "Go down fighting: Short sellers vs. firms," working paper 10659, NBER, 2004.

24. Jonathan Karpoff and Xiaoxia Lou, "Short sellers and financial misconduct," *Journal of Finance* LXV (2010): 1879–1913.

25. Alina Lerman, "Individual investors' attention to accounting information: Message board discussions," working paper, Stern School of Business, New York University, 2010.

26. Individuals' significant demand for and action upon timely information is evident from Dey and Radhakrishna, who report that individual investors account for 30% of all trades around companies' earnings announcements and 11% of the volume. See M. Dey and B. Radhakrishna, "Who trades around earnings announcements? Evidence from TORQ data," *Journal of Business Finance and Accounting* 34 (2007): 269–291.

27. *Barron's*, December 3, 2007.

28. Peter DeMarzo, Dimitri Vayanos, and Jeffrey Zwiebel, "Persuasion bias, social influence, and unidimensional opinions," *The Quarterly Journal of Economics* 118 (2003): 909–968.

29. Brad Barber and Terrance Odean, "All that glitters: The effect of attention and news on the buying behavior of individual and institutional investors," *The Review of Financial Studies* 21 (2008): 785–818.

30. If actual EPS is negative (a loss), you can put the absolute value of EPS in the denominator.

31. The consensus estimates are available from vendors, such as I/B/E/S, or free of charge from Yahoo! Finance. The latter, however, does not provide historical data.

32. The dispersion of analysts' forecasts as a measure of uncertainty was discussed in chapter 5.

33. Benjamin Lansford, Baruch Lev, and Jennifer Tucker, "Causes and consequences of disaggregating earnings guidance," working paper, Fisher School of Accounting, University of Florida, 2010.

## CHAPTER 7

1. Essential technical details: Stock prices are those three months after the end of a company's fiscal year, to allow investors to fully comprehend and react to the release of the annual financial report. Earnings are for the fiscal year, and book value is at the end of the year. The three data items are per share, accounting to some extent for the different sizes and share number of companies. The number of companies in each year's regression increases

from 1,500 to 2,000 in the 1970s and 1980s, to 2,000 to 3,000 in the 1990s and 2000s. All large, midsize, and many small U.S. listed companies are included in the analysis. To avoid certain large variations in $R^2$, the bars in figure 7-1 represent three-year moving averages.

2. A subtle point: figure 7-1 doesn't indicate that the relevance of corporate earnings and asset values decreased drastically; rather the relevance of *reported* earnings and assets, subject to multiple accounting measurement deficiencies and manipulation, dropped sharply.

3. Shuping Chen, Dawn Matsumoto, and Shivaram Rajgopal, "Is silence golden? An empirical analysis of firms that stop giving quarterly earning guidance," *Journal of Accounting and Economics* 51 (2011): 134–150.

4. CNNMoney.com, May 16, 2006.

5. David Aboody and Baruch Lev, "Information asymmetry, R&D and insider gains," *Journal of Finance* 55 (2000): 2747–2766.

6. George Akerlof, "The market for 'lemons': Quality uncertainty and the market mechanism," *Quarterly Journal of Economics* 84 (1970): 488–500.

7. Economists call the process leading to such market degradation "adverse selection" (the "good" exit from the market).

8. The historical returns are from Ibbotson Associates.

9. Such information surprises were apparently present, for example, at Vonage Holdings Corp., whose share price declined by 41.1% during the month subsequent to IPO (May 24, 2006) as investors became better informed about the company and its challenging competitive position.

10. Given the company's future cash flows, if investors increase their required return, share price will drop.

11. These relative spreads were computed as the ask price (for selling) minus the bid price (buying), divided by the bid price.

12. For a formal analysis of the bid-ask spread decision, see Lawrence Glosten and Paul Milgrom, "Bid, ask and transaction prices in a specialist market with heterogeneously informed traders," *Journal of Financial Economics*, 14 (1985): 71–100. The market maker may also decrease the "depth," the number of shares offered at the bid and ask, in reaction to increased information asymmetry. The market maker recoups his or her losses to the better informed from trades with investors who must buy or sell, irrespective of price ("liquidity traders" in the economic jargon).

13. A company's cost of capital is the rate of return its owners can obtain from alternative investments having the same level of risk as the company's (investors' expected return).

14. These cost of capital estimates were obtained from Reuven Lehavy's Web site, http://webuser.bus.umich.edu/rlehavy/vldata.htm.

15. It also reflects other accounting deficiencies, like assets reported at unrealistic historical values, though those are increasingly mitigated by fair value accounting rules.

16. Baruch Lev, *Intangibles: Management, Measurement and Reporting* (Washington, DC: Brookings Institution Press, 2001).

17. S. DiPiazza, A. McDonnell, D. Parrett, W. Rake, M. Samyn, and J. Turley, "Global capital markets and the global economy: A vision from the CEOs of the international audit networks," white paper, 2006, 6.

18. See A. Eberhart, W. Maxwell, and A. Siddique, "An examination of long-term abnormal stock returns and operating performance following R&D increases," *Journal of Finance* 54 (2004): 623–650; and Baruch Lev, Doron Nissim, and Jacob Thomas, "On the informational usefulness of R&D capitalization and amortization," in *Visualizing Intangibles: Measuring and Reporting in the Knowledge Economy*, eds. Z. Zambon and B. Marzo (Burlington, VT: Ashgate, 2007). R&D is, of course, not the only intangible investment of businesses, but it's the only intangible expenditure that has to be separately reported in the income statement and therefore extensively researched. Investments in brands, IT, human resources, business processes,

and like intangibles are "buried" in large expense categories (SG&A, cost of sales), not amenable for research.

19. Dennis Oswald and Paul Zarowin, "Capitalization of R&D and the informativeness of stock prices," *European Accounting Review* 16 (2007): 703–726.

20. The vulnerability of earnings to "management" and manipulation obviously detracts significantly from its usefulness. This issue will not be discussed here, since it's elaborated on in chapter 3.

21. Specifically, this comprehensive research shows that current and past cash flows outperform earnings in predicting future cash flows, and even outperform earnings in predicting future earnings beyond one year. See Baruch Lev, Siyi Li, and Theodore Sougiannis, "The usefulness of accounting estimates for predicting cash flows and earnings," *Review of Accounting Studies* 15 (2010): 779–807.

22. Cisco is in good company. Bhattacharya et al. report for a sample of 1,149 companies that 80 of their pro forma EPS beat the consensus, whereas only 39% of the corresponding GAAP earnings surpassed the consensus. See Nilabhra Bhattacharya, Ervin Black, Theodore Christensen, and Chad Larson, "Assessing the relative informativeness and permanence of street earnings and GAAP operating earnings," *Journal of Accounting and Economics* 36 (2003): 285–319.

23. *Wall Street Journal,* July 6, 2005, p. C1.

24. Securities and Exchange Commission, *Final Rule: Conditions for Use of Non-GAAP Financial Measures,* Release Nos. 33-8176; 34-47226; FR-65, Washington, DC, January 22, 2003.

25. Cisco warns in its 2008 report (p. 76). "In management's opinion, the existing [stock option] valuation models may not provide an accurate measure of the fair value of the Company's employee stock options."

26. M. Bradshaw and Richard Sloan, "GAAP versus the street: An empirical assessment of two alternative definitions of earnings," *Journal of Accounting Research* 40 (2002): 41–65; and Bhattacharya et al., "Assessing the relative informativeness and permanence of street earnings and GAAP operating earnings."

27. Lawrence Brown and K. Sivakumar, "Comparing the quality of two operating income measures," *Review of Accounting Studies* 4 (2003): 561–572.

28. Analysts often refer to such predictive-ability as the "quality of earnings." High-quality earnings are those that will likely recur in the future.

29. Liz Claiborne's 2005 10-K report states: "At February 17, 2006, our order book reflected unfilled customer orders for approximately $881 million of merchandise, as compared to approximately $980 million at February 25, 2005."

30. For elaboration on this measure and its usefulness, see Massimiliano Bonacchi, Kalin Kolev, and Baruch Lev, "The analysis and valuation of subscription-based enterprises," working paper, Yale University, 2011.

31. These R&D breakdowns, essential for evaluating the efficiency of innovation investments, are not required by GAAP to be disclosed to investors.

32. Numerous studies have shown that patent attributes, such as forward citations and claims breadth, are important indicators of patent value and firm's future performance. For an example, see Zhen Deng, Baruch Lev, and Francis Narin, "Science & technology as predictors of stock performance," *Financial Analysts Journal* 55 (1999): 20–32.

33. Several large pharmaceutical companies currently report "innovation revenues."

34. Many confuse brands with known names. Brands without a price premium aren't brands, just known names, like Polaroid or Krispi Crème, which either no longer exist (Polaroid) or cannot command a price premium. Bayer aspirin and Amazon (books), on the other hand, command a price premium and are therefore valuable brands.

35. Bamford and Ernst, McKinsey consultants, report that large companies often have multiple alliances but vague idea of how they are performing. Very few companies

systematically track the performance of their alliances. See Jim Bamford and David Ernst, "Measuring alliance performance," *McKinsey Quarterly*, October 2002.

36. Such disclosures may even deter competitors from embarking on research or Internet developments, seeing your success in such efforts.

37. Christine Botosan, "Disclosure level and the cost of equity capital," *The Accounting Review* 72 (1997): 323–349; and Michael Goldstein, Edith Hotchkiss, and Erik Sirri, "Transparency and liquidity: A controlled experiment on corporate bonds," *Review of Financial Studies* 20 (2007): 274–314.

38. Luzi Hail, "The impact of voluntary corporate disclosures on the ex ante cost of capital for Swiss firms," *European Accounting Review* 11 (2003): 741–743.

39. Rejin Guo, Baruch Lev, and Nan Zhou, "Competitive costs of disclosure by biotech IPOs," *Journal of Accounting Research* (Supplement) (2004): 319–355.

40. Paul Healy, Amy Hutton, and Krishna Palepu, "Stock performance and intermediation changes surrounding sustained increases in disclosure," *Contemporary Accounting Research* 16 (1999): 485–520.

41. Christian Leuz and Robert Verrecchia, "The economic consequences of increased disclosure," *Journal of Accounting Research* 38 (2000): 91–124.

42. Irene Karamanou and George Nishiotis, "Disclosure and the cost of capital: Evidence from the market's reaction to firm voluntary adoption of IAS," *Journal of Business Finance & Accounting* 36 (2009): 793–821.

43. John Graham, Campbell Harvey, and Shiva Rajgopal, "The economic implications of corporate financial reporting," *Journal of Accounting and Economics* 40 (2005): 3–73.

44. Gregory Miller, "Earnings performance and discretionary disclosure," *Journal of Accounting Research* 40 (2002): 173–204.

## CHAPTER 8

1. Louis Lowenstein, *Sense and Nonsense in Corporate Finance* (New York, Addison-Wesley Publishing Company, 1991), 142.

2. In December 2008, BofA succumbed to reality and cut dividends by half, and in March 2009, the bank practically eliminated its dividend.

3. Michael Spence, "Job market signaling," *Quarterly Journal of Economics* 87 (1973): 355–374; and Michael Spence, *Market Signaling: Informational Transfer in Hiring and Related Screening Processes* (Cambridge, MA: Harvard University Press, 1974).

4. Stewart Myers and Nicholas Majluf, "Corporate financing and investment decisions when firms have information that investors do not have," *Journal of Financial Economics* 13 (1984): 187–221.

5. Increased borrowing is also costly for excessively overvalued companies to signal high value, because the future profitability of such companies is low relative to their elevated market valuation (otherwise they are not overvalued), and the added interest burden of the new debt will worsen their profitability.

6. Paul Asquith and David Mullins, "Equity issues and offering dilution," *Journal of Financial Economics* 15 (1986): 61–89.

7. When company founders, like Google's Larry Page and Sergey Brin, perceive the IPO price to be below the intrinsic value of the company, they will retain a large share of its stock. Accordingly, the retained interest in IPOs signals its value to investors.

8. Fischer Black, "The dividend puzzle," in *The Modern Theory of Corporate Finance*, eds. Michel Jensen and Clifford Smith (New York: McGraw-Hill Book Company, 1984), 634–639.

9. Even the small transaction costs involved in selling shares of no-dividend companies can be defrayed, says Black, by a share repurchase plan organized by the nondividing paying company.

10. If anything, the generally higher taxes on dividends than on capital gains (from selling shares) render dividends less attractive than selling shares. This tax differential in the United States, however, was practically eliminated in 2003.

11. In March 2011, Cisco announced the initiation of a modest $.06 per share quarterly dividend.

12. See, for example, Alon Brav, Campbell Harvey, John Graham, and Roni Michaeli, "Payout policy in the 21$^{st}$ century," *Journal of Financial Economics* 77 (2005): 483–527.

13. Importantly, Allegheny's chairman accompanied the dividend cut announcement with: "our board has concluded that a dividend reduction at this time is financially prudent given the challenging economic conditions." Added the CEO: "We are optimistic about our long-term opportunities but cautious about the short-term outlook for many of our major end-use markets." (SEC 8-K Filing, November 14, 2002)

14. Ahead of the Tape, *Wall Street Journal*, July 18, 2006, C1.

15. The dividend pattern for all U.S. companies, not just the S&P 500, is very similar.

16. The bonds-driven leverage (debt/equity ratio) rise also contributed to the EPS increase.

17. EPS, in general, provides an upward-biased picture of a firm's profitability, since its denominator ignores the capital contribution from retained earnings.

18. Erik Lie, "Operating performance following open market share repurchase announcements," *Journal of Accounting and Economics* 39 (2005): 411–436.

19. Not enough, though, to trigger an upward revision of analysts' forecasts of earnings. See Gustavo Grullon and Roni Michaeli, "The information content of share repurchases programs," *Journal of Finance* 59 (2004): 651–680.

20. For the curious about "accretive buybacks": a share buyback affects both the numerator and denominator of EPS. The denominator effect is straightforward: the number of shares outstanding decreases by the buyback. Since the number of shares used to compute EPS is the time-weighted average of outstanding shares during the quarter, a buyback made early in the quarter has a large effect on decreasing the EPS denominator. Countering the EPS denominator effect of the buyback is the numerator effect: the cash used for the buyback decreases earnings from the investments liquidated for the buyback, or from interest on the debt assumed. An EPS accretive buyback is one where the denominator effect overcomes the numerator effect. Hribar et al. show that this will be the case when the foregone return on the investments liquidated (or the interest rate on the debt) is lower than the company's earnings-to-price ratio at buyback. Paul Hribar, Nicole Jenkins and Bruce Johnson, "Stock repurchases as an earnings management devise," *Journal of Accounting and Economics* 41 (2006): 3–27.

21. Ibid.

22. Told by Lowenstein, *Sense and Nonsense in Corporate Finance*, 177.

23. A reverse split, like 1:4—for every four current shares, you get one new share—is relatively rare, generally used by companies recovering from hard times or Chapter 11, where share prices are exceedingly low. With its stock price hovering around $4.50 in early March 2011, Citigroup proposed on March 21 a 1-for-10 reverse split.

24. A stock dividend, generally leading to a lower-than-25% increase in the number of shares, has an accounting impact: the market value of the new shares is transferred from retained earnings to the capital account, thereby restricting dividends somewhat. A stock split doesn't have an accounting impact.

25. Hanock Louis and Dahlia Robinson, "Do managers credibly use accruals to signal private information? Evidence from the pricing of discretionary accruals around stock splits," *Journal of Accounting and Economics* 39 (2005): 361–380.

26. Stock split announcements are sometimes accompanied by good news, such as a dividend increase. But even pure (single news) split announcements trigger, on average, a mildly positive investor reaction.

27. Josef Lakonishok and Baruch Lev, "Stock splits and stock dividends: Why, who and when," *Journal of Finance*, 42 (1987): 913–932.

28. This result was confirmed by subsequent studies; see Jinho Byun and Michael Rozeff, "Long-run performance after stock splits: 1927–1996," *Journal of Finance* 58 (2003): 1063–1086. Ikenberry and Ramnat confirm the lack of performance improvement post-split by showing that split announcements don't affect analysts' earnings forecasts. David Ikenberry and Sundaresh Ramnat, "Underreaction to self-selected news events: The case of stock splits," *Review of Financial Studies* 15 (2002): 489–526.

29. Shlomo Benartzi, Roni Michaely, Richard Thaler, and William Weld, "The nominal share price puzzle," *Journal of Economic Perspectives* 23 (2009): 121–142.

30. The annual *weighted* (by capitalization) average price ranged between $30 and $40, with the 1933–2005 overall mean at $36.56. Larger companies tend to have higher share prices. Benartzi et al., "The nominal share price puzzle," table II.

31. I was told once by an astute investor that if a stock price falls below $5, it will never recover.

32. The 50-to-1 split was put to shareholders' vote in January 2010. At the time of the split announcement, December 4, 2009, the share price was $3,320. Upon the split announcement, the price increased by 0.7%.

33. Yahoo! message boards, for example, were inundated with multiple postings and readers' reactions during the week following the June 19, 2008, Southern Copper stock split.

34. Patrick Dennis and Deon Strickland, "The effect of stock splits on liquidity and excess returns: Evidence from shareholder ownership composition," *The Journal of Financial Research* XXVI (2003): 355–370.

35. Insiders' own *gains from trade* in their company shares are, of course, subject to strict insider trading regulations. See Josef Lakonishok and Inmoo Lee, "Are insider trades informative?" *The Review of Financial Studies* 14 (2001): 79–111.

36. John McConnell, Henri Servaes, and Karl Lins, "Changes in market values and analysts' EPS forecasts around insider ownership changes," working paper, Purdue University, 2007.

37. The market-adjusted stock return is the stock's return over a specified period minus the average return on all stocks during that period. A market-adjusted return thus focuses on the company, net of economywide effects, such as inflation, which affect all stocks.

38. "Inside Track," *Wall Street Journal*, August 13, 2008, C3.

39. *Wall Street Journal*, April 25, 2007, C2.

## CHAPTER 9

1. General Electric, "Investing and Delivering on Ecomagination," *GE Ecomagination Report*, 2007, 1. Page numbers in the quotes refer to this report.

2. If a 1% emission-reduction target in five years fails to impress, GE notes that without this commitment, emissions were predicted to *rise* by 30% (what is it with 30% at GE?).

3. Michael Jensen, "Value maximization, stakeholder theory, and the corporate objective function," *Journal of Applied Corporate Finance* 14 (2001): 9–10.

4. The Copenhagen Consensus Project, founded by the Danish social scientist Bjorn Lomborg, demonstrates how complicated and controversial it is to rank social projects. Over two years, more than fifty economists, including five Nobel Laureates, collaborated to define and suggest solutions to the world's great global challenges, setting priorities in terms of economic costs and benefits. The panel's 2008 benefit-to-cost ranking was: malnutrition and hunger, trade and subsidies, diseases, education, women and development, global warming, sanitation and water, conflicts, air pollution, and terrorism. (A mental exercise: how would you rank these challenges?) How many executives have the time and expertise to perform such social ranking?

5. Milton Friedman, *Capitalism and Freedom* (Chicago: University of Chicago Press, 1963), 133. Friedman continues: "Few trends could so thoroughly undermine the very foundations of our free society as the acceptance by corporate officials of a social responsibility other than to make as much money for their shareholders as possible ... If businessmen do have a social responsibility other than making maximum profits for stockholders, how are they to know what it is? Can self-selected private individuals decide what the social interest is? Can they decide how great a burden they are justified in placing on themselves or their stockholders to serve that social interest?" (133–134). For a more recent and similar view, see Robert Reich, *Supercapitalism: The Transformation of Business, Democracy and Everyday Life* (New York: Knopf, 2007).

6. *The Economist*, January 19, 2008, 8.

7. *The Economist*, June 28, 2008, 18.

8. Renato Orsato, "Competitive environmental strategies: When does it pay to be green?" *California Management Review* 48, (2006): 136–137.

9. Baruch Lev, Christine Petrovits, and Suresh Radhakrishnan, "Is doing good, good for you? How corporate charitable contributions enhance revenue growth," *Strategic Management Journal* 31 (2010): 182–200.

10. There are, of course, lots of CSR definitions, but they aren't operational; they don't provide a practicable guide to decision makers. Consider one such definition of CSR: "voluntary corporate actions designed to improve social conditions." Surely, providing health care to employees is (as of 2009) voluntary, and it "improves social conditions." But few will consider employee health care a CSR initiative.

11. I am not breaking new ground here. This rule applies to any corporate activity, not just CSR. For example, if managers cannot generate a higher yield on invested capital than investors can on their own, that capital should be returned to shareholders (see chapter 8).

12. My corporate capabilities emphasis is inspired by Porter and Kramer, though they argue for philanthropy, which leads to an improvement in the company's competitive situation; this for me, as I argue below, is not a "deal breaker" for CSR. Michael Porter and Mark Kramer, "The Competitive Advantage of Corporate Philanthropy," *Harvard Business Review*, December 2002, 56–68.

13. Ibid.

14. Cisco Networking Academy, Program Overview, www.cisco.com/web/learning/netacad/academy/.

15. Porter and Kramer, "The Competitive Advantage of Corporate Philanthropy," 12.

16. John Peloza, "Using corporate social responsibility as insurance for financial performance," *California Management Review* 48 (2006): 59.

17. Porter and Kramer, "The Competitive Advantage of Corporate Philanthropy."

18. *New York Times*, http://nytimes.com/2008/04/17/US.

19. The Freddie Mac Foundation, Inc., 2006 Form 990-PF, www.guidestar.org.

20. Porter and Kramer, "The Competitive Advantage of Corporate Philanthropy," 84.

21. *The Economist*, January 19, 2008, 6.

22. An intriguing issue is whether firms should engage in CSR initiatives that seriously sacrifice profits. Indeed, some define CSR as "sacrificing profits in the social interest." See Einer Elhauge, "Corporate managers' operational discretion to sacrifice corporate profits in the public interest," in *Environmental Protection and the Social Responsibility of Firms*, eds. Bruce Hay, Robert Stavins, and Richard Vietor (Washington, DC: Resources for the Future, 2005). It is doubtful, however, whether such profit sacrifice is legal, where managers and directors have fiduciary duty to shareholders, or whether it's even economically sustainable in a competitive environment. Indeed, research shows that in general, CSR activities have negligible effect on company profitability. See Joshua Margolis, Hillary Elfenbein, and James Walsh, "'Does It Pay to Be Good?' A meta-analysis and redirection of research on the relationship between corporate social and financial performance," working paper, Harvard Business School, Boston, 2007.

23. Porter and Kramer, "The Competitive Advantage of Corporate Philanthropy," 6.

24. Lev et al., "Is doing good, good for you?"

25. In June 2010, an Indian court convicted seven Indian former employees of Union Carbide of negligence and sentenced them to two years in jail.

26. *Financial Times*, October 2, 2008, 9.

27. Peloza, "Using corporate social responsibility as insurance for financial performance."

28. Walter Blacconiere and Dennis Patten, "Environmental disclosure, regulatory costs, and changes in firm value," *Journal of Accounting and Economics* 18 (1994): 357–377.

29. A similar finding is reported by Blacconiere and Northcut regarding the reaction of the stocks of chemical companies to news about new superfund environmental legislation. See Walter Blacconiere and Dana Northcut, "Environmental information and market reaction to environmental legislation," *Journal of Accounting, Auditing and Finance* 12 (1997): 149–178.

30. Paul Godfrey, Craig Merrill, and Jared Hansen, "The relationship between corporate social responsibility and shareholder value: An empirical test of the risk management hypothesis," *Strategic Management Journal* 30 (2009): 425–445.

31. *The Economist*, January 19, 2008, 12. A 2008 survey by Goodpurpose, a consultancy, highlights an interesting aspect of CSR as insurance. The survey of six thousand consumers in ten countries found that seven in ten consumers said they would remain loyal to a brand during recession, if the brand supports a good cause. See GoodPurposeCommunity.com.

32. Not surprisingly, a mini-consultancy industry sprung up to advise companies on how to prevent mishaps, particularly in their vulnerable supply chains, including inspection of subcontractors. "We don't make it"—Nike's early reaction to the alleged use of child labor by its shoe subcontractors—doesn't cut it anymore. Given the significant vulnerabilities of long supply chains in foreign countries to social and environmental abuse, and the need to comply with local labor laws and product safety regulations across the globe, some companies shorten the chains (produce more in-house) and move weak supply chain links back to their home country, as well as exercise more effective control over them. Nike representatives, for example, met in July 2008 with thirty-seven apparel suppliers in Malaysia to rectify various worker-abuse issues raised by Australian TV. *Wall Street Journal*, August 4, 2008, B10.

33. R. Putnam, "The case of missing social capital," working paper, Harvard University, 1995.

34. Example from *The Economist*, January 19, 2008, Special Report on CSR.

35. Kenneth Arrow, "Gifts and exchanges," *Philosophy and Public Affairs* (1972): 357.

36. Luigi Guiso, Paola Sapienza, and Luigi Zingales, "The role of social capital in financial development," *American Economic Review*, 94 (2004): 526–556.

37. Guiso et al., ibid, demonstrate the economic efficiencies of social capital by recounting how Jewish diamond merchants conduct their transactions informally, without written contracts and agreements, saving legal expenses. The power of the community of diamond dealers is sufficient to enforce the informal contracts. In the capital market context, Guiso et al. define trust as the subjective probability individuals attribute to the possibility of being cheated and note that the percentage of Italians who do not trust major companies is almost 2.5 times bigger than in the States.

38. There are no effective direct measures of social capital. Researchers use proxies, such as participation in trade and civic associations, electoral turnout, charity giving, or voluntary blood donation (when not compensated). Such proxies measure the level of caring about the community, albeit with noise.

39. Stephen Knack and Philip Keefer, "Does social capital have an economic payoff?: A cross-country investigation," *Quarterly Journal of Economics* 112 (1997): 1251–1288. Of course, social capital—leading to cooperation, solidarity, collective action—can be turned toward negative causes, such as the oil cartel restricting output or harmful labor union activities.

40. While product quality is the main driver of reputation, there are additional dimensions to corporate reputation. Companies can be known as "a great place to work in" or "guardians of the environment."

41. Consider the following adulation: "BP integrated agenda begins with a commitment to sustainability that builds on the logic of multistakeholder capitalism but joins social, environmental, and economic sustainability to the long-term survival of the firm ... BP has put into place an integrated governance system that includes a Board-level Ethics and Environmental Assurance Committee ... Heading all of this machinery is Lord John Browne, CEO, who has been the champion of corporate citizenship in BP and a global spokesman for all of industry." Philip Mirvis and Bradley Googins, "Stages of corporate citizenship," *California Management Review*, 48 (2006): 114.

42. Eliciting proposals for a further name change to "Beyond Probes," *Wall Street Journal*, February 7, 2007, C1.

43. *The Economist*, January 19, 2008, 8.

44. *BusinessWeek*, September 29, 2008, 68–70.


## CHAPTER 10

1. CFA Institute and the Business Roundtable, "Breaking the short-term cycle," Symposium Series on Short-Termism, CFA Institute, 2006, 3.

2. U.S. Chamber of Commerce, Commission on the regulation of U.S. capital markets in the 21$^{st}$ century, 2007, 8.

3. Daniel Vasella and Clifton Leaf, "Temptation is all around us," *Fortune*, November 18, 2002, 109.

4. CFA Institute and the Business Roundtable, "Breaking the short-term cycle," 3.

5. Bureau of Labor Statistics, www.bls.gov; and Robert Gordon, "Exploding productivity growth: Context, causes and implications," Brookings Papers on Economic Activity, 2 (2003): Table 1.

6. Bureau of Labor Statistics, "Output per Hour, Hourly Compensation, and Unit Labor Costs in Manufacturing, Twelve Countries, 1950–1986," U.S. Department of Labor, Washington, DC, December 1987.

7. Similar accusations were leveled in the 1980s against corporate raiders who were allegedly looking for short-term gains from breaking up companies and are currently leveled at hedge funds intervening in corporate affairs and strategies; see chapter 11. "There is nothing new under the sun," Ecclesiastes.

8. Robert Denham and Michael Porter, *Lifting All Boats: Increasing the Payoff from Private Investment in the U.S. Economy*, Report of the Capital Allocation Sub-council to the Competitiveness Policy Council, Washington, DC, 1995, 34. The prevailing mood of the time can be gleaned from the following opening to a 1991 widely read book titled *Short-Term America*: "America is experiencing a mid-life crisis. In its year-end 1990 review on competitiveness, *BusinessWeek* observed that 'you can feel America's eroding status in your bones.' A Gallup poll shows most Americans now regard Japan, rather than the United States, as the world's leading economic power ... And pollster Louis Harris observes that Americans fear we will soon drop to number three behind Japan and Germany." Michael Jacobs, *Short-Term America: The Causes of business Myopia* (Boston: Harvard Business School Press, 1991), 1–2. Substitute China and India for Japan and Germany, and the quote sounds similar to the frequent commentaries on the state of U.S. industry at the writing of this book.

9. Peter Drucker, "A crisis of capitalism," *Wall Street Journal*, September 30, 1986, 32. Drucker, who was widely considered a management guru, once quipped that reporters like the term *guru* because charlatan is hard to spell.

10. American Business Conference, *Impact of U.S. Accounting Standards on Capital Formation and International Competitiveness: A Proposal for Change*, Washington, DC, 1991, 1.

11. U.S. Department of Commerce and U.S. Department of the Treasury, *Financing Technology: A Report of the Financing Technology Roundtables*, Washington, DC, 1992, 1.

12. Ibid., 8.

13. U.S. Bureau of Labor Statistics, http://www.bls.gov/lpc.

14. *OECD In Figures*, 2007, www.oecd.org/publishing, 78.

15. John Bogle, *The Battle for the Soul of Capitalism* (New Haven, CT: Yale University Press, 2005), 54, 103.

16. *Financial Times*, April 26, 2007, 2.

17. John Graham, Campbell Harvey, and Shiva Rajgopal, "The economic implications of corporate financial reporting," *Journal of Accounting and Economics* 40 (2005): 14. The survey revealed that CFOs consider exceeding last year's same-quarter EPS the most important earnings target, followed by meeting the consensus analyst forecast. Meeting analysts' benchmark is widely believed to build credibility in capital markets, while missing the benchmark is expected to increase investors' uncertainty about the firm's future (possibly increasing cost of capital) and signal the existence of underlying fundamental operating and financial problems. Interestingly, or rather depressingly, in personal interviews, some CFOs said "you have to start with the premise that every company manages earnings." Ibid., 12. Accordingly, if a company fails to "make the numbers" even in a down quarter, it is considered an ominous sign.

18. It is, of course, also possible that managers don't truly believe in the market's short-termism, but use it as an excuse for not investing in risky, long-term projects, and for an occasional "management" of earnings, "forced upon them" by investors obsessed with quarterly earnings. I try, however, to avoid conspiracy theories.

19. Tom Copeland, Aaron Dolgoff, and Alberto Moel, "The role of expectations in explaining the cross-section of stock returns," *Review of Accounting Studies* 9 (2004): 149–188.

20. Ibid., 183.

21. Similar empirical findings, from different methodologies, samples, and time periods, are reported by Liu and Thomas. Jing Liu and Jacob Thomas, "Stock returns and accounting earnings," *Journal of Accounting Research* 38 (2000): 71–101.

22. The regression was run across a large sample of U.S. companies in selected industries over the five-year period, 2000–2004. The portion of market capitalization accounted for by assets-in-place and next year's earnings is measured by the regression's coefficient of determination, generally known as $R^2$, ranging between 0 and 1. This measure indicates the percentage of the differences across firms' capitalization that is accounted for ("explained") by the differences across companies in assets-in-place and next year's earnings. Accordingly, one minus the $R^2$ indicates the portion of market capitalization *not* accounted for by the two short-term drivers, which primarily reflects long-term growth potential; this is the value displayed in figure 10-1.

23. The low placement of pharmaceutical and telecom companies in figure 10-1 may seem counterintuitive. However, the future growth prospects of these sectors are shrouded in uncertainty. Pharmaceutical companies are beset by myriad problems—thin product pipelines and serious challenges to intellectual property (patents) in East Asia, Africa, and South America—and the large telecom companies face significant challenges to their fixed-line telephone franchise by wireless and Internet technologies. These dimmed future prospects likely account for the relatively low share price portion (40%) reflecting future growth.

24. Jeffrey Coles, Michael Lemmon, and Lalitha Naveen, "A comparison of profitability and CEO turnover sensitivity in large private and public firms," working paper, Arizona State University, 2003. The researchers were careful to control for company size, risk, and industry effects in comparing the public and private firms.

25. Since R&D is expensed in the income statement, a decrease in R&D increases reported income by same amount.

26. John Doukas and Lorne Switzer, "The stock market's valuation of R&D spending and market concentration," *Journal of Economics and Business* 44 (1992): 95–114. The authors were careful to eliminate from the sample confounding cases where the R&D announcement was released with other news (e.g., earnings) that might have affected investors' reaction.

27. Joseph Schumpeter (1883–1950) once declared that he wished to become Europe's greatest lover, horseman, and economist, in that order of preference. On his way to academia, Schumpeter was the Austrian minister of finance in 1919 for less than a year and later the president of a small Viennese bank until it collapsed in 1924. In 1932, Schumpeter relinquished the harsh reality of business and politics for the serenity of Harvard University.

28. Keith Chauvin and Mark Hirschey, "Advertising, R&D expenditures and the market value of the firm," *Financial Management* 22 (1993): 128–140; Theodore Sougiannis, "The accounting based valuation of corporate R&D," *Accounting Review* 69 (1994): 44–68; David Aboody and Baruch Lev, "The value relevance of intangibles: The case of software capitalization," *Journal of Accounting Research* 36 (1998): 161–191.

29. Attributed to John Maynard Keynes, who in addition to being a trail-blazing economist in the 1920s and 1930s, was a very astute investor.

30. Louis Gerstner, *Who Says Elephants Can't Dance? Inside IBM's Historic Turnaround* (New York: Harper Collins, 2004).

31. IBM's and Deere's stock prices are adjusted for stock splits, as of December 2009.

32. This is not to say that there aren't cases of managerial short-term focus at the expense of the long term. Harvard Business School professor Clayton Christensen related to *The Economist* the case of the U.S. Steel Corp., a large integrated steel manufacturer, which considered building low-cost mini-mills. Yet, this promising long-term move was quashed because some executives argued that it is cheaper to continue producing steel from fully paid-off blast furnaces rather than investing in new technology. Managerial mistakes notwithstanding, my argument, proved by the likes of IBM and Deere, is that a successful long-term strategy doesn't have to sacrifice the short term. *The Economist*, Special Report on Innovation, October 13, 2007, 12.

## CHAPTER 11

1. Lauren Talner, *The Origins of Shareholder Activism* (Washington, DC: Investor Responsibility Research Center, Inc., 1983), 2; the brief history of shareholder activism in this section draws on Talner's book.

2. Lewis Gilbert's pursuits, along with those of other early activists, are recounted in his book, *Dividends and Democracy* (Larchmont, NY: American Research Council Inc., 1956). Those who came of age after Enron and Sarbanes-Oxley will be amazed to learn that in the 1930s and 1940s, Gilbert focused on, among other issues, the election of independent directors, opposed staggered boards, and challenged lavish stock option plans and excessive managerial compensation. A truly modern activist.

3. Adam Smith, *The Wealth of Nations*, Canaan ed. (New York: Modern Library, 1776, 1937), 700.

4. Lewis Gilbert (1917–1993) was one of the first advocates of shareholder rights. Gilbert would attend numerous shareholders' meetings and raise issues about managers' compensation, deficient accounting procedures, and directors' responsibilities. Until 1979, he issued public reports on activities at annual shareholder meetings. Gilbert, an army corporal, challenged generals Douglas MacArthur and Lucius Clay because they didn't own shares in companies of which they were directors (*New York Times*, Obituaries, December 8, 1993).

5. See Talner, *The Origins of Shareholder Activism*, for elaboration on social and environmental activism up to the early 1980s.

6. Gilbert's ideological descendants, often termed gadflies, are still active today. Evelyn Davis was until recently the leading gadfly. Holding stocks in more than fifty companies, she advanced governance proposals—limiting directors to six years of service at DuPont and American Express, and annual election of all directors at Lucent and Morgan Stanley, for example—with occasional success. A *Washington Post* article (April 20, 2003) claimed that managers are "scared she'll show up at their shareholder meetings to excoriate, eviscerate and generally rip their heads off with the sheer force of her Dutch-accented voice, which could sandblast granite."

7. Labor laws call for pension funds regulated by ERISA to vote on shareholder proposals. This requires the funds to become familiar with the issues proposed, which is a first step to activism.

8. See, for example, Institutional Shareholder Services, *ISS 2006 US Proxy Voting Guidelines Summary*, www.issproxy.com.

9. Cindy Alexander, Mark Chen, Duane Seppi, and Chester Spatt, "The role of advisory services in proxy voting," working paper, U.S. Securities and Exchange Commission, Washington, DC, 2008.

10. William Bratton, "Hedge funds and governance targets," *The Georgetown Law Journal* 95 (2007): 1375–1433.

11. Filers of Form 13D, required for an investment that equals or exceeds 5% of the company's outstanding shares, have to state the purpose of the transaction—that is, their intention in acquiring the substantial equity position. Such stated intent can be just a passive investment, or various kinds of activism, and is the main source for analyzing empirically the objectives of activists.

12. Alon Brav, Wei Jiang, Frank Patrony, and Randall Thomas, "Hedge fund activism, corporate governance, and firm performance," *The Journal of Finance* 63 (2008): 1729–1775.

13. A 2006 study by Proxy Governance, a proxy-tracking company, indicates that only 38% of the 179 social policy proposals examined received more than 10% shareholder support.

14. Michael Smith, "Shareholder activism by institutional investors: Evidence from CalPERS," *Journal of Finance* 51 (1996): 227–252; and Stuart Gilan and Laura Starks, "Corporate governance proposals and shareholder activism: The role of institutional investors," *Journal of Financial Economics* 57 (2000): 275-305.

15. Management regularly submits proposals too for shareholders' vote. Certain actions, such as M&A bids, stock issues, and managerial compensation involving stock, require a vote on the submission of proposals. A study covering the 1993–1997 period indicates that, of all the proposals submitted to shareholders for voting, management advances 83% and shareholders advance 17%. Ernst Maug and Kristian Rydqvist, "What is the function of the shareholder meeting? Evidence from the U.S. proxy voting process," working paper, Humboldt University, Berlin, 2001.

16. Diane Del Guerico, Laura Seery, and Tracie Woidtke, "Do boards pay attention when institutional investor activists 'just vote no'?" *Journal of Financial Economics* 90 (2008): 84–103.

17. *Wall Street Journal*, April 4, 2006, C1.

18. Jonathan Karpoff, "The impact of shareholder activism on target companies: A survey of empirical findings," working paper, University of Washington, 2001.

19. Brad Barber, "Monitoring the monitor: Evaluating CalPERS' shareholder activism," *Journal of Investing* 16, no. 4 (2007): 66–80.

20. These share price increases translate to a total value increase of $3 billion for the 115 companies targeted, allowing for a neat cost/benefit analysis: Since CalPERS owned, on average, 0.5% of the 115 targeted companies, its investors gained about $15 million (0.5% of

$3 billion), or slightly over $1 million a year (1992–2005). This negligible gain, probably not even covering CalPERS' cost of activism, demonstrates vividly the free-riding problem discussed. I wonder about the reaction of CalPERS investors to this cost–benefit analysis, were they aware of it.

21. While my discussion focuses on the *economic consequences* of activism—that is, the impact on target shareholders and corporate performance—certain actions of the activists, particularly the public pension funds, have express social and political aims. Barber, "Monitoring the monitor: Evaluating CalPERS' shareholder activism" (2007), mentions several cases: in 2000, the CalPERS board voted to divest its holdings in tobacco companies. Ironically, these "sin stocks" have performed rather well in subsequent years. In 2004, CalPERS got involved in a labor dispute at Safeway, siding with the employee union and voting to oust Safeway's CEO (instead, CalPERS chief was subsequently shown the door).

22. *Wall Street Journal*, July 11, 2008, C13.

23. Randall Thomas and Kenneth Martin, "The effect of shareholder proposals on executive compensation," *University of Cincinnati Law Review* 67 (1999): 1021–1081.

24. James Cotter and Randall Thomas, "Shareholder proposals in the new millennium: Shareholder support, board response, and market reaction," *Journal of Corporate Finance* 13 (2007): 368–391.

25. A shareholder proposal, under Rule 14a-8 of the Securities Exchange Act of 1934, enables any shareholder holding shares worth $2,000 or more for at least one year to include one 500-word proposal in the proxy material distributed by the company for its annual meeting. Such proposals request a vote in favor or against a particular issue from all shareholders. The company may ask the SEC, under certain circumstances, to exclude a proposal from shareholders' vote. Vote-no campaigns are attempts to persuade shareholders to withhold their vote from the election of certain directors at the annual meeting. Such campaigns may also raise specific issues, like executive pay.

26. Yonca Ertimur, Fabrizio Ferri, and Volkan Muslu, "Shareholder activism and CEO pay," *Review of Financial Studies* 24 (2011): 535–592. Interestingly, the researchers calculate that moving from the lowest pay quartile (lowest 25% of CEO pay distribution) to the third quartile (50%–75% of the distribution) substantially increases the probability of being targeted by activists, from 29.9% to 38.4%.

27. Brav et al., "Hedge fund activism, corporate governance, and firm performance"; and April Klein and Emanuel Zur, "Entrepreneurial shareholder activism: Hedge funds and other private investors," *The Journal of Finance* 64 (2009): 187–229. Obviously, this measurement assumes that investors, in aggregate, are able to anticipate the consequences of activism ("the wisdom of the crowd").

28. In Korea, when blockholders (large investors) announce a switch of the declared investment purpose from passive to active, investors in the target companies also react with a significantly positive stock price increase. See Woochan Kim, Woojin Kim, and Kap-Sok Kwon, "Value of outside blockholder activism: Evidence from the switchers," *Journal of Corporate Finance* 15 (2009): 505–522.

29. Marco Becht, Julian Franks, Colin Mayer, and Stefano Rossi, "Returns to shareholder activism: Evidence from a clinical study of the Hermes U.K. Focus Fund," *Review of Financial Studies*, 22 (2009): 3093–3129.

30. Mayer Brown Rowe & Maw, "Hedge funds and institutional shareholder activism," *Securities Update*, April 21, 2006, 3.

31. Citigroup, "Hedge funds at the gate," *Financial Strategy*, September 22, 2005, 6. How ironic. Citigroup, whose short-term investments in risky structured securities and subprime mortgages were a contributor to the 2007–2008 financial crisis, blames hedge funds for short-termism.

32. Brav et al., "Hedge fund activism, corporate governance, and firm performance."

33. Greenwood and Schor, examining hedge fund investments made during 1993–2006, report that target companies were more likely to be acquired by other companies than similar nontargets. For these acquisition cases, the investment by hedge funds may seem short term because of the subsequent target acquisition, but the original intent may well have been a long-term investment. See Robin Greenwood and Michael Schor, "Investor activism and takeovers," *Journal of Financial Economics* 92 (2009): 362–375.

34. From Marcel Kahan and Edward Rock, "Hedge funds in corporate governance and corporate control," *University of Pennsylvania Law Review* 155 (2007): 1021–1093.

35. *The Economist*, April 11, 2009, 63.

36. Examples from *The Economist*, April 11, 2009, 63. There are, of course, always contrarians. The *Wall Street Journal* reports on hedge fund Bulldog Investors demanding board seats and strategic changes from four companies. *Wall Street Journal*, December 31, 2008, C5.

37. Bernardo Bortolotti, Veljko Fotak, William Megginson, and William Miracky, "Sovereign Wealth fund investment patters and performance," working paper, Price College of Business, University of Oklahoma, 2009.

38. SWFs invested heavily in financial institutions, sustaining heavy losses in the financial crisis.

39. Brav et al., "Hedge fund activism, corporate governance, and firm performance."

40. Ironically, in February 2011, Deutsche Boerse bid for a larger fish, the New York Stock Exchange. As of this writing, the merger awaits shareholders approval.

41. *Wall Street Journal*, July 14, 2008, B4.

## CHAPTER 12

1. The data for these indicators was provided in January 2011 by The Corporate Library, a leading governance rating and consulting firm.

2. A "poison pill" deters potential acquirers. When triggered, for example, the pill causes the company to issue rights to its shareholders allowing them to convert the rights to a large number of common shares if a suitor acquires a substantial part of the target equity, thereby significantly diluting the acquirer's position. Another example is when the target company takes on a large debt to make itself less attractive to a suitor. A "staggered (classified) board" is one divided into several groups of directors (often three), who serve overlapping, multiyear terms (as in the U.S. Senate). Thus, only a subset of directors can be replaced each year, making the company less attractive to a change-minded acquirer.

3. Often the implications of governance metrics are not unique. A poison pill, for example, deters or prolongs a takeover—generally bad for shareholders—but it also sometimes enables managers and directors to negotiate better deals for shareholders, a good thing. The same holds true for staggered boards. Advocates of staggered boards claim that they provide for stability and continuity—a good-governance attribute—yet they also deter the company's takeover or the replacement of all or most directors by shareholders in a given year. Such conflicting implications of many governance mechanisms complicate the construction of governance quality indexes and scores and their interpretation.

4. Outside or independent directors are generally defined as not having any significant familial or financial ties with the company or its executives. Outside-related directors are nonexecutives who have business relations with the company, like legal counselors or investment bankers.

5. News Corporation recently experienced its share of embarrassments with alleged phone hackings in the UK and reportedly making multimillion dollar settlements with firms claiming uncompetitive practices (Bloomberg News July 18, 2011).

6. An intriguing perk, coming to light in 2009, was John Thain's reported $1.2 million decoration of his CEO suite at Merrill Lynch in the depth of recession (an $88,000 rug, $18,000 George IV chair, two $88,000 guest chairs, $1,400 waste can, and $800,000 interior designer fee). Thain subsequently reimbursed Merrill for the decoration. Thain was recruited in 2007 to rescue the failing Merrill Lynch, which required, after merging with Bank of America, government support. Wikipedia, June 11, 2009.

7. Shareholders wishing such risk diversification can easily achieve it by holding stocks in the two or three merger partners, without the company incurring the heavy costs of actually merging the companies. This, "equivalence principle" (shareholders can do what the company is doing), of course, doesn't hold when the merger offers substantial synergies (cost savings, new market penetration), which individual shareholders cannot achieve on their own.

8. The massive frauds at Enron, WorldCom, Parmalat (Italy), and Satyam (India)—a very partial list—all went undetected for years by the companies' "prestigious" and "big" auditors. For a comprehensive study of who detects corporate fraud and improprieties, documenting the relatively small role auditors play in such detection, see Alexander Dyck, Adair Morse, and Luigi Zingales, "Who blows the whistle on corporate fraud?" *Journal of Finance* 65 (2010): 2213–2253.

9. For the history of shareholder access to director nomination and proxy rules, see Robert Brown, "The SEC, corporate governance and shareholder access to the board room," working paper no. 08-05, Sturm College of Law, University of Denver, 2008.

10. Independent directors seem to be in short supply, since so many of them serve on multiple boards, and not just in the United States. Gerhard Cromme, chairman of the German multinational ThyssenKrupp, for example, also serves on the boards of seven other German companies and three in France (*The Economist*, April 14, 2007, 74). Independent or not, how can one person provide effective monitoring and advice to eleven companies? Indeed, this common "busy director" phenomenon, seriously detracting from directors' attention and effectiveness, was shown by researchers to negatively impact the company's performance and market value. Eliezer Fich and Anil Shivdasani, "Are busy boards effective monitors?" *The Journal of Finance* 61 (2006): 689–724.

11. Who can forget how the SEC failed to detect Bernard Madoff's decades-long multibillion dollar Ponzi scheme, despite multiple alerts by investors leading to several inconclusive SEC investigations. On the relatively small role of the SEC in fraud detection, see Dyck et al. (2010)

12. Audra Boone, Laura Field, Jonathan Karpoff, and Charu Raheja, "The determinants of corporate board size and composition: An empirical analysis," *Journal of Financial Economics* 85 (2007): 66–101.

13. The costs of company misconduct that sees the light of day are high and ultimately hit shareholders' pockets. For example, in 2008 the SEC settled claims for $350 million with the German company Siemens AG under the Foreign Corrupt Practices Act, concerning more than $1 billion bribes that Siemens allegedly paid to various persons. In addition to the $350 million paid to the SEC, Siemens paid $450 million to the Department of Justice and reportedly around $800 million to settle criminal charges in Germany. Effective governance and internal controls should have obviated the bribes and the consequent heavy fines and loss of reputation.

14. Researchers sometimes create their own company-specific governance score by assigning 1 to a good attribute (no poison pill) and 0 to a poor one (a staggered board), and then summing the numbers assigned to the various governance attributes, like my score of 7:3 for Time Warner in this chapter's opening example. This equally weighted score implicitly assumes that all governance mechanisms are equally effective.

15. John Core, Wayne Guay, and Tjomme Rusticus, "Does weak governance cause weak stock returns? An examination of firm operating performance and investors' expectations," *Journal of Finance* LXI (2006): 655–687.

16. A useful reminder: correlation is not necessarily causation. It may be that successful companies provide for generous shareholder rights—they feel less threatened by takeover, say, and will therefore dispose of poison pills. So the causation may be from operating success to better governance, not the reverse. I believe, though, that in the case of governance, the documented correlation between governance and performance primarily indicates causation from the former to the latter.

17. Sanjai Bhagat and Brian Bolton, "Corporate governance and firm performance," *Journal of Corporate Finance* 14 (2008): 257–273.

18. The data on SEC settlements was obtained from NERA, an economic consultancy, and the governance data was obtained from The Corporate Library.

19. To clarify: if company A is more profitable than B and is expected to continue its superior performance, then A's shareholder value will be larger than B's, other things equal. But once the higher capitalization of A, reflecting its better performance, is established, the *return* on A's shares (changes in stock prices plus dividends) will equal B's return, unless A's subsequent profitability changes keep surprising investors (returns, or stock price changes, are generated by investors' surprise).

20. Core et al., "Does weak governance cause weak stock returns?"; and Bhagat and Bolton, "Corporate governance and firm performance."

21. Craig Doidge, Andrew Karolyi, and René Stulz, "Why are foreign firms listed in the U.S. worth more?" *Journal of Financial Economics* 71 (2004): 205–238.

22. April Klein, "Audit committee, board of director characteristics, and earnings management," *Journal of Accounting and Economics* 33 (2002): 375–400.

23. Olubunmi Faleye, "Classified boards, firm value, and managerial entrenchment," *Journal of Financial Economics* 83 (2007): 501–529.

24. Lucian Bebchuk, John Coates, and Guhan Subramanian, "The powerful antitakeover force of staggered boards, theory, evidence and policy," *Stanford Law Review* 54 (2002): 887–951.

25. Re-Jin Guo, Timothy Kruse, and Tom Nohel, "Undoing the powerful anti-takeover force of staggered boards," *Journal of Corporate Finance* 14 (2008): 274–288.

26. Black and Khanna also report that investors in the faster growing Indian companies, more likely to raise equity capital, responded even more favorably to the reform announcement. Bernard Black and Vikramaditya Khanna, "Can corporate governance reforms increase firms' market values: Evidence from India," *Journal of Empirical Legal Studies* 4 (2007): 749–796.

27. Bernard Black, Hasung Jang, and Woochan Kim, "Does corporate governance predict firms' market values? Evidence from Korea," *Journal of Law, Economics and Organization* 22 (2006): 366–413; and Gonzalo Chavez and Ana Silva, "Brazil's experiment with corporate governance," *Journal of Applied Corporate Finance* 21 (2009): 34–44.

28. Rafael La Porta, Florencio Lopez-De-Silanes, Andrei Shleifer, and Robert Vishny, "Legal determinants of external financing," *Journal of Finance* 52 (1997): 1131–1150.

29. Almost unheard of in the United States, here is a hypothetical example of a pyramid: the founding family owns 60% equity of company A at the top of the pyramid, which in turn holds 60% equity in two second-tier companies, B and C. Company B holds 50% equity of D, one of several third-tier companies in the pyramid. The controlling family thus holds (indirectly) only 18% of company D (60% × 60% × 50%), but since it controls A, and A controls B, which in turn controls D, the founding family in effect controls D, and other components of the pyramid, by the rights to appoint managers and determine key decisions. Thus, while D's shareholders provided 82% of equity, they are essentially deprived of real control. For different ownership structures around the world, see Tarun Khanna and Yishay Yafeh, "Business

groups in emerging markets: Paragons or Parasites?" *Journal of Economic Literature* 45 (2007): 331–372.

30. Djankov et al. published in 2008 a firm-specific minority expropriation hazard index (Anti-Self-Dealing index), reflecting, among other things, minority shareholders' ability to reverse self-dealing activities in courts. Simeon Djankov, Rafael La Porta, Florencio Lopez-De-Silanes, and Andrei Shleifer, "The law and economics of self-dealing," *Journal of Financial Economics* 88 (2008): 430–465.

31. Randall Morck, Daniel Wolfenzon, and Bernard Yeung, "Corporate governance, economic entrenchment, and growth," *Journal of Economic Literature* XLIII (2005): table 2.

32. Ronald Anderson and David Reeb, "Founding-family ownership and firm performance: Evidence from the S&P 500," *Journal of Finance* 58 (2003): 1301–1327; and Yakov Amihud and Baruch Lev, "Risk reduction as a managerial motive for conglomerate mergers," *The Bell Journal of Economics* 12 (1981): 605–617.

33. *The Economist*, January 24, 2009, 67.

34. The hereditary nature of management in many pyramids and family groups prompted the following from Warren Buffett: "If we were to pick our United States Olympic team based on the eldest son and eldest daughter of those who represented us in all the events 24 years ago, we would think that was asinine; but to hand the resources of society ... to a bunch of people simply because they happen to have the right last name strikes me as just as foolish." Randall Morck, "The riddle of the great pyramids," working paper no. 14858, NBER, 2009, 5.

35. Randall Morck, David Stangeland, and Bernard Yeung, "Inherited wealth, corporate control, and economic growth: The Canadian disease," in *Concentrated Corporate Ownership*, ed. Randall Morck (Chicago: University of Chicago Press, 2000), 319–369.

36. Randall Morck, and Bernard Yeung, "Family control and the rent-seeking society," *Entrepreneurship: Theory and Practice* 28 (2004): 391–409.

37. Corporate governance and particularly the board of directors are easy targets for blame and attempts to fix because of their apparent simplicity: independent directors are "good," auditors providing consulting services to the auditee are "bad," etc. Unfortunately, legislators are loath to tackle more complex and thorny governance issues like the easy-to-manipulate and relevance-challenged accounting system. "We don't understand accounting and therefore don't touch it," a congressman once told me.

38. Sanjai Bhagat, Brian Bolton, and Roberta Romano, "The promise and peril of corporate governance indices," *Columbia Law Review* 108 (2008): 1803–1882.

39. Robert Daines, Ian Gow, and David Larcker, "Rating the ratings: How good are commercial governance ratings?" *Journal of Financial Economics* 98 (2010): 439–461. The Audit Integrity rating primarily focuses on financial information quality and the risk of fraud, along with certain other governance attributes.

40. Since Institutional Shareholder Services (ISS) provides both a governance rating (CGQ) and advice on shareholder voting, Daines et al. (2010) also examine the association between the CGQ rating and voting advice, and, in turn, the actual shareholders voting record. Surprisingly, no significant relationship was found between the rating and shareholder voting but the advisers' recommendations are, as expected, correlated with the actual voting.

41. The required number of independent directors and the definition of independence changed over time by rules and regulations, such as the 2004 NYSE standards calling for a majority of independent directors on boards, the Sarbanes-Oxley Act mandating that audit committee members must all be independent, and the requirement of the NYSE listing standards that companies have a board nominating committee (all independent directors) to vet and select new board members.

42. *Team of Rivals* is the title of a 2006 biography of Abraham Lincoln by Doris Kearns Goodwin.

43. Gordon traces the beginning of the shift from advising to monitoring to the spate of corporate failures in the 1970s (Penn Central, Equity Funding, LTV, Ampex, and Memorex), calling attention to board members sleeping at the wheel. This perceived failure of the advising board model, exacerbated later on by disclosures of the widespread practice of illegal corporate payments (bribes), led to a shift in expectations from directors—the monitoring board. Jeffrey Gordon, "The rise of independent directors in the United States, 1950–2005: Of shareholder value and stock market prices," *Stanford Law Review* 59 (2007): 1465–1568.

44. The NYSE listing requirements mandate such "regularly scheduled executive sessions."

45. Mark Mitchell and Harold Mulheirn, "The impact of industry shocks on takeover and restructuring activity," *Journal of Financial Economics* 41 (1996): 193–229.

46. Courts, too, were more sympathetic toward managers' resistance to takeover bids if backed by largely independent boards. Gordon, "The rise of independent directors in the United States, 1950–2005," 1523, 1526.

47. Ibid., 1500, and Sanjai Bhagat and Bernard Black, "The non-correlation between board independence and long-term firm performance," *Journal of Corporation Law* 27 (2002): 231–273. There is, however, some evidence that when boards are dominated by independent directors more CEOs are fired for poor firm performance. Volker Laux, "Board independence and CEO turnover," *Journal of Accounting Research* 46 (2008): 137–171; and for the U.K., Jay Dahya, John McConnell, and Nickolaos Travlos, "The Cadbury committee, corporate performance, and top management performance," *Journal of Finance* 57 (2002): 461–483. Interestingly Adams and Ferreira report that a larger proportion of women on boards is associated with a higher frequency of CEO dismissal for poor performance. A "weak gender"? See Renée Adams and Daniel Ferreira, "Women in the boardroom and their impact on governance and performance," *Journal of Financial Economics* 94 (2009): 291–309.

48. Myles Mace, *Directors: Myth and Reality* (Boston: Harvard Business School Press, 1971).

49. In June 2009, Bank of America announced that four directors with experience in banking and financial oversight joined its board. A welcome expertise-strengthening move, to be sure, but why after the battering of BofA in the financial crisis rather than prior to it? Strengthening expertise on boards is not always considered urgent, though. CNNMoney.com (April 23, 2008) reported that despite heavy criticism of Citigroup's board in the annual shareholders meeting, the entire slate of incumbent directors had been reelected. Notably, "Responding to a question about finding board members with particularly significant financial experience, Bischoff [Citi's board chair] said that as members retire, that experience is something Citigroup is taking into consideration." "Haste is from the devil," said Saint Jerome.

50. Anup Agrawal and Sahiba Chadha, "Corporate governance and accounting scandals," *Journal of Law and Economics* 48 (2005): 371–406, and Renée Adams and Daniel Ferreira, "A theory of friendly boards," *Journal of Finance* 62 (2007): 217–250.

51. April Klein, "Firm performance and board committee structure," *Journal of Law & Economics* 41 (1998): 275–304.

52. In certain countries—Germany, China, Holland, and Spain, for example—public companies have two boards: a *supervisory*—mostly monitoring board—and a *management* board in charge of advising managers.

53. Akoke Ghosh and Doocheol Moon, "When the CEO is also the chair of the board," working paper, Zicklin School of Business, Baruch College, 2009.

54. Jay Dahya and John McConnell, "Board composition, corporate performance, and the Cadbury committee recommendations," *Journal of Financial and Quantitative Analysis* 42 (2007): 535–564; Jay Dahya, John McConnell, and Nickolaos Travlos, "The Cadbury committee, corporate performance, and top management performance," *Journal of Finance* 57 (2002): 461–483; and Aiyesha Dey, Ellen Engel, and Gloria Liu, "Determinants and implications of board leadership structure," working paper, Booth School of Business, University of Chicago, 2009.

55. *The Economist*, October 30, 2010, 74.

56. Despite the fact that in the U.K. many companies separate the CEO from the board chair position, shareholders of the large British clothing and food chain Marks & Spencer voted in 2009 for CEO Stuart Rose to be appointed as board chairman too. The likely reason: Rose successfully revamped the retailers' operations, and shareholders may have felt that the adverse economic conditions in 2008–2009 required a unified top command. (Or, perhaps, the free wine, cider, sandwiches, and desserts offered to investors in Marks & Spencer's shareholder meeting did the trick [*Wall Street Journal*, July 10, 2008, C2].)

57. David Yermack, "Higher market valuation of companies with a small board of directors," *Journal of Financial Economics* 40 (1996): 185–211. Coles et al., however, show that for diversified, complex companies there is a positive relation between board size and company performance. Jeffrey Coles, Daniel Naveen, and Lalitha Naveen, "Boards: Does one size fits all?" *Journal of Financial Economics* 87 (2008): 329–356.

58. CEOs can only suggest a change, because the New York Stock Exchange 2003 listing rules removed CEOs from board nominating committees.

59. Lucian Bebchuk, "The myth of the shareholder franchise," *Virginia Law Review* 93 (2007): 675–732.

## CHAPTER 13

1. While CEOs are obviously well compensated, there are "bigger and better" yet. Kaplan and Rauh (2007, p. 3) report that the top twenty-five hedge fund managers' combined earnings in 2004 exceeded the total pay of the 500 S&P 500 CEOs. Steven Kaplan and Joshua Rauh, "Wall Street and main street: What contributes to the rise in the highest incomes?" *Review of Financial Studies* 23, no. 3 (2007): 1004–1050.

2. An earlier and still active critic of executive pay is Graef Crystal, for many years a pay consultant, who in his book *In Search of Excess* and subsequent Bloomberg online commentary thoroughly and systematically dissects companies' executive pay practices. A good read. Graef Crystal, *In Search of Excess: The Overcompensation of American Executives* (New York: WW Norton & Co., 1991).

3. Lucian Bebchuk and Yaniv Grinstein, "The growth of executive pay," *Oxford Review of Economic Policy* 21 (2005): 282–303.

4. Lucian Bebchuk and Jesse Fried, *Pay without Performance: The Unfilled Promise of Executive Compensation* (Harvard University Press, Cambridge MA, 2004). Managerial power grabs are most apparent when executive compensation lacks any justification, such as the multimillion-dollar bonuses given to CEOs of roughly 40% of companies that made large acquisitions for "closing the deal." What else were they supposed to do, leave it open? Yaniv Grinstein and Paul Hribar, "CEO compensation and incentives: Evidence from M&A bonuses," *Journal of Financial Economics* 73 (2004): 119–143. This, despite the evidence that most M&As decrease shareholders' value. Feng Gu and Baruch Lev, "Overpriced shares, ill-advised acquisitions, and goodwill impairment," *The Accounting Review*, forthcoming, November 2011.

5. Bebchuk and Fried, *Pay without performance*.

6. *Wall Street Journal*, May 20, 2009, C1.

7. The rate of increase in the mean total capitalization (market value) of companies—another firm-size indicator—is similar to that of total assets in figure 13-3. For more on the size and compensation issue, see Xavier Gabaix and Augustine Landier, "Why has CEO pay increased so much?" *Quarterly Journal of Economics* 123 (2008): 49–100.

8. Gu and Lev, ibid.

9. Robert Daines, Vinay Nair, and Lewis Kornhauser, "The good, the bad and the lucky: CEO pay and skill," working paper, University of Pennsylvania Law School, 2005.

10. The strength of the performance–pay link is called by economists the "pay–performance sensitivity." For example, if, on average, an increase in shareholder value of $1,000 is associated

with a pay increase of $3.25 (this is the actual finding of Jensen and Murphy), then the pay–performance sensitivity is 0.325%, a rather low sensitivity, insufficient to provide a strong performance incentive to executives. Michael Jensen and Kevin Murphy, "Performance pay and top-management incentives," *Journal of Political Economy* 98 (1990): 225–264. The pay-performance sensitivity increased in the last two decades.

11. Peter Demerjian, Baruch Lev, and Sarah McVay, "Quantifying managerial ability: A new measure and validity tests," working paper, University of Utah, 2011.

12. Ibid., for detail.

13. Some of this skill–performance relation is by design, since I measure CEO skill by the efficiency of generating revenues from deployed resources. The skill score, however, focuses on revenues, while the company performance in table 13-1 is measured by ROA, which focuses on earnings and assets.

14. *Wall Street Journal*, July 31, 2009, 1.

15. Ron Chernow, *Titan: The Life of John D. Rockefeller* (New York: Random House, 1998).

16. Raymond Baumhart, "How ethical are businessmen?" *Harvard Business Review* 39 (1961): 10.

17. The pendulum of the corporate purpose never stops. The recent financial crisis and the protracted recession that followed it resurrected the old arguments about the perils of unchecked profit drive and focus on shareholders. One hears again about the need to broaden the corporate propose and managers' objectives.

18. Jensen, Murphy and Wruck note: "... since it is logically impossible to maximize in more than one dimension, purposeful behavior requires a single-dimensional governing objective. As someone once said, multiple objectives is no objective." Michael Jensen, Kevin Murphy, and Eric Wruck, " Remuneration: Where we've been, how we got here, what are the problems and how to fix them," working paper, Harvard Business School, 2004,15.

19. This conflict is not theoretical. Gorton and Schmid report that in German companies, where employee representatives sit on supervisory boards, the shares of companies with equal representation of employees and shareholders on supervisory boards—a particularly strong employee representation—trade at a 31% discount to companies with only one-third labor representation on the board. Satisfying employees obviously comes at the expense of shareholders. Gary Gorton and Frank Schmid, "Capital, labor, and the firm: A study of German codetermination," *Journal of the European Economic Association* 2 (2004): 863–905.

20. Jensen et al., "Remuneration: Where we've been, how we got here, what are the problems and how to fix them." As Jensen et al. note, this objective assumes that national laws and regulations prevent private monopolies and make companies pay for (internalize) the detrimental effects of their actions on other constituencies and the environment.

21. In France, for example, even severance payments are now conditional on performance. *The Economist*, June 14, 2008, 77.

22. *The Economist*, May 23, 2009, 70.

23. Such investments will carry a significant cost-of-capital charge, reducing residual earnings.

24. For evidence, see Baruch Lev, Siyi Li and Theodore Sougiannis, "The Usefulness of accounting estimates for predicting cash flows and earnings," *Review of Accounting studies*, 15 (2010): 779-807.

25. Jeffrey Gordon, "A remedy for the executive pay problem: The case for compensation and discussion analysis," *Journal of Applied Corporate Finance*, 17 (2005), 28; and Steven Kaplan and Bernadette Minton, "How has CEO turnover changed? Increasingly performance sensitive boards and increasingly uneasy CEOs," working paper no. 12465, NBER, 2006.

26. Justin Wolfers, "Diagnosing discrimination: Stock returns and CEO gender," *Journal of European Economic Association* 4 (2006): 531–541.

27. These are not theoretical concerns. Basic, paradigm-changing research, which was until fifteen to twenty years ago prevalent in the United States, has all but vanished. Bell Labs (now, a much shrunken unit of Alcatel-Lucent), with revolutionary innovations like fax transmission, the transistor, and cellular telephony, along with RCA Labs and Xerox PARC—powerful innovation houses in the past—all but ceased to conduct basic research. Many companies cut their basic R&D too, seriously threatening the growth of the U.S. economy (for a survey, see *BusinessWeek*, September 7, 2009, 35–44). Managers' concerns with the risk of basic research are undoubtedly a major factor in its decline. As for risk-diversifying conglomerate acquisitions that don't benefit shareholders, see Yakove Amihud and Baruch Lev, "Risk reduction as a managerial motive for conglomerate mergers," *The Bell Journal of Economics* 12 (1981): 605–617.

28. For the reader unfamiliar with employee stock options: when granted to employees by the board, stock options specify the *exercise price* of the option (generally the firm's share price at grant date), namely the price the employee will have to pay the company to receive a share upon the option's exercise, and the *vesting period* (often three to five years from grant), after which the options can be exercised. (At roughly half of large U.S. companies, options vest in three years, in four years at about 30% of the companies, and in five years at about 15% of companies. See David Walker, "The challenge of improving the long-term focus of executive pay," *Boston College Law Review* 51, no. 2 (2010): 435–472.) Thus, for example, if the exercise price is $30, the vesting period is three years, and the company's stock price rises to $45 three years after grant, the option-holder employee will gain $15 ($45–$30) for each option exercised and sold.

29. Options were granted with abandon not only to executives. The bulk—90%—of the large increases in stock option grants from 1992 through 2002 went to employees, rather than to top executives (*The Economist*, Special Report, January 20, 2007, 15). Subsequent to the accounting expensing of options (2005), many companies cut significantly option grants, increasing restricted stock grants.

30. Employee stock options should not be confused with the options regularly traded in stock exchanges. IBM's traded options are not issued by IBM. They are bets on IBM's share prices. The options granted to IBM employees, in contrast, when exercised, are issued by the company. The main difference between the two option types is that traded options are *liquid*, they can be bought and sold at any time, whereas employee options are illiquid—they cannot be traded before they vest. This illiquidity of employee stock options decreases their value substantially relative to traded options. It also makes the valuation of employee options for accounting purposes very difficult, because there is no reliable way to price illiquidity.

31. When stock options are granted *in lieu* of cash salary, then their cost is decreased by the salary saved. It appears, however, that in most cases, options were just piled on top of cash salaries: "In practice, however, equity-based pay [options, restricted shares] is often layered on top of existing competitive pay packages without requiring any meaningful offset (through direct payments or reductions in other remuneration)." (Jensen, Murphy, and Wruck, 2004, p. 58).

32. Jap Efendi, Anup Srivastava, and Edward Swanson, "Why do corporate managers misstate financial statements? The role of option compensation and other factors," *Journal of Financial Economics* 85, no. 3 (2007): 667–708.

33. Fabrizio Ferri and David Maber, "Say on pay votes and CEO compensation: Evidence from the UK," working paper, Harvard Business School, 2011.

34. Ertimur et al. examined shareholders' "vote no" campaigns in the United States on executive pay from 1997 to 2007, prior to the say-on-pay legislation. While most of the proposals were initiated by union pension funds, the researchers report that the specific pay issues voted on did not reflect specific labor-related motives. Yonca Ertimur, Fabrizio Ferri, and

Volkan Muslu, "Shareholder activism and CEO pay," *Review of Financial Studies* 24, no. 2 (2011): 535–592.

35. *Wall Street Journal*, June 19, 2009, C2.

36. *The Economist*, June 14, 2008, 77. Vasella apparently took a page from baseball legend Ted Williams, who, upon failing to hit 0.300 in 1959 for the first time in his career, insisted that his 1960 salary be cut almost 30%, from $125,000 to $90,000. While Williams's exploits are surely known to many managers, the salary cut is largely unknown. I wonder why.

## CHAPTER 14

1. See Lawrence Cunningham, "Introduction to the Essays of Warren Buffett: Lessons for Corporate America," Legal Studies Research Paper no. 294, George Washington University Law School (2007), http://ssrn.com/abstract=1000439.

2. The title of a famous 1902 essay by Leo Tolstoy, analyzing the causes of poverty in Russia and prescribing remedies.

3. "Milton Friedman goes on tour," *The Economist*, January 27, 2011, 76.

# Bibliography

Aboody, David, and Ron Kasznik. "CEO stock option awards and the timing of corporate voluntary disclosures." *Journal of Accounting and Economics* 29 (2000): 73–100.

Aboody, David, and Baruch Lev. "The value-relevance of intangibles: The case of software capitalization." *Journal of Accounting Research* (Supplement) 36 (1998): 161–191.

Aboody, David, and Baruch Lev. "Information asymmetry, R&D and insider gains." *Journal of Finance* 55 (2000): 2747–2766.

Adams, Renée, and Daniel Ferreira. "A theory of friendly boards." *Journal of Finance* 62 (2007): 217–250.

Adams, Renée, and Daniel Ferreira. "Women in the boardroom and their impact on governance and performance." *Journal of Financial Economics* 94 (2009): 291–309.

Agrawal, Anup, and Sahiba Chadha. "Corporate governance and accounting scandals." *Journal of Law and Economics* 48 (2005): 371–406.

Agarwal, Vineet, Angel Liao, Elly Nash, and Richard Taffler. "The impact of effective investor relations on market value." working paper, University of Edinburgh Business School, 2008.

Akerlof, George. "The market for 'lemons': Quality uncertainty and the market mechanism." *Quarterly Journal of Economics* 84 (1970): 488–500.

Alexander, Cindy, Mark Chen, Duane Seppi, and Chester Spatt. "The role of advisory services in proxy voting." working paper, U.S. Securities and Exchange Commission, Washington, DC, 2008.

American Business Conference. "Impact of U.S. Accounting Standards on Capital Formation and International Competitiveness: A Proposal for Change." Washington, DC, 1991.

Amihud, Yakov, and Baruch Lev. "Risk reduction as a managerial motive for conglomerate mergers." *The Bell Journal of Economics* 12 (1981): 605–617.

Anderson, Ronald, and David Reeb. "Founding-family ownership and firm performance: Evidence from the S&P 500." *Journal of Finance* 58 (2003): 1301–1327.

Arrow, Kenneth. "Gifts and exchanges." *Philosophy and Public Affairs* 1 (1972): 343–362.

Asquith, Paul, and David Mullins. "Equity issues and offering dilution." *Journal of Financial Economics* 15 (1986): 61–89.

Azzi, Sarah, Ron Bird, Paolo Ghiringhelli, and Emanuele Rossi. "Biases and information in analysts' recommendations: The European experience." *Journal of Asset Management* 6 (2006): 345–380.

Baginski, Stephen, John Hassell, and Michael Kimbrough. "The effect of legal environment on voluntary disclosure: Evidence from management earnings forecasts issued in U.S. and Canadian markets." *The Accounting Review* 77 (2002): 25–50.

Baker, Malcolm, Jeremy Stein, and Jeffrey Wurgler. "When does the market matter? Stock prices and the investment of equity-dependent firms." *Quarterly Journal of Economics* (August 2003): 969–1005.

Baker, Malcolm, and Jeffrey Wurgler. "Investor sentiment in the stock market." *Journal of Economic Perspectives* 21 (2007): 129–151.

Ball, Ray, and Lakshmanan Shivakumar. "How much new information is there in earnings?" *Journal of Accounting Research* 46 (2008): 975–1016.

Bamford, Jim, and David Ernst. "Measuring alliance performance." *McKinsey Quarterly*, October 2002.

Barber, Brad. "Monitoring the monitor: Evaluating CalPERS' shareholder activism." *Journal of Investing* 16, no. 4 (2007): 66–80.

Barber, Brad, Reuven Lehavy, Maureen McNichols, and Brett Trueman. "Can investors profit from the prophets? Security analyst recommendations and stock returns." *The Journal of Finance* LVI (2001): 531–563.

Barber, Brad, and Terrance Odean. "All that glitters: The effect of attention and news on the buying behavior of individual and institutional investors." *Review of Financial Studies* 21 (2008): 785–818.

Barro, Robert. "The stock market and investment." *The Review of Financial Studies* 3 (1990): 115–131.

Baumhart, Raymond. "How ethical are businessmen?" *Harvard Business Review* 39 (1961): 6–19.

Bebchuk, Lucian. "The myth of the shareholder franchise." *Virginia Law Review* 93 (2007): 675–732.

Bebchuk, Lucian, John Coates, and Guhan Subramanian. "The powerful antitakeover force of staggered boards, theory, evidence and policy." *Stanford Law Review* 54 (2002): 887–951.

Bebchuk, Lucian, and Jesse Fried. *Pay without Performance: The Unfilled Promise of Executive Compensation.* Cambridge, MA: Harvard University Press, 2004.

Bebchuk, Lucian, and Yaniv Grinstein. "The growth of executive pay." *Oxford Review of Economic Policy* 21 (2005): 282–303.

Bebchuk, Lucian, Yaniv Grinstein, and Urs Peyer. "Lucky CEOs and lucky directors." *The Journal of Finance* 65 (2010): 2363–2401.

Becht, Marco, Julian Franks, Colin Mayer, and Stefano Rossi. "Returns to shareholder activism: Evidence from a clinical study of the Hermes U.K. Focus Fund." *Review of Financial Studies* 22 (2009): 3093–3129.

Benartzi, Shlomo, Roni Michaely, Richard Thaler, and William Weld. "The nominal share price puzzle." *Journal of Economic Perspectives* 23 (2009): 121–142.

Berle, Adolf, and Gardiner Means. *The Modern Corporation and Private Property.* New York: The McMillan Company, 1932.

Bhagat, Sanjai, and Bernard Black. "The non-correlation between board independence and long-term firm performance." *Journal of Corporation Law* 27 (2002): 231–273.

Bhagat, Sanjai, and Brian Bolton. "Corporate governance and firm performance." *Journal of Corporate Finance* 14 (2008): 257–273.

Bhagat, Sanjai, Brian Bolton, and Roberta Romano. "The promise and peril of corporate governance indices." *Columbia Law Review* 108 (2008): 1803–1882.

Bhattacharya, Nilabhra, Ervin Black, Theodore Christensen, and Chad Larson. "Assessing the relative informativeness and permanence of street earnings and GAAP operating earnings." *Journal of Accounting and Economics* 36 (2003): 285–319.

Bhojraj, Sanjeev, Paul Hribar, Marc Picconi, and John McInnis. "Making sense of cents: An examination of firms that marginally miss or beat analyst forecasts." *The Journal of Finance* LXIV (2009): 2361–2388.

Billings, Mary. "Disclosure timeliness, insider trading opportunities and litigation consequences." working paper, New York University, 2009.

Blacconiere, Walter, and Dennis Patten. "Environmental disclosure, regulatory costs, and changes in firm value." *Journal of Accounting and Economics* 18 (1994): 357–377.

Blacconiere, Walter, and Dana Northcut. "Environmental information and market reaction to environmental legislation." *Journal of Accounting, Auditing and Finance* 12 (1997): 149–178.

Black, Bernard, Hasung Jang, and Woochan Kim. "Does corporate governance predict firms' market values? Evidence from Korea." *Journal of Law, Economics and Organization* 22 (2006): 366–413.

Black, Bernard, and Vikramaditya Khanna. "Can corporate governance reforms increase firms' market values? Evidence from India." *Journal of Empirical Legal Studies* 4 (2007): 749–796.

Black, Fischer. "The Dividend Puzzle." In *The Modern Theory of Corporate Finance*, edited by Michel Jensen and Clifford Smith, 634–639. New York: McGraw Hill Book Company, 1984.

Bogle, John. *The Battle for the Soul of Capitalism*. New Haven, CT: Yale University Press, 2005.

Bonacchi, Massimiliano, Kalin Kolev, and Baruch Lev. "The analysis and valuation of subscription-based enterprises." working paper, Yale University, 2011.

Boone, Audra, Laura Field, Jonathan Karpoff, and Charu Raheja. "The determinants of corporate board size and composition: An empirical analysis." *Journal of Financial Economics* 85 (2007): 66–101.

Bortolotti, Bernardo, Veljko Fotak, William Megginson, and William Miracky. "Sovereign Wealth fund investment patters and performance." working paper, Price College of Business, The University of Oklahoma, 2009.

Botosan, Christine. "Disclosure level and the cost of equity capital." *The Accounting Review* 72 (1997): 323–349.

Bowen, Robert, Angela Davis, and Dawn Matsumoto. "Emphasis on proforma versus GAAP earnings in quarterly press releases: Determinants, SEC intervention, and market reactions." *The Accounting Review* 80 (2005): 1011–1038.

Bradshaw, Mark, and Richard Sloan. "GAAP versus the street: An empirical assessment of two alternative definitions of earnings." *Journal of Accounting Research* 40 (2002): 41–65.

Bratton, William. "Hedge funds and governance targets." *The Georgetown Law Journal* 95 (2007): 1375–1433.

Brav, Alon, Campbell Harvey, John Graham, and Roni Michaeli. "Payout policy in the 21st century." *Journal of Financial Economics* 77 (2005): 483–527.

Brav, Alon, Wei Jiang, Frank Patrony, and Randall Thomas. "Hedge fund activism, corporate governance, and firm performance." *The Journal of Finance* 63 (2008): 1729–1775.

Brav, Alone, Reuven Lehavy, and Roni Michaely. "Using expectations to test asset pricing models." *Financial Management*, Autumn 2005, 5–37.

Brennan, Michael, and Claudia Tamarowski. "Investor relations, liquidity, and stock prices." *Journal of Applied Corporate Finance* 12 (2000): 26–37.

Brown, Lawrence, and Kumar Sivakumar. "Comparing the quality of two operating income measures." *Review of Accounting Studies* 4 (2003): 561–572.

Brown, Robert. "The SEC, corporate governance and shareholder access to the board room." working paper no. 08-05, University of Denver Sturm College of Law, 2008.

Brown, Stephen, Stephen Hillegeist, and Kin Lo. "Conference calls and information asymmetry." *Journal of Accounting and Economics* 37 (2004): 343–366.

Burns, Natasha, and Simi Kedia. "The impact of performance-based compensation on misreporting." *Journal of Financial Economics* 79 (2006): 35–67.

Bushee, Brian, and Gregory Miller. "Investor relations, firm visibility and investor following." working paper, Wharton School, University of Pennsylvania, 2006.

Byun, Jinho, and Michael Rozeff. "Long-run performance after stock splits: 1927–1996." *Journal of Finance* 58 (2003): 1063–1086.

Campbell, Jeremy. *The Liar's Tale: A History of Falsehood*. New York: W.W. Norton & Co., 2001.

Carruthers, Bruce, and Barry Cohen. "Predicting failure but failing to predict: A sociology of knowledge of credit rating in post-bellum America." working paper, Department of Sociology, Northwestern University, 2001.

CFA Institute and the Business Roundtable. "Breaking the short-term cycle." Symposium Series on Short-Termism, CFA Institute, 2006.

Chan, Louis, David Ikenberry, Josef Lakonishok, and Sangwoo Lee. "Are all analysts alike? Identifying earnings forecasting ability." *Journal of Investment Management* 6 (2008): 1–19.

Chan, Louis, Jason Karceski, and Josef Lakonishok. "The level and persistence of growth rates." *The Journal of Finance* LVIII (2003): 643–684.

Chari, Anusha, and Peter Henry. "Firm-specific information and the efficiency of investment." *Journal of Financial Economics* 87 (2008): 636–655.

Chauvin, Keith, and Mark Hirschey. "Advertising, R&D expenditures and the market value of the firm." *Financial Management* 22 (1993): 128–140.

Chavez, Gonzalo, and Ana Silva. "Brazil's experiment with corporate governance." *Journal of Applied Corporate Finance* 21 (2009): 34–44.

Chen, Joseph, Harrison Hong, and Jeremy Stein. "Breadth of ownership and stock returns." *Journal of Financial Economics* 66 (2002): 171–205.

Chen, Shuping, Dawn Matsumoto, and Shivaram Rajgopal. "Is silence golden? An empirical analysis of firms that stop giving quarterly earnings guidance." *Journal of Accounting and Economics* 51 (2001): 134–150.

Chernow, Ron. *Titan: The Life of John D. Rockefeller*. New York: Random House, 1998.

Choi, Stephen, Karen Nelson, and Adam Pritchard. "The screening effect of the Private Securities Litigation Reform Act." *Journal of Empirical Legal Studies* 6 (2009): 35–68.

Citigroup. "Hedge funds at the gate." *Financial Strategy*, September 22, 2005.

Cohen, Daniel, Dey Aiyesha, and Thomas Lys. "Real and accrual-based earnings management in the pre- and post-Sarbanes Oxley periods." *The Accounting Review* 83 (2008): 757–787.

Coles, Jeffrey, Michael Lemmon, and Lalitha Naveen. "A comparison of profitability and CEO turnover sensitivity in large private and public firms." working paper, Arizona State University, 2003.

Coles, Jeffrey, Daniel Naveen, and Lalitha Naveen. "Boards: Does one size fits all? *Journal of Financial Economics* 87 (2008): 329–356.

Collins, Daniel, Oliver Li, and Hong Xie. "The information content of GAAP versus street earnings: Evidence from trading volume." working paper, University of Iowa, 2005.

Copeland, Tom, Aaron Dolgoff, and Alberto Moel. "The role of expectations in explaining the cross-section of stock returns." *Review of Accounting Studies* 9 (2004): 149–188.

Core, John, Wayne Guay, and Tjomme Rusticus. "Does weak governance cause weak stock returns? An examination of firm operating performance and investors' expectations." *Journal of Finance* LXI (2006): 655–687.

Core, John, Wayne Guay, and Randall Thomas. "Is U.S. CEO compensation broken?" *Journal of Applied Corporate Finance* 17 (2005): 97–104.

Cotter, James, and Randall Thomas. "Shareholder proposals in the new millennium: Shareholder support, board response, and market reaction." *Journal of Corporate Finance* 13 (2007): 368–391.

Cotter, Julie, Irem Tuna, and Peter Wysocki. "Expectations management and beatable targets: How do analysts react to explicit earnings guidance?" *Contemporary Accounting Research* 23 (2006): 593–624.

Crystal, Graef. *In Search of Excess: The Overcompensation of American Executives*. New York: W.W. Norton & Co., 1991.

Dahya, Jay, Orlin Dimitrov, and John McConnell. "Does board independence matter in companies with a controlling shareholder?" *Journal of Applied Corporate Finance* 21 (2009): 67–78.

Dahya, Jay, and John McConnell. "Board composition, corporate performance, and the Cadbury committee recommendations." *Journal of Financial and Quantitative Analysis* 42 (2007): 535–564.

Dahya, Jay, John McConnell, and Nickolaos Travlos. "The Cadbury committee, corporate performance, and top management performance." *Journal of Finance* 57 (2002): 461–483.

Daines, Robert, Ian Gow, and David Larcker. "Rating the ratings: How good are commercial governance ratings?" *Journal of Financial Economics* 98 (2010): 439–461.

Daines, Robert, Vinay Nair, and Lewis Kornhauser. "The good, the bad and the lucky: CEO pay and skill." working paper, University of Pennsylvania Law School, 2005.

Davis, Angela, and Isho Tama-Sweet. "Managers use of pessimistic tone across alternative disclosure outlets: Earnings press releases versus MD&A." working paper, Lundquist School of Business, University of Oregon, 2008.

Dechow, Patricia, and Catherine Schrand. *Earnings Quality.* Charlottesville, VA: The Research Foundation of the CFA Institute, 2004.

DeFond, Mark, and Mingyi Hung. "Investor protection and corporate governance: Evidence from worldwide CEO turnover." *Journal of Accounting Research* 42 (2004): 269–312.

Del Guercio, Diane. "The distorting effect of the prudent-man laws on institutional equity investment." *Journal of Financial Economics* 40 (1996): 31–62.

Del Guerico, Diane, Laura Seery, and Tracie Woidtke. "Do board pay attention when institutional investor activists 'just vote no'?" *Journal of Financial Economics* 90 (2008): 84–103.

DellaVigna, Stefano, and Joshua Pollet. "Investor inattention and Friday earnings announcements." *Journal of Finance* 64 (2009): 709–749.

DeMarzo, Peter, Dimitri Vayanos, and Jeffrey Zwiebel. "Persuasion bias, social influence, and unidimensional opinions." *The Quarterly Journal of Economics* 118 (2003): 909–968.

Demerjian, Peter, Baruch Lev, and Sarah McVay. "Quantifying managerial ability: A new measure and validity tests." working paper, University of Utah, 2011.

Demers, Elizabeth, and Clara Vega. "Soft information in earnings announcements: News or noise?" working paper, INSEAD, France, 2010.

Deng, Zhen, Baruch Lev, and Francis Narin. "Science & technology as predictors of stock performance." *Financial Analysts Journal* 55 (1999): 20–32.

Denham, Robert, and Michael Porter. "Lifting All Boats: Increasing the Payoff from Private Investment in the U.S. Economy." Report of the Capital Allocation Sub-council to the Competitiveness Policy Council, Washington, DC, 1995.

Denis, David, Paul Hanouna, and Atulya Sarin. "Is there a dark side to incentive compensation?" *Journal of Corporate Finance* 12 (2006): 467–488.

Dennis, Patrick, and Deon Strickland. "The effect of stock splits on liquidity and excess returns: Evidence from shareholder ownership composition." *The Journal of Financial Research* XXVI (2003): 355–370.

Dey, Aiyesha, Ellen Engel, and Gloria Liu. "Determinants and implications of board leadership structure." working paper, Booth School of Business, University of Chicago, 2009.

Dey, Malay, and B. Radhakrishna. "Who trades around earnings announcements? Evidence from TORQ data." *Journal of Business Finance and Accounting* 34 (2007): 269–291.

Dichev, Ilia, and Vicki Tang. "Matching and the changing properties of accounting earnings over the last 40 years." *The Accounting Review* 83 (2008): 1425–1461.

DiPiazza, Samuel, David McDonnell, William Parrett, Mike Rake, Frans Samyn, and James Turley. "Global capital markets and the global economy: A vision from the CEOs of the international audit networks." International Audit Networks (2006).

Djankov, Simeon, Rafael La Porta, Florencio Lopez-De-Silanes, and Andrei Shleifer. "The law and economics of self-dealing." *Journal of Financial Economics* 88 (2008): 430–465.

Doidge, Craig, Andrew Karolyi, and René Stulz. "Why are foreign firms listed in the U.S. worth more?" *Journal of Financial Economics* 71 (2004): 205–238.

Doukas, John, and Lorne Switzer. "The stock market's valuation of R&D spending and market concentration." *Journal of Economics and Business* 44 (1992): 95–114.

Drucker, Peter. "A crisis of capitalism." *Wall Street Journal*, September 30, 1986, 32.

Durfee, Don. "Management or manipulation?" *CFO Magazine*, December 1, 2006.

Dyck, Alexander, Adair Morse, and Luigi Zingales. "Who blows the whistle on corporate fraud?" *Journal of Finance* 65 (2010): 2213–2253.

Eberhart, Allan, William Maxwell, and Akhtar Siddique. "Returns and operating performance following R&D increases." *Journal of Finance* 59 (2004): 623–650.

Eberhart, Allan, William Maxwell, and Akhtar Siddique. "An examination of long-term abnormal stock returns and operating performance following R&D increases." *Journal of Finance* 54 (2004): 623–650.

Eccles, Robert, Robert Herz, Mary Keegan, and David Phillips. *The Value Reporting Revolution*. New York: John Wiley & Sons, 2001.

Efendi, Jap, Anup Srivastava, and Edward Swanson. "Why do corporate managers misstate financial statements? The role of option compensation and other factors." *Journal of Financial Economics* 85, no. 3 (2007): 667–708.

Elhauge, Einer. "Corporate managers' operational discretion to sacrifice corporate profits in the public interest." In *Environmental Protection and the Social Responsibility of Firms*, edited by Bruce Hay, Robert Stavins, and Richard Vietor, 13–76. Washington, DC: Resources for the Future, 2005.

Englmaier, Florian. "A brief survey of overconfidence." ICFAI *Journal of Behavioral Finance* 31 (2007): 329–345.

Ertimur, Yonca, Fabrizio Ferri, and Volkan Muslu. "Shareholder activism and CEO pay." *Review of Financial Studies* 24 (2011): 535–592.

Fahlenbrach, Rudiger, and Rene Stulz. "Managerial ownership dynamics and firm value." *Journal of Financial Economics* 92 (2009): 342–361.

Faleye, Olubunmi. "Classified boards, firm value, and managerial entrenchment." *Journal of Financial Economics* 83 (2007): 501–529.

Fama, Eugene, and Kenneth French. "Financing decisions: Who issues stock?" *Journal of Financial Economics* 76 (2004): 549–582.

Fama, Eugene, and Kenneth French. "The cross-section of expected stock returns." *The Journal of Finance* 47 (1992): 427–465.

Feng, Mei. "Why do managers meet or slightly beat earnings forecasts in equilibrium? An endogenous mean-variance explanation." working paper, University of Pittsburgh, 2008.

Ferri, Fabrizio, and David Maber. "Say on pay votes and CEO compensation: Evidence from the UK." working paper, Harvard Business School, 2011.

Fich, Eliezer, and Anil Shivdasani. "Are busy boards effective monitors?" *The Journal of Finance* 61 (2006): 689–724.

Field, Laura, Michelle Lowry, and Susan Shu. "Does disclosure deter or trigger litigation?" *Journal of Accounting and Economics* 39 (2005): 487–507.

Financial Accounting Standards Board (FASB). Statement of Financial Accounting Standards No. 86, Accounting for the Cost of Computer Software to be sold, Leased or Otherwise Marketed, 1985.

Fisher, Dan. "Accounting tricks catch up with GE." Forbes.com, August 4, 2009.

Francis, Jennifer, Donalt Pagach, and Jens Stephan. "The stock market response to earnings announcements released during trading versus nontrading periods." *Journal of Accounting Research* 30 (1992): 165–184.

Frank, Ted. "Arbitrary and unfair." *Wall Street Journal*, May 31, 2007, A14.

Frankfurt, Harry. *On Bullshit*. Princeton, NJ: Princeton University Press, 2005.

Friedman, Milton. *Capitalism and Freedom*. Chicago: The University of Chicago Press, 1962.

Frost, Carol. "Characteristics and information value of corporate disclosures of forward-looking information in global equity markets." working paper, Dartmouth College, 2003.

Gabaix, Xavier, and Augustine Landier. "Why has CEO pay increased so much?" *Quarterly Journal of Economics* 123 (2008): 49–100.

Gerstner, Louis. *Who Says Elephants Can't Dance? Inside IBM's Historic Turnaround.* New York: Harper Collins, 2004.

Ghosh, Aloke, and Doocheol Moon. "When the CEO is also the chair of the board." working paper, Zicklin School of Business, Baruch College, 2009.

Gilan, Stuart, and Laura Starks. "Corporate governance proposals and shareholder activism: The role of institutional investors." *Journal of Financial Economics* 57 (2000): 275–305.

Gilbert, Lewis.. *Dividends and Democracy.* Larchmont, NY: American Research Council, Inc., 1956.

Glass Lewis & Co. "Getting it wrong the first time." March 2, 2006.

Glass Lewis & Co. "The errors of their ways." February 27, 2007.

Godfrey, Paul, Craig Merrill, and Jared Hansen. "The relationship between corporate social responsibility and shareholder value: An empirical test of the risk management hypothesis." *Strategic Management Journal* 30 (2009): 425–445.

Goedhart, Marc, Timothy Koller, and David Vessels. "Do fundamentals—or emotions—drive the stock market?" *McKinsey on Finance* 15 (2005): 1–6.

Goldstein, Michael, Edith Hotckiss, and Erik Sirri. "Transparency and liquidity: A controlled experiment on corporate bonds." *Review of Financial Studies* 20 (2007): 274–314.

Gordon, Jeffrey. "A remedy for the executive pay problem: The case for "compensation discussion and analysis." *Journal of Applied Corporate Finance* 17 (2005): 24–35.

Gordon, Jeffrey. "Executive compensation: If there is a problem, what's the remedy? The case for 'compensation discussion and analysis.'" *Journal of Corporation Law* 30 (2005): 675–702.

Gordon, Jeffrey. "The rise of independent directors in the United States, 1950–2005: Of shareholder value and stock market prices." *Stanford Law Review* 59 (2007): 1465–1568.

Gordon, Robert. "Exploding productivity growth: Context, causes and implications." *Brookings Papers on Economic Activity* 2 (2003): 207–298.

Gorton, Gary, and Frank Schmid. "Capital, labor, and the firm: A study of German codetermination." *Journal of the European Association* 2 (2004): 863–905.

Graham, John, Campbell Harvey, and Shiva Rajgopal. "The economic implications of corporate financial reporting." *Journal of Accounting and Economics* 40 (2005): 3–73.

Greenwood, Robin, and Michael Schor. "Investor activism and takeovers." *Journal of Financial Economics* 92 (2009): 362–375.

Grinstein, Yaniv, and Paul Hribar. "CEO compensation and incentives: Evidence from M&A bonuses." *Journal of Financial Economics* 73 (2004): 119–143.

Grullon, Gustavo, George Kanatas, and James Weston. "Advertising, breadth of ownership, and liquidity." *Review of Financial Studies* 17 (2004): 439–461.

Grullon, Gustavo, and Roni Michaeli. "The information content of share repurchases programs." *Journal of Finance* 59 (2004): 651–680.

Grundfest, Joseph. "The class-action market." *Wall Street Journal*, February 7, 2007, A15.

Gu, Feng, and Baruch Lev. "Overpriced shares, ill-advised acquisitions, and goodwill impairment." *The Accounting Review* (forthcoming 2011).

Guiso, Luigi, Paola Sapienza, and Luigi Zingales. "The role of social capital in financial development." *American Economic Review* 94 (2004): 526–556.

Guo, Re-Jin, Timothy Kruse, and Tom Nohel. "Undoing the powerful anti-takeover force of staggered boards." *Journal of Corporate Finance* 14 (2008): 274–288.

Guo, Rejin, Baruch Lev, and Nan Zhou. "Competitive costs of disclosure by biotech IPOs." *Journal of Accounting Research* (Supplement) (2004): 319–355.

Hail, Luzi "The impact of voluntary corporate disclosures on the ex ante cost of capital for Swiss firms." *European Accounting Review* 11 (2003): 741–743.

Hall, Brian. "Six challenges in designing equity-based pay." *Journal of Applied Corporate Finance* 15 (2003): 21–33.

Healy, Paul, Amy Hutton, and Krishna Palepu. "Stock performance and intermediation changes surrounding sustained increases in disclosure." *Contemporary Accounting Research* 16 (1999): 485–520.

Heinzl, Mark. "Nortel to restate several years' results to fix revenue-booking flub." *Wall Street Journal*, March 11–12, 2006, A3.

Hensley, Scott, and Peter Landers. "If drug firm's star falls, does anyone hear it?" *Wall Street Journal*, February 24, 2004.

Himmelberg, Charles, Glenn Hubbard, and Darius Palia. "Understanding the determinants of managerial ownership and performance." *Journal of Financial Economics* 53 (1999): 353–384.

Hirshleifer, David, and Siew Hong Teoh. "Limited attention, information disclosure, and financial reporting." *Journal of Accounting and Economics* 36 (2003): 337–386.

Hirshleifer, David, Sonya Lim, and Siew Hong Teoh. "Disclosure to an audience with limited attention." working paper, The Ohio State University, 2004.

Hochberg, Yael. "Venture capital and corporate governance in the newly public firm." working paper, Northwestern University, 2008.

Holmstrom, Bengt, and Steven Kaplan. "The state of U.S. corporate governance: What's right and what's wrong?" *Journal of Applied Corporate Finance* 151 (2003): 8–20.

Huberman, Gur, and Tomer Regev. "Contagious speculation and a cure for cancer: A non-event that made stock prices soar." *Journal of Finance* 56 (2001): 387–396.

Hong, Harrison, Jeffrey Kubik, and Jeremy Stein. "The only game in town: Stock-price consequences of local bias." *Journal of Financial Economics* 90 (2008): 20–37.

Hong, Harrison, and Ming Huang. "Talking up liquidity: Insider trading and investor relations." *Journal of Financial Intermediation* 14 (2005): 1–31.

Houston, Joel, Baruch Lev, and Jennifer Tucker. "To guide or not to guide? Causes and consequences of stopping quarterly earnings guidance." *Contemporary Accounting Research* 27 (2010): 143–185.

Hribar, Paul, Nicole Jenkins, and Bruce Johnson. "Stock repurchases as an earnings management devise." *Journal of Accounting and Economics* 41 (2006): 3–27.

Huberman, Gur, and Tomer Regev. "Contagious speculation and the cure for cancer: A non-event that made stock prices soar." *Journal of Finance* 56 (2001): 387–396.

Hutton, Amy. "Determinants of managerial earnings guidance prior to regulation Fair Disclosure and bias in analysts' earnings forecasts." *Contemporary Accounting Research* 22 (2005): 867–914.

Jacobs, Michael. *Short-Term America: The Causes of Business Myopia.* Boston: Harvard Business School Press, 1991.

Jensen, Michael. "Value maximization, stakeholder theory, and the corporate objective function." *Journal of Applied Corporate Finance* 14 (2001): 8–21.

Jensen, Michael. "Value maximization, stakeholder theory, and the corporate objective function." *European Financial Management Review* 7 (2001): 297–317.

Jensen, Michael. "The agency costs of overvalued equity and the current state of corporate finance." *European Financial Management Journal* 10 (2004): 549–565.

Jensen, Michael, and William Meckling. "Theory of the firm: Managerial behavior, agency costs and ownership structure." *Journal of Financial Economics* 3 (1976): 305–360.

Jensen, Michael, and Kevin Murphy. "Performance pay and top-management incentives." *Journal of Political Economy* 98 (1990): 225–264.

Jensen, Michael, Kevin Murphy, and Eric Wruck. "Remuneration: Where we've been, how we got here, what are the problems and how to fix them." working paper, Harvard Business School, 2004.

Jenter, Dirk, and Fadi Kanaan. "CEO turnover and relative performance evaluation." working paper no. 12068, NBER, Cambridge, MA, 2006.

Johnson, Marilyn, Karen Nelson, and Adam Pritchard. "Do the merits matter more? The impact of the Private Securities Litigation Reform Act." *The Journal of Law, Economics & Organization* 23 (2007): 627–652.

Kahan, Marcel, and Edward Rock. "Embattled CEOs." *Texas Law Review* 88 (2010): 987–1051.

Kahan, Marcel, and Edward Rock. "Hedge funds in corporate governance and corporate control." *University of Pennsylvania Law Review* 155 (2007): 1021–1093.

Kahneman, Daniel, and Amos Tversky. "Prospect theory: An analysis of decision under risk." *Econometrica* 47 (1979): 263–291.

Kahneman, Daniel, and Amos Tversky. "Intuitive prediction: Biases and corrective procedures." In *Judgement Under Uncertainty: Heuristics and Biases*, edited by D. Kahneman, P. Slovic, and A. Tversky, 414–421. Cambridge, U.K.: Cambridge University Press, 1982.

Kaplan, Steven, and Bernadette Minton. "How has CEO turnover changed? Increasingly performance sensitive boards and increasingly uneasy CEOs." working paper no. 12465, NBER, 2006.

Kaplan, Steven, and Joshua Rauh. "Wall Street and main street: What contributes to the rise in the highest incomes?" *Review of Financial Studies* 23, no. 3 (2007): 1004–1050.

Karaoglu, Emre, Tatiana Sandino, and Ranolph Beatty. "Benchmarking against the performance of high profile 'scandal' firms." working paper, Leventhal School of Accounting, University of Southern California, 2006.

Karamanou, Irene, and George Nishiotis. "Disclosure and the cost of capital: Evidence from the market's reaction to firm voluntary adoption of IAS." *Journal of Business Finance & Accounting* 36 (2009): 793–821.

Karpoff, Jonathan. "The impact of shareholder activism on target companies: A survey of empirical findings." working paper, University of Washington, 2001.

Karpoff, Jonathan, Scott Lee, and Gerald Martin. "The consequences to managers of financial misrepresentation." *Journal of Financial Economics* 88 (2008): 193–205.

Karpoff, Jonathan, and Xiaoxia Lou. "Short sellers and financial misconduct." *Journal of Finance* LXV (2010): 1879–1913.

Kasznik, Ron, and Baruch Lev. "To warn or not to warn: Management disclosures in the face of an earnings surprise." *The Accounting Review* 70 (1995): 113–134.

Kedia, Simi, and Thomas Philippon. "The economics of fraudulent accounting." *Review of Financial Studies* 22 (2009): 2169–2199.

Khanna, Tarun, and Yishay Yafeh. "Business groups in emerging markets: Paragons or Parasites?" *Journal of Economic Literature* 45 (2007): 331–372.

Kim, Woochan, Woojin Kim, and Kap-Sok Kwon. "Value of outside blockholder activism: Evidence from the switchers." *Journal of Corporate Finance* 15 (2009): 505–522.

Kim, Woojin, and Michael Weisbach. "Motivations for public equity offers: An international perspective." *Journal of Financial Economics* 87 (2008): 281–307.

Kimbrough, Michael. "The effect of conference calls on analyst and market underreaction to earnings announcements." *The Accounting Review* 80 (2005): 189–219.

Kimbrough, Michael, and Henock Louis. "Voluntary disclosure to influence investor reactions to merger announcement: An examination of conference calls." *The Accounting Review* 86 (2011): 637–668.

Klein, April. "Firm performance and board committee structure." *Journal of Law & Economics* 41 (1998): 275–304.

Klein, April. "Audit committee, board of director characteristics, and earnings management." *Journal of Accounting and Economics* 33 (2002): 375–400.

Klein, April, and Emanuel Zur. "Entrepreneurial shareholder activism: Hedge funds and other private investors." *The Journal of Finance* 64 (2009): 187–229.

Koh, Kevin, Dawn Matsumoto, and Shivaram Rajgopal. "Meeting or beating analyst expectations in the post-scandal world: Changes in stock market rewards and managerial actions." *Contemporary Accounting Research* 25 (2008): 1067–1098.

Kothari, S.P., Susan Shu, and Peter Wysocki. "Do managers withhold bad news?" *Journal of Accounting Research* 47 (2009): 241–276.

Knack, Stephen, and Philip Keefer. "Does social capital have an economic payoff?: A cross-country investigation." *Quarterly Journal of Economics* 112 (1997): 1251.

Krishna, Vijay, and John Morgan. "Cheap talk." In *The New Palgrave Dictionary of Economics*, edited by Steven Durlauf and Lawrence Blum. Houndsmill, UK: Palgrave Macmillan, 2008.

Lakonishok, Josef, and Baruch Lev. "Stock splits and stock dividends: Why, who and when." *Journal of Finance* 42 (1987): 913–932.

Lakonishok, Josef, Andrei Shleifer, and Robert Vishny. "Contrarian investment, extrapolation, and risk." *The Journal of Finance* XLIX (1994): 1541–1578.

Lakonishok, Josef, and Inmoo Lee. "Are insider trades informative?" *The Review of Financial Studies* 14 (2001): 79–111.

Lamont, Owen. "Go down fighting: Short sellers vs. firms." working paper 10659, NBER, 2004.

Lansford, Benjamin, Baruch Lev, and Jennifer Tucker. "Causes and consequences of disaggregating earnings guidance." working paper, Fisher School of Accounting, University of Florida, 2010.

La Porta, Rafael, Florencio Lopez-De-Silanes, Andrei Shleifer, and Robert Vishny. "Legal determinants of external financing." *Journal of Finance* 52 (1997): 1131–1150.

La Porta, Rafael, Florencio Lopez-de-Silanes, and Andrei Shleifer. "Corporate ownership around the world." *Journal of Finance* 54 (1999): 471–517.

Laux, Volker. "Board independence and CEO turnover." *Journal of Accounting Research* 46 (2008): 137–171.

Lehavy, Reuven, and Richard Sloan. "Investor recognition and stock returns." *Review of Accounting Studies* 13 (2008): 327–361.

Lerman, Alina. "Individual investors' attention to accounting information: Message board discussions." working paper, Stern School of Business, New York University, 2010.

Leuz, Christian, and Robert Verrecchia. "The economic consequences of increased disclosure." *Journal of Accounting Research* 38 (2000): 91–124.

Leuz, Christian, Dhananjay Nanda, and Peter Wysocki. "Earnings management and investor protection: An international comparison." Working paper, Wharton School, University of Pennsylvania, 2002.

Lev, Baruch. "On the usefulness of earnings and earnings research: Lessons and directions from two decades of accounting research." *Journal of Accounting Research*. Supplement (1989): 153–192.

Lev, Baruch. *Intangibles: Management, Measurement and Reporting*. Washington, DC: Brookings Institution Press, 2001.

Lev, Baruch. "Corporate earnings: Facts and fiction." *Journal of Economic Perspectives* 17 (2003): 27–50.

Lev, Baruch, Siyi Li, and Theodore Sougiannis. "The usefulness of accounting estimates for predicting cash flows and earnings." *Review of Accounting Studies* 15 (2010): 779–807.

Lev, Baruch, and Gershon Mandelker. "The microeconomic consequences of corporate mergers." *The Journal of Business* 45 (1974): 85–104.

Lev, Baruch, and Doron Nissim. "The persistence of the accruals anomaly." *Contemporary Accounting Research* 23 (2006): 193–226.

Lev, Baruch, Doron Nissim, and Jacob Thomas. "On the informational usefulness of R&D capitalization and amortization." In *Visualizing Intangibles*, edited by S. Zambon and G. Marzo, 97–128. Burlington, VT: Ashgate Publishing Co., 2007.

Lev, Baruch, Christine Petrovits, and Suresh Radhakrishnan. "Is doing good, good for you? How corporate charitable contributions enhance revenue growth." *Strategic Management Journal* 31 (2010): 182–200.

Lev, Baruch, Stephen Ryan, and Min Wu. "Rewriting earnings history." *Review of Accounting Studies* 13 (2008): 419–451.

Lev, Baruch, and Ramu Thiagarajan. "Fundamental information analysis." *Journal of Accounting Research* 31 (1993): 190–215.

Levine, Ross, 2005, Chapter 12 of "Finance and growth: Theory and evidence," *Handbook of Economic Growth*, Volume 1, Part 1, 865–934.

Levitt, Arthur. "The earnings game." http://www.sec.gov/news/speech/speecharchive/1998/spch220.txt, 1998.

Li, Feng. "Annual report readability, current earnings, and earning persistence." *Journal of Accounting and Economics* 45 (2008): 221–247.

Libby, Robert, Robert Bloomfield, and Mark Nelson. "Experimental research in financial accounting." *Accounting, Organizations and Society* 27 (2002): 775–810.

Lie, Erik. "Operating performance following open market share repurchase announcements." *Journal of Accounting and Economics* 39 (2005): 411–436.

Lie, Erik. "On the timing of CEO stock option awards." *Management Science* 51 (2005): 802–812.

Liu, Jing, Doron Nissim, and Jacob Thomas. "Equity valuation using multiples." *Journal of Accounting Research* 40 (2002): 135–172.

Liu, Jing, and Jacob Thomas. "Stock returns and accounting earnings." *Journal of Accounting Research* 38 (2000): 71–101.

Loughran, Tim, and Anand Vijh. "Do long-term shareholders benefit from corporate acquisitions?" *The Journal of Finance* LII (1997): 1765—1790.

Louis, Hanock, and Dahlia Robinson. "Do managers credibly use accruals to signal private information? Evidence from the pricing of discretionary accruals around stock splits." *Journal of Accounting and Economics* 39 (2005): 361–380.

Lowenstein, Louis. *Sense and nonsense in corporate finance*. New York: Addison-Wesley Publishing Company, 1991.

Lu, Yvonne. "Have defendant firms of shareholder securities litigation manipulated earnings?" working paper, University of Southern California, 2006.

Mace, Myles. *Directors: Myth and Reality*. Boston: Harvard Business School Press, 1971.

Margolis, Joshua, Hillary Elfenbein, and James Walsh. "Does It Pay to Be Good? A meta-analysis and redirection of research on the relationship between corporate social and financial performance." working paper, Harvard Business School, 2007.

Matsumoto, Dawn. "Management's incentives to avoid negative earnings surprises." *The Accounting Review* 77 (2002): 483–514.

Matsumoto, Dawn, Maarten Pronk, and Erick Roelofsen. "Conference call disclosure and firm performance: An empirical analysis of the length and content of earnings-related conference calls." working paper, University of Washington, 2007.

Maug, Ernst, and Kristian Rydqvist. "What is the function of the shareholder meeting? Evidence from the U.S. proxy voting process." working paper, Humboldt University, Berlin, 2001.

Mayer Brown Rowe & Maw. "Hedge funds and institutional shareholder activism." *Securities Update*, April 21, 2006.

McConnell, John, Henri Servaes, and Karl Lins. "Changes in insider ownership and changes in the market value of the firm." *Journal of Corporate Finance* 14 (2008): 92–106.

McKinsey & Co. "The misguided practice of earnings guidance." *McKinsey on Finance*, Spring 2006, 1–5.

McNichols, Maureen, and Stephen Stubben. "Does earnings management affect firms' investment decisions?" *The Accounting Review* 83 (2008): 1571–1603.

McVay, Sarah. "Earnings management using classification shifting: An examination of core earnings and special items." *The Accounting Review* 81 (2006): 501–531.

Mercer, Molly. "How do investors assess the credibility of management disclosures?" *Accounting Horizons* 18 (2004): 185–196.

Mikhail, Michael, Beverly Walther, and Richard Willis. "When security analysts talk, who listens?" *The Accounting Review* 82 (2007): 1227–1253.

Miller, Gregory. "Earnings performance and discretionary disclosure." *Journal of Accounting Research* 40 (2002): 173–204.

Mirvis, Philip, and Bradley Googins. "Stages of corporate citizenship." *California Management Review* 48 (2006): 104–126.

Mitchell, Mark, and Harold Mulheirn. "The impact of industry shocks on takeover and restructuring activity." *Journal of Financial Economics* 41 (1996): 193–229.

Morck, Randall. "The riddle of the great pyramids." working paper no. 14858, NBER, 2009.

Morck, Randall, Andrei Shleifer, and Robert Vishny. "Management ownership and market valuation: An empirical analysis." *Journal of Financial Economics* 20 (1988): 293–315.

Morck, Randall, David Stangeland, and Bernard Yeung. "Inherited wealth, corporate control, and economic growth: The Canadian disease." In *Concentrated Corporate Ownership*, edited by Randall Morck, 319–369. Chicago: University of Chicago Press, 2000.

Morck, Randall, Daniel Wolfenzon, and Bernard Yeung. "Corporate governance, economic entrenchment, and growth." *Journal of Economic Literature* XLIII (2005): 655–720.

Morck, Randall, and Bernard Yeung. "Family control and the rent-seeking society." *Entrepreneurship: Theory and Practice* 28 (2004): 391–409.

Myers, Stewart, and Nicholas Majluf. "Corporate financing and investment decisions when firms have information that investors do not have." *Journal of Financial Economics* 13 (1984): 187–221.

National Investor Relations Institute (NIRI), Executive Alert: NIRI issues 2006 survey results on earnings guidance practices, news release, 2006, Vienna, VA, 2006.

Orsato, Renato. "Competitive environmental strategies: When does it pay to be green?" *California Management Review* 48 (2006): 127–143.

Oswald, Dennis, and Paul Zarowin. "Capitalization of R&D and the informativeness of stock prices." *European Accounting Review* 16 (2007): 703–726.

Peloza, John. "Using corporate social responsibility as insurance for financial performance." *California Management Review* 48 (2006): 52–72.

Peng, Lin, and Ailsa Röell. "Executive pay, earnings manipulation and shareholder litigation." *Review of Finance* 12 (2008): 141–184.

Perino, Michael. "What we know and don't know about the Private Securities Litigation Reform Act of 1995." Testimony before the subcommittee of Finance and Hazardous Materials of the Committee on Commerce, U.S. House of Representatives, October 21, 1997.

Petersen, Mitchell. "Information: Hard and soft." working paper, Kellogg School of Management, Northwestern University, 2004.

Plancich, Stephanie, and Svetlana Starykh. "Recent trends in securities class action litigation: 2009 year-end update." National Economic Research Associates, Inc., New York, December, 2009.

Polk, Christopher, and Paola Sapienza. "The stock market and corporate investment: A test of catering theory." *The Review of Financial Studies* 22 (2009): 187–217.

Porter, Michael, and Mark Kramer. "The Competitive Advantage of Corporate Philanthropy." *Harvard Business Review*, December 2002, 56–68.

PricewaterhouseCoopers Advisory. Securities Litigation Studies, 2007.

PricewaterhouseCoopers. "Harnessing the Required: Equity Compensation's Evolving Role in Total Compensation." 2007 Global Equity Incentives Survey, 2008.

Putnam, Robert. "The case of missing social capital." working paper, Harvard University, 1995.

Rajan, Raghuram, and Julie Wulf. "Are perks purely managerial excess?" *Journal of Financial Economics* 79, no. 1 (2006): 1–33

Reich, Robert. *Supercapitalism: The Transformation of Business, Democracy and Everyday Life*. New York: Knopf, 2007.

Ritter, John. "The long-run performance of initial public offerings." *Journal of Finance* 46 (1991): 3–27.

Schrand, Catherine, and Sarah Zechman. "Executive overconfidence and the slippery slope to fraud." working paper, University of Pennsylvania, 2010.

Shannon, Claude, and Warren Weaver. *The Mathematical Theory of Communication*. Urbana, IL: The University of Illinois Press, 1964.

Shleifer, Andrei. *Inefficient Markets: An Introduction to Behavioral Finance*. Oxford, UK: Oxford University Press, 2000.

Simon, Herbert. *Administrative Behavior*. 3rd ed. New York: Free Press, 1976.

Skinner, Douglas. "Earnings disclosures and stockholder lawsuits." *Journal of Accounting and Economics* 23 (1997): 249–282.

Skinner, Douglas, and Richard Sloan. "Earnings surprises, growth expectations, and stock returns or don't let an earnings torpedo sink your portfolio." *Review of Accounting Studies* 7 (2002): 289–312.

Sloan, Richard. "Do stock prices fully reflect information in cash flows and accruals about future earnings?" *The Accounting Review* 71 (1996): 289–315.

Slovic, Paul. "Psychological study of human judgement: Implications for investment decision making." *Journal of Finance* 27 (1972): 779–799.

Smith, Adam. *An Inquiry into the Nature and Causes of the Wealth of Nations*. 5th ed., Canaan edition. London: Methuen and Co., Ltd., 1776, 1904.

Smith, Adam. *The Wealth of Nations*. Canaan edition. New York: Modern Library, 1776, 1937.

Smith, Michael. "Shareholder activism by institutional investors: Evidence from CalPERS." *Journal of Finance* 51 (1996): 227–252.

Sougiannis, Theodore. "The accounting based valuation of corporate R&D." *Accounting Review* 69 (1994): 44–68.

Spence, Michael. "Job market signaling." *Quarterly Journal of Economics* 87 (1973): 355–374.

Spence, Michael. *Market Signaling: Informational Transfer in Hiring and Related Screening Processes*. Cambridge, MA: Harvard University Press, 1974.

Spindler, James. "Why shareholders want their CEOs to lie more after Dura Pharmaceuticals." *The Georgetown Law Journal* 95 (2007): 653–692.

Stulz, Rene. "The limits of financial globalization." *The Journal of Finance* LX (2005): 1595–1638.

Sullivan, Evelin. *The Concise Book of Lying*. New York: Farrar, Straus and Giroux, 2001.

Swanson, Edward, Senyo Tse, and Rebecca Files. "Does the format of a press release announcing a restatement affect the market response and litigation?" working paper, Texas A&M University, 2007.

Talner, Lauren. "The Origins of Shareholder Activism." Investor Responsibility Research Center, Inc., Washington, DC, 1983.

Tetlock, Paul, Maytal Saar-Tsechansky, and Sofus Macskassy. "More than words: A study of decision-making in administrative organization quantifying language to measure firms' fundamentals." *Journal of Finance* 63 (2008): 1437–1467.

Thomas, Randall, and Kenneth Martin. "The effect of shareholder proposals on executive compensation." *University of Cincinnati Law Review* 67 (1999): 1021–1081.

Tucker, Jennifer. "Is openness penalized? Stock returns around earnings warnings." *The Accounting Review* 82 (2007): 1055–1087.

Tucker, Jennifer, and Paul Zarowin. "Timeliness of firms' voluntary disclosure of good and bad news." working paper, University of Florida, 2006.

U. S. Chamber of Commerce. Commission on the Regulation of U.S. Capital Markets in the 21st Century: Report and Recommendations, 2007.

U.S. Department of Commerce and U.S. Department of the Treasury. *Financing Technology: A Report of the Financing Technology Roundtables*. Washington, DC, 1992.

Varchaver, Nicholas. "CA: America's most dysfunctional company." *Fortune*, November 16, 2006.

Vasella, Daniel, and Clifton Leaf. "Temptation is all around us." *Fortune*, November 18, 2002, 109.

Walker, David. "The challenge of improving the long-term focus of executive pay." *Boston College Law Review* 51, no. 2 (2010): 435–472.

Wolfers, Justin. "Diagnosing discrimination: Stock returns and CEO gender." *Journal of European Economic Association* 4 (2006): 531–541.

Wu, Min. "Earnings restatements: A capital market perspective." working paper, New York University, 2002.

Yermack, David. "Higher market valuation of companies with a small board of directors." *Journal of Financial Economics* 40 (1996): 185–211.

# Index

# About the Author

BARUCH LEV is the Philip Bardes Professor of Accounting and Finance at New York University's Stern School of Business and the director of the Vincent C. Ross Institute for Accounting Research. Formerly at the University of Chicago, UC Berkeley, and Tel Aviv University, Lev is a permanent visitor at École Nationale des Ponts et Chaussées (Paris) and LUISS Business School (Rome). Lev has extensive experience in public accounting, worked in investment banking, was a partner in a consulting firm, and served on several boards.